RULING RUSSIA

POLITICS AND ADMINISTRATION
IN THE AGE OF ABSOLUTISM
1762-1796

STUDIES OF
THE HARRIMAN INSTITUTE
COLUMBIA UNIVERSITY

The W. Averell Harriman Institute for Advanced
Study of the Soviet Union, Columbia University,
sponsors the *Studies of the Harriman Institute* in
the belief that their publication contributes to
scholarly research and public understanding. In
this way the Institute, while not necessarily en-
dorsing their conclusions, is pleased to make available the results of some of the research conducted
under its auspices. A list of the *Studies* appears at
the back of this book.

JOHN P. LeDONNE

RULING RUSSIA

Politics and Administration

in the Age of Absolutism

1762-1796

PRINCETON UNIVERSITY PRESS

PRINCETON, NEW JERSEY

Published by Princeton University Press, 41 William Street,
Princeton, New Jersey 08540
In the United Kingdom: Princeton University Press,
Guildford, Surrey

Library of Congress Cataloging in Publication Data will be
found on the last printed page of this book

ISBN 0-691-05425-8

Publication of this book has been aided by a grant from
the Andrew W. Mellon Foundation

This book has been composed in Linotron Sabon

Clothbound editions of Princeton University Press books
are printed on acid-free paper, and binding materials are
chosen for strength and durability.

Printed in the United States of America
by Princeton University Press
Princeton, New Jersey

PREFACE

This book follows the publication of Isabel de Madariaga's magisterial study of the reign of Catherine the Great, but focuses on the internal administration of the Empire. No comprehensive study of the great reforms of 1775-1785 has yet been written, although they are as important as those of the 1860s. Some very valuable work has been done on the bureaucracy and the nobility, but Russian law and procedure as well as finance have been almost completely ignored; and no systematic survey of Great Russia's relations with its borderlands is yet available. Scholars seeking to take up the challenge face a choice: they may treat any of these subjects in some detail, or attempt in a general work to present a global view of Russian internal administration at one of the most interesting periods of its history. Without the benefit of preliminary monographs and fully conscious of the many pitfalls attending such an enterprise, I have chosen the second course in the belief that a general work describing institutions and procedures will give scholars interested in more specific aspects of domestic administration a framework and a background lacking until now.

Archival materials have been used to supplement basic references to the Collection of Laws of the Russian Empire; they have been most useful for a study of military-budget procedures, a subject on which virtually nothing has been written. In order to help students of institutions I have tried to identify as many officials as possible within the scope of a general work, a difficult task without access to the rare Calendars of administrative personnel published from 1765 on. For background material on the Legislative Commission, the Organic Law, and the Charters of 1785 the reader is referred to Professor de Madariaga's work.

This book attempts to meet the need for the facts of Russian administration; it is also an investigation of the social foundations of political power. Certain fundamental questions must be asked in Russian historiography if we are to proceed beyond the sterile assumption that the Russian political order was ruled by an "autocrat" commanding mindless "bureaucratic servitors," scattered among a passive nation. Did a Russian state really exist in the eighteenth century? Was a bureaucracy subservient to the ruler the center of gravity of the political order? And, if it was not, what was the ruling class of the Empire? Who sustained the legitimacy of both the ruler and the ruling class, and what forces fashioned a consensus without which there could be no effective government? There are no simple answers to these fundamental questions, but this book will suggest approaches for solving them.

Why the reign of Catherine? It is customary to see the accession of Alexander I in March 1801 as marking the beginning of the third and last period of the Romanov dynasty, while the middle period is made to begin with the reforms of Peter the Great and end with the chaos seemingly created by Paul. Any periodization serves a purpose in our search for order, but it also obscures the fundamental continuity of the historical process which creates, affirms, and submerges intricate patterns of ever-changing relationships and carries along great men and women toward the fulfilment of their destiny. Catherine's reign marked both an end and a beginning, and the great reforms of 1775-1785 which filled its middle years marked the turning point. In the 1770s the uneasy combination of Petrine and Muscovite institutions was laid to rest, the central government was radically transformed, and a comprehensive reorganization of local administration was completed. The centralist reaction, which began under Paul and reached its zenith under Nicholas I, cannot be understood without an appreciation of the import of Catherine's great reforms and of their motivation. Here these reforms are seen as the response to a vast social movement engulfing not only central Russia but the borderlands as well, and compelling a redistribution of authority between the political leadership and the rank-and-file nobility, a movement of such scope that the central government was no longer viable in 1796 and required drastic overhaul. It has often been claimed that Catherine's reign was the golden age of the Russian nobility; it remains to be shown why such a claim could be made.

I wish to thank Professor Marc Raeff for his persistent encouragement over many years and for the patience with which he listened to various theories suggested by a scholar in search of a unifying theme in a very difficult work; Professors John Keep and Richard Wortman for their interest and constructive criticism; Professor Charles Lelong for teaching me to appreciate the geographical context of historical developments; Ruth Mathewson for her invaluable editorial assistance; and Nina Lencek for good cheer in moments of discouragement. This work would not have been completed without the financial assistance of the American Council of Learned Societies and the Russian Institute of Columbia University and a travel grant from the International Research and Exchange Board; their help is gratefully acknowledged. Thanks are due to Professor Mikhail Timofeevich Belavskii, my adviser at Moscow University; Svetlana Romanovna Dolgova at TsGADA, and Elena Nikolaevna Dmitrochenkova at TsGVIA, who

gave me valuable material on military finance. And those who have
worked at TsGADA in recent years remember the gracious hospitality
of Zoia Sergeevna Murasheva which contributed to making work in
the archives such a pleasant experience.

The portraits are from the Slavonic Division, The New York Public
Library, Astor, Lenox, and Tilden Foundations.

TABLE OF CONTENTS

CONTENTS

ABBREVIATIONS

AE	Arkheograficheskii Ezhegodnik
AHR	American Historical Review
C-ASS	Canadian-American Slavic Studies
CSS	Canadian Slavic Studies
Chteniia	Chteniia v Imperatorskom Obshchestve istorii i drevnostei Rossiiskikh pri Moskovskom Universitete
CMRS	Cahiers du monde russe et soviétique
DNR	Drevniaia i Novaia Rossiia
ES	Entsiklopedicheskii slovar' (Brokaus i Efron)
FOG	Forschungen zur Osteuropäischen Geschichte
IuV	Iuridicheskii Vestnik
IESS	International Encyclopedia of Social Sciences, 1968
IV	Istoricheskii Vestnik
IZ	Istoricheskie Zapiski
JGO	Jahrbücher für Geschichte Osteuropas
LN	Literaturnoe nasledstvo
OV	Osmnadtsatyi vek
PSZ	Polnoe Sobranie Zakonov
RA	Russkii Arkhiv
RBa	Russkaia Beseda
RB	Russkoe Bogatstvo
RBS	Russkii Biograficheskii Slovar'
RH	Russian History
RHMC	Revue d'Histoire moderne et contemporaine
RIZh	Russkii Istoricheskii Zhurnal
RS	Russkaia Starina
RV	Russkii Vestnik
SA	Sovetskie Arkhivy
SEER	Slavonic and East European Review

SIRIO	Sbornik Imperatorskago Russkago Istoricheskago Obshchestva
SR	Slavic Review
UZGU	Uchenye Zapiski Gor'kovskogo gosudarstvennogo universiteta
UZIMU	Uchenye Zapiski Imperatorskago Moskovskago Universiteta
VE	Vestnik Evropy
VI	Voprosy Istorii
VIMO	Vremennik Imperatorskago Moskovskago Obshchestva istorii i drevnostei Rossiiskikh
VIRGO	Vestnik Imperatorskago russkago geograficheskago obshchestva
VLU	Vestnik Leningradskogo universiteta (N.8: Istoriia, iazyk, literatura)
VMU	Vestnik Moskovskogo Universiteta (N. IX, istoriia)
VP	Vestnik Prava
VS	Voennyi Sbornik
ZhMIu	Zhurnal Ministerstva Iustitsii
ZhMNP	Zhurnal Ministerstva Narodnago Prosveshcheniia
ZhGUP	Zhurnal Grazhdanskago i Ugolovnago Prava

PART I

THE SETTING

It is not as easy as you think . . . [to see your will fulfilled]. In the first place, my orders would not be carried out unless they were the kind of orders which could be carried out; you know with what prudence and circumspection I act in the promulgation of my laws. I examine the circumstances, I take advice, I consult the enlightened part of the people, and in this way I find out what sort of effect my laws will have. And when I am already convinced, in advance, of general approval, I issue my orders, and have the pleasure of observing what you call blind obedience. *And that is the foundation of unlimited power.* But believe me, they would not obey blindly were orders not adopted to customs, to the opinion of the people, and were I to follow only my own wishes, without thinking of the consequences. In the second place, you delude yourself if you think that everything is done only to gratify me. On the contrary, it is I who must seek to oblige everyone, according to his deserts, merits, tastes, and habits; . . . it is much easier to please everyone than to get everyone to please you.

CATHERINE'S REMARKS
TO HER SECRETARY, V. POPOV.
Quoted in N. Shil'der,
Imperator Aleksandr I,
vol. I, 279-280.

CHAPTER I

THE ISSUES

Our understanding of a given historical situation is often clouded by the indiscriminate use of the troublesome concepts of class, ruling class, state, and bureaucracy. On the one hand, the social sciences need definitions expressing the inner simplicity of a complex aggregate of phenomena; on the other, the flow of history keeps creating original combinations that escape deciphering. The result is that definitions often become rigid constructs unable to encompass the wealth and variety of social relationships;[1] and the attempt to adapt them to changing conditions threatens to destroy their consistency and to render them unrecognizable. Therefore, the meaning of terms to be used in this study of a historical period must be clearly stated at the outset.

In a preindustrial society such as Russia, a social class was a distinct group occupying a definite position in the social hierarchy, with a specific function to fulfill, and with a consciousness of its peculiar status. Function, consciousness, and status were thus fundamental criteria. Social and economic functions still served a narrow spectrum of stable needs and conferred a status rigidly defined in accordance with the system of values characteristic of that society. But the highest— because the most responsible and the most comprehensive—function was the political, by which is meant setting the goals which a human collectivity pursued at a given time; working out programs of action to reach them (in which fiscal considerations are of the utmost importance); settling disputes in ways acceptable to maintain the social compact; and protecting the peace against attacks on the core of the ideological consensus and the security of individuals.

If every social function important enough to attract a substantial group capable of developing a consciousness of its separateness and insistent upon the creation of privileges to define and protect it generated a social class, it follows that the exercise of political responsibilities had to be vested in a political class. What distinguished a preindustrial society was the monopoly of the political function by the ruling class, and the sharper division separating the constituent classes of that society, imbedded in a vertical structure governed by the principle of strict social hierarchy. The ruling class, then, embodied in its totality the moral unity of a definite human collectivity; it har-

[1] A. Gouldner, "On Weber's Analysis of Bureaucratic Rules," in Merton, 48.

monized diversified interests and resolved group conflicts. And the ultimate justification of its existence was protection of the collectivity against external danger.[2]

The ruling class was not a caste founded upon the principle of religious or racial exclusiveness, nor an army of occupation, alien to the society in which it operated. It possessed a social constitution by which it formulated the social relationships between its constituent elements and coopted new members; it worked out a political constitution by which it apportioned political responsibilities at various levels; and it sought ways to define the character of its symbiosis with the rest of society.

If, as Raymond Aron suggests,[3] the term "ruling class" is not suitable to describe the political class of a modern society, where a small group of elites share the political function, it is eminently relevant to the analysis of a preindustrial society. It does not follow that in such a society the ruling class was so homogeneous that its constituent parts could not be distinguished. The process of modernization, by diversifying socio-economic functions, dislocates the traditional hierarchy, creates free-floating status groups with a claim to a share in the political function and enough power to enforce their claims, and ultimately produces a ruling class in which the autonomy of each constituent group becomes so strong as to end the pretense of homogeneity. At an earlier time, however, the small size of the ruling class in relation to the rest of society, coupled with its monopoly of the political function and the consciousness of its exclusive privileges, still imposed a unity overriding every tendency to internal differentiation.

The Russian ruling class, which reached maturity in the reign of Catherine, had its origin in the massive social revolution engineered by the policies of Ivan the Terrible in the sixteenth century. A new class of "servitors," supporters of an assertive ruling house against the political claims of certain well-established aristocratic families, was consolidated by the political disintegration of the Times of Troubles and the initial weakness of the new Romanov dynasty. With the passage of time the structure of this new ruling class came to resemble a cone. At the top stood the Romanov house, itself the product of that same social revolution which engendered the ruling class. Tsars continued until the eighteenth century to marry native members of that class, a practice which the keeping of a favorite by the eighteenth-century empresses resembled in a slightly different form. By the 1750s

---

[2] S. Keller, "Elites," in IESS, V, 27. I have benefited greatly from von Stein, *Social Movement*, Sjoberg, *Preindustrial City*, Eisenstein, *Political Systems*, and Mosca, *Ruling Class*.

[3] Aron, 2, 9-10.

a top stratum of the ruling class had crystallized, consisting of the Naryshkins, the Saltykovs, the Golitsyns, and the Vorontsovs, among others, together with their own related families, extremely stable from one generation to another, whose supremacy was unchallengeable short of a political revolution directed against the ruling house itself.

Ranking just below this top leadership and gathered as it were in a circle around it stood the officer corps, i.e., those whose occupation embodied the very function that defined the ruling class, the defense of the collectivity against foreign (and domestic) enemies. The importance of this first sub-group was capital. In no other country perhaps had the sense of insecurity been so pervasive as in Russia, where national unity was achieved against odds that seemed overwhelming on more than one occasion, and where the threat of a mobile frontier was coupled with the tantalizing challenge of the proximate sea. The officer corps was, to use Suzanne Keller's term in a different context,[4] a strategic elite within the ruling class, wielding an influence extending far beyond the administration of the army and military planning. Officers did not constitute a technical corps but a political association which placed its members at all levels of responsibility. Conversely, even those members of the ruling class who did not make the army a career received their education in the Cadet Corps, from which they graduated to serve their stint in the army, then retired after receiving what amounted to a certificate of admission to the social core of the ruling class. Count Langeron, who left us such interesting memoirs on the composition of the Russian army, emphasized this predominantly social and political character of the officer corps.[5] They were "servitors" indeed, but servitors who set the tone and defined the options of political life.

There were three more constituent groups within the ruling class, of inferior status but gravitating around the core with which they were inextricably bound. One consisted of those nobles—for it must be obvious that by ruling class is meant the *dvorianstvo*—who did not serve either in the army or the civil service but chose to remain on their estates. They belonged to the ruling class by right and had inherited their status, but they did not take part in the political responsibilities of their class, unless the public power they exercised as private individuals over their peasants be looked upon as a political activity. They were the reserve of the ruling class, a pool from which officers were selected whenever a nobleman chose to enter the wider world. Another subgroup included those who served exclusively in the civil

---

[4] Keller, 26.
[5] Langeron, 159-170, 188-190.

service. Few hereditary nobles still chose that path in the eighteenth century, and this group consisted of men whose origin was diverse and who had entered the ruling class by a process of cooptation whenever the demand rose for this essentially secretarial personnel. The last group does not quite fit in the conical structure of concentric circles arranged in order of decreasing status because its members are found everywhere. It consisted of members of the ruling classes of the various borderlands—Germans, Poles, Ukrainians, and the tribal leadership of Turkic hordes along the southeastern and Siberian borders. They were found at court as favorites, in the officer corps, where they were initiated into the social and the religious world of the Great Russian ruling class, and they were leaders in their native territories; probably few had yet joined the secretarial staff, and this chiefly among the interpreters.

The internal dynamism of the ruling class was generated by radial channels of influence, intertwined and overlapping, originating at the very top of the cone or anywhere below it. These channels fostered social mobility by creating incentives: ruling families, including the Romanov house, built parties and cliques to strengthen their hand in the division of the spoils; subordinate families sought upward mobility by a more active participation in the politics of their class. The central location of Moscow, the fusion of ethnicity and religion, the geographical uniformity of central Russia and the unstable frontier surrounding it generated centripetal forces favoring leadership and imposing obedience. The Russian nobility, as Helmut Rüss has shown in a very suggestive book,[6] never was provincial and always displayed a strong anti-regionalist bias. Irresistibly drawn toward Moscow, its field of action was the entire national territory and its political commitment a total one. The scattering of its properties all over central Russia, its lack of attachment to particular communities, was the reverse side of an intense commitment to the unity of the Russian land and to the integrity of its leadership.

The ruling class, then, was not a completely homogeneous body, socially, culturally, or materially. A wide chasm separated the great lord at Court from the petty noble without means, the officer who knew from his travels the wide expanse of the Russian land—not to mention the allurements of Poland and the dangers of the Turkish frontier—from the hidebound landowner on some distant estate in the interior. The crucial factor, however, was not the inevitable gradation of status within such a ruling class, but the overwhelming consciousness of its exclusive monopoly over the exercise of the political function

---

[6] Rüss, 6-7.

and of its exclusive privilege in the ownership of peasant labor to turn into wealth the possession of land. This alone justifies calling the Russian nobility a ruling class.

What gave a fundamental unity to the two and a half centuries stretching from the accession of the Romanov dynasty to the reign of Alexander II was the existence of serfdom. It kept expanding against a seemingly contradictory background of gradual economic development and rising national power, reached its apogee in the reign of Catherine,[7] then receded during the first fifty years of the nineteenth century. In such an overwhelmingly agrarian socioeconomic order the range of rewards was very narrow. The possession of money still depended in most cases on the ownership of land and of peasants to till it, peasants bound to a master as the guarantee of his income. "The unification of the elite is inseparable from the concentration of all economic power in its hands,"[8] and the history of the period witnessed the expansion of the ruling class as the chief beneficiary of serfdom. The old system of conditional tenure by which the ruling house had sought to bind its supporters gradually but inexorably gave way to full ownership, as the ruling house abandoned its age-old claims to the ownership of all the land in favor of a system of property law based on the marketability of land. The progress of the idea that landed property, once distributed from the pool of state lands as a reward for services, might remain in the family of the original beneficiary reflected the growing strength of the landed nobility as a whole vis-à-vis the presumptive claims of the ruling house. It was certainly no coincidence that the first massive grants of land in full ownership took place in 1610 and 1612, when insecure rulers were seeking political support, and that the almost complete disappearance of conditional tenure in the heart of central Russia by the end of the seventeenth century ran parallel to the consolidation of the Romanov dynasty. Against such a background Peter the Great's order of 1714, abolishing the distinction between conditional and hereditary tenure, i.e., allowing the latter to supersede the former, merely gave legislative sanction to a fait accompli.

The growth of landownership paralleled with the extension of serfdom. Veselovskii has described in masterful fashion how over some twenty-five years the peasants' right to move was gradually restricted and how it would take another fifty years (until the Code of 1649) before the peasants lost their illusion that the prohibition was only

[7] Liashchenko, 277, 286; Troitskii, *Absoliutizm*, 353; Kahan, 57-60.
[8] Aron, 132.

temporary.[9] The extension of serfdom reached its completion in the reign of Catherine, in the neat and almost even division of the peasant world between the serfs of private landowners and all others, including those of the ruling house. Its victory was so complete, even if it soon proved to have been a Pyrrhic one, that serfdom was not a negotiable issue in the eighteenth century. It was the social creed of the ruling class and the cement of its unity. Not all members of that class owned serfs, it is true, but all enjoyed the prescriptive right to acquire them if the opportunity presented itself. In the absence of other rewards, those who did not or could not afford to own serfs were compelled to participate directly in the exercise of the political function. They received an income in the form of a salary, together with the more important perquisites resulting from bribery and extortion, officially discouraged but unofficially taken for granted. Although that salary had the same source as the landowners' income: taxes levied upon either all peasants (the capitation) or upon the so-called state peasants kept, so to speak, in trust for the needs of the ruling class (the quitrent), the ownership of land and peasants sustained the existence of a subgroup within the ruling class characterized by a more exalted class consciousness and with interests that did not always coincide with those of their non-possessing brethren. However, despite differences in the origin of the constituent groups making up the ruling class and in their status within it, there existed a fundamental unity on essentials: the social order was inviolable; serfdom and the ruling class were interdependent; and social membership in the ruling class gave power to use public resources for private purposes.

That the ruling class was not a caste implies that it was open to outsiders when circumstances required. The core could always draw upon the landowners to rejuvenate its ranks and replace casualties, but demand and supply were not always in equal relation. As Russia's international prominence rose and the responsibilities of its ruling class widened, the demand for additional members grew accordingly. Thus, there was constantly at work what Mosca has called the "democratic tendency" by which a ruling class replenishes itself from the social classes whose status is closest to its own,[10] a tendency most likely to prevail in unsettled times and in periods of economic expansion. The complaint of Vasilii Tatishchev in the 1730s and of Mikhail Shcherbatov in the 1760s against the influx of outsiders into the nobility is adequate testimony of the existence of social mobility and of the

[9] Veselovskii, 51-52, 95-98; see also Got'e, *Zamoskovnyi krai*, 255-256, 263-265, 283.

[10] Mosca, 413-415.

disquiet of the socially conservative at this incipient threat to the relative homogeneity of the ruling class.

The main channel of access to the ruling class was the army, and the criterion was either administrative talent, valor in battle, or crass favoritism. The soldiers and non-commissioned officers constituted an inexhaustible reserve of men who already belonged to the structure of power since the army was the coercive arm of the ruling class. Those who were already hereditary members and served in the ranks suffered no social disability and were admitted into the officer corps as a matter of course. The others had to wait until they were coopted by army and corps commanders or the College of War, but even then they were assigned to positions that were not part of the command hierarchy of the officer corps, such as adjutants, quartermasters, and law clerks (*auditory*) of the courts-martial.[11] Yet, cooptation into the officer corps made them ipso facto hereditary members of the ruling class. The inferior status of those who entered by cooptation into the secretarial staff resulted from the fact that these men were admitted only for their lifetime and did not bequeath their status to their children (except in rare instances, when they were promoted to positions of considerable responsibility). Preference was given to sons of clergy, merchants, and others who belonged to that intermediate zone separating the ruling class from the great mass of Russians required to pay the capitation, that badge of social inferiority. Thus access to the social core of the ruling class required a stage of apprenticeship, either in the army or in the menial tasks of that class. Exceptions only confirmed the rule. Direct access to the core from the merchant class or even the peasantry was possible. The soldiers who served in the Life Company that supported Elizabeth on that fateful night of November 1741 became hereditary noblemen. Dispensing ranks among merchants' sons who served pro forma in the Guard seems to have become an ordinary phenomenon bordering on scandal in the reign of Catherine.[12] On the whole, however, access to the ruling class was not a matter of right, but a social privilege granted by cooptation for subjective or political reasons.

If the social constitution of the ruling class rested on the monopolistic ownership of peasant labor, the cooptation of outsiders, and the acceptance of a hierarchical relationship, its political constitution sought to define the position of the ruler and the role of the bureaucratic element in Russian politics.

In such a hierarchically structured organism of concentric circles

[11] Langeron, 165.
[12] Vorontsov, 99.

bound together by radial channels of influence exercised by the leading families and clans, the question of the ruler's legitimacy was of
crucial importance. In the absence of a succession law each candidate
had to vie for acceptance among the leading families, and the final
choice embodied a consensus on both his person and his program.
The ruler, in addition, had to be perceived by the collectivity at large
as the embodiment of its values and the bearer of its expectations.
Legitimacy was recognized when acceptance crystallized among those
immediately subordinated to the ruler and beyond them among the
rank-and-file of the ruling class. This recognition was an act of collective psychology that could not be forced. Likewise, the legitimacy
of a ruler's orders was taken for granted when the compulsion to obey
became a moral force; and the decision as to whether an order had
authority or not lay with the persons to whom it was addressed.[13] In
distinguishing between the legitimacy of the person of the ruler and
that of his decisions, one touches upon the distinction between authority and power. The tsar had the authority of his office by virtue
of his occupying the exalted position at the apex of the ruling class.
Power, however, is something acquired, earned, developed by an individual personality and his accomplishments. It accrues with a long
series of suggestions, recommendations, compromises, and outright
commands which are accepted at the various levels of the ruling class
because they reflect a collective mood or embody a collective program.
"The theoretically unlimited power of the Russian autocracy," David
Ransel has written, "was in fact very narrowly circumscribed . . . the
articulation of tsarist will depended upon the familial and personal
patronage networks that dominated the court and upper administration . . . (and) supplied the organizational cohesion that made for
effective policy implementation."[14]

One of the most striking characteristics of the top leadership of the
Empire after the death of Peter the Great, who is thought by many to
have begun a new chapter in Russian history, was its continuity with
the leadership of Muscovite Russia. Some ninety percent of those in
the first four classes of the Table of Ranks in 1730, the so-called
generalitet, belonged to families which had held high office in the
seventeenth century, and the generation that would govern the Empire
in the 1770s and 1780s was born to these families at about that time.[15]

[13] Ch. Barnard, "A Definition of Authority," in Merton, 180-181.

[14] Ransel, *Politics*, 1.

[15] Pipes, 125, Meehan-Waters. Mrs. Waters put it very aptly when she wrote of the
fathers of the men who governed under Catherine that "their expertise was leadership,
and their qualifications were distinguished birth and distinguished service"; see "Social

In both the military and civil service there was a significant group of families whose sons were born to govern and to compete for the key positions irrespective of the person of the crowned ruler. A strong ruler like Peter, who could not alter the foundations of a social order that had begun to crystallize before his reign and would continue to harden after him, could not operate without the cooperation and the support that these families were able to generate for transforming Russia into a great power. The weakness of the rulers who followed him, women whose favorites exacerbated the struggle for positions, heightened the tension between the leading families and the throne, resulting in depositions and assassinations carried out with the assistance of the Guard. Peter's elimination of the succession law further undermined the legitimacy of the ruler and made him more dependent upon political cliques for which the maintenance of autocracy and serfdom was a guarantee of their future prospects. The ruler could play off some groups against others and become the arbiter of the political struggle for power and influence, but he could not afford to antagonize the political community as Peter III and Paul, whose reigns bracket Catherine's, found out to their misfortune. One can agree, although with some reservations, with Richard Pipes's conclusion that "after 1762 the monarchy became in large measure the captive of groups which it had originally brought into existence" and that "the trappings of imperial omnipotence served only to conceal its desperate weakness—as well as to camouflage the actual power wielded by dvoriane and chinovniki."[16]

Nevertheless—Pipes's conclusion notwithstanding—there was bound to exist a permanent tension between the Romanov house and the ruling class, if only because the exercise of leadership often entails a degree of frustration for those who must follow. The house was not simply just another ruling family; it was the richest and the most powerful. Although the ideology of the ruling class exalted the majesty and the independence of the sovereign, certain eighteenth-century developments were already pointing to a gradual estrangement between the ruling class and its head at the very time when the victory of serfdom seemed to create an indestructible bond between the two.

While legitimacy is bestowed by the core of the ruling class, it needs to be rationalized in terms that appeal to all classes of society. The eighteenth century was a secular century when the divine right of kings became less and less acceptable as the religious source of legitimacy,

---

Career Characteristics of the Administrative Elite, 1689-1761" in Pintner and Rowney, 105.

[16] Pipes, 138; see also Wortman, 20.

and especially so in a country where on several occasions the ruler was brought to power by officers of the Guard, the most politically active minority within the ruling class. The need was felt to legitimize the power of the ruling house by appealing to secular principles. Here, however, lay the source of a monumental contradiction.[17] The appeal was made to the "general good," i.e., the welfare of the entire society, but in order to reach that goal the ruler needed to frame policies favoring social differentiation and economic liberalism, policies which in an overwhelmingly agrarian and conservative society threatened to undermine the internal stability of the ruling class and destroy the very foundations of the ruler's strength. To look beyond the status quo to a situation where economic development would create a new social order was to anticipate a realignment of political forces that would profoundly affect the power of the ruling house. It has been noted that an organization fails when "individuals in sufficient numbers regard the burden involved in accepting orders as changing the balance against their interests" and that "politically significant moral anger comes from the application of new principles that work to the disadvantage of substantial numbers of people."[18] Promoting socially dependent but qualified people over socially established individuals could generate powerful reactions—as Speranskii found out fifteen years after the death of Catherine—and it was obvious that any attempt to alter the foundations of the social order grounded in serfdom would have created an unacceptable risk. This, indeed, was the most constricting limitation upon the ruler's power and the most inhibiting factor in political life.

Without the possibility of fashioning a domestic program that would appeal to broad strata of the population beyond the ruling class, the ruler could seek to develop his autonomy by removing himself from the social politics of the ruling class. It was perhaps no coincidence that neither Anna nor Elizabeth or Catherine chose to marry (or remarry) while empresses. The choice of a favorite did not have the same consequences: his position remained insecure, he did not always come from the established families, and he fathered no children.[19] The three empresses never became the prisoners of their husbands' relatives and were able to create a certain privacy in their family life, although Catherine, who already had a son by the time she was crowned, was perhaps less successful than her two predecessors. But when one remembers the horrible scenes which Peter the Great had to witness as

---

[17] Krieger, 254-255.
[18] Barnard, "Definition," 180-181, and Moore, 16-17.
[19] Or, if he did, his children were illegitimate.

a child, the progress was considerable. A second way by which the ruler could develop his autonomy was to rely increasingly upon the clerks, specialists in their trade and reliable in their loyalties because they were too miserable socially to dare change them. But to do so was again to favor a dangerous course leading to increased differentiation within the ruling class, and that is a policy which none of Catherine's predecessors or Catherine herself could afford to follow because it was ultimately bound up with an attack upon the integrity of the social order.

In such conditions there was no need to institutionalize the legislative power. Such a need would arise later, from the generalization of power, its diffusion in society, and from the dislocation of the vertically integrated society characteristic of preindustrial Russia. Divergent interests reflecting the increasing complexity of the social and economic world would require a forum where divergences could be reconciled into a consensus, in horizontal fashion so to speak, among juridically equal groups, and no longer between social leaders and their followers. The concentration of all political power in the ruling class founded on serfdom entailed a structuralization of decision making giving considerable leeway to the social leadership of that class. The leadership of the ruling class which bestowed legitimacy upon the ruler by recognizing his authority and accepting his power, even maximizing it in order to maximize its own, depended on the rank and file for the recognition of its own authority and power, and differences were reconciled within the clans with large followings. Much of the political function was still expressed in administrative terms, i.e., in the modalities by which an agreed-upon program was carried out, rather than in legislative terms establishing substantive norms of political action. The leadership kept a very tight control over the final settlement of differences and left it to the ruler to create new legislative norms, on the tacit understanding that his decisions were made within a framework taken for granted by the ruling class. By the middle of the eighteenth century the domestic program amounted essentially to a systematic attempt to make power more efficient while maintaining the status quo.

A fundamental distinction still existed between the ruling class and the bureaucracy. Hierarchy of offices, specialization, impersonal relationships governed by abstract legal norms, fixed and universal rules of promotion, allegiance to the "state," full-time and remunerated work—such are the basic criteria of bureaucratic organization;[20] yet

[20] M. Weber, "The Essentials of Bureaucratic Organization: An Ideal-Type Construction," in Merton, 18-27. See also Raeff, *Origins*, 107-108.

they were hardly characteristic of the Russian political order. The absence of hierarchy among the levels of provincial government and even between the central colleges and the governors was striking: all were equally subordinated to the Senate. Specialization of functions was noticeable at the center but not in the provinces, and members of the ruling class were generalists without training in the specialized activities of their agencies. Relationships at all levels and promotions expressed social and political choices. And if work was full time and remunerated for some it was neither for those who exercised their political responsibilities outside the network of agencies.

The ruling class, it is true, had in the Table of Ranks its own principle of internal organization; it did not thereby become a bureaucracy. To claim that "bureaucracy is simply institutionalism written large, . . . merely an accentuation of characteristics found in all [institutions] . . . a matter of degree, of the combination of components"[21] is to deny the importance of definitions as frames of reference and to persist in applying abstract concepts to situations which they cannot explain. The Table of Ranks set criteria by which political and administrative tasks were allocated according to an ascending scale and created a subdivision of functions within the ruling class. Consciousness of the link between rank and prestige reflected the importance accorded to the political function in a society where the division of labor had not yet created alternative sources of rewards. The major subdivision was between those who ruled over society as a whole in a public capacity and the non-serving nobles who exercised in a private capacity the public power over their serfs. The first three classes of the Table of Ranks were reserved for the top leadership of the ruling class, with direct access to the ruler both socially and in the exercise of their responsibilities. These men also possessed the crucial power to coopt outsiders into the ruling class, to bestow rank upon them, and to promote them into the middle group consisting of those who served in classes four to eight. The nobles in this group formed the political core, filled the management level, of the ruling class. They were the clients of the ruling families and of the Romanov house; their views had to be taken into account because it was they who carried out policy. Below this middle group the Table of Ranks diversified responsibilities and status. Captains and lieutenants and their subordinates down to class fourteen enjoyed the greater status conferred by military service: they were all hereditary noblemen. The others who

---

[21] M. Dimock, "Bureaucracy Self-Examined," in Merton, 397-398; see also Sjoberg, 237-244.

had served and risen exclusively in the civil service were looked upon as retainers reserved for secretarial and other executive functions.

The essential point is that these junior members did not consider themselves a special group, separated, if not alienated, from the society of the well-born. Being nobles by birth, or aspiring to be coopted into the core of the ruling class, they did not see their interests as a mere constituent part of a national interest but submerged the latter into their class interest. Hence the importance of persons rather than office, the personal whims, the loyalties to the patrons rather than to the ruler, the graft, not only to supplement one's income but also as expected return for a favor, and the procrastination when kinship ties were not involved or inducements forthcoming.[22] Rules governing promotions were few and did not apply to the higher ranks. Political advancement reflected social recognition and, as Robert Jones put it, "service was a dead-end street rather than a road to opportunities" for those without family connections or wealth.[23] Noblemen entered military service as children, "retired" even before they served, reentered public life in the civil service, and retired again often merely to take advantage of the rule granting promotion upon retiring.[24] In its composition, attitudes, and behavior the Russian nobility was not a bureaucracy.

However, there already existed an incipient bureaucracy. A glance at the table of organization of agencies reveals that the overwhelming majority of their personnel did not occupy graded positions. The clerks of various denominations, the military scribes, and the non-commissioned officers (except those who were nobles) constituted not only the social pool from which the ruling class replenished itself but a political world of its own, with interests that were not necessarily identical with those of the ruling class. It was among these men, still socially excluded from the ruling class, yet already members of the power structure, that the search for an autonomous legitimation would inevitably proceed. Their insistence upon stable impersonal and non-political norms and procedures, upon regular remuneration for full-time work, upon regular promotions in accordance with universal criteria, upon the routinization of work, and protection against the intrusion of social prejudices created a political program whose importance must not be underestimated. The nature of the clerks' work demanded consistency, logic, and uniformity if records were to have any meaning as a basis for decision making. The clerks served a

[22] Hassel, "Table of Ranks," 294, de Madariaga, *Russia*, 56, Sjoberg, 239-240.
[23] Jones, *Emancipation*, 41.
[24] See Mertvago's own case in Mertvago, 38.

subfunction within the political function, but one likely to become so important with the growth of Russia's power that they would seek a measure of autonomy as a status group with a claim to legitimation distinct from that of the ruling elite.[25] For such claims to become effective, however, there must already have begun that differentiation of society of which the dislocation of the ruling class is but a reflection. By the end of the eighteenth century the evolution of Russian society still had not reached the stage where the relationship between the ruler, the ruling class, and the bureaucracy becomes a triangular one. Rather, it remained a linear one in which ruler and ruling class had a common interest in maintaining the social and political status quo, and this interest included the social and political subordination of the non-noble clerks to the membership of the ruling class. Indeed, there occurred in the reign of Catherine a last-ditch reaction against the growing power of the clerks, which took the form of a dismantling of the central government apparatus and a scattering of the clerks in the provinces of the Empire, where, presumably, they were to lose their esprit de corps and become a more pliant tool of the ruling class.

An awareness of the distinction between ruling class and bureaucracy is necessary if the concept of state is to make any sense. Perhaps no other term has been so misused in political literature, and one authority has been led to conclude that "it is impossible to offer a unified definition of the state that would be satisfactory even to a majority of those seriously concerned with the problem."[26] Yet how many concrete actions have been imputed to a concept that resists definition!

When the ruling class is still homogeneous, i.e., when its constituent elements, despite their different origin and status, still possess an overriding consciousness of their exclusively political function buttressed by a monopoly over specific privileges, the state is simply synonymous with the leadership of the ruling class and the network of institutions by which this class transforms its political power into administrative directives; it has no separate existence. It is social differentiation and the resulting instability within the ruling class that raises for the first time the need for a definition. As social institutions multiply, representing new social forces released by economic development and cultural progress and seeking a political solution of the issues concerning them, the resolution of conflicts requires the formulation of the concept of state in both abstract and tangible terms. In abstract terms "the state is nothing more than the organization of all social forces that

[25] Eisenstadt, 159.
[26] M. Fried, "State: The Institution," in IESS, XV, 145.

have a political significance . . . the resultant of the coordination and disciplining of . . . all the elements in a society that are suited to exercising political functions."[27] In tangible terms the state is embodied in institutions such as a legislature, where the battle of interests then affecting the whole of society seeks to forge a more elusive consensus, and a bureaucracy whose size and specialization grow with the differentiation of society. A new *rapport de forces* develops, constantly subject to change, between the new elites, the bureaucracy, and the legislature, and between all of them and the ruler. Its nature depends on society's ability to integrate new forces into its political tradition.

The idea of the state in eighteenth-century Russia was still in its infancy. Without a society whose structural elements enjoyed an independent existence, possessed an internal consistency, and wielded enough power to create a useful tension seeking its resolution in political action, there could be no state interest transcending the parochial interests of the ruling class. Only in foreign policy had a complex of motives, circumstances, and capabilities already created an autonomous state interest with a dynamism of its own. In domestic affairs the concept of the general welfare did envision an interest transcending that of the ruling class, but its implications belonged to the future and did not go at the time beyond fiscal (*kazennye*) concerns. In the vertically integrated society of eighteenth-century Russia there was no room for loyalty to the "state," which as a result had only a shadowy existence. There was a sense of community fostered by a strong ethnic and religious unity. There was personal loyalty to the leadership of the ruling class and to the ruler, but that was not the same thing as loyalty to the state.

A ruling class also needs to define its relationships with the socially dependent. Preindustrial society was characterized by the dominion of one class over the rest of society, a dominion particularly harsh where serfdom still prevailed, and it seems almost irrelevant to inquire into the nature of the mutual ties binding nobles, townsmen, and peasants into a single human collectivity. Yet these ties were of vital importance in sustaining the legitimacy of the ruling class and the development of its power.

Eighteenth-century Russia resembled the model suggested by Joseph Obrebski, consisting of "the folk-society or the peasant strata living under their traditional non-literate culture and the national culture group bound to the folk-mass by a political order or a class system." The two cultures were mutually exclusive and hostile, each finding no

[27] Mosca, 158.

place for the cultural forms and values of the other.[28] An imported
civilization alien to traditional Muscovite ways did indeed begin to
seep into Russia in the seventeenth century and conquered the ruling
class in the next. Expanded cultural contacts with France and the
German states brought about an increased awareness of the Western
world. New forms of entertainments, new social customs, new governmental agencies made their appearance. Language, too, felt the
impact of foreign influences, and a knowledge of European literature
gradually became part of an educated man's baggage. These new developments reinforced the exclusiveness of the ruling class, while the
merchants, townsmen, and peasants remained in the affective world
of their ancestors.[29]   The mutual hostility of the two cultures, however, did not exclude cooperation. Indeed, "in its drive for expansion,
continuity and realization the national culture group proceeds to as-
similate and incorporate into its structure the individual members of
the folk groups and the folk society as a whole" while at the same
time "it evolves mechanisms of stratification and segregation which
relegate the new segments to an inferior class position and allow them
to participate in the national society on a reduced scale, socially and
culturally."[30] This process of gradual absorption of the strata found
just below the ruling class, without which it could not govern, was
matched by a similar influence of the socially dependent upon their
superiors. In the private sphere, the abundance of domestic help which
every observer of the Russian scene has found to be characteristic of
noble households created a crucible in which the old and the tendency
to the new fought to create the synthesis of a new culture. Socially,
as Johnson discovered for Prussia, "instead of the army molding the
peasants the peasants steadily molded the army and the lower ranks
of the civil service," a phenomenon which Mosca has called a "ferment
of endosmosis and exosmosis between the upper classes and certain
portions of the lower."[31]

In this grey zone overlapping the very real division between the
world of the ruling class and that of the masses were found several
status groups with definite functional responsibilities, whom Wittfogel

[28] Obrebski, 9-10, 14.

[29] Certain differences, however, suggest that the national community had not yet
completely coalesced by the beginning of Catherine's reign. Obrebski (23-24), for example, claims that there was no difference in the functions of the two communities
(while that of the ruling class was precisely to rule) and that the national group was
no longer bound by personal ties of kinship.

[30] Obrebski, 12.

[31] Johnson, 27, Mosca, 65.

calls the secular semi-officials.[32] They were very close to the clerks who staffed the bureaucracy, and they lived in the same cultural world, but they were unequally wedded to the power structure. Among them we find the leadership of the guilds, including the tax farmers, whose ready cash enabled them to purchase influence and, in favorable circumstances, direct cooptation into the ruling class, and the town and village officials elected by their communities, with the sanction of the ruling class. A wider circle included the wealthier peasants, who still found it hard to overcome their legal disabilities, the priests' numerous offspring who sought to anchor themselves in the ruling class, and the soldiers' children who still vacillated between the world of their fathers and civilian life. All these men formed the indispensable channels through which messages were relayed from the depths of society and orders from the ruling class were given the necessary legitimacy.

This issue of legitimacy is, once again, central in determining the performance of a political system, in the ability of the ruling class to mobilize resources. To be effective, power must be exercised within a network of clearly defined hierarchical roles and thus routinized.[33] Routinization implies the diffusion of authority or its "nesting"[34] so that greater and greater resources can be tapped when the application of power to a definite object is not immediately effective. One must marvel, for example, at the ability of the Russian police to track down fugitive serfs several hundred miles away from their villages, given the difficulty of communications and the sparsity of the population. Legitimacy, then, as was previously noted, depended upon the acceptance by the socially dependent of orders sent through recognized channels, upon the observance of an unwritten social contract between ruling class and society. Even if the theory of social contract is now found disreputable, as Barrington Moore has remarked, it provides a significant insight: a set of limits on what rulers and subjects can do. Unless we accept the theory of absolute power—and there are no absolutes in human affairs—or believe that "fear, fraud, and force" are the sole basis of human society,[35] some set of mutual obligations must exist between the ruling class and society.

The men who occupied the intermediate stratum between the ruling class and the mass of townsmen and peasants formed separate segmental elites[36] who received their orders from the subordinate individuals of the ruling class, the same individuals who by their acceptance

[32] Wittfogel, 317.
[33] Ho, 474.
[34] The term is used by Peabody in "Authority," in IESS, I, 474.
[35] Moore, 10, 17-18.
[36] Keller's term: 26.

conferred legitimacy upon the program of the political leadership. They carried out their orders when they fell within that "zone of acquiescence," where orders are acceptable without the conscious questioning of their authority,[37] i.e., when they were consistent with the values of their social order. The village headman—if not the landowner himself—determined whether fugitives or criminals should be turned over to the police; the elected representatives determined how taxes apportioned by head at the highest level of the ruling class should be apportioned territorially among rural communities, etc. Of crucial importance was the congruence of the style of authority of the ruling class with other authority patterns in society.[38] The symbiosis between ruling class and folk-society facilitated a natural understanding between the lower levels of executives of the political organization—the clerks, the nonserving landowners, on the one hand, and the elite of the peasantry and townsmen, on the other. Bribes were expected because they were freely given and vice versa. The peasant who beat his wife and sons took for granted his beating by the land captain.

Orders, however, will be challenged if they fall outside the zone of acquiescence: a test of power will ensue in which sheer coercion will be pitted against either passive resistance or outright rebellion. Individual acts are quickly put down if they find no resonance within a class or society. But if an order strikes at the foundation of the social order or the religious beliefs which constitute a community's most intimate conception of the meaning of its existence, strong resistance is bound to result. In extreme cases rebellion—and with it rejection of the ruling class—is brought about when social norms are introduced or are retained which are or have become remote from the way of life of those to whom they apply. The Pugachev rebellion is an excellent example. It was not a peasant revolt, but the last stand of Cossacks who had fled the progress of serfdom in other Cossack territories and were pushed against the wall by the relentless advance of that social order; of Bashkirs who sought to remain free nomads in the face of advancing civilization; and of industrial workers who felt the norms of serfdom were incompatible with their new status. The rebellion

[37] Barnard, "Definition," 181-182, and H. Simon, "Decision-making and Administrative Organization," in Merton, 189-190. Simon prefers the term "zone of acquiescence" to "zone of indifference" used by Barnard, but the two are not synonymous. In one case obedience is unconscious; in the other a conscious acceptance of the validity of the order is assumed. Langeron (148-149) gives an illustration of these limits beyond which an officer's power would be challenged: if he used the monies deposited by the men of his company or regiment in the treasury of the *artel* and intended for their own use.

[38] Peabody, "Authority," 475.

found no dangerous echo beyond pre-reform Kazan gubernia, in the areas where serfdom was reaching its apogee: there was no "perception of injury," "no moral anger," where serfdom was taken for granted.

On the eve of Catherine's reign at least two trends were clearly emerging, sometimes complementary, sometimes threatening to cancel each other. One was a trend toward internal consolidation in society as a whole and within its major constituent groups—the nobility, the peasants, the townsmen, and the clergy—a desire to define by statute the boundaries of social categories. The blurred social contours of the elite resulted in general insecurity, which itself pointed to the openness of access to the ruling class and to its organic link with the rest of society. But the rapid growth of the nobility, from 37,326 males in 1744 to 49,777 in 1762, a 33 percent increase in eighteen years,[39] helped generate a current of opinion seeking an objective definition of status. A society in search of security is a society in process of consolidation, and this pursuit already presaged the more restrictive social policies of the early decades of the nineteenth century.

The second trend was the result of outside pressures upon the machinery of the Imperial government during the Seven Years War. The Enlightenment, Peter Gay has told us, was a cultural climate in which "criticism achieved a creative role."[40] Criticism proceeds from premises considered rational to create an orderly arrangement of phenomena capable of producing a desired result. The eighteenth century witnessed, in Marc Raeff's words, "a continuous desire to maximize all resources [of society] and to use this new potential dynamically for the enlargement and improvement of its way of life."[41] This desire followed the completion in most European states of a modern monarchy sustained by a ruling class which gave it a political base and a social underpinning, and demanded the creation of an efficient administrative machinery capable of effectively bringing about the new quality of life which the vital elements of society were yearning for.

War and finance are two sides of the same coin, and international wars, prolonged and extremely expensive, were a dominant feature of eighteenth-century history. Military preparedness became the test of governmental efficiency, which could be achieved through changing the awkward administrative system created in the late 1730s out of Muscovite and Petrine elements. This system tried to operate in accordance with the self-contradictory proposition that a highly centralized administration could function without the necessary personnel

[39] Kahan, 42.
[40] Gay, I, x, 141, 150.
[41] Raeff, "Well-Ordered Police State," 1222.

in a vast and sparsely populated land. The administrative reform therefore would have three components: a more rational territorial division
of the country and a concomitant clarification of local jurisdictions;
a reorganization of the judiciary to give the nobility the means to
enforce its dominant status; and reform to give the police a free hand
to maintain order and to speed up the flow of funds from the peasant
communities to the treasury.

These two trends, in turn, combined to compel a comprehensive
definition of Great Russia's relationships with its borderlands. Russia,
like other European countries was a "still incomplete state,"[42] and the
powerful current toward "systematization," to use George Yaney's
term,[43] was bound to accelerate an uncertain evolution toward political
integration and unification. The realization that the growth of serfdom
and its spread into the borderlands of the south were creating everywhere a ruling class with common interests to defend led to the absorption of the nobility of both Great Russia and the borderlands into
a single and truly Imperial ruling class, a development with momentous
consequences for both its social and political constitutions.

[42] Gagliardo, 82.
[43] Yaney, 5. A similar trend was noticeable in literature and is analyzed in Kurilov,
passim.

CHAPTER II

THE IMPERIAL GOVERNMENT, 1762-1774

THE POLITICAL LEADERSHIP

The Empress Catherine, always "with a book in her pocket,"[1] came to the throne imbued with the generous ideas of the Enlightenment and driven by a fervent desire to improve the condition of her adopted country and raise its prestige among the other European states. She was also endowed with an eclectic approach to politics and a cynicism learned during her hard apprenticeship at the Russian Court, which her unhappy private life tended only to deepen—hence a contradiction between a liberal impulse toward change and a deep distrust of its consequences. In foreign policy she was harsh and brutal and took full advantage of the favorable circumstances ripening along her Polish and Turkish borders. Her economic program rejected monopolies, supported free trade, and favored agriculture as the major source of wealth, yet gave considerable support to the development of the Ural mines. She patronized literature and tolerated criticism more than any of her predecessors; she encouraged the development of a third estate, but was aware of its social implications. She wanted a powerful monarchy with fundamental laws, thinking perhaps that the two were compatible and that they would be acceptable to her entourage. The torture of prisoners and the inhumane punishments offended her sensibility; so did the brutality of serfdom, but she soon became aware of the "passion and fury" with which even the kindest man could defend the social order.[2]

The political program of a ruler, especially one put together with quotations from the leading figures of the Enlightenment, none of whom was Russian, must first be accepted as legitimate by those who have to reconcile in the course of its execution the inevitable contradictions between intentions and realities. And not only the program must withstand the scrutiny of the political leadership, the legitimacy of the Empress herself had to be acknowledged. The elevation of Catherine, wrote David Ransel, "represented a more flagrant breach of the traditional succession system than any other that had occurred

[1] Madariaga, 9.
[2] *Ibid.*, 587, 581, 554.

in the eighteenth century."[3] Yet, without any substantial opposition, the former German princess of Anhalt-Zerbst found herself within a few months in full possession of the Imperial authority. Supreme legislator and supreme judge, she was in a position to choose the men who would carry out her orders. She had the authority to appoint all senators, presidents, members and procurators of all colleges and other central agencies, all governors general, governors, and vice-governors, men who would police the realm, administer justice, and collect the revenue, all army, brigade, and regimental commanders to lead the armies, which she, as a woman, could not command in person. In a word, she had the authority to select men for all the graded positions which constituted most of the political core of the ruling class, down to class VI of the Table of Ranks. But she could not know all these men personally—the active list of general officers in the first four classes alone numbered 82—and even if she did, they had to be selected from a pool of candidates submitted by the ruling families. It was these families which in the final analysis would pass upon the legitimacy of the Empress's program and select the candidates for membership in the political core. As Mosca put it so well, one cannot enter paradise over the veto of the saints.[4]

There were three clusters of political families at the outset of the reign, and the distribution of appointments indicates that a conscious effort was made to achieve a representative apportionment not only in the government as a whole but even within individual agencies and councils. The judicious distribution of leadership positions among the three clusters gave the ruling families a voice in shaping policies, perpetuated rivalries, and shaped a consensus on current issues which the Empress could use to her advantage.

One cluster of political families included the Kurakins, the Nepliuevs, and the Sheremetevs, among the leaders of military and foreign policy under Peter the Great. Another consisted of the Saltykov and Trubetskoi families, also of boyar origin; they must be considered the core of what can be called the Senate or domestic establishment. A third cluster, sharply different in origin but giving its true measure to the vitality of the ruling class, included families or individuals who rose to prominence in the wake of important favorites. In two remarkable instances in the eighteenth century these men came from the borderlands: the Razumovskiis from the Ukraine and the Potemkins

³ Ransel, 68.

⁴ Mosca, 402-403. The "constitutional" position of the autocrat during the eighteenth century has received little attention, much less indeed than that of his Muscovite predecessor. Valuable insights may be found in Cracraft, 27-49, Pipes, 112-138, Szamuely, 49-55, 59-64.

from the Smolensk nobility. It may be an exaggeration to call them representatives of the borderlands, in contrast to the old families from Great Russia, because many of these were of Lithuanian or Tatar background. But since they were of more recent origin they certainly symbolized the union of Great Russia with its borderlands and brought new blood to an aristocratic world that had ruled Russia for several generations.

It is tempting to isolate a number of Court families into another cluster, but it is not clear whether one existed as such. If one did exist, its core was probably the Golitsyns and above all the Naryshkin family, linked with the Saltykovs, the Nepliuevs, and the Rumiantsevs. The Saltykov family gave Peter's half-brother a wife who became Anna Ioanovna's mother, and from the Naryshkins came Peter the Great's mother. Rumiantsev was almost certainly Peter's illegitimate son. The Vorontsovs finally were closely related to Catherine I. Thus the Romanov house was enmeshed in a network of marital alliances binding some of the most important ruling families.[5]

The division of the elite into three or four clusters must not be overdone, since nothing in politics is ever permanent or straightforward; it is, however, a very useful guide to the intrigues and rivalries that were a permanent feature of Russian political life. Although there were crossovers, it seems that in most cases marriages took place within each of the two clusters of Great Russian families while the favorites' relatives gradually became absorbed into either one. These families were among the largest landowners, the Sheremetevs owning more than 100,000 souls and each of the others more than 10,000. The political elite thus included the richest families as well, the chief beneficiaries of serfdom and those most interested in its retention.

In the administrative structure which these men were called upon to staff there were three major centers of patronage. In a century marked by repeated wars and constant preparation for war, the three colleges of Foreign Affairs, War, and Navy and the regional military commanders assumed a vital importance in shaping the foreign policy of the Empire. To benefit an elite that stood to gain from military expansion and new territorial conquests, they set a social and fiscal policy designed to extract immense resources from the population. This foreign-policy and military establishment, as a source of patronage, found its counterpart in the Senate establishment and the staff of the colleges in charge of domestic administration. It was the Senate and its Procurator General who were ultimately responsible for the

[5] Dolgorukov, Rŭssiisk. Rodoslovnaia kniga, and Rummel are the two major sources for the study of genealogies. See Appendix A.

less glamorous but no less vital tasks of day-to-day administration and for finding the resources to support both the army and an active foreign policy.

The first decade of Catherine's reign was marked by the emergence of Nikita Panin as the dominant influence in the formulation of a foreign policy oriented toward Prussia and Denmark and active support of the Russian party in Poland and Sweden, even though he was never given the title of Chancellor borne for many years by his predecessor Bestuzhev-Riumin.[6] Panin was also the tutor to Grand Duke Paul, who many considered to have been wronged when his mother usurped the throne in 1762. The Panin family had given two pages to the Court of Ivan the Terrible and at least two voevodas in the seventeenth century. Its position within the ruling elite was determined by its alliance with the family of Peter the Great's favorite—Nikita's father married the niece of Menshikov—and with the Kurakin family—his two sisters married a Kurakin and a Nepliuev.

In the College of Navy the dominant figure was not Grand Duke Paul, its President and Grand Admiral of the Fleet, but its Vice-President Ivan Chernyshev, who reported personally to the Empress on naval affairs. His brother Zakhar was appointed Vice-President of the College of War in 1763 and President ten years later with promotion to field marshal. The Chernyshevs and the Panins were related by marriage, and these two families were thus the current leaders of the old clans whose influence had been decisive in the formulation of foreign and military policy. Among the eight commanding generals of military regions created in European Russia in 1763 we find Peter Panin (Finland), Nikita's brother; Zakhar Chernyshev again (Smolensk); Marshal Buturlin (Lifland), another descendant of a boyar family and related to the Kurakins.

The other commands, however, were given to representatives of the other two great political families. The Petersburg command went to Marshal Kirill Razumovskii, the last hetman of the Ukraine and brother of Elizabeth's favorite. The Moscow command was given to Marshal Peter Saltykov, brother-in-law of Elizabeth's former Procurator General, Prince Nikita Trubetskoi. Troops along the Ukrainian border were placed under Peter Rumiantsev, who occupied a key position in the network of families: he was related to both the Kurakins (through his wife, a Golitsyna) and the Trubetskois (through his sister).[7]

---

[6] The role of Panin and his supporters is the object of Ransel's careful study *Politics*.

[7] Data on appointments to various military and civil positions everywhere in this book are culled from the *Mesiatseslovy*. A significant fact, yet one overlooked by Ransel, is that the Orlovs, to whom he attaches such importance, received no major appointment

What made all these men so influential was the power to dispense the patronage they possessed by virtue of their administrative positions. Appointment to central agencies, to the post of governor and voevoda and to subordinate commands, whether made in the last resort by the Empress, the Senate, or the Colleges of War and Navy, depended on recommendations by superiors who in the Russia of the 1760s were men born to govern.

The Senate establishment had been headed since 1764 by an outstanding administrator, Prince Alexander Viazemskii. The scion of a family that gave one of the leaders of Ivan the Terrible's *oprichnina* but then ceased to be politically active, he owed his appointment to General Rumiantsev, to whom he referred later in life as "the source of my happiness." In 1768 he married the daughter of Nikita Trubetskoi, and as a result the clan led by the Saltykov and Trubetskoi families controlled the chief administrative posts in the Empire and the governor generalship of the enormous Moscow gubernia, together with the military command vested in Peter Saltykov. Thus the overwhelming majority of requests for appointments, promotions and rewards, for leaves and transfers in the entire civil service, passed through agencies under the immediate control of these two families.

The third center of power and influence—and this is a development peculiar to Catherine's reign—was the Cabinet. The Empress was a forceful ruler who kept in close touch with important developments and maintained an enormous correspondence. Governors general, governors, and regional commanders reported to her directly, as did a number of college chiefs. A great many petitions were addressed to her personally, seeking redress, requesting pensions or an appointment, submitting a project. A stream of Imperial orders on an immense variety of subjects flowed from her office to a multitude of agencies. To handle the ruler's private and public correspondence a cabinet had been in existence since the reign of Peter, an agency whose jurisdiction also included at various times the management of the ruler's wealth such as the Altai gold mines, the Nerchinsk silver mines, and the Siberian fur trade. This dual function was reflected in the distinction made between the Cabinet proper and the Secretariat, although the term as such did not exist. A state secretary (*stats-sekretar'*) might very well be asked to examine items in the Imperial family's budget or the management of its palaces.[8]

The Director of the Cabinet was an important personage who be-

---

that was also a source of patronage. Grigorii was only Commanding General of the Artillery and head of the Chancery for the settlement of foreign colonists.

[8] There exists no separate study of the Secretariat save a short survey in *Dvukhsotletie Kabineta*, 351-407. See also Amburger, *Geschichte*, 82-83, 85-86.

Alexander Alexeevich Viazemskii

PETR SEMENOVICH SALTYKOV

longed to the ruler's immediate entourage. Adam Olsuf'ev, married to a Saltykova, was appointed to the post by Elizabeth in 1758 and remained in it until his death in 1784, a long tenure similar to Prince Viazemskii's twenty-eight years in the post of Procurator General. Considered one of the best-educated men of his time, he had the unusual distinction of being simultaneously a member of the College of Foreign Affairs and of the First Department of the Senate.

The Secretariat proper took shape about a year after Catherine's accession, when three secretaries were appointed "to receive petitions addressed to Her Majesty": Ivan Elagin, Grigorii Teplov, and the same Olsuf'ev.[9] Actually, during the first decade of the reign, the Secretariat

[9] PSZ, 1763, N. 11867-11868.

consisted of four or five individuals. One of the secretaries was Sergei
Kozmin, the son of a senior secretary of the Senate and former Vice-
President of the College of Revenue. Teplov, the son of a Novgorod
smelter, was a direct protégé of Razumovskii and the only secretary
"with special responsibilities" (*u sobstvennykh del*), a reference perhaps to his role as legislative adviser. Grigorii Kozitskii was a protégé
of the Gudovich family related to the Razumovskiis. The other two,
Elagin and Stepan Strekalov, had long been associated with the Court.

Finally, the need to provide a coordinating body where the three
clusters would be represented together was met by the creation of the
Council "attached to Her Majesty's Court" in 1768. The event was
symptomatic of the clash of opinions and interests caused by the
Turkish war. The Court had traditionally been the arena where the
struggle for preeminence among the ruling families developed. The
creation of the Council marked a major step in the institutionalization
of a semi-legislative body where major policy goals would be set, but
its major function was still to discuss foreign policy and military planning—it was sometimes called the Military Council[10]—and Prince Viazemskii was the only representative of the domestic establishment.
Razumovskii and Grigorii Orlov, the current favorite, were members.
The diplomats and the military were represented by the Panin brothers,
Zakhar Chernyshev and two Alexander Golitsyns. Strekalov served
as secretary. Thus the political constellation surrounding the new Empress was relatively simple, and did not consist of mere courtiers adept
at satisfying the ruler's whims. These men thrashed out the issues,
recommended options, and set the limits of the possible before an
assertive ruler whose dynamic mixture of idealism and cynicism needed
at times to be guided and restrained. And when the Empress submitted
to some of them the instruction containing her political program they—
in Catherine's own words—erased "what they pleased and struck out
more than half of what (she) had written," especially in the chapter
where the amelioration of serfdom was contemplated.[11]

SENATE AND COLLEGES

The Senate was the central body most likely to represent the ruling
families. It "was not a bureaucratic office in the usual sense. It was
the seat of the noble families in the country and represented the interests of the entire elite of servicemen."[12] Staffed with members who

[10] PSZ, 1770, N. 13476.
[11] Madariaga, 158.
[12] Ransel, 61. The standard history of the Senate in the eighteenth century is *Istoriia Prav. Senata*, vols. I-II.

all belonged to the top stratum of the ruling class, the Senate selected on its own authority the subordinate members of that class. Its decisions, based on precedents, provided continuity in the business of government and gave the stamp of legitimacy to the ruler's initiatives.

Created in 1711 as the "first agency in the state," its jurisdiction, however, never included foreign policy and operational matters in the army and navy, and the colleges of Foreign Affairs, War, and Navy gradually built up an autonomy that came to be sanctioned by tradition. The Senate became chiefly a committee to coordinate the activities of specialized agencies, to maintain some uniformity in the interpretation of the law, and to act as a court of last resort in all but the most important cases reserved for the final decision of the Empress or those in which she expressed a personal interest.

The membership of the Senate grew throughout the eighteenth century. There were originally nine senators but their number had reached twenty-one in 1762. Its size and the requirement that all senators had to take part in the discussion of its business—no specialization being allowed—reflected the participation of the elite in the highest council of government, but also impaired its efficiency. Unsuccessful attempts were made on two occasions to divide it into departments, but not until Panin's project was accepted by the Empress in December 1763 did the need for a more orderly examination of governmental business become generally recognized.[13]

In theory, under Panin's plan, all six departments—four in Petersburg and two in Moscow—were equal; in fact they were not. The responsibilities assigned to the First Department were so much greater than those of the other five that it was clearly seen as the core of the new Senate. Its jurisdiction encompassed "state and political affairs," but the reference to political, i.e., foreign, affairs, included chiefly relations with border commissions under the College of Foreign Affairs and the settlement of colonists. The department also received business from the Synod and the College of Economy, civil-service matters from the Heraldmaster, and proposals to codify legislation from the Commission established to draft a new code of laws. But the department's jurisdiction was above all financial: the Colleges of Revenue and Audit, the Treasury, the Mint, the Colleges of Commerce and Mining reported to it. Its higher status also was evidenced in the appointment of the Procurator General himself to be its senior procurator and in the fact that the general assembly of the four Petersburg departments met in the department's chambers.

The creation of the First Department was a major step toward a

[13] PSZ, 1763, N. 11989, pt. 1-3. Ransel, 92-94.

separation of functions, of administrative matters from judicial proceedings. The concept had been in the air for some time, but it was
still imperfectly realized in the reform. The other departments continued to combine administrative and judicial functions, even at times
with a territorial jurisdiction. The Fourth Department, for example,
received matters—chiefly personnel questions and military contracts—
from the Colleges of War and Navy, from the army and navy cadet
corps, and matters related to the Smolensk nobility and New Serbia.
The Third Department received appeals from the Academy of Sciences,
Moscow University and other educational institutions, and from the
western borderlands where Russian law did not apply. The Second
Department was given "judicial affairs and investigations," and shared
this jurisdiction with the Sixth Department in Moscow. The Fifth took
over the duties of the old Senate Branch (*Kontora*) to which five
senators had been appointed in 1763. The Governor General of Moscow was a member, and its major responsibility was to watch over
the performance of the colleges and their branch offices in Moscow,
to compel them to follow their instructions, and to receive complaints
against their decisions or their dilatoriness. It might seem at first glance
that the Fifth Department became the Moscow equivalent of the First,
since the most important colleges had their headquarters in Moscow,
but this did not take place for at least three reasons: all college business
requiring higher-level decision had to be sent to the First Department;
petitioners had the choice of sending their complaints to Moscow or
Petersburg and might choose the latter because everyone knew that
final decisions were made there; and provincial agencies, aware that
the Fifth Department served as the branch of the First for current
administrative matters in the center and south, began to bypass it and
to send their requests to Petersburg. After the completion of the local
government reform in the early 1780s which closed the colleges in
Moscow, the Fifth Department became a third judicial department.

In the first decade of the reign the turnover among the three to five
members of each department was fairly rapid, as if to reflect the
jockeying for position among the leading families. If we consider only
the senators who remained several years, it appears that the Court
was represented chiefly in the First (Olsuf'ev and Elagin) and Second
Departments (Skavronskii). The Procurator General's party was strong
in the Second (Peter Trubetskoi) and the Fifth (Saltykov and Mel'gunov),
the party of the favorites in the Fourth (Razumovskii) and the Third
(Teplov). Other families, notably the Vorontsovs and the Murav'evs,
were represented in the Third and Sixth Departments. It is likely that
this mixed membership was intentional; and each department may be
seen as a representative cross-section of the ruling elite. As a result,

the Senate as a whole, in general assembly, was the council where a consensus was reached on major issues of domestic policy.[14]

Procedural rules throw some light on this attempt to make the Senate a forum for the settlement of differences. Each of the four Petersburg departments was required to discuss the business presented to it by a senior secretary or, in rare cases, by a senator, and to base its decision on existing law alone. If its decision was unanimous it had the force of law as if it had been made by the entire Senate; therefore, departmental decisions were issued in its name, irrespective of the department making them. Delays were sometimes caused by the requirement to obtain the votes of all the current members of a department, some of whom might be ill or away on a mission.

A department's decision was not final in four cases: if no unanimity was reached; if the department annulled one of its previous decisions; if its decision contained an amendment to existing law; or if a new law was required. When senators could not reach agreement, the senior procurator presented a "proposal" and asked for a unanimous vote. If he could not sway the dissenters or when new legislation was indeed required, the matter was taken to a general assembly of the four departments, where a similar procedure was repeated. If differences were reconciled and unanimity was obtained, the matter rested there. Otherwise, the Procurator General referred the proceedings to the Empress. When new legislation was required, the Senate submitted a "respectful report" (*vsepoddaneishii doklad*) through the Procurator General, and the final decision was left to the Empress. In Moscow, similar procedures were followed, but these reflected the subordinate position of the two departments there. If their general assembly could not reach unanimity or new legislation was required, the matter was sent to the Procurator General, who brought it before the general assembly of the Petersburg departments.

The Empress did not take kindly to the senators' inability to decide a case for personal reasons dictated by interests or conscience. She expressed her annoyance at being asked to settle such matters and insisted on a consensus.[15] This procedure was designed to maintain a sharp separation between the coordination of existing procedural and substantive norms and the introduction of any new rules. The conclusion is sometimes drawn that this meant a distinctly secondary role for the Senate while the legislative power remained the prerogative of the Empress. Yaney has emphasized the Senate's essentially passive

[14] See LeDonne, "Appointments."

[15] PSZ, 1763, N. 11989, pt. 2, 5-6; 1772, N. 13889; *Istoriia Prav. Senata*, II, 389-391; PSZ, 1773, N. 14049.

activity, contrasting it with the more forceful role played by the "bureaucracy." This is to over-emphasize the dynamism of government in the eighteenth century. The Senate was a conservative body in a conservative society, the repository of tradition, or, as the law put it, the "depository" (*khranilishche*) of the laws.[16] Against a background of a seemingly unchanging social order, the chief function of the Senate was to settle disputes, to grant lucrative contracts, and to manage the civil service, i.e., to share the rewards which the system had to offer among the subordinate members of the ruling class, while contentions among the ruling families and the division of spoils among them belonged to the arbitration of the Empress.

The history of the Senate was closely bound with that of the Procurator General's office. The post was created in 1722 to serve as the "eye" of the Tsar in the Senate's deliberations. Since the tsars seldom participated personally in its meetings, relations between the "first agency in the state" and the ruler were limited to the submission of written reports and the issuance of written orders. The Procurator General introduced a human element in this relationship, and his strength came to rest on a power base among the ruling families, on his privilege of direct and permanent access to the ruler, and on his control of the staff (*kantseliaria*) of the Senate. This position made him a potential prime minister, but the growth of his office was retarded by the unstable political situation that followed the death of Peter. The long tenure of Prince Nikita Trubetskoi (1740-1760) despite the emergence of the Shuvalovs, a powerful family of favorites, who later became integrated into the domestic establishment—Andrei, Alexander's nephew, head of the secret police under Elizabeth, married a daughter of Peter Saltykov—laid the political base which gave Catherine's Procurator General his immense power.[17]

Prince Alexander Viazemskii was born in 1727, two years before the Empress, in the ancient family of the princes of Viazma between Smolensk and Moscow. His father was a mere naval lieutenant, but his mother was a Pozniakova, a family well established in the Senate establishment. During the Seven Years War he was chief of staff to General Rumiantsev, whose command became a nursery of future governors and governors general. After the war he was sent to the Urals to put down a miners' revolt, and his ruthlessness, efficiency, and intelligent recommendations marked him out among the potential close collaborators of the Empress. He became Procurator General in

[16] Tel'berg, 5, Yaney, 29, 77-78, 80.

[17] Dmitriev, *Istoriia*, 507-511, 519-520; *Ist. Prav. Senata*, II, 392-393; Ransel, *Politics*, 162-163.

1764 and was instructed to share with Nikita Panin his knowledge of
"secret matters," a fine illustration of accommodation between two
of the three major political families. He soon became de facto head
of the secret police. In 1765, together with Peter Panin, he sat on the
commission to review land survey legislation and to prepare the instruction of 1766 which became the basis for a systematic land survey
of European Russia. In 1767 he was appointed chairman of the Legislative Commission summoned to draft a new code of laws, and he
joined the Council the following year. His most constructive work
was in financial administration, and he is certainly one of the architects
of the reform of 1775 although very little is known about his role.[18]

   Two aspects of the Procurator General's activities help us understand the source of his influence and power. He was, first of all, one
of the most important legislative advisers of the Empress. Not bound
like senators to settle cases in accordance with existing law, he could
suggest remedies and new departures. His right of access to the throne
at least twice a week in his official capacity was a vital element of his
power, and his long tenure illustrates how close the relationship must
have been. Second, the Procurator General possessed vast powers of
patronage by virtue of his office, power which the Empress's confidence
must have increased considerably. He appointed, dismissed, and rewarded the entire staff of the Senate, except the senior procurators.
Each Senate department had a senior secretary and a staff of clerks
who received the documentation and the evidence pertaining to each
case, prepared briefs for the senators, and wrote the final draft of the
decisions. This senior secretary and the senior procurator who watched
over the proceedings and upheld legality were directly responsible to
the Procurator General. And in most colleges, in all gubernias and
provinces, the Procurator General appointed (with Senate approval)

---

[18] A portrait of the young Viazemskii is in Ivanov; another can be seen in the Treti'iakov
Gallery. The many negative assessments of Prince Viazemskii are largely due to the fact
that he was not accessible to foreigners and had many enemies, if only because of the
crucial position he occupied for so long in the Imperial government. He may very well
have been the object of a systematic campaign of defamation by some members of the
military-foreign policy establishment, like Bezborodko, Potemkin, and Vorontsov, who
had every reason to resent his conservative fiscal policy, and the downgrading of his
abilities—which reached its lowest point in Turgenev's comment that he could hardly
express himself without the help of a clerk—must be taken for what it is. That the
Empress, who, according to the universal opinion of her contemporaries, was an intelligent, hard-working, and witty woman should have placed the three key sectors of
domestic administration in the hands of a blockhead and kept working with him for
twenty-eight years simply defies commonsense. For some negative comments bordering
on the grotesque, see Turgenev, 1887, I, 86-87, Goertz, 55-56. Very positive assessments
are in Makushev, 20, Chichagov, 76-78, 113, Bantysh-Kamenskii, I (1836), 366-369.
See also Hassell, 24, 29.

procurators who reported directly to him. Promotion lists were prepared in his office and routed through the general assembly of the
Petersburg departments. Appointments not subject to Senate confirmation were made by him directly.

He was the head of the civil service in other ways as well. In central
and local agencies his procurators kept the attendance records; even
governors could not come to the capital without his authorization. He
granted leaves of absence exceeding twenty-nine days. Procurators sent
him copies of their objections to an agency's interpretation of the law.
Thus the Procurator General became in addition the final interpreter
of the law; only the Empress could reverse his decision. In the nineteenth century, when the creation of independent ministries directly
responsible to the Tsar reduced the Procurator General to the modest
role of Minister of Justice and terminated the Senate's role as coor-
dinator of the entire internal administration, many would lament the
loss of the unity maintained under the earlier system.

The specialized agencies of the Imperial government were the colleges. Nine were established by 1718, seven years after the creation
of the Senate, in order to reduce the burden of work placed upon that
body. Because the sheer volume of government business required a
specialization of functions, the number of colleges or chanceries, as
some of these agencies were called, continued to grow.

References are often found in eighteenth-century documents to the
"two capitals," Petersburg and Moscow. This was no mere flattering
tribute to the former importance of Moscow at a time when the decision had irrevocably been made to leave the Court and the Senate
in the northern capital. The central location of Moscow made it more
accessible from almost anywhere in European Russia. The nobility's
estates were concentrated in the Moscow region, and the city was still
the largest in the country. Petersburg was located 763 kilometers to
the north, its physical environment was inhospitable, the cost of living
was high. By removing all central agencies to Petersburg, the Imperial
government would have risked making itself inaccessible to the population. As a result, a compromise was found by which some agencies
were housed in Petersburg while others remained in Moscow, with
each agency maintaining a branch office (*kontora*) in the other capital.
There was no comprehensive table of organization for all colleges until
1763, but it was generally accepted that each college had to have a
president and a vice-president, two councillors and two assessors, and
that each branch office would consist of a third councillor and a third
assessor, subordinated to the college and operating under the orders
(*po ukazam*) of the main office. A confusing situation resulted which
considerably blurred relationships between the colleges and the Senate.

The table of organization of December 1763, the first such comprehensive document in the history of Imperial administration, listed
eighteen major central agencies: eleven had their headquarters in Moscow and maintained a branch in Petersburg, with jurisdiction over the
three northern gubernias of Petersburg, Novgorod, and Arkhangelsk.
Thus, if Petersburg was definitely the political capital of the Empire,
Moscow remained its administrative heart.

Presidents and vice-presidents were chosen by the Empress and were
generally in class III or IV; four members and the procurator were
appointed by the Senate. The staff was large but varied greatly from
one agency to another.[19] Altogether, leaving out a few small agencies
and the higher educational establishment, about three-fourths of a
force of some two thousand people were in Moscow.

The colleges were the embodiment of the bureaucratic principle, yet
they were divided along class lines. The presidents and the members
belonged to the ruling elite; it is probable that an attempt was also
made here to place candidates from various groups and achieve a
balance similar to that found in the Senate departments. But a reading
of the table of organization immediately shows that these members
were a small minority among the clerks, "subclerks," and copyists
who, under the guidance of secretaries, constituted the backbone of
the organization. These men were of uncertain social origin, although
many seem to have come from "dynasties" of clerks. The clerks belonged to a social milieu often despised by the elite—most strongly,
one must assume, by those whose origins were best left obscure. The
elite, as a political class, believed in making deals by personal contacts;
in the give and take of politics, they gave preference to content over
form. The clerks insisted on accuracy, consistency, and efficiency—
relative terms, to be sure, in the overly centralized administration of
such a vast country—yet very real constraints on the nobles, who were
made to pay for the services they required.

It is perhaps this distrust of the bureaucracy that explains the very
subordinate role of the colleges in the central government. Rather than
independent bureaucracies operating at the bidding of the ruler for
the greater good of the "state," they were screening committees of the
Senate departments with authority to dispose of only the least con-
troversial cases. Only after the Senate had ignored three requests for
assistance was a college allowed to refer the matter directly to the
Empress.[20]

[19] PSZ, 1763, N. 11991, vol. 44², 59-67.
[20] Procedures in the colleges were still regulated by the *General'nyi Reglament* of
1720 (PSZ, 1720, N. 3534); see also 1763, N. 11989, pt. 9-12, 27-28; 1765, N. 12382;
1772, N. 13784; 1781, N. 15193, Dmitriev, *Istoriia*, 497-498.

And yet, by a paradox often found in complex organizations, the colleges had developed an autonomy which could cause only disquiet among the political leadership. It was the product in part of the unsettled political situation after the death of Peter and the weakness of the rulers, especially Elizabeth; it was also built into the undifferentiated jurisdiction originally given to the colleges. Government was not at the time divided into administrative, judicial and fiscal functions, but rather into blocks of activities such as mining, manufacturing, commerce, municipal administration, etc. Each college could make appointments (to very subordinate positions), try and punish, and also collect funds. Thus, a college possessed all the ingredients of autonomous existence, even if, as a rule, it did not have its own local agencies. Nowhere was this autonomy so damaging as in financial administration. Since almost every college was also a separate treasury with a natural self-interest in hiding the total amount of its receipts and in keeping a reserve for its own needs, the College of Revenue was never able to establish its authority as the budget office, even for domestic agencies, despite the provisions of its statute.

To counter the growing autonomy of the colleges, a strong anti-bureaucratic trend was emerging in the 1760s in which the ruling class sought to eliminate the incipient threat to its supremacy. Marc Raeff has noted that non-noble clerks came to symbolize the impersonal machine of the state,[21] but their growing strength faced the Empress with a dilemma. To form what might seem a natural alliance with the bureaucratic element by governing directly through the colleges would have made possible an active domestic policy capable of dealing with the intractable issue of serfdom. To do that, however, would have violated the unwritten social contract and generated that moral indignation which precedes political disobedience. The Empress could not afford to take that course in the 1760s, when the legitimation of her power was not yet complete, and ten years later she no longer even had that choice.

The anti-bureaucratic trend took the form of a gradual sapping of the colleges' power. A new instruction sent to the governors in 1764 abolished their subordination to the colleges and placed them directly under the Senate and the Empress, thus removing a major source of irritation among those key managers of the ruling class. The creation in the spring of 1773 of the Expedition of State Revenues (*Ekspeditsiia Gosudarstvennykh Dokhodov*) for the express purpose of preparing an annual budget dealt a major blow to the financial autonomy of the colleges. The Expedition, it is true, was a bureaucratic agency par

---

[21] Raeff, *Origins*, 53; see also Jones, *Emancipation*, 34 and Pipes, 133-134.

excellence, but it was not a college subordinated to the Senate with an autonomous sphere of activity; it was only an extension of the Procurator General's staff. The reforms of 1775-1785 broadened the anti-bureaucratic offensive of the ruling class, scattered the clerks to the four corners of the Empire, and closed the colleges, an unusual occurrence indeed in a state where the absolute monarch supposedly ruled without the consent of the estates. Before we turn to the analysis of these reforms, however, we should examine the structure of local government in the 1760s.

GOVERNORS AND VOEVODAS

Central Russia—the Empire without its Baltic and Ukrainian border-lands and without Siberia—was divided into ten gubernias, eight of which were further divided into provinces (*provintsii*). A governor was appointed in each gubernia and a voevoda in each province save that of which the gubernia capital was the center. Most of the provinces in turn consisted of uezds, headed likewise by a voevoda, but one of lower rank.

Twenty-eight govenors were appointed in central Russia in the first decade of Catherine's reign.[22] Almost all were military men, about half of them in their fifties and sixties. For them a gubernatorial appointment was a reward for distinguished military service, a form of pension to give a general the means to live honorably after retirement. There were also a few younger men, some inclined toward civilian affairs and diplomacy; at least one of them, the Baltic German Jakob von Sievers, became one of the great administrators of the reign. Most governors were class III or IV officials—major or lieutenant generals—but all received the same annual salary (1,875 rubles) as that of the president of a college in Moscow. Although appointed by the Empress in person, they owed their recommendation to the army commanders under whom they had served during the Seven Years War, chiefly Rumiantsev and Saltykov, or the commanding generals of the military regions. Recommendations were sent to the First Department of the Senate or directly to the Secretariat, and if it is true that Sievers was selected from among some thirty candidates the competition must have been severe.[23] Next to an appointment in the two capitals a gover-

[22] The standard work on governors is still Blinov, *Gubernatory*. The term "central Russia" includes the 26 gubernias created after the reform and populated by Great Russians. Other gubernias are included in the "borderlands" discussed in Chapter Five.

[23] See LeDonne, "Catherine's Governors." For examples illustrating the procedures of appointment, see *Arkhiv Senata*, XII (1907), 392-393, XIV (1910), 202, 417-418. On Sievers, see Ilovaiskii, "Graf Iakob Sivers," in *Sochineniia*, I (1884), 465.

norship was the finest reward the elite could distribute among its members, and it formed one of the two links—the other was the post of gentry marshal—between the political leadership and the rank-and-file nobility in the provinces and uezds. Governors were not appointed for any length of time: only two remained at their posts during the entire pre-reform period, and about a third served more than five years. Most died in office or retired on their estates. The repeal at the end of 1765 of the 1740 law forbidding them to acquire property in their gubernias[24] makes it quite likely that during the last decade of their lives some governors acquired an estate sufficient to endow their daughters and sustain the promotion of their sons in the service.

Each governor had a chancery headed by two deputies (*tovarishchi*), two classes below him; these received 600 rubles a year. It included the gubernia procurator, three secretaries, and thirty-seven clerks. Thus the entire gubernia administration of central Russia consisted of 70 officials in graded positions (including 30 secretaries) and 370 clerks. The Instruction of 1764 sought to establish a symmetry between the chancery and a central college. The chancery was under the direct authority (*v tochnoi direktsii*) of the governor, who, "like the president of a college," distributed the business of the agency among its members, and, if he could not take part in the debates in person, especially in judicial proceedings, compelled the chancery to proceed expeditiously. Voting took place in accordance with the *General'nyi Reglament* in collegial fashion, the junior members voting first.[25]

The Instruction made it a point to strengthen the political role of the governor. It abandoned the condescending attitude characteristic of the 1740s, and proclaimed that he would enjoy the personal confidence of the Empress. The governor was removed from the jurisdiction of the colleges and placed directly under the Senate and the Empress; she alone would fine or reprimand him, on recommendation of the Senate or the Procurator General. This in fact placed him higher in the hierarchy of the ruling class than the presidents of at least some colleges and stressed his political rather than his bureaucratic status.[26]

The new standing of the governor reflected the emphasis now placed on the principle of territorial administration. Area administration can be territorial or functional, although it is often a combination of the two in which one form or the other predominates. Administration is

[24] PSZ, 1765, N. 12554; 1740, N. 8145.

[25] PSZ, 1763, N. 11991, vol. 44[2], 68-69; 1764, N. 12137, II; 1775, N. 14394; 1759, N. 10998, Dmitriev, *Istoriia*, 456-457, Eroshkin, 145.

[26] PSZ, 1764, N. 12137. A separate instruction was given to the governors of Moscow and Petersburg in the following year: 1765, N. 12306. See LeDonne, "Evolution," 97-103.

territorial when it is concentrated in an individual or a body looked upon as the recipient of all orders and requests from the central government, whether these impulses come down in the form of separate beams issuing from individual central agencies or are first concentrated into a single beam issuing from the coordinating organ of the central government, and when these orders are then retransmitted either horizontally to other agencies housed in the area capital or vertically to subordinate agencies at lower levels. Administration is functional when the beams issuing from the central agencies are directed to the local agents of these agencies who exercise a specialized jurisdiction in a given area and are not coordinated by any authority in the area. Thus, territorial administration is multifunctional when it absorbs all, or nearly all, the functions of government, while functional administration is linear and unifunctional because it is specialized.[27]

Such theoretical formulation, however, must have a social context. Functional administration recognizes the fragmentation of society into groups whose interests must be given representation in the central government. The colleges, especially the Colleges of Mining and Commerce and the Central *Magistrat*, and the nineteenth-century ministries were functional structures. Territorial administration, on the contrary, assumes the preeminence of a single class to which all other groups in society must be subordinated. The governor as the local representative of the ruling elite now became the nexus through which a ruthless class policy must be carried out. The tilt of governmental policy was quite apparent, even if it did not yet go as far as Prince Shakhovskoi's suggestion to appoint governors general in each gubernia with even higher pay and authority than the presidents of colleges;[28] but it was the initial move in the assault against the principle of functional-bureaucratic administration through colleges.

Despite the fact that the governor was such an important personage, it is impossible to find in the legislation of the period any systematic outline of his powers. The instruction declared him to be the head and master (*khoziain*) of his gubernia but was silent on the meaning of this term.[29] Yet, there is paradox only if one persists in looking upon the governor as a bureaucratic agent. In fact, his power derived from his status as a member of the social and political core of the ruling class and needed no restrictive definition in a legal document. His mission was to govern the dependent population of his gubernia in his dual capacity of social leader and political boss and to maintain

[27] I am greatly indebted to Fesler's very valuable book for this brief study of the distribution of governmental authority: see especially 1, 6-16, 60.

[28] TsGADA, f. 370, d. 21, fol. 1-6, 34-37.

[29] PSZ, 1764, N. 12137, I; see also Keep, "Light and Shade," 8.

discipline among the junior members of the ruling class and the clerks who served under him. The instruction considerably broadened the responsibilities of the governor. For the past thirty years he had been essentially the agent of a punitive government bent on extracting by compulsion the resources to maintain its great power status. In the 1760s a more enlightened attitude gained the upper hand: the view that the functioning of the whole depended on the proper operation of the parts,[30] that the might of the Empire rested on the prosperity of its provinces. It was the responsibility of the governor to improve communications, to encourage trade and agriculture, to build a well-ordered community to serve as one of the building blocks of an enlightened state. But the instruction did not create new agencies to carry out this ambitious program, and the governor was left to operate with the old institutional framework.

Over the members of the gubernia chancery he possessed few powers. His deputies were appointed by the Senate and the procurator by the Procurator General, and could be dismissed only with their approval. The instruction empowered him to dismiss secretaries, voevodas, postal officials, salt officials, etc., appointed by the Senate from lists prepared by the Heraldry, but he had to give the reasons for his actions, and only the Senate could appoint replacements. Short of dismissal, the governor gave warnings and reprimands and imposed fines for dereliction of duty, in amounts fixed by the ukase of July 1766. Only the governor (and not the provincial voevoda) could impose a fine; his decision was sent to the treasury, where the amount was deducted from the official's salary. The dismissed officials, however, had the right to appeal the governor's decision to the Senate, which reported the conflict to the Empress. The case of Captain Golokhvastov, a member of a well-connected family and local representative of the College of Economy in Novgorod, shows that a governor had to tread carefully. The quarrelsome Governor Sievers ordered him jailed with common criminals for "several hours," on the ground that too many complaints had been received against his performance. The captain complained to the Secretariat, the case was investigated in the Petersburg branch of the College of Justice, and the governor was ordered to ask for "Christian forgiveness" and to pay compensation (*bezchest'e*). The Senate found this decision offensive (*predosuditel'no*) to the office of governor, but Sievers nevertheless was reprimanded as ordered. If a governor chose to prosecute officials, the case was referred automatically to the College of Justice.[31]

---

[30] PSZ, 1764, N. 12137.

[31] *Ibid.*, IV-V, XIV, 1765, N. 12417; *SIRIO*, II (1868), 419-424. Governors, however,

The governor possessed certain less drastic powers which reinforced his authority. All officials in the gubernia were under him, and leaves of absence for up to twenty-nine days required his approval. When a provincial official was transferred to another post, or asked to retire, requested a pension, a decoration, or some other favor, his file had to contain the recommendation (*attestat*) of the governor, a document which could break his career if it contained unfavorable remarks.[32] Since gubernias varied so greatly in size, it is difficult to say how many officials were thus subject to the governor. In a large gubernia like that of Kazan there were about eighty-five, in a small one like Smolensk about twenty.

But these officials, members of the ruling class, were only a small part of the provincial administration. The clerks, about 350 in Kazan and 90 in Smolensk, were at the mercy of the governor, with no appeal provided. They were hired and dismissed by the governor and the voevoda, but criminal prosecutions followed the ordinary channels and ended in the gubernia chancery, where all but death sentences were confirmed. We have the case of Protopopov, a clerk in the Zvenigorod chancery who had inserted derogatory comments in the file of the voevoda. He was dismissed, whipped "without pity," drafted into the army and banished to a Siberian garrison.[33] Thus the governor, as local representative of the elite, possessed over the clerks, most of whom were of non-noble origin, those powers of compulsion and arbitrary treatment which the ruling class exhibited toward its social subordinates. The civil service then, instead of being an autonomous body professionally regulated, was, like the army, a microcosm of society governed by the same rules of social behavior. Indeed, the sharp distinction made between the governor's disciplinary power over members of the ruling class and over the clerks shows how inappropriate it is to combine both into a single "bureaucracy."

The governor was also in full command of the police. Some gubernia capitals were garrison towns, and the troops took their orders from him and from the College of War. Regular units, however, were responsible to their field commanders, who were required to give as-

had no power to promote officials on their own authority. This was the major objection made by the four governors in their report of 1768: TsGADA, f. 16, d. 374, fol. 5-7.

[32] PSZ, 1764, N. 12137, I-III, VI, XII, *Ist. Prav. Senata*, II, 365-366, Gradovskii, *Vysshaia admin.*, 234-235; on the permission to come to Petersburg, see *Arkhiv Senata*, XIV (1910), 521, 556, 585; XV (1913), 146. For examples of requests supported by the governor see *Ibid.*, XV, 843-844, 847; on leaves, see PSZ, 1775, N. 14272. On the importance of the *attestat*, see the case of custom official Gavrilov in TsGADA, f. 44, d. 50, II, fol. 144-149.

[33] PSZ, 1766, N. 12714.

sistance to the governor if he requested it. Garrison troops formed the police force of the gubernia capital while their duties as escorts and messengers in the rest of the gubernia were taken up by the "provincial companies" (*shtatnye komandy*) created in 1763 and placed exclusively under the command of the governor. These two units gave the governor a monopoly of force, although the size of the gubernia, poor communications, and sparse population still made it difficult to cope with bandits—"enemies of the Fatherland and of humanity"—who roamed the countryside and made travel hazardous.[34]

The power to punish considerably strengthened the power to prosecute. Before the reform, both powers were in the hands of the governor. Courts hardly existed, and the totality of the judicial power was vested in the chanceries of the voevodas and the governors, where judicial cases vied with other matters for the attention of overworked clerks. Until 1753 governors were empowered to confirm death sentences. After that date, when the application of the death penalty was suspended unless confirmed by the Empress, all such sentences were sent to the governor, who forwarded them to the Senate. Pending examination and final decision by the Empress, they were replaced by banishment to hard labor and took effect upon confirmation by the governor. All other sentences, except those stripping a nobleman of his noble status, were confirmed by the provincial voevoda in his province and by the governor in the province of which the gubernia capital was the center.[35] These were truly extraordinary powers, especially at a time when the penal law was so generous with the more severe forms of punishments, and among peasants, clerks, and ordinary townspeople the governor was indeed the local incarnation of autocratic power. The Tsar was far away, perhaps, as the proverb goes, but the governor was close at hand. Nothing indeed illustrates so vividly the power of the elite to impose its will upon the socially dependent as this judicial power of the governor over non-noble defendants.

This all-powerful governor, however, feared by so many, could not spend one kopeck without the approval of central agencies. In no area was he so limited by the letter of the law as in fiscal affairs. Yet, this restriction was logical and in no way undermined his position. As we shall see in Chapter IV, the major source of revenue collected locally was the capitation and the sale of vodka produced by the nobility. The proceeds of the capitation and a share of the vodka revenue went

[34] PSZ, 1764, N. 12137, VIII-X, XVI-XVII, 1769, N. 13298. For more details, see Chapter Two.
[35] See Chapter Three.

to support the military establishment, i.e., the institutionalized core of the ruling class. In his capacity as fiscal agent the governor was the provincial treasurer of the elite. He channelled the funds to his fellow commanders in the brigades and regiments, and it was in the common interest that there should be no delay. But there were consolations for him elsewhere. Contracts—for the sale of vodka, for the sale of provisions to the army, to rebuild part of a town destroyed by fire, for example—were negotiated in the gubernia chancery and approved without further reference to central agencies if the amount did not exceed 3,000 rubles. Here, as can be seen from the case of Belgorod gubernia, there was much room for bribery and collusion with other members of the elite and for exploitation of townsmen and peasants to defraud the treasury.[36]

The ten governors of central Russia were the administrative superiors of 29 provincial and about 200 uezd voevodas. Originally a field commander, the voevoda became in the seventeenth century the direct representative of the central government in all towns, large and small, and the instrument through which the central agencies (*prikāzy*) carried out their duties. The natural hierarchy of towns in such a vast area as central Russia created an implicit hierarchy of voevodas, and the appointment of governors in strategic towns in the early years of the eighteenth century completed the establishment of a three-tiered structure of local administration: the governor, the provincial voevoda, and all other voevodas. Their relationships, however, remained undetermined, and their activities, in fact, were regulated by an identical instruction;[37] the Instruction of 1764 was the first one explicitly addressed to the governor alone. Paradoxically, it was drafted at a time when some provincial voevodas were growing in stature as provincial capitals assumed a more prominent role in the economic life of central Russia, and about a decade before the reform combined most of the provinces into twenty-six gubernias and turned provincial voevodas into governors.

Provincial voevodas were appointed by the general assembly of the Petersburg Senate departments from lists submitted by the Heraldry. Chiefly retired officers without a pension and eager to acquire an estate

---

[36] PSZ, 1764, N. 12138, *Arkhiv Senata*, XV (1913), 624; on contracts, see 1766, N. 12809. Contracts valued at between 3,000 and 10,000 rubles were confirmed by the College of Revenue; all others were negotiated in the Senate's First Department. See also *SIRIO*, X (1872), 323, 333-334, PSZ, 1774, N. 14041, and Chapter Four. On the periodic reports, see 1775, N. 14322. The governor was also authorized to spend the 400 rubles appropriated for "chancery expenditures" more or less as he pleased. On the Belgorod case, see PSZ, 1766, N. 12781.

[37] Chicherin, 74-99; PSZ, 1728, N. 5333.

in the provinces, they depended for selection on finding a patron and on their ability to bribe the right officials in the Heraldry. There were many applicants and few vacancies, but an appointment was well worth waiting for. It guaranteed a reasonable income of 600 rubles a year and opened possibilities to supplement it with the many favors which were the perquisites of an official position. The voevoda was lodged in government quarters, and if there were none in the town, he was allowed three rooms in a private home. A provincial voevoda was placed in class VI (army colonel), but men of other ranks were also appointed. Among the twenty-nine appointed or retained in 1764, sixteen were in class VI, nine below, and four above. The career of Bavykin may well have been typical. A nobleman who entered military service in 1742 and served in many campaigns, he rose from the ranks to become a captain, was promoted to class VIII upon his retirement in 1759, and was appointed voevoda in Sudai, retired in 1763 on ground of illness, and became provincial voevoda in Izium in 1765 while still in class VIII.[38]

A voevoda was a middle-rank nobleman retired from military service and given a province or an uezd as an "estate" in conditional tenure in return for service. There was truly no fundamental difference, historically speaking, between a nobleman's being given such an estate, consisting of plowland, hayfields, and woods, or an administrative area. By the reign of Catherine the former had long since become marketable family properties, while the latter obviously could not be so transformed, but we are witnessing an unmistakable trend toward letting the voevoda join the local community of landowners. The two-year term of the voevoda was extended to five years in 1760, and it was announced that the Senate would consider a reappointment if favorable reports were received from landowners and townsmen. In 1764 the old prohibition of 1672 that voevodas might not acquire real property in their towns or uezd was lifted, and the way was open to the transformation of the voevoda into a local official elected by influential landowners and approved by the leadership in the Senate.[39] It is difficult to find a pattern in the tenures of these provincial officials. Some remained less than a year—and it would be interesting to know what happened thereafter—others served more than ten years. The record was held by Alexei Vorontsov, who remained over fourteen years in Vladimir.

Like the governor, the provincial voevoda had a chancery, but a

[38] PSZ, 1775, N. 14349, *Arkhiv Senata*, XIV (1910), 323-326; PSZ, 1773, N. 14040 (Bavykin); the voevoda of Alatyr in the 1770s was a soldier's son: "Zapiski Mertvago," 25-34.

[39] PSZ, 1760, N. 11131, 1764, N. 12181, Dmitriev, *Istoriia*, 459-461.

smaller one. There was only one deputy, also appointed by the Senate, and a procurator. Both positions were new. The chancery proper included two secretaries, nineteen clerks, and the executioner, altogether twenty-five persons.[40] Thus, in the 29 provinces of central Russia there were 77 voevodas, deputies, and procurators, 58 secretaries, and almost 600 clerks. If we combine gubernia and provincial chanceries, which, as we shall see, constituted the top level of local administration between the colleges and the uezds, we obtain a total of 39 governors and provincial voevodas, 49 deputies, 39 procurators, 88 secretaries, and 950 clerks, a total staff of 1,165.

The position of the provincial voevoda in the administrative hierarchy was not clear. The persistence of the Muscovite tradition that direct links between the central government and all voevodas must remain unimpaired meant that the colleges and the Senate issued orders directly to them in individual cases although it was common practice in matters of general interest to send orders to the provincial chanceries from which they were then distributed among the voevodas of the province.[41] The provincial voevoda was the local agent of each central college, reported to it periodically on the execution of its orders, requested instructions from it, and turned to the First Department only when the matter under consideration was not in the jurisdiction of any college. He had no access to the Empress. He owed his appointment to the Senate, and at the end of his five-year term he was required to go to Moscow, where he was "audited" (*sochten*) by the College of Audit. Until he received a clean bill of health he could not be promoted or receive a pension.[42] His retirement or transfer to another post depended on the Senate alone, and his offenses, like those of other officials, were investigated in the College of Justice and tried in the Senate.

The ambiguity was also fostered by the lopsided territorial division of the country and the inconvenient location of some gubernia capitals. The city of Moscow was perfectly located at the center of its huge gubernia. It was also the seat of all important colleges responsible for domestic administration, and the eleven provincial voevodas, together with the Moscow governor, reported to them directly. But in other gubernias, Arkhangelsk and Novgorod, Belgorod and Voronezh, especially, several provincial capitals were in fact much closer to Moscow than the gubernia capital located on the periphery of the gubernia. The resulting delays in channelling correspondence were recognized

---

[40] PSZ, 1763, N. 11991, vol. 44², *kn. sht.*, 69.

[41] Orders even came from the Secretariat: *SIRIO*, X (1872), 215-217; for transmission of orders through the gubernia and provincial chanceries, see PSZ, 1770, N. 13455.

[42] See for example *Arkhiv Senata*, XV (1913), 843-844, 847.

in the early 1730s, when provincial voevodas were allowed to report
directly to Moscow if the direct route to the city was shorter than the
itinerary via the gubernia capital.[43] This, of course, further confused
an already complicated pattern of relationships between the central
government and its local agents, as some provincial voevodas found
themselves dependent on the governor while others were virtually
independent.

In matters of personnel administration the provincial voevoda was
definitely subordinated to the governor. He received recommendations
from him, and he applied to his chancery for leaves of absence not
exceeding one month. Over the officials of his province, including the
voevodas in the uezds, he had no power. Prosecutions, fines, reprimands, and recommendations were attributes of the governor's power;
requests to be allowed to retire or to be reappointed, requests for
promotion or other favors were channelled through the governor's
office. Even "society" had to turn to the governor first to express its
disapproval of a voevoda. When the Heraldry reported to the general
assembly of the Senate that the nobility of Staryi Oskol did not want
their voevoda reappointed but wanted his deputy to succeed him, the
Senate rejected their position on the ground that no complaint had
been made to the governor.[44] On the eve of the reform, when another
effort was made to keep a census of all civil servants, governors were
instructed to send to the Heraldry service records (*posluzhnye spiski*)
on every official in their gubernia, showing their service, rewards, and
punishments. The clerks of course were hired and dismissed by the
voevoda, but they were in short supply, and voevodas were forbidden
in 1775 to let anyone retire even on the ground of illness or old age
without the approval of the governor.[45]

The provincial voevoda had no military powers. If there were garrison troops in his city, their commandant reported to the governor.
The *shtatnaia komanda* in each province took its orders from the
voevoda, who was responsible for the maintenance of order in his
province to the same extent as the governor in his own. But their
judicial authority was not the same. All death sentences were sent to
the Senate through the gubernia chancery, and provincial voevodas
were stripped in 1763 of their authority to apply torture to prisoners.
When the law allowed torture, the prisoners were sent to the governor.
Deeds of purchase and mortgages were notarized in either the voevoda's or the governor's chancery if their value did not exceed one

[43] I have discussed this in LeDonne, "Evolution."

[44] PSZ, 1773, N. 14040, 1770, N. 13467.

[45] PSZ, 1774, N. 14175, 1775, N. 14324. See also 1772, N. 13815; for the census
of children of priests and sacristans, see 1769, N. 13306.

hundred rubles. In financial matters, the voevoda had even less power than the governor, and no reference was made to him in statutes giving the governor the right to approve contracts not exceeding 3,000 rubles.[46] But he was a great writer of forms, which he sometimes sent in triplicate to the governor, the gubernia chancery, and the procurator, as well as to the central colleges and the Senate—an occupation that made him highly visible in the colleges but gave him no power.

Thus the provincial voevoda, on the eve of the reform, appears before us as a local agent doubly subordinated to the central government and to his governor—primarily to the Senate, to which he owed his appointment, promotion, and permission to retire; and secondarily to the governor, with whom he shared in his province the same universal competence as the governor in his gubernia. But the governor wore three hats. He was the regional supervisor—for some gubernias were truly administrative regions—of the provincial voevodas whom he prodded, watched, and compelled to carry out the same obligations as his own. And he possessed certain powers which to a very limited extent made him a regional authority, intermediate between the colleges and the provincial voevoda.

LOCAL GOVERNMENT

The traditional view of Russian administration in the eighteenth century as a bureaucratic phenomenon ignores completely the vital links binding the elite with the remainder of Russian society into a social and political community of extraordinary strength. Troitskii in a minuscule footnote drew his readers' attention to the fact that there existed below the bureaucratic world a vast network of individuals elected by their communities about which little is known because historical scholarship has almost entirely overlooked it.[47] Yet, even within the narrow limits of our knowledge, it is not difficult to show the extensive role played by the vital elements of society in sustaining the leadership role of the ruling class.

Many towns, especially the gubernia capitals and most of the provincial centers, were already focal points of economic and administrative activity. They were the residence of the elite, the governors, the voevodas and their staffs, and the nobility who spent their long

---

[46] For the jurisdiction of the voevoda in military matters, see PSZ, 1767, N. 12822; in police matters, see 1762, N. 11672; in judicial matters 1781, N. 15313 and 1775, N. 14278 for abuses committed by the Tambov voevoda in crushing the opposition of the *odnodvortsy* to survey of their lands. For more details, see Chapters Two and Three. See also PSZ, 1774, N. 14201, 1775, N. 14332.

[47] Troitskii, *Absoliutizm*, 220.

winters there and stimulated the production and transportation of "luxuries." They were the junctions at which many strands of human activity met, where the elite collected and forwarded the revenue, concentrated its police forces, and settled disputes. But the elite was only a transient part of the towns' population. It came and went, and used for the performance of its tasks and the satisfaction of its needs a network of agents elected from among the townsmen. These agents were the link between the ruling class and society, and, under favorable circumstances, membership in the elite was open to them.

A townsman (*grazhdanin*) was not simply an individual who lived in a town. Such "territorial" definition was not yet in use. Petrine legislation included among the townsmen a top layer of *gosti* and the *gostinnaia sotnia* who were chiefly Moscow merchants; bankers, traders, shipmasters, doctors, who registered in the first merchant guild (*gildiia*), and retail traders, who registered in the second, if they declared a capital of 500 and 300 rubles, respectively; and the inhabitants who registered in craft guilds (*tsekhi*).[48] Since access to these social categories was based on the knowledge of a craft or the ownership of capital, it should have been open to all, and in fact it was, juridically. But the elite was anxious to retain control over the size of the body of townsmen. Urban development was a secondary consideration, while the maintenance of a pool of socially dependent individuals just large enough to carry out the supportive functions without which the elite could not maintain itself was a vital preoccupation: hence the hesitation noted in the government's policy toward admission to the guilds, ranging from non-interference to outright refusal to confirm registration on the rolls.

Guild merchants formed the extension of the power of the elite into the towns and even the countryside. In the absence of a true bureaucracy reaching deep into the recesses of society and governed by an abstract conception of the state rather than subservient to the elite, it was the representatives of these merchants who collected the capitation and other taxes in the town or sold salt and liquor in villages and towns. They transported these public funds from the place of collection to the agencies to which they were assigned. They served in the custom houses and as accountants in government offices or as appraisers of goods to be sold by the government to recover debts and arrears. They

---

[48] The major works on municipal administration and urban classes are Ditiatin, *Ustroistvo*; Kizevetter, *Posadskaia obshchina*; Klokman, *Sotsial'no-ekon. istoriia*; and Rozman, *Urban Networks*. See also PSZ, 1721, N. 3708 (*Reglament* of the Central *Magistrat*) and 1724, N. 4624 (Instruction for the *magistraty*). There are some very interesting comments on several *kuptsy* families in Smirnaia; see also Garshin, Dmitriev, A.

were required to billet troops stationed in the towns, kept a census of houses and taxable souls, and were responsible for the policing of markets.[49]

In order to supply these services, resented by some if they interfered with their businesses but appreciated by others as a source of substantial enrichment, the guild merchants elected representatives, usually for one year, named after the function they performed, and a corporate agency called the *magistrat* (or *ratusha* in smaller towns), consisting of a president and a small number of burgomasters and councillors (*ratmany*), depending on the size of the town.[50] The hierarchy of local town and provincial *magistrat* was capped by the Central *Magistrat* in Moscow. Its Petersburg branch was also the *magistrat* for the northern capital until the establishment of a separate municipal *magistrat* in 1774.[51] In addition, and presumably only in the larger towns, each merchant guild elected a council of several members to assist the *magistrat*, and this council elected in turn a "headman" (*starosta*) and a deputy with responsibility for all matters concerning the good of the town, who submitted their recommendations to the *magistrat*.[52]

The *magistrat*, a corporate body chosen by the well-to-do elements of the merchant class, was responsible for the registration of new members and their expulsion, for giving certificates of solvency which served as security in the negotiation of contracts with government agencies, and passports without which they could not leave on extended trips. It was a public body responsible for the municipal police in the widest sense of the term, for the collection of revenue and for the settlement of disputes in which both parties or the plaintiff were merchants.[53] How many individuals were drawn into these public and semi-public activities is difficult to say. We know that 209 *magistraty* and *ratushi* were in the jurisdiction of the Central *Magistrat* in 1765. If we are satisfied with the 175 towns listed by Kizevetter in which he found almost 15,000 elected officials,[54] this is about four times the

[49] PSZ, 1763, N. 11762, 1771, N. 13710; SIRIO, CVII (1900), 274-276.

[50] PSZ, 1721, N. 3708, VI, 1724, N. 4624, pt. 2. Since 1744 a president was elected only in the *magistrat* of the gubernia and provincial capitals. In other towns the *magistrat* consisted of two burgomasters and four ratmans. In towns consisting of less than 250 houses (*dvory*) there was a *ratusha* consisting of one burgomaster and two ratmans; see PSZ, 1744, N. 9018.

[51] PSZ, 1763, N. 11991, vol. 44², *kn. sht.*, 65-66, 1774, N. 14161, 1778, N. 14824.

[52] PSZ, 1724, N. 4624, pt. 16-17, Ditiatin, 385, PSZ, 1766, N. 12801.

[53] PSZ, 1724, N. 4624, 1762, N. 11692, 1737, N. 7211, 1773, N. 14045.

[54] PSZ, 1765, N. 12395; Kizevetter, *Posad. obshchina*: see below p. 297-298. If the gubernia and provincial staff consisted of 1,165 persons and that of 177 uezd chanceries of 2,478 persons, this is about one-fourth of 15,000 officials elected in towns.

total number of governors, voevodas, procurators, and secretaries. Thus, in the towns alone, and this in an overwhelmingly agrarian society, the political elite depended on the cooperation of four times its number of socially dependent individuals to carry out the essential tasks without which it could not survive.

Similarly, to keep its hold on the countryside and extract from it the resources in money and men vital to maintain the military establishment and sustain the process of "westernization," the elite needed the cooperation of an even larger number of individuals. The existence of an elite in a preindustrial society is unthinkable without an army of non-commissioned officers, drawn from the peasantry, who can persuade, cajole, and threaten the peasant masses to part with a substantial share of their resources for the benefit of their masters and who, in turn, can provide the elementary services—order and the settlement of disputes—essential to any human community. The structure of rural administration is more difficult to analyze because it took various forms according to local customs and activities and the size of the agglomerations. Some isolated villages (*derevni, seleniia*) had no more than ten male souls; others (*sela*) had a few thousand and were larger than some uezd centers. Some villages or serfs were owned by several lords; others were part of the estate (*votchina*) of a single lord. Yet all had some representatives, some "best men," who linked them with the elite into an organic whole.

Over half of the peasantry belonged to the elite as a private domain, but in very unequal shares. Some three-fifths of the 45,000 landowners, or 27,000, possessed shares of less than 20 souls, and these peasants constituted only 5 percent of the total serf population of 5.6 million souls (1762). They were scattered all over central Russia, on estates that some of their masters had never even visited. Yet, they provided their masters with a crucial source of income, and if lord and peasant resided on the estate, the connection between elite and peasantry formed an indivisible whole. Another 12 percent (about 4,950 lords) possessed nearly 80 percent of the serfs in shares of over 150 souls. Some of them owned several thousand and the largest landowners, the Sheremetev family, owned about 140,000 souls, the size of more than one pre-reform province.[55] On such large estates an administrative link was necessary between the lord, who resided permanently in Moscow or Petersburg, and his far-flung estates. It usually consisted of a central office (*kontora*) at the residence of the lord and a local office on each estate. The latter consisted of a steward (*upravitel', prikazshchik*) appointed by the lord, and usually an outsider. If no steward was ap-

55 Dukes, 11-12; "P. B. Sheremetev," in *RBS*, XXIII (1911), 189.

pointed, the estate was managed by a team consisting of a *starosta* elected by the community of heads of families (*mir* or *mirskii skhod*) for one year or more. His election was confirmed by the lord, who sometimes also imposed his choice. His principal assistants were the treasurer (*kaznachei, tselovalnik*), the tax collectors (*sborschiki*), also elected, and the clerks (*zemskie*). The executive agents of the *starosta* were the "hundredsmen" (*sotskie*) and their subordinates, who were appointed for groups of one hundred, fifty, and ten houses (*dvory*), although the number varied from place to place.[56] It is probably impossible to determine the number of these private servants of the elite who translated the consent of their people into victuals, money, wood, and cloth, but they certainly ran into the tens of thousands, and it was by their effort and with their consent that substantial sums were siphoned off from the countryside not only to support the standing of the ruling class but also to maintain the army and civil administration.

The remainder of the peasantry was divided into three major groups. There were the peasants of the Court who should simply be considered peasants of the top stratum of the elite, whose contribution served to defray part of the expenditures of the Court. These peasants were administered by their *starosty* and *sotskie* and were grouped into volosts headed by "administrators" (*upraviteli*) appointed by the Chancery for Court Peasants, which combined the functions of higher tribunal and treasury. There were also the former peasants of the Church who passed in 1763 under the jurisdiction of a new College of Economy. They were widely scattered in many uezds, one of which had only one such peasant (!), while others had more than 15,000. They too had their elected *starosty* and *sotskie*, but the key link was the "treasurer" appointed over one or two uezds by the college. There were altogether 60 treasurers with 94 deputies for just under 900,000 peasants in central Russia.[57]

Finally, there were the state peasants, about 2.8 million in 1762. Most were Russians; others included Votiaks and Tatars and other aborigines in the eastern provinces. They included large clusters of *odnodvortsy* in Voronezh and Belgorod gubernias. Until 1761 they were administered by *upraviteli* appointed by the College of War and subordinated to the governors, and thereafter by their *sotskie*—or *sotniki* since they headed a *sotnia*. Offenses were tried before the *mir*,

---

[56] There are three very good books on the administration of private estates, besides Semevskii's *Krest'iane*: Alexandrov, *Sel'skaia obshchina*, esp. 125-127, 166-169; Confino, *Domaines et seigneurs*, esp. 44-94; and Shchepetov, *Krepostnoe pravo* summarized in *Iz zhizni*. See also "Ukazy grafa Sheremeteva" and Orlov-Davydov, esp. 208-213.

[57] PSZ, 1764, N. 12087, 1764, N. 12226, 1767, N. 12839, 1770, N. 13487.

and appeals were made to the governor. It is to these *sotskie*, no doubt, that the Instruction of December 1774 was addressed—a code of rural police spelling out their duties in detail.[58] These peasants, although called state peasants, should instead be called peasants held in trust by the elite. They paid the capitation and the quitrent to the treasury, but they were also a potential source of serfs. The ruthless social struggle between noble and *odnodvorets* in the south is witness to this, while in the north few nobles cared to have estates, and in the east political considerations still restricted the expansion of private domains. The abolition of the class of state peasants, if it had been possible, would have entailed the loss of financial resources for governmental activities, which would have had to come from somewhere else. But the elite did try, if not to enserf the state peasants, at least to exploit them and reduce their holdings, a step short of enserfment.

These many local posts were the channels through which the power of the ruling class was routinized. In a vertically integrated society marked by the dominion of that class over the rest of society their role was largely passive. Yet it would be a mistake to reduce the relationship to a one-way transmission of orders; passivity alone, indeed, can exercise a powerful influence. The townsmen and peasants who filled these posts, together with the clerks who had already entered the periphery of the power structure, were the men who kept renegotiating the terms of the social contract, i.e., who determined the limits of power. Orders were executed if they fell within the "zone of acquiescence" which the personal interests of these men and the collective experience of their communities had gradually defined and kept defining in response to external challenges. There are countless references in Russian documents to government orders not being executed, and "waiting for the third ukase"—after which sanctions might be taken—was a proverb of sorts. Thus it was at this level that the legitimacy of the social order and of the ruling class was ultimately recognized, not by an official act, of course, but by the patient meshing of two cultures, mutually hostile at times, yet bound together in the inner workings of a common civilization.

It seems a paradox that the nobility, alone of the three estates, should have neither corporate organization nor elected representatives at the beginning of Catherine's reign. As long as it remained largely identical with the officer corps and the civil "bureaucracy," the internal structure of the nobility almost merged with the military hierarchy (regiments and brigades) and the civilian hierarchy. The nobility, however, had its central agency, the Heraldry, where the sons of hereditary

---

[58] Dmitriev, *Istoriia*, 491-493; PSZ, 1774, N. 14231, Zaitsev, 1-41.

nobles were registered. This agency combined the functions of keeper of vital statistics with that of a clearing house for all middle and lower-level appointments; the College of War performed similar functions for the military, but was not represented in the provinces and uezds.[59]

The growth of the ruling class and the final demobilization of the landed nobility in 1762—the other nobles had nowhere to go outside the service—precipitated a reassessment of its privileges and its position vis-à-vis other classes in Russian society. The nobles wanted, first of all, to be more sharply distinguished from their fellow men by social, judicial, and economic privileges that would belong to them alone, to systematize what had been taken for granted. For the very fluidity of social categories meant that noble, peasant, and merchant still lived, despite class differences, in the same world of religious emotions and mental perceptions, while an elite needed at least external symbols of separateness. "Westernization" alone could provide such symbols: hence the emphasis on dress, on manners, on types of conveyance, and on speaking foreign languages. Second, these nobles wanted to meet periodically in their uezds, like the merchants in their towns, to elect their own officers who would provide the services which the voevoda alone, and an outsider at that, could no longer deliver to an aggressive elite, conscious of its strength: quick and effective justice responsive to their needs, protection against banditry and the violence committed by passing troops, trusteeships over minors and the feeble-minded. Moreover, the nobles claimed jurisdiction for their elected representatives not only over the nobles of the uezd, but also over the peasants of the Court, the treasury, and the College of Economy.[60] Thus the elite now claimed an immediate, almost personal, jurisdiction over all social groups which it had previously exercised only from afar and intermittently.

The outbreak of the first Turkish war in 1768 imposed a lull on the turbulent social scene, but the success of Russian arms, of which Rumiantsev was the main architect, brought fundamental issues back to the center of the stage. These victories gave the Empress the legitimacy she needed, and the issue of serfdom was now buried for the

[59] There were three presidents of the College of War between 1763 and 1796: Chernyshev, Potemkin, and Saltykov, who have already been discussed. The four Herald-masters were Mikhail Priklonskii (1765-1770), Pr. Mikhail Shcherbatov (1772-1777), Alexander Volkov (1779-1783), and Luk'ian Talyzin (1784-1794).

[60] Dukes, 160-161, B-va, 77-79, Sipovskii, 382-383, 537. For a portrait of an enterprising pomeshchitsa, see Ponomarev. Augustine's "Portrait" is a fine survey of the attitudes of the nobility. For different opinions on the meaning of the emancipation of the nobility, see Raeff, Origins, 10-12, 51-52, Romanovich-Slavatinskii, 134-135. There is a summary of the controversy in Pipes, 130-134.

remainder of the reign, despite a brave attempt in the Manifesto of March 1775 to leave open the possibility of individual emancipation. A new orientation in Russian foreign policy was taking shape, and a new team was necessary to guide it. A second demobilization of the officer corps was impending, and positions had to be found for the junior officers, who sought recommendations from the established families but could not be placed in central agencies. The Pugachev rebellion—never a real threat to the political leadership, yet an annoying diversion in the midst of a victorious war—exposed the lack of organization of the elite in the east and southeast and the absence of an administrative mechanism to strengthen its leadership in an unsettled territory. Both the rebellion and the expansion of the southern borders to the Black Sea raised complex problems of borderland administration and whetted the appetite of the nobility for land and positions. This renewed social turbulence formed the background of the sweeping changes of 1774-1775 which led to the great reforms of the following decade.[61]

[61] They began with the Organic Law (hereafter OL) of November 7, 1775 (PSZ, N. 14392) and ended with the Noble and Municipal Charters of April 21, 1785 (N. 16187-16188). For a general treatment, see de Madariaga, *Russia*, 281-305 and especially Jones, *Empancipation*, 210-243.

CHAPTER III

THE IMPERIAL GOVERNMENT, 1774-1796

THE NEW POLITICAL LEADERSHIP

The decisive event of 1774 in domestic politics was the summoning to Petersburg of General Grigorii Potemkin, who served at the time in Rumiantsev's command. The new favorite came from Smolensk gubernia, a borderland that was just beginning to join the Great Russian world. There had been other favorites before Potemkin, and there would be many more after him, yet none made such an impact on the imagination of his contemporaries and on the formulation of policy. Potemkin was no plaything of the Empress but a statesman in his own right. The greatness of a man does not depend on his qualities and his political fortune alone. He must also be the embodiment of dynamic social forces, must be seen by lesser men to have achieved what they would like to realize or can accomplish only on a smaller scale. Potemkin embodied the aspirations of the rank-and-file nobility, their lust for recognition, their greed, and their ruthlessness. In his combination of functional and territorial commands he was the very denial of bureaucratic logic and hierarchy. His activities gave direction and consistency to a powerful social current turning away from the traditional concentration on Moscow and Petersburg and directed toward the revitalization of the region, the province, and the uezd. The land survey, the passion for maps and topographic descriptions, the voyages of discovery by Gmelin, Pallas, Lepekhin, among others, across central Russia and the borderlands—all testified to a change of emphasis among the ruling class. Romanovich-Slavatinskii has noted the opposite pull of two tendencies within the nobility: to serve in a political capacity; to return to their estates because it was "better to be first in the uezd than second in the capital."[1] This second tendency came to the fore in the 1760s and was strengthened by the war. It fed the anti-bureaucratic trend, and the reforms of 1775-1785 were the administrative translation of these new concerns.

The emergence of the new favorite from the borderlands compelled a realignment of forces within the ruling elite. The Panins and the Chernyshevs were the major losers. Panin's authority was damaged

[1] Romanovich-Slavatinskii, 181.

ZAKHAR GRIGOR'EVICH CHERNYSHEV

GRIGORII ALEXANDROVICH POTEMKIN

reduction in the central apparatus, leaving the ruling families unhampered by bureaucratic restrictions, and from the multiplication of the levers of power in the provinces henceforth to be manned by the subordinate families; these now depended more than ever on their social superiors for assistance in placing their sons in the military service and settling the endless squabbles dividing local society. This aristocratic reaction, characteristic of the period not only in Russia

by the new southern orientation of Russian foreign policy and by the coming to majority of Grand Duke Paul in 1773, at the very time when military successes were consolidating his mother's position, thus quashing whatever hope Paul may have entertained to ascend the throne.[2] Ivan Chernyshev remained at the head of the College of the Navy, but its jurisdiction did not extend to the new Black Sea Fleet, which was from the beginning under Potemkin's command. Potemkin replaced Ivan's brother Zakhar in the College of War, gaining at one stroke control over the machinery of military patronage.

The new favorite, however, operated within a political framework which he, like everyone else, could not afford to neglect. His leadership of the army was acceptable only if other ruling families were properly represented. Indeed, his position was made more difficult by his modest social origins and the enormous power which he and his family began to accumulate. Among the regional military commands restored after the war, the Ukraine remained under Rumiantsev, while Potemkin took command of the troops stationed in New Russia. The Petersburg command remained under Razumovskii until the end of the reign. Troops in Lifland came under Marshal Alexander Golitsyn, who doubled up as de facto governor general of Petersburg. Prince Nikolai Repnin, from another boyar family and nephew of the Panins by marriage, emerged as an important figure in the military hierarchy, and his relationship with Potemkin was not cordial. The Saltykov family, despite the disgrace of the old marshal because of his inability to cope with the 1771 plague in Moscow, became the leader of the opposition to Potemkin. Count Ivan, the marshal's son, and his relative Nikolai (the future prince), who joined the suite of Paul and became the tutor of the future Alexander I, were given the Kazan and Estland commands, respectively, and Vasilii Dolgorukov in various appointments must be considered one of their supporters. The command of the Guard likewise, formally unified in the person of the Empress, was distributed among the three political families. The Preobrazhenskiis and the Cavaliers were handed over to the favorites (Alexei and Grigorii Orlov in the 1760s, then Potemkin and Zubov); the Semenovskiis to men from the Saltykov clan (Vadkovskii, Brius, and Nikolai Saltykov); the Izmailovskiis and the Horse Guard were given to each in turn (Razumovskii and Repnin; Volkonskii, Grigorii Orlov, and Rumiantsev). The distribution of the spoils within the strictly military establishment, however, seems to have created an unstable situation, unlike that of the 1760s, and put further pressure on Potemkin to

[2] The evolution of the domestic crisis of 1773-1774 can be traced in Ransel, *Politics*, 227-241 and de Madariaga, *Russia*, 256-263.

widen the circle of his supporters by finding additional positions for them outside the military establishment.

By contrast, a remarkable consolidation of the domestic establishment took place. Another decisive event of 1774 was the appointment in September of a separate procurator in the First Department of the Senate. The Procurator General severed his immediate ties with the departments and was raised above the Senate, with special jurisdiction over "political and financial affairs" (*gosudarstvennye i interesnye dela*). He ceased to be, as a historian of the First Department has noted, the eye of the Sovereign in the Senate to become in fact a prime minister over all sectors of domestic administration. This consolidation followed a similar development in Prussia, where Ludwig von Hagen rose from minister in one of the departments of the Directory to become director of the Directory as a whole in the 1760s.[3] In both countries the impulse behind the reform was dissatisfaction with the cumbersome machinery of financial administration, and the result in Russia was the concentration of financial responsibilities in the hands of Prince Viazemskii. The Procurator General remained the de facto "chairman" of the general assembly of the Petersburg departments, where appointments were made to positions below class VI and recommendations were prepared for appointments and promotions reserved for the Empress. His position as the main dispenser of patronage in the civilian administration was well realized by those in search of a position, as it appeared from the letter of a modest local procurator who addressed him as the person "to whom Her Majesty has entrusted the state."[4]

Yet, this strengthening of Prince Viazemskii's position, and by extension of that of the Saltykov clan, must not be seen as a trend toward greater bureaucratization. The efficiency of the Imperial government as a whole was not yet conceived in purely bureaucratic terms, and the implications of the realignment of 1774 were twofold. On the one hand, a new core bureaucracy was shaped by Prince Viazemskii to staff the Expedition of State Revenues, which now became the heart of the central government, but the size of the expedition was modest, at least at the beginning. On the other hand, the creation of the expedition marked the first phase in the dismantling of the colleges carried out in the 1780s. This development, curiously overlooked in studies of the period, revealed the truly anti-bureaucratic direction of the reform. Efficiency, therefore, was seen to result from a significant

[3] PSZ, 1774, N. 14192, Nolken, 108, Johnson, 210-219.

[4] TsGADA, f. 248, d. 6512, fol. 74 (Nikolai Bakhmetev to Prince Viazemskii, 15 Jan. 1782).

but in Prussia as well, was characteristic of a profoundly conservative movement, the natural expression of an age of consolidation.

The neglect of the peasants, the worsening of their legal status, and the very fact that state peasants—let alone the serfs of landowners— did not receive a "charter" in the 1780s like that received by the nobility and the townsmen, evidenced the belief of a class of established and prospective landowners that it should have a free hand, without the interference of a centralized bureaucracy, to exploit the labor of the servile population and the resources of the public domain. The Empress herself became convinced that the time was less ripe than ever to tackle an issue which determined the direction of social and fiscal policy. "Whenever you touch it," she said, "it does not yield," and, as Isabel de Madariaga coyly puts it, she abandoned the idea of a peasant charter "possibly because the magnitude of the peasant problem was too much for her."[5] It was no coincidence that the first serious attempt to protect the state peasants and state property against the greed of the landowning class should have to wait until the reign of Nicholas I, often considered to mark the apogee of bureaucratic government. As in Prussia, where Frederick II also sought to break loose from the constraints imposed by bureaucratic procedures, Catherine consolidated the natural alliance of the Romanov house with the aristocratic families against her own bureaucracy and supported the centrifugal movement of the rank-and-file nobility led by Potemkin. In so doing she secured the gratitude of the entire ruling class and won the final recognition of her legitimacy.

Such a trend, however, did not mean a reduction of her stature, and Catherine remained one of the most dynamic rulers in modern Russian history. The best evidence of her forcefulness after 1774 was the emergence of a powerful Secretariat, usually of six men who represented the three clusters of political families. Two were Ukrainians: Alexander Bezborodko (1775-1793) and Peter Zavadovskii (1776-1793), who owed their appointment to Rumiantsev's recommendation. Two were former secretaries of Potemkin: Peter Turchaninov (1779-1796) and Vasilii Popov (1786-1793). Alexander Khrapovitskii (1783-1793) was probably a Potemkin protégé, and Peter Soimonov (1779-1793), nephew of Elizabeth's famous Siberian governor, came from the Procurator General's party.

The star of the new Secretariat was undoubtedly Bezborodko, whose family was closely associated with Rumiantsev's. His talent and industry, his extraordinary memory and excellent prose (but his handwriting is a nightmare for the modern scholar) made their mark upon

<hr>

5 Madariaga, 299.

ALEXANDER ANDREEVICH BEZBORODKO

the Empress. Reporter (*dokladchik*) of the College of Foreign Affairs after Panin's death in 1783, Director of the Postal Department, member of the Council and *Ober-Hofmeister*, he became the Empress's right-hand man in both foreign and domestic administration. He sat on various committees to discuss financial problems, synodal administration, communications, the introduction to the reforms, and urban provisioning. He negotiated peace with the Turks in 1791 and sent instructions to Prince Repnin, commander of the occupation forces after the second partition of Poland. It is no exaggeration to say that in the eighteen years between 1775 and 1792 the Empire was governed by a triumvirate of Bezborodko, Potemkin, and Prince Viazemskii under the watchful eye of the Empress.

It is difficult to determine precisely the scope of a secretary's activities; in the case of Bezborodko it is impossible. The activities of the Secretariat as a whole were conterminous with the interests of the Empress, which knew no bounds. It is likely that some division of labor existed, but much certainly depended on the pressure of business, and nothing prevented the Empress from assigning the jurisdiction of one secretary to another. Some specialization is apparent in the fact that certain secretaries were at the same time the heads of other agencies. Olsuf'ev and Soimonov had special responsibilities for the management of the mines belonging to the Court, Elagin for the management of Court properties, Zavadovskii for finances and education. Turchaninov directed the supply of the army in Finland during the Swedish war of 1788-1790. But, whatever the extent of their responsibilities, all secretaries received reports and petitions formally addressed to the Empress and transmitted them to her. A governor general like Tutolmin, for example, submitted his reports to the Empress with a covering letter addressed to Bezborodko. Although a governor general had access to the Empress, the access was filtered through the desk of a secretary. What was expected from this official is extremely revealing: to put in a good word for the report, to choose the convenient time for submitting it, to second a recommendation for a promotion, a transfer, a decoration.[6] The implication is quite clear that the role of state secretary was not a passive one. Before the last instance, against which there was no appeal, an ill-intentioned secretary could insure the rejection of a request by submitting it at the wrong time. Petitions likewise were submitted to the Empress together

[6] TsGDA, f. 16, d. 804, I, 243-244, 287-288, II, 104-106, 146-151, 165-166, 270, 425-427, etc.; "Sobstvennoruchniaia pis'ma" gives a good idea of the variety of topics requiring the Empress's attention.

with the oral report of a secretary, who later communicated her decision to the interested parties.[7]

The Secretariat thus developed as the third great center of influence in the Imperial govenment. The final choice of candidates for the top-level positions was made here, and only the President of the College of War and the Procurator General had enough authority to appeal to the Empress directly to support their own candidates. But, for almost everyone else, save the few who were the social companions of the Empress, including those whose commands were far from the capital, the Secretariat was the inevitable intermediary. Its members owed their influence both to their patrons and to their knowledge of the Empress's moods, nurtured by many years of almost daily contact.[8] Capable and highly educated, some were aristocrats, others were of humble origin. Several were sons of the western and southern borderlands, and their role in formulating the expansionist policies of the 1780s and 1790s remains to be studied. Their presence at the core of Catherine's government certainly enhanced the primacy of foreign policy considerations in the drafting of a national policy, with disastrous consequences for the financial stability and the social peace of the country.

The membership of the Council, where fierce battles were fought in the 1780s over the costs of territorial expansion, also came to reflect the realignment of political forces.[9] Razumovskii and Ivan Chernyshev remained until the end of the reign, and Prince Viazemskii until his death. Nikolai Saltykov was appointed in 1787. The Secretariat was represented by Strekalov and Zavadovskii. The other most important members represented the military-foreign-policy establishment and the borderlands: Potemkin, Rumiantsev, Bezborodko, Alexander Vorontsov, and Vice-Chancellor Ivan Osterman. The secretary was Alexander Samoilov, Potemkin's nephew.

The same desire to provide representation for the various ruling families was evident in the staffing of the Senate. After the fairly rapid turnover of the 1760s came to an end, most new appointments were lasting ones. This would seem to show that the Senate was not in full decline, as is sometimes suggested, but, on the contrary, that it became more consistently than ever the machinery through which a consensus was reached in domestic administration. This was most obvious in the First Department, where Elagin was the Empress's personal repre-

---

[7] TsGADA, f. 10, d. 545 contains petitions kept in the papers of Secretary Kozmin (1775); see also "Chelobitnaia," "Pis'mo Tauberta," and "Proshenie."

[8] According to Gribovskii, Bezborodko saw the Empress every day at 11 o'clock; the Procurator General saw her twice a week: Zapiski, 27.

[9] On the State Council see Ransel, Politics, 76-98, 117-124, 134-138, "Council Project," and Chechulin, "Proekt."

sentative, Marshal Golitsyn represented the military establishment, Zavadovskii and Passek the borderlands, and Brius the domestic establishment. The membership of the other departments will be examined briefly in subsequent chapters.

This middle period of the reign came to an end with the death of its two greatest men, Potemkin and Prince Viazemskii, the former in late 1791, the latter in January 1793. A glance at the appointments in the Secretariat, the Senate, and among the governors shows that a second massive change of the guard took place in 1792 and inaugurated the third but short period ending with the death of the Empress in November 1796. Suffice it to say that the new Procurator General was Alexander Samoilov, who married Nikita Trubetskoi's grand-niece, a fine illustration of the lasting influence of this family in domestic administration. In the College of War Nikolai Saltykov succeeded Potemkin, whose influence he had successfully undermined by producing the young and irresponsible Platon Zubov. Zubov's father was a protégé of Prince Viazemskii, and his brother married the Prince's daughter. In a striking reversal of roles, the Senate establishment had produced the last favorite and the Potemkin party the last Procurator General. This third period is of little importance to the subject matter of this book—Isabel de Madariaga dismisses it as an epilogue[10]—because it followed the great reforms and witnessed the continuation of earlier trends.

It is generally agreed that these reforms represented a hallmark in Russia's political history; the nature of the impulse that brought them to a successful conclusion remains, however, an object of debate. For Robert Jones, who has devoted the most substantial monograph to the subject, Catherine's concern for the Empire's welfare and power required a redirection of the bureaucratic absolutism she had inherited, and the chronic shortage of manpower forced the state to rely on elected officials. Compromise with the nobility, suggested by other, chiefly pre-Revolutionary, scholars, played an insignificant role.[11]

There may be only two major approaches to the analysis of a comprehensive reform. One is to see it as a result of dissatisfactions and pressures to remove obsolete and defective practices and to bring structures and procedures in line with the demands of the times as they are expressed by the most influential elites in society. Reforms are seen here as a compromise among these elites, a compromise requiring the sanction of the political leadership. The other approach sees in the authoritarian state the source of all initiatives and assumes

---

[10] De Madariaga, 562-566.
[11] See Jones, *Emancipation*, vi, 122, 226-227, 238.

that reforms proceed from an understanding of an objective situation arrived at in the higher spheres of government and are then imposed on the country without much consideration for the views of society at large. Although these two approaches, like inductive and deductive reasoning, are not mutually exclusive, the first presupposes that a consensus must be reached among the constituent groups of the ruling class before their outlines are worked out at the highest political level.

Anyone choosing to believe that the reforms were merely an attempt by a forceful Empress to improve the efficiency of a bureaucratic system must explain, among other things, why one of its major consequences was the closing of the colleges, those very bastions of bureaucratic government, and why Paul, who did strive to lay the foundations of bureaucratic government, was led to scrap most of his mother's program. There can be no efficiency without acceptance by those asked to carry out a political reform of its premises and its purpose, especially in local government, which was the main object of the reform; and acceptance, which cannot be coerced here, requires that those who accept find it in their interest to do so. Much confusion could be avoided if historians stopped hiding behind the concept of the state, and examined the underlying social and political reality: it would dispel the assumption that the rulers are authoritarian, while society, or social groups necessarily seek greater freedom.

What follows is a discussion of the reforms as a compromise within the ruling class as a whole—the nobility and the Romanov house— seeking to combine two imperatives that proved incompatible in the long run: the demand for administrative efficiency and the freezing of the social order.

GOVERNOR GENERAL AND GOVERNOR

The reform abolished the post of provincial voevoda, creating in its stead twenty-six governorships in central Russia alone, and introducing a new regional office, that of governor general (namestnik). This innovation is extremely interesting because it illustrates Potemkin's need to deliver additional positions in civil administration to those who supported him in expectation of his patronage. It demonstrates, too, that as a result of the alliance between the Empress and representatives of the elite a non-bureaucratic type of administration was beginning to take shape.

To be sure, the post of governor general was not entirely new. Governors general were appointed in Riga and Kiev, and in the 1760s there was one in Smolensk and another in Glukhov (for Little Russia). In central Russia proper, however, governors general were appointed in Moscow alone, as personal delegates of the ruler, and the post seems to have been a near monopoly of the Saltykov family. The Organic Law of November 7, 1775 called for the appointment of a governor general in each new gubernia capital, but this provision was never carried out. As provinces were combined into gubernias, governors general were appointed to preside over two or three, sometimes even four, gubernias, but in the 1780s the norm became one governor general for two gubernias.[12] Nothing was said about their rank, but it can be determined from the list of thirty governors general appointed in central Russia between 1775 and 1796. Fifteen were lieutenant generals and eight were full generals, the military equivalent of class III and IV officials. More than half were generals who had made their mark during the first Turkish war, and most of these had served in the First Army of Marshal Rumiantsev. Thus, their background was very similar to that of the pre-reform governor, but they were one or two ranks higher. A few came from the upper levels of the civilian leadership and had been presidents of colleges. The salary of a governor general was pegged to his rank, not to his post. A lieutenant general received a basic salary of 2,160 rubles, a full general 3,600 rubles a year. In addition, each governor general received 6,000 rubles for entertainment, was given an escort of 24 dragoons, and a young nobleman in each uezd was assigned to his suite.[13]

All this reflected the Empress's desire to give governors general the trappings of authority as her personal representatives. There was no need to repeat in the Organic Law the expressions of confidence that were such a novelty in the Instruction of 1764 because such confidence

---

[12] The distribution of gubernias varied from time to time but remained very close to the following table. The italicized city was the seat of the governor general and the gubernia in parentheses belonged to the borderlands:

Petersburg (and Vyborg)	*Nizhnii Novgorod* and Penza
Tver and Novgorod	*Smolensk* and Pskov
Petrozavodsk and Arkhangelsk	*Kursk* and Orel
Iaroslavl' and Vologda	*Vladimir* and Kostroma
Perm (and Tobolsk)	*Riazan* and Tambov
Kazan and Viatka	*Kaluga* and Tula
Simbirsk (and Ufa)	*Voronezh* (and Khar'kov)

The governor general of *Moscow* had jurisdiction only over the (post-reform) gubernia. Saratov was at first associated with the North Caucasus, then with Voronezh and Khar'kov. Thus, governors general were appointed in fifteen cities in central Russia. Six were former gubernia capitals; seven were former provincial capitals. Perm was a new city. Kursk replaced Belgorod as gubernia capital. Novgorod and Arkhangelsk lost their status as regional centers. An outline of the reform is in LeDonne, "Territorial Reform," I.

[13] See LeDonne, "Catherine's Governors," PSZ, 1794, N. 17494, vol. 44[2], 253; OL, art. 92-93, also PSZ, 11735, vol. 43[1], 40-41.

was now taken for granted. Officials of the first three classes formed
a charmed circle in the Imperial leadership. Governors general received
personal commands from the Empress and reported to her in person
as well as to the Senate and the Procurator General. They were even
ex officio senators who attended the sessions of the general assembly
when they were in the capitals and sat in the department, where matters
concerning their gubernias were being examined. There they were
allowed to act as the representatives (*khodatai*) of their *namestnichestvo*.[14] Thus a governor general was both a central government
official and a regional administrator, a combination which put him in
a class apart from the pre-reform governor. What a stir must have
been caused by the arrival of such a personage in a former provincial
capital where the highest official had been a colonel!

The governor general was the new regional agent, the intermediary
between the governor and the Senate. As agent of territorial administration and member of the elite his responsibility was to enforce
without equivocation the consensus reached in the Senate departments.
An Imperial ukase of September 1780 reminded him that he, no more
than any other "commander" (*nachalnik*), was empowered to set norms
that were not already contained in existing legislation and that he must
limit himself to the strict application of the letter of the law. Should
he find it necessary, however, to introduce innovations "for the good
of the service, the increase of Our revenue and above all for the welfare
and tranquillity of Our subjects," he was allowed to submit his considerations to the Empress through the Senate.[15] Despite these restrictions, there was not a word in the Organic Law on how the governor
general would be held to account, and it is quite likely that none was
intended. The personal relationship with the Empress was not a figure
of speech, as it had been in the Instruction of 1764, intended to raise
the authority of the governor in the eyes of other officials. Governors
general were personally known to the Empress and had lived at the
Court. Some had dined and played cards with her. Moreover, even if
she had reservations about some (Prozorovskii, for example), almost
all belonged to the aristocracy, and a few were even related to the
Imperial family. As such they could be held to account by no one but
the Empress. The Senate was packed with their supporters, and only
an extraordinary scandal could force her to intervene.

The jurisdiction of a governor general over the personnel of his
namestnichestvo was much more extensive than that of the pre-reform

---

[14] OL, art. 91. What the term *namestnichestvo* meant was never clear. One suspects
that it sometimes meant the two or three gubernias over which a governor general was
appointed; in fact, it was often equated with a single gubernia.
[15] PSZ, 1780, N. 15068.

governor because many more officials were now serving in the gubernias and the uezds. Yet, over members of the ruling class in graded
positions a governor general had no more power than a pre-reform
governor. He granted leave, recommended for promotion, gave *attestaty*, and imposed fines, but he was forbidden by an express order of
the Empress to transfer anyone to another post.[16] However, following
the closing of the College of Justice, he was empowered to bring
officials for investigation and trial before the criminal chamber. He
confirmed its sentences, but his decisions required the confirmation of
the Senate. Over the several officials appointed by the Empress he had
few powers of constraint. The election of all representatives chosen
by the nobility, townsmen, and state peasants required his confirmation; the clerks were chosen, dismissed, and punished at his discretion. In police and military matters it was even more evident that
hardly anything distinguished his powers from those of a pre-reform
governor. The town and rural police was subordinated to him and
kept him informed of all developments, which he summarized in semi-
monthly reports addressed to the Empress personally. A glance at these
reports shows that little was considered worth mentioning apart from
an occasional fire in the sleepy towns and uezds, where life unfolded
with the same tedium and monotony so well depicted by Chekhov a
century later. Garrisons were subordinated to him, and their commandants reported both to him and to the College of War. Regular
units remained subordinated to their field commanders, and only in
a few cases in central Russia, notably in Smolensk and Moscow, did
the governor general combine a civil and military command.[17]

In judicial and financial administration the reform introduced important structural changes, but few substantive modifications. Two
judicial chambers and a treasury chamber were created to administer
civil and criminal justice and to collect the revenue, matters which
had been concentrated in the gubernia chancery. Although these new
agencies were subordinated to the governor general, he did not take
part in their meetings. He was no longer a judge, but all sentences to
flogging with the knout and the whip were submitted to him for
confirmation. Death sentences still had to be referred to the Senate.
Noblemen were immune from corporal punishment (after 1785) and
could not be stripped of their nobility without Imperial approval. If
we overlook these few restrictions, the governor general was still the

[16] PSZ, 1777, N. 14618; see also 1784, N. 16075.
[17] PSZ, 1776, N. 14435, art. 2, 1781, N. 15141, art, 23, 1783, N. 15810, 1784, N.
16074. On the clerks see 1779, N. 14831, 1781, N. 15193, 1782, N. 15401; some
protection was introduced by the ukase of 1784: N. 16022. See also OL, art. 84, 90;
PSZ, 1783, N. 15821, 1780, N. 14990. See also Chapter II.

same powerful last instance for the majority of offenders. In financial matters, however, the reform gave him greater discretion. Various financial statutes of the 1780s provided for the annual allocation of lump sums, earmarked for definite purposes but placed at the disposal of the governor general. Contracts were now negotiated in the treasury chamber and were confirmed by him if their value did not exceed 10,000 rubles.[18] This had been the limit of the jurisdiction of the College of Revenue, but, given the rate of inflation in the 1780s, one may wonder whether the governor general's actual power was much greater here than that of the pre-reform governor. Thus it appears that the reform created in the post of governor general a regional agent belonging to the top stratum of the ruling class, with a great deal in common with the pre-reform governor. What set apart the governor general was his social standing, his access to the throne, his commanding position in the army, and his connections with other members of the inner core of the ruling class. If, then, the difference between the governor general and the governor was essentially a social one, what relationships existed in the exercise of their functions? To answer this question we first need to know the position of the new governor according to the Organic Law.

Seventy-seven governors were appointed in central Russia after the reform. Their background was remarkably similar to that of their predecessors. Almost all were military men. Many were graduates of the first Turkish war and probably owed their recommendations to Rumiantsev or Potemkin. Only one was a former provincial voevoda.[19] Thus the tradition was retained that a governor was not a civil servant, although his post was a civilian one, but a military man, demobilized after a war and shipped off to the provinces to make a living in a civilian occupation. Since the size of the Russian army was increased in wartime, more high-ranking officers became available at the conclusion of the peace, but seldom was the invasion of the countryside by major generals so sudden and so extensive as in the late 1770s. The result was to raise the status of the central government's representative in all the new gubernia capitals by one or two ranks over that of his predecessors.

Each new governor received a salary of 1,800 rubles—the basic salary of a major general—and 1,200 rubles a year for entertainment expenses. In fifteen gubernias the allowance was replaced by an assignment of 600 state peasants, who supplied the provisions and pro-

[18] OL, art. 82, 86, 113; Trefolev, "Mel'gunov," 938-941, PSZ, 1787, N. 16513, Lopukhin, Zapiski, 12-17. PSZ, 1776, N. 14544, art. 1, 1781, N. 15140, art. 13, 1783, N. 15760, 1786, N. 16492, 1789, N. 16745. See also Chapter IV.
[19] There is a nearly complete list of governors in Turkestanov.

vided the kitchen staff and other household services.[20] Such an allowance, and the much larger one of the governor general, reflected the renewed emphasis placed upon the representative of the elite as the social leader of his gubernia, around whom the local nobility would gather at public ceremonies to affirm their class solidarity and strengthen their personal contacts.

New agencies were created in gubernia capitals to cope with the enlarged jurisdiction of the provincial administration. The two judicial chambers consisted of five officials each and the treasury chambers of six, including the vice-governor. The old chancery proper was now called the gubernia board (*pravlenie*) and consisted of the governor, two councillors in class VI at an annual salary of 600 rubles each, five secretaries, one procurator and his two deputies (*striapchie*). Thus, a single agency consisting of the governor and six officials had grown into a cluster of agencies staffed with twenty-seven officials, including five secretaries. To continue the parallel with the pre-reform administration, the staffing of the 10 gubernia and 29 provincial chanceries, which had required 215 officials, including 88 secretaries, now required 702, including 130 secretaries in twenty-six gubernias. Clerks were hired at the discretion of the gubernia board. If we assume that there were about 40 clerks in each capital their number would approximate 1,040.

This was a substantial increase, but it must not be forgotten that it took place while the central colleges were being dismantled. These figures show well the immense scope of deconcentration of governmental authority that took place in the 1780s. The judicial chambers (*palaty*) were given the authority of departments of the Colleges of Justice and Landed Estates, and the treasury chambers that of a department of the Colleges of Revenue and Audit. The gubernia board, however, continued to be equated with a full college and was thus placed above the new chambers. It remained the focal point of the gubernia administration and became the intermediary between the chambers and the Senate. These agencies, as a rule, did not meet as a body unless an "important or extraordinary matter" was received from Petersburg, or a new law was not considered "expedient" (*udoben*) in the gubernia. Then they were summoned by the governor general to meet with the gubernia board, and were allowed to submit a unanimous recommendation to the Senate.[21] In such conditions the board was much more than a shrunken gubernia chancery. The parallel with

---

[20] PSZ, 1796, N. 17494, vol. 44², 253-254, 264. In 1780 the assignment of peasants was replaced by an appropriation of 1,200 rubles a year: 1780, N. 14989.

[21] OL, art. 101 and 413.

Senate procedure comes to mind: it was, within the confines of its gubernia, the equivalent of the First Department, where other departments met in general assembly, and the governor general was a provincial procurator general.

The Organic Law clearly reinforced the position of the governor vis-à-vis the two councillors appointed to assist him (*dlia vspomozheniia*). They discussed official business, but they had to carry out the governor's decision even if they found it violated the law or civil service rules or did not serve "the general good." The board's decisions were binding on all police agencies and courts in the gubernia, but appeals were allowed to the Senate as the guardian of legality.[22] Thus the reform split the old gubernia chancery into specialized agencies which remained closely associated with the new board headed by a governor higher in rank and more independent of his subordinates than his predecessor.

The relationship between the governor general and the governor is one of the confusing aspects of the reform, and only a detailed study of their official correspondence might disclose a pattern. We must limit ourselves to an outline of the problem.

Despite the redistribution of the province between the gubernia and the uezd, the administrative reform sought to retain the three-tier division. To the large pre-reform gubernia there now corresponded a smaller *namestnichestvo*, to the much smaller province a larger gubernia. The governor general assumed the responsibilities of the pre-reform governor and the governor that of the provincial voevoda. The retention of the old title, however, gave the governor a prestige which the voevoda never had—hence the confusion surrounding any discussion of the relationship between governor general and governor. It is enough to say here that when the governor general was at his post the two governors—to take the standard case—were subordinated to him; when he was absent, his post ceased to exist, and the governor was restored in his powers under the Instruction of 1764 and assumed in his gubernia the powers which the governor general exercised in two. This confusing situation explains why the origin of the post of governor general in the reign of Catherine remained a mystery for students of Russian administration, notably Gradovskii.[23] They noted its essentially non-bureaucratic nature and its great powers, and condemned it as an anomaly which had done much harm to the orderly process of government. When an attempt was made to restore the post

---

[22] OL, art. 103, 99-100; Blinov, 136-137.
[23] Gradovskii, "Istoricheskii ocherk," 309, Strakhovskii, 50-53, Sokolov, 134, 140-141.

during the reign of Alexander I, the objections came from the ministries, especially the Ministry of Finance, and it was discovered that no law or instruction could be found outlining its jurisdiction and powers. As long as governors general are studied from a legalistic point of view, they must be seen merely as regional authorities exercising functions of supervision over two or three governors. In the borderlands their appointments, in addition, reflected the government's concern over the political situation, and their presence helped to retain the unity of a territory divided into smaller units for the sake of administrative convenience. But what purpose did they really serve in central Russia?

Most governors general belonged to the leadership of the military and foreign policy establishment; some were clearly protégés of Potemkin, others were his rivals. They were not, like the governors as a rule, retired generals whose military career had come to an end, but army commanders for whom no military command could temporarily be found. The fact that Prince Repnin and Zaborovskii, who had married into the Kurakin clan, or Gudovich, who married the daughter of Marshal Razumovskii, returned to active service during the second Turkish war is enough evidence that their appointment as governors general was merely a peacetime assignment. Tutolmin, on the other hand, was appointed to Petrozavodsk after a disagreement with Potemkin. This strongly suggests that the post of governor general was a sinecure devised by Potemkin for important generals whom he wished to conciliate in order to obtain their support in his own political struggle or remove from his immediate command without hurting their feelings.

Such motivation is one way of accounting for the creation of an apparently useless post. A second explanation has to do with the more active role of the Empress after 1774 and the anti-bureaucratic alliance between Catherine and the ruling elite. It was easier to govern with fifteen governors general than with twenty-six governors, and the aristocratic origin of most facilitated personal relationships, unencumbered by bureaucratic procedures and delays. Finally, the post of governor general symbolized the shift of the center of political gravity from the center to the provinces. Not only did the ruling elite consolidate its position at the center; it fanned out into the provinces as well. The large number of new positions created by the reform, as we shall see in subsequent chapters, gave the junior members of the ruling class a broad opportunity to participate in the exercise of the political function and to enhance the interests of their class; it also called upon the ruling elite to come down to the provinces to dispense their patronage and coopt new members. What was required of the governors general was not an administrative power greater than that of the governor, but high social status and greater political influence. The fact that a governor general "represented" his two gubernias in the Senate enabled local factions to enlist their supporters in the government to protect their interests and advance their claims. Thus the post of governor general embodied the political content of the reform as a redistribution of authority within the ruling class.

THE PROCURACY

The anti-bureaucratic thrust of the reform can also be seen from the activities of the local procuracy. At first glance, no other element of the Imperial administration was so bureaucratized, and nowhere, it seems, was the interest of the "state" so well protected. Procurators were first appointed in the gubernias in 1733 and in the provinces thirty years later. Each of the ten gubernia procurators was placed in the rank of colonel (class VI) and received 450 rubles, while the provincial procurators were majors who received 375 rubles a year. Each procurator was assisted by two clerks.[24] This was altogether a simple organization well suited to respond to the demands of an active and ambitious procurator general.

The reform brought about radical change. It enlarged the total staff of the local procuracy by more than fifteen times and diversified it. The gubernia procurator remained in class VI, but his salary was raised to 600 rubles. His office became a collegial one when two *striapchie* (deputies) in class X were appointed to help him, one with fiscal affairs, the other with criminal cases. Each of the three intermediate courts also received a procurator and two *striapchie*, and a *striapchii* in class XI was appointed in each uezd.[25] Thus, the pre-reform staff of 39 procurators had grown, in central Russia alone, to 104 procurators, 208 *striapchie* as deputy procurators, and 321 uezd *striapchie*. The total cost to maintain this force rose in a few years from 15,525 to 145,700 rubles! This phenomenal increase reflected the growing strength of the Procurator General in the high councils of government, not only as guardian of legality—his bureaucratic function—but also as chief dispenser of patronage in the civil administration.

Until the reform, procurators were guided by the Instruction to the Procurator General of 1722, the Instruction of 1733, and various other directives issued from time to time by the Procurator General.[26] The

---

[24] Grigorev, *Reforma*, 87, Blinov, "Nadzor," 46-47, 50; Dmitriev, *Istoriia*, 510; PSZ, 1763, N. 11991, vol. 44², 68-69, 1766, N. 12565.

[25] OL, art. 42-46, 49-51, 53-54; PSZ, 1796, N. 17494, vol. 44², 254-255, 257.

[26] PSZ, 1722, N. 3979, 1733, N. 6475, Veretennikov, 91.

Organic Law devoted seven long articles (art. 404-410) to the duties of procurators and *striapchie*, but introduced no major change in what must have been by then a well-established practice among central and local procurators. Therefore, we can examine the jurisdiction and procedures of the procuracy under the same heading both before and after the reform.

The jurisdiction of a procurator was defined in the broadest possible terms. He watched over the execution by the governor and other officials of their duties as provided in the laws, instructions, and regulations, saw to it that there were no delays, and that their decisions were carried out at all levels not only on paper but in fact (*samym deistvom*). He was responsible for the observance of the provisions of the *General'nyi Reglament*, the procedural code of the entire Imperial administration. These procedures included the keeping of minutes, the despatch of regular reports to central agencies, the registration of all incoming mail, and regular attendance. Provincial and gubernia procurators sent to their voevoda and governor quarterly forms showing who absented himself without cause, but the power to impose a fine was the prerogative of the governor. In police and judicial matters the procurator was responsible for the inspection of prisons, to check whether prisoners were not kept unduly long without trial, an activity in which a dedicated procurator could do much good.[27]

In order to carry out this monitoring of the literal application of the law by all local agencies, the procurator attended their meetings and was considered one of their members. He did not vote, however, and was required to leave the room when the other members were ready to reach a decision.[28] Therefore the procurator exercised his functions in a dual capacity, as member of an agency and as an official to whom decisions reached without his vote were referred. In his capacity as member the procurator acted chiefly as legal consultant. Whenever a new general law was received in the gubernia, the procurator was asked to give a finding (*zakliuchenie*) on its object and to state whether it amended or annulled existing legislation. At agency meetings he chose the laws that the members had to keep in mind and ordered the clerks to read them. And if any doubt was raised during the debate concerning the true significance of a text or its application to the matter under consideration, the agency requested a finding from

---

[27] OL, art. 404, 405, pt. 13; 1765, N. 12417, 1798, N. 18574; 1777, N. 14581, 1798, N. 18342; 1779, N. 14858, 1784, N. 15996, 1790, N. 16831; Grigorev, 293. On the procurator as interpreter of the law see TsGADA, f. 16, d. 200, fol. 9-10, 15-16.

[28] PSZ, 1767, N. 12867, OL, art. 406, pt. 9, 1791, N. 16948.

the procurator. This finding, however, was not binding and the members were free to follow their own convictions.[29]

Every decision, even trifles, required the procurator's seal of approval. The gubernia procurator especially, like his colleague in a central college, must have been overworked, so busy, in fact, that a cluttered desk was symbolic of his office.[30] If the procurator found that a decision violated a law or that procedures had not been observed despite his reminders, he had to suspend the execution of the decision and report the matter to the Procurator General within three days. Objections by the procurators of the intermediate courts and the uezd *striapchii* resulted in the referral of the case to the gubernia procurator.[31]

While the governor was the personal representative of the Empress and the representative of the entire Senate, the procurator was the personal delegate of the Procurator General. Thus there existed before the reform a symmetry between Senate and Procurator General, on the one hand, and between the gubernia or provincial chancery and the local procurator, on the other. Hence there was a natural tension between governor and procurator, sharpened by the difference in rank of the two officials which made it all the more imperative for the procurator to protect his independence if he was to carry out his duties effectively.

Provincial procurators were not subordinated to gubernia procurators, but both reported directly to the Procurator General, who had appointed them and who gave them instructions, clarified their responsibilities, settled misunderstandings, and dismissed or transferred them at discretion. In a word, as the law put it, while the Procurator General was the "eye of the Sovereign" in the Senate, local procurators were the eye of the Procurator General. Thus the reports of a local procurator were likely to receive strong support by a forceful Procurator General who was kept informed by regular correspondence.[32]

Behind this imposing facade of bureaucratic centralization, however, we can observe a social reality that denied the very principles of bureaucratic action. It seems likely that only the gubernia procurators

---

[29] PSZ, 1733, N. 6475, pt. 2-3, OL, art. 405, pt. 1-3, 6-7; PSZ, 1782, N. 15612, 15568, pt. 3, 1800, N. 19394; Grigorev, 291-292.

[30] The Empress, writing to the Governor General of Moscow in 1763, asked to be excused for overlooking two of his reports "car vous savez que ma table a toujours l'air d'un bureau de procureur": "Pis'ma imp Ekat. Vel.," 21.

[31] PSZ, 1733, N. 6475, pt. 2-3, 1767, N. 12867; Dmitriev, *Istoriia*, 510-511, Grigorev, 294.

[32] PSZ, 1733, N. 6475, pt. 7, 1785, N. 16133; Dmitriev, *Istoriia*, 512, *Ist. Prav. Senata*, II, 601; see also PSZ, 1771, N. 13708, 1782, N. 15568, Veretennikov, 91-98.

were appointed from civil service lists submitted by the Heraldry. In one case, probably not an isolated one, one such procurator was appointed without Prince Viazemskii's even having a copy of his service record, an indication that the appointment was a favor to a powerful friend. Whatever the source of the candidacy, these procurators seem in most cases to have been outsiders in the gubernia, junior members of the elite whose connections and talent earned them a share in the division of the spoils. The other procurators and *striapchie* were certain to be local landowners who simply applied for the position to the Procurator General or who were recommended by gubernia agencies, which naturally selected local candidates.

The post was attractive because the procuracy had a finger in every pie and bestowed legality on various deals serving the interests of the local elite. This was especially true where state peasants and state domains were involved. In Vologda, for example, one of the local procurators was on leave to inspect his properties. In Kursk gubernia, we find a Pereverzev among the local procurators whose family was engaged in selling vodka to the public, an illegal activity since noblemen had to sell their production to state-owned stores. In Putivl uezd of the same gubernia the *striapchii* was a local landowner who protected his relatives in a civil suit with other landowners involving, among other things, the illegal acquisition of secularized church lands which should have become state property.[33] Examples such as these could be multiplied by studying the correspondence of gubernia procurators with Prince Viazemskii. What emerges quite clearly is the absorption of the procuracy by local society and the undermining of its chief activity as the guardian of the law, its transformation into yet another source of patronage. This was a natural phenomenon if we keep in mind the anti-bureaucratic nature of the reform and the role played by the governor general in politicizing local administration. If the hapless Vologda procurator Brant could be humiliated by Governor Makarov[34]—the Makarovs were Vologda landowners—other procurators would think twice before antagonizing a governor general. The Organic Law even required procurators who appealed to Prince Viazemskii to refer their objections to the governor general as well, and this either exposed them to a double censure or embroiled them in personal quarrels among members of the elite. This is not to say that such antagonisms did not exist—witness the feud between the irascible Prince Prozorovskii in Kursk and Procurator Stromilov[35]—

[33] TsGADA, f. 248, d. 6512, I, 18-20 (Chemesov), d. 6519, II, 31-32 (Vologda), d. 6560, I, 96 (Putivl), II, 230-231 (Pereverzev).

[34] PSZ, 1783, N. 15822; background in TsGADA, f. 248, d. 6519, II, 37-41.

[35] TsGADA, f. 248, d. 6560, I, 35-36, 119-124.

but they must be seen as part of the politics of the ruling class rather than as a conflict between bureaucracy and society.

LOCAL SOCIETY AND THE REFORM

The expansion of society was most visible in the gubernias and uezds, where it proceeded rapidly in the wake of the reform. The electoral law of December 1766 allowed nobles possessing an estate in the uezd concerned to elect a marshal (*predvoditel'*). This new post was probably patterned after the *starosta* of the town, who represented the community before the *magistrat*. The marshal, whose functions were no more clear than those of the *starosta*, was bound to become the rival of the uezd voevoda[36] who, however, was being gradually integrated into the landowning class. The territorial reform of 1775-1782 that increased the number of uezds in central Russia from 177 to 321 multiplied the number of marshals accordingly. The Organic Law and Charter of 1785 incorporated the nobility of each gubernia into a corporation (*obshchestvo*) electing an assembly—not unlike the town *duma*—in which only landowners had the right to vote and be elected. It also introduced the new post of gubernia marshal in class VII in each of twenty-six gubernias and created a vast array of new posts to be filled, with the confirmation of the governor, at triennal elections: in each uezd a judge in class VIII, a land captain in class IX, and four assessors in classes IX and X; in each gubernia a judge of the court of equity and two chairmen of the upper land court in class VI and twelve assessors in class VII—altogether in twenty-five gubernias[37] and some 300 uezds 2,500 new posts, all paid for from the state budget!

The creation of these posts was the first stage in the integration of the entire local administration of the countryside under the close surveillance of the elite. The reform affected profoundly the administration of state peasants and even those of the Court. In each uezd where their number was large enough they were allowed to elect six assessors and in each gubernia an additional twelve, who were given no rank but received sixty rubles a year. These peasant assessors sat together with an elected or appointed noble to discuss police and judicial matters affecting members of their communities; and below them the network of *sotskie* remained unchanged. But the College of Economy and even the Chancery for Court Peasants were abolished, and in each gubernia a "director of economy" in class VI was given responsibility

---

[36] For an example of conflict see PSZ, 1772, N. 13757.

[37] OL, art. 18-19, 22-23, 50-53; PSZ, 1796, N. 17494, vol. 44², 254-257. There were very few nobles in Arkhangelsk gubernia, and I exclude it from this tabulation of posts.

for their welfare and the collection of their taxes. Thus, with the police and judiciary firmly in their hands, the local elite now blocked nearly every challenge to their rule over state peasants.

Their hold over the town was no less complete. Townsmen, too, yearned for recognition, protection, and status. This was granted, but at a price. The reform of March 1775 introduced, or recognized, a much greater social differentiation than had been the case. Guild merchants were divided into merchants (*kuptsy*) and shopkeepers (*meshchane*), and only the former were allowed to remain in the guilds. A merchant had to declare a capital of 500 rubles, a minimum raised to 1,000 rubles in 1785 and 2,000 rubles in 1794. He was exempted from paying the capitation of seventy kopecks, but was required instead to pay one percent of his declared capital, a minimum of five rubles. The reform divided the 218,630 guild merchants into 24,470 *kuptsy* and 194,160 *meshchane*, thus creating an elite among the townsmen, just below the ruling class, whose size was determined by the government's social policy. The Municipal Charter of 1785 abolished most of the services which they had been required to perform. It divided the merchants into three guilds and created a new top layer, like the old *gosti*, of "distinguished townsmen," who declared a capital of over 50,000 rubles. The three guilds and the shopkeepers elected every three years a *duma* and a *magistrat* whose jurisdication was intended to be purely judicial. The *duma* chose a committee of six members under a "headman" (*glava*), whose function seems to have been the management of town properties and revenues. In fact this *duma* showed a strong resemblance to the council of *starshiny* referred to in the Instruction of 1724, and it is quite likely that in many a town with a small population the *magistrat* remained the executive body and retained its old jurisdiction.[38]

But this greater social differentiation, which paved the way for the integration of the upper layer of merchants into the elite, was accompanied by an even greater subordination of the town to the elite. The Central *Magistrat* was abolished and replaced by a *magistrat* in each gubernia capital through which appeals to the judicial chambers were routed. Its two chairmen were placed in class VII during their three years in service.[39] Final decision depended on the judicial chambers,

[38] PSZ, 1775, N. 14275; Klokman, *Sotsial'no-ekon, istoriia*, 90-93; OL, art. 156-175, PSZ, 1785, N. 16188, art. 102-119, 123, 132-137. Even the Moscow and Petersburg *magistraty*, divided into four departments in 1784, retained jurisdiction over executive matters and municipal revenues: PSZ, 1784, N. 15917 and 15952.

[39] Every town with a full complement of new posts would elect fourteen people (excluding the *duma*), and ten more would be chosen to serve as chairmen and assessors

which were in the hands of the landed nobility. It must not be forgotten that the return to the countryside implied in the emancipation of the nobility was also a return from the two capitals to the provincial towns. The elite did not rule from their estates, but from the new uezd centers which dotted the countryside and from the gubernia capitals, where their presence was more visible than ever. The most important of their corporate positions was that of gubernia marshal, who, merely by virtue of the fact that he represented the entire gubernia, was the spokesman of the nobility and of the socially dependent groups. The position conferred prestige—we find very distinguished names among the marshals. Moreover, there is evidence from the correspondence of the Vologda marshal with Prince Viazemskii, in the case of a provincial voevoda dismissed for offending the local nobility, that personal relationships existed between these marshals and the Procurator General, and it is almost certain that they were among the major dispensers of local patronage.[40] The gubernia marshal, indeed, became the natural ally of the governor—or his enemy if the latter forgot his duties to his class—and their alliance formed the link between the purely local interests of the nobility and its wider responsibilities as the ruling class. The representatives elected by the nobility, the townsmen, and the state peasants now met in agencies created by the reform to replace the single chancery of the voevoda. A land court of three nobles and two state peasants, an uezd court of three nobles, a *rasprava* of four peasants and a *magistrat* shared jurisdiction in the uezd; in gubernia capitals an upper land court, and upper *rasprava*, and a gubernia *magistrat* elected separately by nobles, state peasants, and townsmen acted as appellate courts over the uezd and town courts.

This luxuriant proliferation of offices, all elected and supported by the state budget to replace the modest office of voevoda, embodied a consensus among the three major social groups in which each obtained a share in the administration of its own affairs, but under the overall leadership of the landed nobility. The conduct of investigations, the settlement of a large number of civil disputes, above all those involving boundaries, and to a large extent the collection of taxes in the countryside passed under the control of elected landowners, whose influence in the gubernia capital was strong enough to checkmate state peasants seeking protection against them. There landowners and appointed officials met on common ground. The aspirations of the nobility in the third quarter of the eighteenth century were not directed toward

in the gubernia capital, altogether for 26 gubernia and 321 uezd capitals 4,754 people; but these are maximum figures.

[40] TsGADA, f. 248, d. 6519, II, fol. 89-90.

constitutional change. They aimed at securing control over land and peasants as sources of wealth, and the reforms gave them the mechanism to do so.

It is puzzling to read in many scholarly works that the nobility obtained social power while political power eluded it, that, as Robert Jones put it, it was not "a political force capable of imposing a political program on the Empress.[41] If political power implies the autonomy of the ruling class and its ability to wring concessions from the monarch in duly constituted parliaments, the nobility did not possess it. But if it means the ability to impose a consensus on the nature of social relationships and to frame policies expressing that consensus, then it did have it. There was in the reign of Catherine no fundamental conflict of interest between the ruling class and a ruling house that also derived its wealth from the exploitation of servile labor and natural resources. If the information presented in this chapter is correct, the various factions of the elite were represented in all major agencies of government. The new orientation toward the Black Sea that began in the late 1760s was a response to domestic pressures for a more extensive division of the spoils than was possible within the confines of central Russia.[42] The shaping of foreign policy, of a tariff and tax policy, of a social policy to extract the maximum from servile labor, and of a comprehensive reform aimed at making more responsive to the needs of the nobility the administration of police and justice—these constituted the very essence of political power. The closing of the colleges in the 1780s was merely a footnote to an essentially anti-bureaucratic movement. Only the Colleges of Foreign Affairs, War, Navy, and Commerce remained, but even the latter was scheduled to be closed as of January 1, 1797. The ancient role of Moscow as the administrative capital came to an end with momentous implications for the future. There were to be no more presidents whose influence could rival that of the Procurator General and no more bureaucracies to restrain the greed and caprices of governors general and local elites.

[41] Jones, *Emancipation*, vi.

[42] See de Madariaga, "Catherine II and the Serfs," on the grant of estates in newly occupied territories and her interesting comments on Potemkin's attitude on the Polish question: *Russia*, 399, 418, 424, 428.

PART II
THE POLICE

POLICE ORGANIZATION

CENTRAL AGENCIES

The police controlled the movement of the tsar's subjects by means of internal passports, pried into private lives, and entangled all public activities in a web of distrust and denunciations. The secrecy in which it has wrapped Russian life and the operations of the government has made the police in the eyes of outsiders the incarnation of the Russian political order, the essence of its mystery, and the source of the fear it has always sought to inspire. Therefore, it should come as a surprise to find that no separate police administration existed, either at the center or locally. Rather, police activities were distributed among several central bodies; in the provinces, governors and voevodas continued to exercise until the reform the totality of governmental functions.

Some police responsibilities were vested in the First Department of the Senate. The Secret Expedition, nominally at least, was subordinated to it; so were the Central *Magistrat* and its local *magistraty*, responsible for the municipal police, including fire-fighting, sanitation, and public construction. Reports on natural catastrophes and requests for military assistance were sent to this department as well. The Procurator General, who headed the chancery of the Senate, was of course the first to receive these communications addressed to the Senate, but the First Department was much more than a police agency and its jurisdiction was chiefly financial. Censorship was the responsibility of the Academy of Sciences, Moscow University, the Imperial Theater, the Petersburg Custom House, the Senate's Third Department, the Synod, and the Post Office. It was not until 1796 that local censorship agencies were created, in Riga, Odessa, and Radzivilov in Volhynia. Thus, there did not exist in the reign of Catherine a central agency exclusively responsible for police administration, such as we find in the nineteenth century in the Ministry of Internal Affairs. The Secretariat, the Procurator General's office, the Academy, the University, and the Church all shared in police administration, yet their jurisdiction also encompassed such a vast number of other activities that they can in no way be called exclusively police agencies. In the still relatively simple conditions of eighteenth-century political life, when two cities absorbed so much of the nation's energy, and a consensus still largely prevailed on the bases of the social order, police functions remained intertwined with several others in a common body of general administration.

There was, however, one specialized agency whose activities extended over the entire territory of the Empire. Its jurisdiction remained uncertain, and its reach was as limitless as its methods were irresistible. This modest Secret Expedition already had a long history. Without going back into the seventeenth century to the Secret *Prikaz* of Tsar Alexis, we can find its immediate predecessor in the Secret Chancery of Peter the Great, abolished in 1729 but reopened in 1731 to deal with the so-called "first two points," i.e., crimes of lèse majesté and treason. The Chancery was headed by the famous Alexander Shuvalov from 1747 to 1762, and again abolished at the same time the nobility was emancipated from compulsory service in February 1762.[1]

For a short period after the coup of June 1762 there seems to have been no formal agency of political police. Secret matters were handled by Nikita Panin and Procurator General Glebov, replaced in February 1764 by Prince Viazemskii. The historian Sivkov claims that both men continued to report jointly to the Express until Panin's death in 1783,[2] but this is doubtful since there were certainly cases in which the Procurator General acted alone or, for example, with Marshal Golitsyn, the de facto Governor General of Petersburg in the 1770s. At any rate, Prince Viazemskii was surely the head of the secret police and remained so until his retirement in 1792. Thereafter, the picture is less clear. Platon Zubov may have succeeded him; State Secretary Popov as well as Procurator General Samoilov are also mentioned in political trials; and the ubiquitous Bezborodko may very well have had some responsibility in fighting subversion.

These men, however, handled secret police matters as part of their extensive political responsibilities and needed the services of a specialized agency if the prosecution of state crimes was to remain effective. And indeed, less than a year and half after the coup, the order of December 10, 1763 announced the appointment of Senate secretary Stepan Sheshkovskii to assist Panin and Glebov. This man, with long experience in the Secret Chancery, who had already gained the ear of the Empress, became the head of a new Secret Expedition of the Senate, subordinated to the First Department. The Expedition operated in a wing of the former palace of Shuvalov, which now belonged to the Procurator General. Its archive and its library were housed in the Senate building, and the most dangerous prisoners were kept in the Peter and Paul fortress, whose commandant, in political cases, received his instructions from Sheshkovskii and the Procurator General.[3]

[1] PSZ, 1762, N. 11445, esp. pt. 1 and 10.

[2] Sivkov, Ocherki, 8, 12-13.

[3] Amburger, *Geschichte*, 143-144, says that the Secret Expedition was established by the Manifesto of October 19, 1762 (N. 11687) confirming Peter III's own Manifesto

Sheshkovskii, born in 1720, was of recent Polish ancestry. His grandfather came from Grodno, was taken prisoner by Peter the Great, converted to Orthodoxy, and served at the Court. His father died in the post of policemaster of Kolomna. By 1740 Sheshkovskii was already a clerk in the Secret Chancery, and his ability to please Shuvalov

Stepan Ivanovich Sheshkovskii

of February (N. 11445), but I find no confirmation of this in the text. See also Kulakova, 236.

guaranteed his success. He rose through the ranks and became secretary in the Senate in 1762. Catherine soon valued his services so
highly that she charged him with the investigation of Arsenii Matseevich in 1763 and the Mirovich case in 1764, two of the most
important political cases of the early part of the reign. When the Senate
was divided into departments he was appointed senior secretary attached to (pri) the First Department. The Empress was pleased with
his investigation of Pugachev in 1774, and his subsequent career was
assured. A state councillor (class V) in 1775, he was promoted to class
IV in 1781 and class III in 1791. That he accepted "gifts" is certainly
true, but that he was "immensely rich," as Radishchev's son contended, is not. After his death in 1794, his widow received 10,000
rubles from the Treasury, but his debts amounted to 16,000 rubles,
and all his real property seems to have consisted of 780 souls in Nizhnii
Novgorod gubernia and another 100 elsewhere. His successor was
Alexander Makarov, who had been a secretary of Governor General
Brown (Riga) and of Procurator General Samoilov.

The man was unusual, but in certain respects true to type. A mas-
ochist who had himself flogged by cadets of the Corps of Pages and
enjoyed being taunted and despised, he was also very religious and
took communion every day. He conducted his interrogations in a room
filled with icons, not only to remind his victims that the crimes of
which they were accused were both violations of the civil law and
transgressions against the divine law requiring confession and repentance, but also to remind himself that his role as grand inquisitor
was a priestly function, the protection of the leadership, and the defense of political dogma. He was much feared, and his lean figure, his
hands adorned with rings stuck in the pockets of his grey frock coat,
was well known in Petersburg. Catherine admired his skill in con-
ducting investigations and his knack of winning the trust of simple
people. But he also tortured prisoners, knouted and whipped them
with his own hands, reserving his talents for the nobles while leaving
the smaller fry to his subordinates. Potemkin teased and despised him,
but the less fortunate, like Radishchev, fainted when they heard that
their case had gone to him.[4]

Thus, despite the appearance of a "liberal" reign, a powerful agency
of political repression was reconstituted at the very beginning. What
relationships developed between Sheshkovskii and Prince Viazemskii
is not clear. Both reported directly to the Empress, but Sheshkovskii
was also subordinated to the Procurator General as well in all cases

[4] Sheshkovskii's biography is in RBS, XXIII (1911); see also Kulakova, 237-238,
Kashkin, 9-10, and Gernet, "Politicheskii sysk," 26-27.

in which the Empress took no personal interest. He conducted the investigations, but it was probably the Procurator General who wrote the final report and recommended the penalty. If we consider the totality of police functions scattered among several agencies, it becomes clear that Prince Viazemskii was the single most important high police official. As Procurator General he was the de facto chairman of the First and Third Departments; local procurators kept him informed of police matters not properly reported; he was the head of the secret police. His office was indeed the precursor of a ministry of internal affairs.

One agency occupied a special place. Neither central nor local, it owed its existence to the overwhelming importance in the national life of Petersburg and Moscow as large agglomerations and seats of the Imperial government. The post of Policemaster General—the so-called "central police" (*glavnaia politsiia*) and the equivalent of a governorship of Petersburg—was far on the way to becoming a ministry of police when policemasters were appointed in twenty-three towns of central Russia and after the creation of various police units in the 1750s. But the trend was cut short in January 1762 when dissatisfaction with these vertical police structures led to their abolition and to the restoration of the powers of the governor and the voevoda over the police of their territories.

The new Policemaster General, appointed in 1763, occupied his post for fourteen years. Nikolai Chicherin, probably related to Procurator General Glebov, had been senior commandant in Kiev. He became the most important member of a commission established in 1766 to prepare construction projects for the expansion of Petersburg. After his promotion to lieutenant general in 1766 and full general in 1773, his inability to cope with a catastrophic flood of the Neva in September resulted in a semi-disgrace until his retirement in 1777. His successor, Dimitri Volkov, banished to Orenburg for his role in the reign of Peter III, had been President of the College of Manufactures in 1764-1777 and Governor General in Smolensk. Neither man belonged to the Saltykov-Trubetskoi clan, and the fall of Chicherin, resulting in the downgrading of his post after 1774, may have been connected with the increasing influence of Prince Viazemskii.

The table of organization of 1763 provided for a senior policemaster in Moscow in the rank of colonel. The reason for his comparatively low rank was the presence of a governor general. Traditionally, this high official administered the old capital in the ruler's absence, as his personal representative, and governors general were usually members of the aristocracy close to the Court. In September 1763 Catherine appointed Marshal Peter Saltykov, who had been commander-in-chief of the Russian army against Prussia in 1759. His old age explains in part his loss of nerve during the 1771 plague epidemic, and he was soon replaced by Prince Mikhail Volkonskii, nephew of former Chancellor Bestuzhev-Riumin. The next six governors general followed one another in quick succession, as if to make sure that the two major clans would receive, each in turn, the prestigious position: Vasilii Dolgorukov, the conqueror of the Crimea (1780-1782); Zakhar Chernyshev (1782-1784); Iakov Brius, Dolgorukov's nephew (1784-1786); Peter Eropkin (1786-1790); Prince Alexander Prozorovskii, Volkonskii's son-in-law (1790-1795); and Mikhail Izmailov (1795-1797).

The power of the Moscow Governors General rested on several factors.[5] Some, like Volkonskii and Brius, were very close to the Empress and the Court. The Governor General was a senator in the Fifth Department and as such, at least before the reform, a kind of deputy Procurator General in Moscow. The branch of the Secret Expedition was subordinated to him. And he was also the commanding general of the Moscow military region, which was more or less conterminous with the pre-reform Moscow gubernia. Thus, the Governor General was a regional political, administrative, judicial, and military authority, ranking in importance just below the President of the College of War and the Procurator General.

We can now understand why the Policemaster General could not evolve into a ministry of police. With the return to the principle of territorial administration, separate police agencies in the central provinces were abolished, and those remaining in the borderlands were not enough to justify the separate existence of a central police agency. The senior policemaster in Moscow was perforce subordinated to both his superior in Petersburg and to the governor general. In addition, any attempt to raise the office to the status of a ministry of police would have been incompatible with the concentration of governmental authority in the person of the Procurator General, as it would inevitably have encroached upon some of his major responsibilities. This did eventually take place, but not until after Catherine's death.

The jurisdiction of the Policemaster General became in fact limited to the city of Petersburg, and the abolition of the post marked a symbolic termination of whatever hopes had been placed on it as the nucleus of a national police ministry. The creation of a new post of Petersburg Governor General in 1786 seemed to show a desire to

⁵ No instruction, to my knowledge, was ever published for the Moscow Governor General, but see "Reskript i Nakaz." A draft of the rescript is in SIRIO, XIII (1874), 191-196.

enhance the status of the police authority, but that was not the case.[6] The recall of Brius from Moscow and his appointment in Petersburg, where he received the command of the troops stationed in the capital and in Vyborg gubernia, was motivated by an unusual situation. After his death in November 1791, no new governor general was appointed and the senior policemaster once again reported to the Empress directly.

In Moscow there was a decline in the status of the governor general after 1786, a result of the reduced role of the city following the territorial reform and the closing of the colleges. Eropkin was not so close to the Court as his predecessors had been. We know that the Empress did not feel, and could not feel by temperament, close to Prozorovskii, whose well-known narrow-mindedness and brutality had so distressed Potemkin. Toward the end of the reign the Moscow military region had practically ceased to exist as more and more troops were stationed in the newly annexed territories; the branch of the Secret Expedition may have been closed; and Izmailov was not even a military man. Thus, in the end, the status of the chief of police in the two capitals had been much reduced. The Policemaster General was gone, and the Moscow Governor General shrank from a powerful regional authority to the more modest condition of "policemaster general" of Moscow.

LOCAL AGENCIES

Outside the two capitals there existed no separate police organization. Each uezd had its voevoda and additional voevodas were also appointed in small towns which were not centers of separate uezds. These local officials were usually majors and captains who received 375 rubles a year and had a deputy and a staff of thirteen clerks. Their jurisdiction in no way differed from that of their provincial counterparts, a characteristic feature of pre-reform administration, which refused to recognize a hierarchy of responsibilities. All voevodas possessed the same universal competence as police authorities, courts of

---

[6] There had been no governor general in the northern capital because it was the residence of the Empress, although Marshal Golitsyn was a defacto governor general from the mid-1770s until his death in 1783 and acted as the surrogate of the Empress when she retired to Tsarskoe Selo during the summer months. In 1786, however, tension with Sweden required a strong authority in the capital, and Brius, a dour man with close connections at Court, was a very good choice for the post. Brius died in November 1791, and no successor was appointed. Arkharov, however, may have been the defacto governor general in 1796. See Golitsyn's reports in TsGADA, f. 16, d. 500, and Turgenev, 1886, I, 71.

justice, and tax-collecting agents. The countryside was left very much
to its own devices. With hardly any police force at his disposal, the
voevoda had to rely on the landowners, the *upraviteli*, and the treasurers in the villages of state peasants, and on the network of *sotskie*
and parish priests to carry out his orders.[7] The situation was so chaotic
that in areas hospitable to bandits and fugitives no civil society could
find the stability and security necessary for its consolidation and peaceful development.

Larger towns were administered by *magistraty*, smaller ones by
ratushi. They were responsible for the maintenance of order, the election of the night watch and firemen, the supervision of trade and
sanitation. This municipal administration, however, was flawed by the
excessive burden placed upon the population registered in the census;
peasants trading in the towns did not share the responsibilities inherent
to town life. This division among the urban population created the
need for a municipal police to serve the interests of the town as a
whole, but the ruling class, ambivalent toward the development of
towns—sources of wealth but also potential centers of opposition to
its hegemony—refused for long to see the urgency of the problem.

The abolition of the policemasters in 1762, together with the downgrading of the central police apparatus, must be placed in the context
of the political struggle for positions among the new leadership in the
early 1760s. Their appointment had been a source of patronage for
the Policemaster General, but their activities interfered with established
relationships between town and countryside—as when peasants ceased
to bring their products to Serpukhov after the new policemaster decided to inspect their passports—and they were a form of bureaucratic
interference in the patriarchal world of the landed nobility.[8] Yet, there
was a need for a separate police administration in the towns, especially
the large ones. The Instruction of 1764, which proclaimed the governor
to be the "lord and master" of his gubernia and the "guardian" of its
population, placed the *magistraty* under his jurisdiction as well as that
of the Central *Magistrat*. An active governor could not remain indif-
ferent to what seems to have been a general pattern of neglect of
municipal economy, and provincial voevodas, in imitation of their
governor, began to complain that the *magistraty* neglected their police
functions and to appoint retired officers to serve as de facto policemasters to be paid from city funds. Complaints came from Murom,

    7 Got'e, I, 53-56, 197-202, 315-321; PSZ, 1728, N. 5333.
    8 PSZ, 1733, N. 6378, 1762, N. 11401, 11573, 11628; Eroshkin, 146-147. Projects
continued to be made, however, for the appointments of policemasters and a staff in
every town of Great Russia and Siberia: see the very valuable document in TsGADA,
f. 16, d. 208.

Arzamas, Elets, and Kungur, and the Senate in October 1766 forbade this practice but reaffirmed the right of the governors to watch over the execution of police functions by the *magistraty.*[9]

In some towns with military garrisons police functions were the responsibility of a commandant. These retired officers reported to the governor and to the College of War, which had appointed them, and they were grouped into loose regions under a senior (*ober*) commandant. Most of these were major generals who received 1,200 rubles, and most of the commandants were colonels who were paid half that amount. Their duties included the day-to-day administration of the local garrison and the maintenance of order in the fortress and the town. In the 1760s there were five senior commandants in central Russia (Petersburg, Moscow, Kazan, Arkhangelsk, and Smolensk) and twenty commandants, and very few changes were made later in the reign.[10]

The reform—whose goal was to create an apparatus extensive enough to enforce the status quo and to facilitate the extraction of resources from the dependent population—abolished the voevodas and created an entirely different situation. It broke up their undifferentiated jurisdiction and vested police responsibilities, judicial administration, and tax collection into separate agencies. In addition, it separated the administration of the town from that of the uezd and established no link between them. The voevoda had no successor. In each uezd the reform created a lower land court (*nizhnii zemskii sud*) consisting of a land captain (*ispravnik*) and two or three assessors, elected for three years by the landowners of the uezd and confirmed in office by the governor if they had no clear "vices" (*porok*). In uezds where state peasants were to be found in large numbers, two of the eight assessors elected by them to serve in various capacities were assigned to the land court. In uezds where there were few nobles, usually in the north, the land captain was chosen by the gubernia board from three names submitted by the upper *rasprava*. The land court (a misnomer actually since it was not a judicial agency) met only when its services were necessary.[11] Thus, the entire court was elected by the nobles of the

[9] PSZ, 1763, N. 11838, 1766, N. 12764. An exception was made for Tula (1762, N. 11724), where the district (*sloboda*) occupied by gunsmiths remained under the Weapon (*Oruzheinaia*) Chancery responsible to the Commanding General of the Artillery.

[10] For the commandants, see PSZ, 1764, N. 12135 and 1769, N. 13390, 1797, N. 17767 and 17878; Got'e, I, 134-135. For individual cases see 1777, N. 14583, 1780, N. 14990, 1781, N. 15181, 1784, N. 15926, 1786, N. 16331, 1797, N. 18206 and 1799, N. 18929; also Minkh.

[11] OL, art, 22-23, 35, 52-53, 66-67, 223, 234; PSZ, 1792, N. 17019, 1796, N. 17494, vol. 44², *kn. sht.*, 257.

uezd, and the state peasants were represented on it, although their position was clearly a subordinate one. A secretary was appointed to keep the minutes and the record of the investigations: the possibility that the captain might be illiterate could not be excluded.

The expansion of the apparatus of general administration and police was indeed striking. If we assume that there were about 200 voevodas before the reform—leaving the deputy of each voevoda to deal with judicial and financial affairs—there were now some 320 land captains and 640 noble assessors, or 960 local landowners elected by other landowners in their uezds.[12] The claim of this new elected nobility on the state budget was very substantial, and one can only speculate on the extent to which this infusion of funds to support the land court and other elected uezd agencies spurred the local economy, local construction, and in general the progress of "westernization." Unlike the old voevodas, these men had local roots and were sensitive to pressures to uphold the interests of those who elected them in conflicts with the peasantry and those of the strong in conflicts with the less fortunate members of the local nobility.

The land captain could not be, by virtue of his rank alone, a highly respected individual. He was required by law to be a local landowner, but he must have been a poor one. A man could even be elected land captain against his will since landowners did not "run" for office but were elected by secret ballot without a list of candidates being presented. The procedure may indeed have been used to punish certain individuals whom their peers considered too independent or too self-righteous. To some, then, the election must have been unwelcome. The position required long trips to isolated villages to carry summons, investigate "events," and collect arrears. In small communities the land captain could play the bully, but on large estates he ran the risk of being whipped or having the dogs unleashed after him. If he was found to be at fault, any agency in the gubernia capital could give him a hard time, and the gubernia board could fine him or turn him over to the criminal court. He was often the intermediary between the landowners and the administration, but he was more often their errand boy and had to fear both.[13]

On the other hand, electing a poor nobleman was the equivalent of giving him a good pension and a free hand to "feed himself" off the state peasantry. In this sense it was a form of division of the spoils among the needy members of the nobility. The post was certainly a

---

[12] Less in fact, because the insufficient number of nobles in the northern uezds required that the land captains and their assessors be appointed.

[13] "Razgovor," 491.

boon to the unscrupulous. The landowners had wanted to place the affairs of the uezd in the hands of their elected representatives. Once their interests were protected against the arrogance of an appointee of the central government, they had no objection to giving him a free hand in bullying the peasants, if not those of other landowners, at least the various categories of state peasants. At a time when landowners were seeking to maximize their revenue from the exploitation of their own serfs, the possibility of tapping the resources of the state peasants unhindered by any representative of the central government was attractive.

In the opinion of the state peasants of Saratov gubernia, who claimed that they were better off when a voevoda lorded it over them, the reform certainly made serfdom more oppressive. The captain was a fool, the assessors were thieves, and the secretary was a cheat; all demanded money, chickens, fish and sheep, flax and wool in the spring, carts and horses all year round to visit their relatives; they scattered like wolves at Eastertime and helped themselves to piglets and fowl, and used the peasants at their hunting parties to start hares and ducks.[14]

The reform gave the nobility the instruments to assert its dominance over the entire peasant population. It confirmed the victory not of the state interest but of that of a social class bent on extracting from the population the resources necessary to maintain its privileged position. The uezd police was also the executive agency of the entire gubernia administration. It conducted investigations, the crucial stage in a judicial system marked by the prevalence of written procedures; it carried out judicial decisions, sometimes in such an arbitrary fashion as to nullify the effect of the decision; it collected arrears, a tempting form of fiscal repression; it prosecuted vagrants, a source of cheap labor. The land court was truly the corporate agent of the nobility of the uezd and the guardian of its interests.

The division of the spoils among members of the privileged class was also evident in the reform of municipal administration. The policing of the towns could not be left to absentee merchants and committees of shopkeepers. On the other hand, the need to recognize the status of the townsmen, who were pushing for recognition, required that the preeminence of the privileged class be recognized. What emerged was a compromise in which both elements were integrated, and the unity of uezd administration, otherwise broken by the creation of separate agencies for the administration of the town and the country-

[14] Iudin, "Zhaloba." A similar case (in Orel gubernia) is in "Proshenie ekon. krest'ian," and "Zhaloba" (in Tambov gubernia). See also Sipovskii, 528-529 (the facts were ignored because state peasants were the plaintiffs).

side, was to a large extent retained. This was especially true in the smaller uezd centers created by the reform out of former villages, where townsmen were no more than state peasants under another name. The voevoda was replaced by a sheriff (*gorodnichii*) appointed in all towns except Petersburg and Moscow by the Senate on recommendation of the gubernia board. It was likely, therefore, that he would be a local nobleman and perhaps even a landowner. In class VIII, he even ranked higher than the land captain. He received 300 rubles and an additional 130 rubles for clerks and expenditures.

The Police Code of 1782 went a step further and transformed the office of sheriff into a collegial agency called the police board (*uprava blagochiniia*) by adding two deputies (*pristavy*) for civil and criminal affairs, appointed by the gubernia board on recommendation of the sheriff, and two members of the *magistrat*, who were the intermediaries between the sheriff and the merchants and shopkeepers. There was no provision for a secretary. The deputies were in class IX, like the land captain, and were paid 250 rubles; the other members were neither ranked nor paid. The new agency was subordinated to the gubernia board, where ultimate control was exercised over the police of the entire gubernia.[15]

Certain towns were divided into districts (*chasti*) and wards (*kvartali*), and instructions were sent to the governors general to draw up tables of organization for the police of each town, depending on its size, location, and layout. Each district was to consist of between 200 and 700 houses (*dvory*) and was headed by an officer (*pristav*) in class X appointed by the gubernia board. He was expected to be of good conduct, display common sense and good will, and be impartial, and had to live in his district. The gates (*zastavy*) in the district were in his jurisdiction. He assigned the night-watch to their places, reported to the police board every morning, and received his orders directly from the sheriff.

Wards were subdivisions of the district or, if the town was small, were simply subdivisions of the town. Each ward had from fifty to one hundred houses and was headed by a supervisor (*nadziratel*) in class XI appointed by the police board on recommendation of the *pristavy* and the community of the ward. The only truly elected official of this police organization was his assistant, elected for three years by the members of the ward; his election required the confirmation of the police board.[16]

[15] OL, art. 25, 51, 71, 253, 262, 265, 276, 427; Police Code (1781, N. 15379), art. 1-2, 4, 28-29, 40; *SIRIO*, XXVII (1880), 200-206.

[16] Police Code, art. 5-20, 24-27, 77-78, 93-97, 127-128, 146-159; on the night watch,

Two examples will illustrate the new police organization. Kazan, for instance, was divided into two districts and (probably) ten wards. The first district included the fortress and the town, together with an adjacent *sloboda* along the Kazanka river. The second was the working-class district, divided into four wards; the new and the old Tatar *slobody*; one village of 240 souls; and the cloth factory with surrounding *slobody*. Novgorod likewise was divided into two districts and ten wards. However, only two of the eight uezd centers (Staraia Rusa and Tikhvin) were divided into districts; elsewhere there were only wards.[17]

The new municipal police apparatus gave the junior members of the ruling class—captains, lieutenants, and ensigns, and needy landowners—an opportunity to participate directly in the exercise of the political function and to draw an income from the treasury. The penetration of the ruling class into the life of the socially dependent was deeper in the towns than in the countryside because of the higher density of the urban population and the greater variety of municipal services. The subordination of municipal life to the interests of the nobility, always taken for granted, now became a fact supported by organization. However, the appearance of landowners and retired officers in the districts and the wards on a daily basis affected the relationship between the two cultures and raised more forcefully the problem of legitimacy. Contacts required compromise, or orders would remain without effect. This was also true in the countryside, where dominion over the peasant did not exclude understanding. What kind of understanding developed is a question to which Russian anthropology must urgently address itself.

---

see 137, 150; on police personnel, see 1782, N. 15472, 1783, N. 15792, 1784, N. 16006.

[17] Klokman 283; for Tula, see "Zhurnal reliatsii," 5-7; PSZ, 1782, N. 15430, 1799, N. 18985; for Petrozavodsk, see TsGADA, f. 16, d. 804, fol. 281-285. Petersburg and Moscow were a class apart. Moscow was the largest city in the Empire, with a total population of about 300,000 in the summer and about 400,000 in the winter. Before the reform, the municipal police consisted of the senior policemaster, two deputies, and a staff of 39. The city was divided into 12 *komandy*, each run by a captain. After the reform, it was divided into 11 districts and 45 wards. The police board consisted of the senior policemaster, one policemaster (a new post), and two deputies, two secretaries, and two members of the *magistrat*. The staff in each district and ward followed the general pattern. Petersburg was much smaller than Moscow, but grew steadily. There were 150,000 inhabitants in 1761 and 218,000 in 1790. The reform raised the number of districts from four to ten, seven on the left bank of the Neva, including the three Admiralty districts, the heart of the city, and three on the right bank including Vasil'ev island. The police board was similar to that of Moscow, but pay scales were higher. See Chebotarev, 3-4, 45-50; "Moskva 1785 goda," *Gorodskiia poseleniia*, VI (1864), xxxi; VII (1864), xxiv-xxv; and *SIRIO*, XXVII (1880), 200-205.

Police Forces

Governors and voevodas before the reform governors, land captains
and sheriffs after the reform, relied for the performance of their duties
on the support of two kinds of police forces. Some were chosen by
the communities which benefitted from their services: they were the
night watch, the firemen, and various people who assumed responsibility for sanitation and street lighting, together with the network of
sotskie and desiatskie in the uezds. Other forces were military or para-
military formations constituting the repressive arm of the provincial
administration. These forces consisted of units of the regular army, of
garrison troops, and shtatnye komandy.

In the 1760s fifty-one regiments were stationed on the territory of
the twenty-six post-reform gubernias and in 1780 only forty-two, or
about 80,000 men. But regiments were often kept below strength in
peacetime, and the tense international situation after 1788 resulted in
the dispersion of more and more troops in the borderlands. Perhaps
half that amount would be closer to reality, not a very compelling
presence among the 9.5 million male peasants registered in the census
of 1782.[18]

Regular troops were used against recalcitrant peasants when a steady
form of pressure was considered necessary. This presence took the
form of the so-called dragonnades (ekzekutsii), the billeting of a company in peasant homes without payment for food and forage in order
to compel payment of tax arrears. Troops were used to put down
violent manifestations against the authorities, to catch escaped prisoners and highway robbers, and even to watch over the suspicious
activities of villagers. But these were relatively rare forms of participation by the regular army in police administration. So few troops
were stationed outside the immediate vicinity of the two capitals that
their use had to be limited to emergencies or to the application of
exemplary punishment. The dragoons, however, were present in every
important town, and they probably constituted the most efficient police
force at the disposal of the governor and the police boards.[19]

Garrison troops in central Russia were more important than the
regular army as an executive force of general administration and an
instrument of police control. Their geographical distribution depended

[18] Beskrovnyi, Russkaia armiia, 311-330, 339; "Rospisanie russkikh voisk (1763)";
SIRIO, XXVII (1880); on the absence of troops in Moscow, see Solov'ev, "Moskva v
1770 i 1771 gg." See also Maslovskii, 5-49. Troops stationed in Petersburg in 1775,
including the Guard, regular troops, and the garrisons, numbered slightly over 24,000
men: TsGADA, f. 16, d. 500, fol. 28-82.

[19] On the dragoons, see PSZ, 1763, N. 11735, pt. 10, 1764, N. 12157 and 12304,
1775, N. 14236, 1786, N. 16376.

on two considerations: the location of fortresses, where the officers staffed the administration and the men policed the grounds and sometimes the town as well, and the need to maintain a military presence in areas where no regular troops were stationed. Thirty-two battalions—each consisting of 772 officers and men—were stationed in central Russia, giving a total strength on paper of 24,700 men.[20]

The duties of the garrison troops were many. In towns where regular troops were also stationed, all guard duties in the fortress were taken over by the army, which also became responsible for the pursuit of bandits and for putting down peasant disorders. Elsewhere, the duty of garrison troops had traditionally been to provide assistance to the civil administration wherever armed protection was necessary. They were used to guard government offices, the post office, the local treasury, churches, public gardens, and prisons; as convoys to watch over funds sent to the army or to the treasury, or prisoners to their place of exile in the Orenburg Territory or Siberia. They were also used in the collection of taxes and arrears, in catching robbers and criminals, even in compelling subordinate agencies to carry out their responsibilities, such as sending accurate reports on time. But the result of this confusion between guard duties and the functions of an executive police was that garrison troops ceased to be the compact forces they were intended to be, and were often unavailable in sufficient numbers when some forceful action was required.[21]

One example will illustrate how difficult it was to muster an adequate police force in any extraordinary situation. In July 1776 Governor Golovtsyn wrote from Arkhangelsk to the Procurator General that sixty escaped convicts were roaming the countryside in Vologda uezd, breaking into the homes of nobles to steal guns, food, and vodka. The Vologda and Galich provincial chanceries were unable to gather enough of a force against them. The Governor wrote to the Fifth Department in Moscow, asking the Governor General to send a detachment from the two companies stationed in Iaroslavl, but nothing was done. From the Arkhangelsk garrison—837 km away!—the Governor could afford to send only thirty men and had to draft the soldiers' children, who were in school, to replace them. He asked the Procurator General to intercede with the Empress to order the College of War to send a military force to Vologda, but the Empress thought the Governor was making a mountain out of a molehill.[22]

Neither the regular army nor the garrison troops, then, could pro-

---

[20] PSZ, 1763, N. 11818, 1764, N. 12135 and 1769, N. 13390, 1777, N. 14583, 1795, N. 17291, 1797, N. 18206; Beskrovnyi, 326-327.

[21] PSZ, 1761, N. 11347, 1764, N. 12135, pt. 5-6.

[22] SIRIO, XXVII (1880), 101-105.

vide a permanent and adequate force to carry out the functions of the governors and the voevodas. An additional solution was sought in the creation of the *shtatnye komandy*, so called because they were included in the table of organization (*shtat*) of every voevoda chancery. Both these units and the garrisons were the forerunners of what was later called the "internal guard" of the Empire.[23]

Detachments of various size were assigned to different levels. Each gubernia chancery received a detachment of 132 commanded by a captain, each provincial chancery one of 58, and each voevoda chancery half that number. For the whole of central Russia in 10 gubernia capitals, 29 provincial capitals, and about 200 voevoda chanceries there was, then, a total force of about 8,830 men. The local government reform of the 1770s increased this force substantially. The gubernia detachments (*gubernskie roty*) remained of the same size, but their number rose to 26; the uezd detachments were enlarged to consist of 34 men; and their number rose to 321. This gives us a total of about 14,550 officers and men. The *shtatnye komandy*, attached to specific agencies and uniformly distributed across the territory, were the true executive police of the provincial and local government, under the authority of the governor and maintained by appropriations from the civilian budget.

Yet, the fact remains that even in peacetime the *komandy* and the garrisons provided an inadequate police force. In Nizhnii Novgorod gubernia, for example, even after the reform, when the situation had already much improved, one garrison detachment and twelve uezd *komandy* amounted to a force of 1,312 men. Many of these men were old or sick. Even assuming that as many as 900 were available, it was not a very large force for a gubernia of some 580,000 inhabitants, where diversified economic activities along the Volga created a constant demand for the maintenance of order and various forms of administrative and judicial assistance. And other gubernias were even less policed. Viatka gubernia, with a population of nearly 830,000 inhabitants, had a force of only 540 men.

We may conclude from our study of police organization that, with the exception of the Secret Expedition, there was no central police agency and that none was created by the reform. The Expedition enforced the terms of a political consensus and a conception of uniformity. Police administration, however, had not yet developed as a branch separate from military and general administration, and the reassertion of the territorial principle in the 1760s militated against the creation of functional services while favoring the defense of class interests within the confines of compact administrative areas. The vast increase in the number of administrative personnel which is such a salient feature of the reign of Catherine was certainly no part of a process of bureaucratization. On the contrary, it represented a division of the spoils on a grand scale and benefited chiefly the rank-and-file nobility. The officers of the *shtatnye komandy*, lieutenants and captains, who otherwise would have been abandoned to their fate or at best sent to live in monasteries, were now distributed, after their selection by commanders of military regions and the College of War, among the gubernia capitals and uezd centers and paid a reduced salary, which nevertheless allowed them to retain their dignity. The creation of a land court and a police board to replace the voevoda and his chancery, together with the vast increase in the number of uezds, multiplied the number of posts at least fourfold. The crucial point was that these positions were no longer filled as a rule by the central government but by the gubernia board from among retired junior officers of the gubernia. The new men may or may not have been landowners, although the law required them to be, but, if they were not, they were certain to associate with landowners and to seek to obtain by hook or by crook the status symbol represented by land and above all by serfs. Patronage here was distributed, no longer by the top stratum of the elite, but by the governors and gubernia marshals who were very close to it. If anything, the reform was an anti-bureaucratic phenomenon which shifted the center of gravity to the gubernias and uezds, where the nobility won the right to exploit the state peasantry and to satisfy their "hunger for land that was not theirs"[24] without interference. Finally, a paradoxical result of the reform was the creation of a rudimentary police organization in the person of the sheriff and the *shtatnye komandy* and an attempt for the first time to define the functions of the police. Thus here, too, the extension of class rule and the rationalization of the process of governing worked together to create a more efficient and more oppressive local apparatus to enforce serfdom and to facilitate the exploitation of natural resources for selfish ends.

[24] Augustine, 402.

CHAPTER II

THE JURISDICTION OF
THE POLICE

The function of the eighteenth-century Russian police was dual: to guard
the hegemony of the ruling class and to provide services to the socially
dependent in towns and countryside. The first derived from the political supremacy of that class, the second from its social responsibility
toward the collectivity of which it was the most exalted part.

Aron has made the telling point that "a unified elite means the end
of freedom."[1] This is a convincing sociological explanation of ideological uniformity anywhere; and it applies as well to Catherine's
Russia, where the unity of the ruling class was still undisturbed by the
emergence of social groups bent upon challenging its political monopoly and the integrity of the social order. To this explanation must
be added another, the product of the country's historical experience.
Police attitudes in Russia pervaded the entire body politic, compelling
unity and repressing dissent, sensitive to the smallest deviation, and
all-encompassing in the fervor of their compulsion. Such a mood was
derived from two mutually reinforcing concomitants of the Russian
political order: the close relationship between the church and the
political leadership and the identification of church with nation.

The police was indeed the soul of the Russian political and social
order,[2] not merely a passive reflection of its constitution or a mood
suffusing the entire body politic, but an active antidote against all
attempts to tamper with its ideological foundations. The term "political police" is in fact a misnomer, and it is used here only for the sake
of convenience. It implies the existence of two jurisdictions, identifies
"political" with "extraordinary," and distinguishes between procedures regulated by law and arbitrary actions dictated by the security
interests of the leadership. At the root of the distinction between
ordinary and political police lies the old duality in the allegiance of
man, to God and to Caesar.[3] In the absence of such a duality in Russia,

[1] Aron, 143.

[2] PSZ, 1721, N. 3708, X (Statute of the Central *Magistrat*).

[3] Matthew, 22:21, Mark, 12:17, Luke, 20:25. This section is based on various read-
ings, notably Vernadskii, Szamuely, and Ware. The classic discussion of the church and

all police are potentially political, and if there must be agencies with responsibility for the sensitive cases their jurisdiction is not restricted to them but can be extended to include any actions considered injurious to ideological purity.

If church and state lived in "symphony" and not in latent opposition to each other, man's dual allegiance was considerably muted and could not have the dynamic quality that compelled western thinkers to ground in rational and legal arguments man's relationship with the secular leadership. The relationship remained a fluid one, and when the ruling house gained ascendancy over the church, the duality was naturally resolved into unconditional allegiance to it. It was his inner life, his spiritual life, the care of his soul, that western man had refused to render unto Caesar. By rendering total allegiance to Caesar, the Russian Orthodox believer (except the mystic who withdrew from the world entirely and the sectarians who sought protection against persecution behind a barrier of forests and swamps) renounced the sanctity of his private life. The claims of the leadership extended to man's private life as well, and interference into the religious and spiritual as well as the family life of individuals was justified, not as an exception in emergencies, but as a normal pattern of behavior. On reading the Instruction of the Policemaster General's chancery submitted to the Legislative Commission, Got'e wrote that there was "no corner of private [and] social life into which the proposed police could not poke its reasonable, beneficient, and all-powerful nose. You read this and wonder if this is not some committee of public security administered by highly placed bureaucrats under the highest guidance of the autocratic sovereign."[4] There should have been no cause for him to wonder, since this interference in everyday life was already a matter of course. We find indeed in this Instruction not only all the activities of ordinary police identical with municipal administration in general, but also claims to policing churches during services, to decreeing fashions worn by men and women, supervising private entertainment and domestic living, and watching over private activities. These activities formed a grey area where both political and ordinary police overlapped. Supposedly innocent meetings and words acquired a political coloration, depending on the sensitivity of the environment.

A considerable extension of the realm of intervention of the political police derived from the association of church and nation. When the two are separate and even in opposition, acts committed in defiance

---

state relationship in the west is in Carlyle, I, 175-193; III, 6-9, 129; IV, 384-395; see also Huizinga, 151-166, 178.

[4] Got'e, I, 15; Papmehl, "Problem," 282.

of the authority of one do not impinge upon the authority of the other but may even be rationalized and justified. The right to rebel, the supreme defiance of authority, can be justified if there is civil encroachment upon religious freedom. When the church is associated with the nation, the community of subjects is also the community of believers, and if there is no salvation outside the church, then there is no freedom outside the order created by the ruling class. Political thought and political actions acquire an extended resonance because they cannot remain individualized, and they carry a religious connotation going far beyond their original intent. Political dissent, in the many forms it can take—in private thought, in action, in writing—is not merely the rejection of certain policies; it is heresy which exposes the dissenter not only to political persecution but also to the flames of hell. If he goes so far as to question and reject the entire political order, the dissenter removes himself from the political community and deserves to be cast away by excommunication from the community of believers. Emigration is also apostasy. One cannot reject the political creed without challenging religious dogma and the foundations of national consciousness. The identification of the Russian Orthodox Church with Russia, not only the largest Orthodox state but the only one not to have fallen under Turkish domination and been defiled by it, implied the sanctification of the land and of its people and of its political order. Dissent endangered the physical freedom of the dissenter, his salvation, and his national identity.

Finally, the organic unity of state and ruling class gave police activities an extended political content. The alliance of nobility and autocracy strengthened social conservatism and gave any criticism of the existing order subversive implications that could not remain unpunished. The reign of Catherine marked the culmination of this alliance. It also witnessed the first stirrings of opposition to it as the issue of serfdom began to generate a debate over the compatibility of the social foundation of autocracy with industrial development, while the French Revolution challenged the very foundations of the old order everywhere. It became the task of the police to maintain the existing arrangement between the ruling house and the nobility and to repress the resentment of those whose economic power or education justified claims to a share in it. Such social questions were potentially vital challenges to the integrity of the political order. The police became an instrument of social conservatism to preserve the status quo at all cost.

Such considerations help us gauge the intensity of those radial influences binding, on the one hand, the rank and file of the ruling class with its leadership, and, on the other, the ruling class as a whole with the remainder of the collectivity. Ideological uniformity—and who has not been struck by the absence of political literature in pre-industrial Russia?—favored centralization and consensus, and created centripetal currents. Obedience to the hierarchy became a value in itself because it was tied up with a social and religious attitude. Thus Orthodoxy and social conservatism enhanced the leadership function of the ruling class and fostered unity with it. Likewise, the union of religion with ethnicity created a bond, still indissoluble in the eighteenth century, between the ruling class and the peasantry and townsmen. Westernization was a process spread over several generations and exhibiting different degrees of realization. A Russian did not become a "Western man" in the eighteenth century because he read Voltaire, smoked tobacco, and no longer kept his wife in seclusion. Prince Volkonskii, among others, despite his position in the "Westernized" elite, remained in his private life very close to the merchants who clung to the old ways and who stood so far below him. What the association of religious orthodoxy, political conformity, and social conservatism achieved was to keep in existence, despite the emergence of two cultures, a single civilization whose tenets still upheld social hierarchy and vested the ultimate interpretation of its doubts in its political leadership.

THE POLITICAL POLICE

The activities of the political police thus covered a broad spectrum, and found no limitations either in social mores or political prejudices. Some cases depended very much upon the whims of the Empress. The Secret Expedition, for example, was also a kind of household police. The Empress ordered Sheshkovskii to whip—for making caricatures of Potemkin—two ladies-in-waiting who were none other than the daughter-in-law of former Policemaster General Divov and the wife of her secretary Turchaninov; and to arrest at a public masquerade the wife of Major General Kozhin, known for her idle and pretentious chatter, and to have her whipped in Expedition headquarters. Most of its cases, however, were much more serious.

There were, first of all, attempts to overthrow the Empress and manifestations of political discontent with the conduct of her private life. As early as October 1762 a plot was discovered, led by Peter Khitrovo and the Gur'ev brothers, to put Ivan VI on the throne. The plotters were banished. But in July 1764 a captain Basil Mirovich drew up a manifesto accusing the Empress of being a usurper and a regicide and forced his way to the cell of the unfortunate Tsar in the Shlisselburg fortress. The coup failed, and the investigation of the captain was one of the first important cases entrusted to Sheshskovskii. Ten years later, the Pugachev rebellion in the eastern provinces coincided with the majority of Grand Duke Paul and fed speculation as to whether the Empress ought not to abdicate in favor of her son. The Secret Expedition, however, was not given major responsibility for the investigation of the uprising; instead, independent commissions were established for that purpose in Kazan and Orenburg. Piontkovskii, who studied the files of the Expedition, found only seventeen related cases, mostly from outside the area affected by the rebellion. They involved chiefly rumors spread by runaway soldiers and prisoners. Each case was processed with unusual rapidity—within four to six days of the arrest. The investigation was conducted locally by the procurator and was sent by the Governor to the Procurator General, who submitted a summary to the Empress. In the case of a soldier stationed in Petersburg and brought to the Expedition on March 31, 1774, the Empress gave her decision the next day. In another case Sheshkovskii's investigation was returned as inconclusive, and Prince Viazemskii was ordered to supplement it. Pugachev, however, after his arrival in Moscow, was investigated by Sheshkovskii.[5]

Other political cases affecting the Empress directly included the opposition of the archbishop of Rostov, Arsenii Matseevich, to the secularization of ecclesiastical properties. The opposition, although it turned into bitter personal enmity, went beyond personal considerations. It was a challenge to the assault mounted by the nobility to turn those properties into a fund for the extension of private landholding and state domains. The removal of the archbishop was facilitated by the lack of extended support by fellow churchmen. Plans were made by Fedor Khitrovo and a group of friends in 1763 to murder the Orlov brothers in order to put an end to their influence and prevent a possible marriage of the Empress with Grigorii Orlov. The ghost of Peter III continued to roam the southern provinces. A soldier Dmitriev was heard to say in a drunken state in Tsaritsyn that the former emperor was with an army in the Crimea and that Marshal Rumiantsev had decided not to oppose him. Some individuals continued to claim from time to time that they were the deceased emperor. Personal comments on the Empress and members of the Imperial family were called "indecent" (*nepristoinye slova*) and were investigated by the Secret Expedition as coming under the "first two points." Interest in Grand Duke Paul also attracted attention. In 1775 a former voevoda of Dedilovo wrote a manifesto in the name of Paul; in 1778 a lampoon (*paskvil*) on a speech supposedly made by Paul in the Senate was found

---

[5] "Istoricheskie razskazy," 137-138; Bilbasov, II, 170-180; Sivkov, Ocherki, 376; Piontkovskii, 91-100; *Sbornik istor. materialov*, 95-101.

circulating in Orel. In 1785 a peasant named Baibakov from Kholm uezd saw in a dream the Grand Duke surrounded by fire and threatened by snakes. Greatly perturbed, he went to Gatchina to tell his story, but on Paul's orders he was sent to Sheshkovskii.[6]

The Secret Expedition also had jurisdiction over the so-called *slovo i delo* cases, in which someone claimed to have something important to tell the sovereign. Such persons were automatically sent to Petersburg for interrogation, but the Empress did not take kindly to the sordid reasons that often lay behind these claims, and the manifesto abolishing the Secret Chancery sought to discourage this ingrained habit, which had done so much harm during the preceding reigns. In 1784, in a reversal of the usual procedure, Sheshkovskii was sent to Moscow to take the deposition of Natalia Passek, who had written the Empress that she had a "secret" to tell.

Espionage and counterfeiting cases were investigated by the Secret Expedition. In 1773 a conspiracy to print forged assignats was discovered, engineered by none other than Fedor Sukin, the Vice-President of the College of Manufactures, and two Pushkins, one of whom was a member of the college. In 1790 a secretary of the College of Foreign Affairs, Valts, was investigated for selling information to the French ambassador. We can include here the case of the Irkutsk Governor General Ivan Iakobi, accused in 1788 of a variety of crimes, including treasonable activities; he was saved only owing to his energetic defense by Derzhavin. Political dissent fed by the unpopular second Turkish war (1788-1791) and the irresponsible resort to the printing press was repressed by censorship and brutal police methods. Governor General Brius forced out of office the chairman of the Moscow criminal chamber Ivan Lopukhin for martinist sympathies, the first move in the campaign against the masons completed by his successor Prozorovskii. Kniazhnin's play *Vadim of Novgorod* was hounded out of circulation. Sheshkovskii investigated Novikov and the students Nevzorov and Kolokoltsov in 1791-1792 for publishing and distributing "monstrous creations (*iurodivye porozhdeniia*) of the so-called Encyclopedists," as the archbishop of Moscow put it. In 1795, after Sheshkovskii's death, the archbishop told the curator of Moscow University that a German named Melman, a professor of philosophy and rhetoric, knew nothing about the principles of the Christian religion. The investigation by the Governor General of Moscow was conducted on the direct orders of the Procurator General and the Empress.[7]

[6] For the Matseevich case, see Barsov and Ikonnikov. For the other cases see "Iz bumag Viazemskago," Sivkov, Ocherki, 197, 226, "Delo o Baibakove," Longinov, "Neskol'ko izvestii," 346.

[7] *Krest'ianskaia voina*, 359; Efremov, 269; Longinov, "Materialy," 631-650; "Delo

Finally, if we exclude a number of cases that defy classification—
such as those of peasants who linked the unfavorable weather to the
Empress's accession, who did not like to see a woman on the throne,
and found that too many people were being recruited—mention must
be made of what might be called cases of deviant social behavior by
nobles who thereby challenged the foundations of both the social and
the political order. Radishchev's *Journey from Petersburg to Moscow*
could be prosecuted on a variety of grounds, but the Empress's anger
(incited by Platon Zubov, who was the evil influence behind the throne
during the last five years of the reign) was no doubt directed against
the criticism of the social foundations of autocracy by a nobleman
whose wife had ties at Court. Even if the ominous developments taking
place in Paris had not been known, the reaction of the Empress to the
publication of such a book in wartime was understandable. Similar
considerations probably played a role in the sentencing in 1777 of a
Captain Bogdanov accused of giving support to Latvian peasants who
complained against their German overlords. The case was tried by
court martial in Riga and resulted in a sentence of banishment to a
distant garrison. But, following the intervention of Governor General
Brown, it was removed to the Secret Expedition. The most interesting
of such cases was probably that of naval captain Kravkov, who committed the unprecedented offense for a nobleman of wearing a beard,
preferring Russian dress, and living with sectarians, albeit at a time
when the persecution had been suspended. Such unusual conduct puz-
zled the Balakhna land captain, who reported it to the Nizhnii Novgorod Governor General. That official in turn expressed to Prince
Viazemskii his concern over its harmful consequences. This brought
about the intervention of the Secret Expedition and a harsh sentence
for preferring "life with perverted boors to the society of people protected by the laws and the faith." This accusation summed up the
triple alliance of autocracy, orthodoxy, and the ruling class seen as
the embodiment of the nation. By straying from his class and his
church, the captain had become a political criminal.[8]

The Secret Expedition alone was not considered enough to muzzle
political dissent and to impose that unity which is seen in Russia as
the greatest source of strength. The ordinary police had the major task
of insuring that all forms of discontent were channelled out of the

---

o Mel'mane," 199-200 and 86-120; "Iz rozysknago dela," Bogoiavlenskii, 25-26, 29,
42.

   [8] Sivkov, Ocherki, 100, 102; Sivkov, "Podpol'naia," 69-89; Lopukhin, "Vopl." See
also Esipov, 203-211; V. Lamanskii, "Evdokim Mikhailovich Kravkov, dvorianin-sta-
rover," in *Pamiatniki novoi istorii*, I, otd. 1, 36-49; and "Volneniia krest'ian v Lifliandii
v 1777 godu," *ibid.*, otd. 2, 17-38.

environment and effectively neutralized. This was achieved by the simple expedient of forbidding people to assemble in public and even in private without the authorization of the police, and banning all public announcements not approved by the police.

The Instruction submitted by the Policemaster General to the Legislative Commission suggested that all gatherings in private houses (fancy dress balls, lotteries, theatricals) be forbidden unless permission had been granted by the local police. In Petersburg and Moscow public entertainment, including theatrical performances, required the approval of the Empress and in provincial capitals that of the governor. The Police Code stated explicitly that unauthorized gatherings of people must be dispersed by the *pristav* in his district and that any society, association, or brotherhood, unless sanctioned by law, must be abolished by the police, especially if it was likely to cause "harm, damage, or loss."[9] The term "harmful" was one of the favorite expressions of Russian public-security legislation. A vague term at best, it was highly political and moral in content, and subject to the most extensive interpretation to fit the requirements of political expediency.

The banning of any unapproved public announcement reflected the absolutist claim of the police to preempt every type of public activity. In each town, or in each district, a spot was reserved for a post (*stolb*) where all orders of the police board—its own or those transmitted from the Senate or the gubernia board—were tacked, and no other public announcement, including "advertising" or proclamation, could be made without the approval of the police board.[10] Thus the political leadership, through the governors and a few hundred police boards, claimed to be the only source of public news. It was easier to make such a claim than to enforce it, even in the simpler conditions of eighteenth-century life, but its persistence until our own day is characteristic of an attempt to channel the entire flow of information through a police filter and to release only those elements considered neutral or favorable to current ideological concerns.

Censorship was considered the best way to combat the growing influence of a body of native and imported literature which could not simply be banned without rejecting the entire policy of opening a window on Western Europe, symbolized by the transfer of the Court to Petersburg. It had been centralized in the Academy of Sciences, in Moscow University, and in the Synod because books were printed either in Petersburg or Moscow and belonged to the two broad cat-

---

[9] Drizen, 546-554, *SIRIO*, XLIII (1885), 314 passim; Papmehl, "Problem," 281-282; "Pis'ma imp. Ekat. Velik.," 19, Police Code, art. 64-65, 124.

[10] Police Code, art. 111-112. The present Soviet practice of posting copies of *Pravda* and *Izvestiia* in various public places and along streets reflects a similar attitude.

egories of secular and ecclesiastical books.[11] The experiment with private, so-called "free" presses in the 1770s[12] must have been reassuring to the leadership and led to the famous ukase of January 1783, in which presses were declared to be a form of enterprise or handicraft (*rukodelie*) which anyone might freely establish without requesting preliminary authorization. The local police board, however, had to be informed of the location of the press. The order also implicitly authorized the installment of presses in the gubernia boards, where much clerical work could be saved by printing copies of government orders.[13]

But freedom to establish presses did not imply freedom of the press, and criteria were set up to govern the "inspectors" who passed on the acceptability of manuscripts. The jurisdictions of the secular leadership and the Church were not clearly demarcated. Thus books published in ecclesiastical presses were subject to the censorship of the Synod under the Spiritual Regulation and laws of 1726, 1727, and 1743. On the other hand, books published in governmental and private presses were also subject to ecclesiastical censorship if they contained religious material. In view of the fact that a considerable amount of printed matter still belonged to a type of literature that flourished in Muscovite Russia, it must be said that the true guardian of ideological purity was still the Church. The concessions given to Hartung and others in the 1770s contained similar provisions. The printed work itself must contain nothing offensive (*predosuditel'no*) to the Christian religion, to the government, and to morality (*dobronravie*), and must not "arouse temptations" (*klaniashchiesia k soblaznu*). Imported books were inspected by the custom authorities in Petersburg, then had to receive the imprimatur of the Academy of Sciences. Domestic manuscripts were submitted to the Academy or to Moscow University, and after the local government reform to the police board (in Petersburg and Moscow) or to the gubernia board. The authorization had to be printed at the beginning of the book, together with the name of the publisher. Any announcements (*ob'iavleniia*) in the printed work had to be cleared by the police. In addition, publishers were required to print catalogues of their publications and to send a copy of each work to the library of the Academy of Sciences, a very worthy measure but one which instituted a form of ex-post facto censorship.[14] Thus, censorship was

[11] *SIRIO*, XLIII (1885), 302-373.

[12] For officials and secular presses, see PSZ, 1763, N. 11795, 1779, N. 14911, 1780, N. 14985, 1783, N. 15633; for ecclesiastical presses, see 1780, N. 15019, 1796, N. 17508; see also 1771, N. 13572, 1776, N. 14495, 1779, N. 14927, 1783, N. 15756, 1784, N. 16048 and 16086, Kulakova, 192-193.

[13] PSZ, 1783, N. 15634; Salias, 97-98.

[14] PSZ, 1780, N. 15019, 1783, N. 15671, 1797, N. 18094.

very real in the 1760s and 1770s, and a mechanism was already in place to make sure that no printed work would reach the public without the approval of the police or the ecclesiastical authorities. What seemed to be lacking was the conciousness of a threat and the stimulus that it gives to repressive measures. The "free press" order of January 1783 showed a certain blissful ignorance of danger, but things were to change very quickly.

The offensive against the publisher Novikov began in 1784 after the death of Zakhar Chernyshev, who had been favorable to him. The new Governor General of Moscow, Brius, was ordered in December 1785 to have the gubernia procurator make a list of "strange" books published by Novikov and to send them to Platon, the Archbishop of Moscow, who in addition was to test Novikov's beliefs (*ispytivat' v zakone nashem*). Brius was also ordered to appoint with the agreement of Platon two churchmen who, together with lay censors, would examine books already published by Novikov and other private presses, to prevent the dissemination of anything concerning the faith or ecclesiastical matters. In 1786 all but six of Novikov's books were found harmless and released for distribution, but Novikov and private printers were warned to refrain from publishing "strange philosophies" or "downright fallacies" on pain of confiscation of the books and loss of their concession.[15] The first round was over, but six years later Novikov was finally destroyed by Prozorovskii.

The repressive measures ordered by Brius signalled a general offensive of the Church against the publication of religious matter in secular presses. If religious literature was still the main staple of popular reading, religious books must have sold well, and the new private presses could not miss the opportunity to print and sell prayer books (*molitvenniki*) and books devoted to the Scriptures, the interpretation of dogma, and the lives of the saints. Early in 1786 Archbishop Gavril was ordered, like Platon in Moscow, to appoint two ecclesiastical censors (he appointed two archimandrites) to examine religious books published in Petersburg secular presses. In July 1787 all such presses and bookstores were forbidden to print and sell religious books, which were to be printed and sold only by the Church and the Commission on Popular Schools. The following month a directive of the Synod developed this Imperial order. In all towns the police, together with ecclesiastics appointed by the diocesan bishop, were to seize any religious books in lay bookstores and send them to the Synod in Petersburg and Moscow, to the bishop elsewhere. Gubernia boards were

---

[15] PSZ, 1785, N. 16301, 1786, N. 16362; "Bumagi Novikova," "Podlinnye reestry," "Novye dokumenty," and Makogonenko, 515-525.

ordered to show constant vigilance to ensure that religious books were no longer published and sold by laymen, especially at fairs, and church authorities were enjoined to report to the police their presence in unauthorized places.[16] The offensive of the Church was not, and could not be, limited to the establishment of a monopoly over the printing and the distribution of religious books. It also extended to lay publications containing religious expressions and symbols. In 1786 Fedor Krechetov, an unsuccessful publicist, came under investigation because Archbishop Gavril objected to the use of liturgical words in a secular work. He was forbidden to quote texts from the Scriptures which "he poorly understands," or to write about freemasons.[17]

The accelerated repression of the printing trade in the 1790s marked by the arrest of Radishchev and Novikov, led to the improvement of the censorship machinery at the very end of the reign, and inaugurated a period of reaction against the import of foreign ideas. No longer was there the generous acceptance of western ideas that had marked most of the eighteenth century as long as their subversive implications were neither seen nor felt. It became necessary to reassert the purity of the ideology of Church and State in the face of subversion from abroad. While it would take some time to give shape to this ideology— it had never really been articulated because it had always been taken for granted—a more efficient machinery of control was easier to devise. The orders of September and October 1796 systematized the roles of the police, the educational establishment, the church, the customs administration, and the post office in blocking the progress of subversion. The order of January 1783 was revoked, and only private presses established with the agreement of the government were allowed. A network of new specialized censorship agencies was created for the first time in 1796, but no censorship code was published, and they were simply guided by the old regulations that no book must be published if it contained anything against religion, "state rules," and morality. The censorship of periodicals remained the responsibility of the two post offices under the authority of Bezborodko, the Director of the Post Office.[18]

The policing of the mind to prevent the spread of intellectual dissent from official dogma was one weapon in the hands of the political leadership and the Church. The other was the policing of private and social morality, aiming at gaining entrance into the recesses of the soul

[16] PSZ, 1786, N. 16378, 1787, N. 16556 and 16564. A general survey is in Barsov, "O dukh. tsenzure," 238-257. On Archbishop Gavril, see Pokrovskii.

[17] Kulakova, 180, Chulkov, 459, 465-468.

[18] PSZ, 1796, N. 17508 and 17523; PSZ, vol. 45, kn. tarifov, Tarify po evropeiskoi torgovle 1782-1822, 100.

and at maintaining a certain code of behavior peculiar to each class
for the purpose of enforcing the social order.

The Church-State symbiosis, so characteristic of the Russian political system, required not only that the political leadership help the
Church to carry out its mission among the faithful but also that,
conversely, the Church help the leadership in their common task to
keep Russians both faithful subjects and good Orthodox Christians.
It was the duty of the police to ensure that all inhabitants went to
confession and received communion at least once a year, and Imperial
orders kept reminding local officials that this was no obsolete pre-
scription but a very real obligation. Not only the peasantry but all
classes were subject to these police reminders of their religious duty.
The Instruction to the *sotskii* of December 1774 *began* with this duty
to make sure that, on pain of a fine, the peasants and their officials
and the landowners went to church on Sundays and holidays and to
confession at Lent.[19]

It was also the duty of the police to repress heresies. Their presence
had to be reported by the *sotskii* to the voevoda. It is true that Catherine was much more tolerant of other religions and of the Old Believers than her predecessors, but we should not delude ourselves about
the scope of that toleration. When a sect appeared near Kaluga in the
early 1760s, troops were stationed in villages to watch over the activities of the peasants. The orders came directly from Petersburg over
the objections of the Governor General of Moscow, who felt that there
was not really anything to discover.[20]

The control of social morality took the form, among others, of
sumptuary laws and the prohibition of certain card games. The passion
of the Russians for games of chance is well known; and its destructive
consequences were a cause of concern to the government. In a letter
to Governor General Saltykov, Catherine expressed her surprise that
the Muscovites had returned to their passion as soon as she left the
city. She was not so much concerned about the fate of individuals who
had lost a fortune at cards as over the fact that games of chance were
a social solvent which not only ruined noble and merchant families
alike but made it possible for townsmen to acquire landed property.
Therefore, playing games of chance was not only a crime against
individuals, a form of fraud, but a crime against the social order and
by extension a threat to the political system as well.[21] Sumptuary

---

[19] Got'e, I, 348-349; PSZ, 1774, N. 14231, pt. 1. Visits to the confessional were
registered in so-called *ispovednye rospisi*; these documents were accepted as evidence
in civil cases: see PSZ, 1817, N. 26684.

[20] PSZ, 1774, N. 14231, pt. 2; "Pis'ma imp. Ekat. Velik.," 34-35.

[21] Police Code, art. 67-69; "Pis'ma," *ibid.*, 15.

legislation also made the police the guardian of the social order. Gold-
and silver-embroidered clothing, hat feathers, swords, and certain colors
were reserved for the privileged classes. A specific number of horses
was assigned to the equipages of various ranks. This legislation sought
to limit the importation of expensive materials, to prevent the ruin of
families who tried to live above their station, to bridle vanity in the
proud, to reduce the demand for food and forage necessary to maintain
large numbers of servants and horses.[22] It was also an exercise in self-
defense by the nobility, suspicious of the wealth of individuals from
the lower orders. Whatever the reasons, it gave the police a very
effective means of prying into the private lives of individuals in order
to maintain the status quo.

Finally, order was preserved by having the police enforce a number
of moral precepts regarding family and social relationships. The Police
Code began with such precepts, which were at the foundation of family
life sanctified by the Church. Then similar precepts were extended to
govern social relationships, on the assumption that society was a large
patriarchal family with its privileged and unprivileged members under
the watchful eye of a revered leader. Young people must respect their
elders and servants their masters. The police must quell harmful and
slanderous rumors, combat spitefulness, and curb fortune telling.[23]
Russian society, once again, was not only a secular society. It was an
Orthodox world, a community of believers in which social norms were
also moral norms, and moral norms were sanctified by religious law.
Authority was sacred, and disrespect toward it was blasphemy. When
moral norms were given a religious sanction, their violation became
a sin. Disrespect for authority became sinful pride and called upon
the sinner the full retribution of the law. Thus the imposition by the
police of the observance of sanctified moral and social norms became
a demand for the unconditional acceptance of the social order, on
pain of exclusion from the community.

There is certainly much evidence to show that the operations of a
Sheshkovskii were not a "dissonance" in the supposedly liberal reign
of Catherine.[24] A broad pattern of police repression remained in force
from the beginning. The first half of the reign, it is true, was marked
by an extensive social movement and a successful war culminating in
the reforms of 1775-1785, which gave the nobility very much of what
it had asked for in its *nakazy*. Such circumstances were favorable to
the maintenance of domestic peace and unity. Yet, by the mid-1780s

[22] Police Code, art. 66.
[23] Police Code, introduction, art. 154. For comparisons with De la Mare's Traite de
Police (1722), see Grigor'ev, "Zertsalo."
[24] Korsakov, 656.

the baneful consequences of the infatuation with the ideas of the Enlightenment became apparent. A threat to the consensus appeared, repression began in earnest as the Church counterattacked, as Russian armies marked time before the Turks, and the French Revolution confirmed the fears of the conservatives, who felt relaxation had gone too far. The reaction was not so much a swing of the pendulum as the reassertion of a natural state in which social conservatism, ortho- dox traditionalism, and Russian ethnocentrism combined to reimpose a deadly uniformity.

GENERAL ADMINISTRATION

If the word "state" is largely a discovery of the seventeenth century, the term "police" did not come into being in Russia until the eighteenth and then with a meaning very different from today's. The emergence of the "absolutist" monarchies after a long period of internecine con- flicts between competing families was followed by the creation of an increasingly complex machinery of government to collect revenue, to administer justice among the various social groups, and to run a mil- itary establishment strong enough to support the continued claims of one monarchy against another. To administer the collectivity was to police it, to formulate a single *policy* of interdependent parts. In the late eighteenth century, among the cameralists who so popularized the term, "police" still included financial administration, since almost every sector of government had a fiscal component. But the process of func- tional differentiation continued into the nineteenth century, in Western Europe especially, where social and economic progress compelled an ever greater fragmentation of responsibilities. In Russia, however, where social stratification lagged far behind that of Western Europe and a vertically integrated society meant the absorption of the concept of state into that of dynastic and class rule, the division of functions never acquired that precision and legal definition which is the product of a compromise between the competing claims of rival social groups. The scope of judicial and financial administration remained much nar- rower, still closely integrated in the concept of general administration. In consequence, the same imperatives governing the entire political order—traditionalism, intellectual uniformity, and social conserva- tism—continued to pervade judicial and financial administration as well as the maintenance of order and those related activities gradually emerging as the specific objects of police administration.

Governmental activity was largely concentrated in the towns, and it is there that the term "police" was first used in its etymological sense of *politeia*, or the governing of the city state. The general administration of the countryside became the police of the town. In all the great documents of eighteenth-century legislation on central and local agencies the term police—*politsiia* borrowed from the German *Polizei*, or the Russian *blagochinie*—is used only in connection with municipal administration: the *punkty* addressed to the Policemaster General—who was the true governor of Petersburg—and the Instruction to the senior policemaster of Moscow of 1718 and 1722, the statutes of the Central *Magistrat* and the local *magistraty* of 1721 and 1724, the supplement to the *Nakaz* of 1768, the Instruction to the commandant of the Palace of 1771, and the Police Code of 1782—all use the term, but it is not to be found in the Instruction to the governors and voevodas of 1728 and that of 1764, nor in the instruction to the *sotskii* of 1774.²⁵ The reason was a simple one. The town was a concentrated aggregate of human beings, still sharply differentiated from the surrounding countryside by its walls, its stone buildings and churches, and the high density of its population. A large town was a center of administration, a market for products, perhaps a center of industry, the residence of the rich, a cultural center. It was a place where houses and government buildings had to be built according to plan because space was limited, where streets had to be cleaned, where fires were a greater danger than in the countryside, where thieves abounded and the poor had to be cared for, where the provisioning of the population had to be assured, where money circulated and the speculators were strong. These problems either did not exist in the countryside or were less pressing.

The policing of streets and markets was done by men from the *shtatnye komandy* and by the inhabitants of each ward. Main streets were blocked at their ends by turnpikes (*rogatki*) kept open in the daytime but closed at night. These checkpoints were manned by the inhabitants of the streets chosen by their neighbors or appointed by the *magistrat* in each ward consisting of from fifty to one hundred houses. An elected night watch of twelve men per ward paid for each night's work was at the disposal of the ward supervisor. Some kind of rotation probably existed so that all males of the street could take their turn. Fires were kept burning day and night, at least in the larger towns, for the watch and the occasional passer-by. In the event of a street fight or a burglary or when vagrants were found loitering in the street and the policeman on the spot was not strong enough to arrest the troublemakers, a rattle box was used to sound the alarm, the gates

²⁵ PSZ, 1718, N. 3203 and 1722, N. 4047; 1721, N. 3708, 1724, N. 4624; 1768, N. 13075; 1771, N. 13711; 1782, N. 15379; 1728, N. 5333; 1764, N. 12137; 1774, N. 14231.

were closed, and everyone had to come out to give assistance. The culprits were then sent to the voevoda or the sheriff for investigation.[26] All this was fairly simple and, given the small size of most towns, was probably efficient enough if the community was strong and homogeneous. Where class dissensions had developed—between the townsmen proper and the *raznochintsy*, for example—this reliance on self-help by the inhabitants of each street and ward may have broken down.

Another function of the municipal police was the maintenance and repair of public buildings. In the 1763 table of organization of the Petersburg and Moscow police we find an architect in each city "to supervise construction and the drawing of plans," with three assistants and eight students, one mason, and a few clerks. Obviously, such a small staff was inadequate, and public construction in the two cities was the task of special commissions. Elsewhere, little interest was paid to public construction until after the local government reform. It remained the responsibility of governors and voevodas who had no funds at their disposal and who had to rely on compulsory labor (*nariady*). Agencies had to repair their own buildings from the inadequate sum assigned for office expenditures. After the reform we find one architect assigned to each gubernia board. Each supervisor had to watch over the safety of buildings and the observance of prescribed exteriors (*fasady*) in his ward. He was also enjoined to encourage the inhabitants to build in vacant lots along the streets. In each district the Police Code called for the establishment of a housing agent (*chatnoi makler*). Anyone wanting to build or tear down a building, or sell, buy, mortgage, or rent a house or part of it had to appear before the agent and state the particulars of the transaction. The agent also kept a book containing the cubic measurement of each house. It is not clear how he was chosen, but his books were at the disposal of the police. The maintenance and paving of streets, the building of lampposts and street lighting, were contracted out in each ward. Many of these activities must have remained on paper: Russian towns were not known for their polished appearance. Although these activities were the responsibility of the police, they were discharged by the community, with or without remuneration. In the two capitals the duties of the police were more extensive. The maintenance and repair of bridges across the Neva came from the police budget; so did the funds to build and repair over 2,000 lampposts. In Moscow, likewise, all bridges and ferries (*perevozy*) in 1762 were placed under the senior policemaster's chancery, which had to keep them clean and in working order. The maintenance

[26] Police Code, art. 142, 144; PSZ, 1728, N. 5333, pt. 40-41, 47.

of stone pavements (*mostovye*) in front of state agencies and all city gates was also under police management.[27]

One of the most important responsibilities of the police was the prevention and fighting of fires. Because there were so few stone and brick houses, fires were the scourge of Russian towns and large-scale destruction was an all-too-frequent occurrence. Once a major fire had started, if the winds were favorable to its spread, there was little that men could do to extinguish it with the equipment at their disposal. A major fire was seen as an act of God, and, as soon as it was over, prefabricated houses were rolled into place and life gradually returned to normal. Preventive measures were part of the "construction code" which the police had to enforce. Firemen were chosen, like the night watch, in accordance with the number of houses, but they received no pay. Fire-fighting was a community affair, although a more systematic approach was already noticeable in the larger towns. The table of organization of 1763 ignored this activity altogether, but a serious attempt was made in the 1780s to create a fire-fighting force in post-reform towns. In a city like Novgorod, for example, whose table of organization seems to have been a model for other towns, the force consisted of 12 drivers, 24 horses, and 168 firemen in two districts, 30 drivers, 30 horses and 80 firemen in ten wards, a total force of 290 men and 54 horses. But no changes were made in the men's status: they remained unpaid.[28]

Sanitation, the control of diseases, the building and maintenance of markets were also the responsibility of the police. The climate did not encourage good sanitation. Refuse froze until the spring, when mud turned the streets into swamps, created an abominable smell, and nourished abundant vermin. Legislation, here as in much else concerning the functions of the municipal police, remained merely admonitory. To upgrade, nay, create, municipal services was part of the process of modernization. It was necessary if the elite was to find in the towns a milieu suitable to the exercise of its political functions; it embodied its social responsibility toward those elements in society from which candidates were recruited for membership in the ruling class. On the other hand, the quality of municipal life could not be improved by administrative orders alone but depended on the cooperation of the townsmen themselves. The success of the "police" as

[27] PSZ, 1763, N. 11991, vol. 42², *kn. sht.*, 67; 1776, N. 17494, vol. 42², 255; Police Code, art. 136-142, 158, 179-180. For Petersburg, see PSZ, 1770, N. 13451, 1782, N. 15479; for Moscow, see PSZ, 1762, N. 11675, 1769, N. 13311; for Arkhangelsk, see Podvysotskii.

[28] PSZ, 1728, N. 5333, art. 39; 1774, N. 14231, pt. 8 and 12; 1782, N. 15430, vol. 44², 190-193; 1786, N. 16335.

municipal administration depended on the allocation of very sparse funds and on the acceptance of this responsibility of the ruling class as a legitimate program. At the end of the eighteenth century it seems that such acceptance was still not forthcoming, largely because the level of economic development did not yet require an extensive program of urban modernization.

In two areas, however, there was a recognition that common action was necessary. Public welfare appealed to the communal instincts of the population. The support of the poor was necessary not only for humanitarian reasons but also to save them from a life of degradation and crime, since begging was forbidden. These poor included retired soldiers, clerks, and clergy with their wives and children who could not fend for themselves and old people who belonged to no community able to support them. In the 1760s these poor were arrested by the police and given two kopecks a day for living expenses. In the 1770s a poorhouse (*bogadel'nia*) was established in Moscow where they received four kopecks a day, also from police revenues. Children too young to work were placed in the House for Foster Children (*Vospitatel'nyi Dom*). For those who could not work but preferred to loiter and beg, a workhouse (*rabochii dom*) was opened under police supervision, and they were employed in tasks determined by the police such as cracking stones for the paving of streets and construction; women were given spinning work. Both men and women were paid three kopecks a day for living expenses. These activities were in fact public works under police auspices, and there are references to their being used elsewhere in the country, notably in Penza province in the 1770s and in Arkhangelsk and Olonets gubernias in the 1780s.[29]

The second area was the provisioning of the towns. High prices sometimes simply reflected the operation of the law of supply and demand. The price of grain was a most sensitive barometer because the diet relied so heavily on bread. The generally low yield of agriculture, the vagaries of the weather, and an inadequately developed transportation network combined to create scarcity. In such cases the mechanism was largely beyond the control of the police unless grain stores were available. But when high prices were also caused artificially by speculators (*skupshchiki*) who manipulated the supply to their advantage, a remedy was found in separating wholesale from retail selling. Peasants who brought their grain and other food products to the market were allowed to sell only to retail buyers from the time the *magistrat* raised a flag over the marketplace until one o'clock in

---

²⁹ PSZ, 1765, N. 12441; 1775, N. 14357; OL, art. 252, 275; Police Code, art, 119. On public works, see PSZ, 1774, N. 14222, 1776, N. 14418, 1785, N. 16204, pt. 2.

the afternoon. Thereafter, what was left could be sold to anyone. There were, of course, ways by which speculators could obtain the grain they wanted by buying it up from the peasants at the approach to the larger towns or directly in the villages. Within the town, however, it was the responsibility of the police to maintain, if not a "just price," at least one acceptable enough to prevent widespread discontent.[30]

But this responsibility of the sheriffs to keep the government informed of the movement of prices encouraged falsification and inflation. A book kept by each sheriff showing the monthly market prices (*torgovye tseny*) of grain and food products (*kharcha*) was sent to the gubernia board, where tables for the entire gubernia were drawn up and forwarded to the First Department of the Senate at the end of each quarter. These tables were used in the Audit Expedition to verify the expenditures claimed by various disbursement agencies. In Moscow, at least after 1784, grain prices were printed each week in the *Moskovskie Vedomosti*: the largest market of the nation was given maximum publicity in order to encourage the free movement of grain. But sheriffs and land captains supposed to supply the data seem to have been delinquent here: when they did send reports, they inflated prices far above the real ones.[31] The reasons are not hard to find. Higher prices meant larger appropriations for the army and the provincial administration, and larger profits for the grain traders, who split the profits with the police. Thus, police involvement with prices resulted in two conflicting activities. It was in the interest of the sheriff for reasons of security to keep prices as low as possible, but in his official reports he inflated real prices in order to share in profits from government procurements. The result was chaos in price statistics and embezzlement of treasury funds.

A closely related function was the maintenance of grain stores to keep the price of bread within reasonable limits and to provide grain and seeds to the peasant when a poor harvest threatened to cause famine. The difficulty of transporting grain from surplus to deficit areas, the existence of the large Petersburg market at considerable distance from the grain-rich regions, yet highly sensitive in political terms, required the police to interfere in transportation and marketing for the public welfare.

The government's concern with granaries was evident from the beginning of the reign, when a blunt ukase of Catherine ordered in August 1762 their establishment in all towns "so that the price of grain may

[30] PSZ, 1784, N. 16023; 1774, N. 14231, pt. 6; 1782, N. 15576.
[31] PSZ, 1780, N. 15095; 1785, N. 16137 and 16143; 1790, N. 16837; 1796, N. 17648.

always be in My hands."[32] The need for stores, however, was not felt equally everywhere. In Petersburg a granary was established in August 1766 under the jurisdiction of the Policemaster General with a staff of twenty and a guard from the garrison to contain 200,000 *kuli* of rye flour, 10,000 *chetverti* of rye, 2,000 *chetverti* of groats, and 25,000 *chetverti* of oats and barley. Competition between the army and the city administration was reflected in the fortunes of the store. In the early 1770s it was placed under the overall jurisdiction of Marshal Golitsyn, the "governor general" of Petersburg; its immediate chief was Colonel Mavrin, who also reported directly to the Empress. After Golitsyn's death Mavrin became vice-governor of Petersburg in 1783 and then head of the Provision Chancery in 1784. This had the effect of reducing competing claims by centralizing provisioning in the army. In 1786, however, in the wake of a heavy concentration of troops in the Petersburg area, Mavrin asked to be relieved of his responsibility for the city store. It was placed once again under the vice-governor, and its annual turnover was raised to 300,000 *chetverti* of grain. The situation remained unchanged until the end of the reign.[33]

In Moscow there was a police granary in the 1760s. We learn from a letter of the Empress to Governor General Saltykov that she had accepted the offer of Prince Meshcherskii, a landowner of Tver province, to sell it 20,000 *chetverti* of grain, mostly oats, at one ruble a *chetvert*. But it may very well have been closed later because a ukase of February 1785 ordered Governor General Brius to establish "gradually" a grain store modelled after the Petersburg granary. The new store was opened in the fall of 1786 and placed under the governor general. The delay may have been due to the location of the city, more easily accessible from the rich regions of the south, and to the fact that many of its inhabitants were peasants and domestics of the landowners, who came to spend the winter months in the city and fed their people with foodstuffs grown on their estates. But rising prices caused the government to act.[34]

Elsewhere in the country public granaries seem to have been established chiefly in the northwest and the north. Their stocks were made available not only to townsmen but to state peasants as well. One such store was opened in Arkhangelsk in 1764; others were later

---

[32] PSZ, 1762, N. 11649. The problem of urban provisioning is discussed in Tilly, ed., 392-412. See also "Sekretnyi ukaz," "Mnenie," "Dukh Ekateriny II," 1279-1781, "K istorii," 448-449, and Romanovich-Slavatinskii, "Goloda," 38-65.

[33] PSZ, 1766, N. 12718; 1769, N. 13238; 1771, N. 13670; 1775, N. 14416; 1786, N. 16406, 16445, 16458, 16487; TsGADA, f. 16, d. 532, fol. 3-20, 75-78.

[34] PSZ, 1785, N. 16143; 1786, N. 16446; "Pis'ma imp. Ekat. Velik.," 41-42, TsGADA, f. 16, d. 532, fol. 55-60.

opened in Olonets, Vologda, Novgorod, and Tver gubernias.[35] State peasants or townsmen brought a statement (*bilet*) from the *starosta* indicating how much they needed, a procedure intended to prevent the wealthier peasants from buying a surplus and selling it to poor peasants. Grain, usually rye, was issued either in its natural state, or already ground into flour for immediate consumption. The grain was lent at interest, and both the loan and the interest were repayable in kind or in money. In the north, where peasants received the bulk of their income from non-agricultural pursuits, a money payment was almost the only one possible. This welfare function was expected to be profitable as well. The Olonets store, for example, planned to amortize its original investment of 35,730 rubles within sixteen years and make a profit thereafter.[36]

[35] For Arkhangelsk see PSZ, 1764, N. 12247, 12276; 1770, N. 13529; 1772, N. 13787; 1785, N. 16204; for Vologda, see 1785, N. 16161; for Olonets, 1783, N. 15669; for Novgorod and Tver, 1764, N. 12247, pt. 3, 1786, N. 16363; 1799, N. 18856.

[36] PSZ, 1766, N. 12562; 1772, N. 13787; 1783, N. 15669; 1786, N. 16406, 16445.

CHAPTER III

THE POWERS OF THE POLICE

The extensive jurisdiction of the police required for its successful enforcement a panoply of powers whose effectiveness depended upon the widespread support of the population. Nowhere was it more obvious than here that tacit consent was the prerequisite of effective government, that the legitimacy of orders had to be recognized before they were carried out and that, despite the development of a national culture borrowed from abroad, the folk society continued to respond to the leadership of its ruling class.

DENUNCIATIONS AND PASSPORTS

One of the most readily accepted methods of keeping the police informed of violations of the law and deviations from orthodox norms of political and social behavior was the denunciation (*donos*), either by police spies or by other individuals who felt they were serving a good cause or had accounts to settle. The widespread use of denunciations reflected the absorption of private into communal life characteristic of the Russian social order. This symbiosis expanded immeasurably the scope of the police, who could depend on the cooperation of countless individuals in all walks of life, from university professors who censored their colleagues to maids and cooks who reported the secrets of their masters. The Manifesto of 1762 abolishing the Secret Chancery had much to say about the nefarious effects of these denunciations: "evil, lowborn and lazy people" hoped to postpone indefinitely the punishment they deserved, vented their spite by denouncing their superiors and their enemies, and led the innocent to the torture chamber.[1]

The Manifesto did not outlaw denunciations—this was impossible—but tried, for the sake of convenience, to establish a procedure to prevent the transformation of minor crimes into political cases. Agencies were forbidden to accept denunciations from criminals sentenced to exile and hard labor because this was merely a means to gain a temporary suspension of sentence. On the issue of *slovo i delo* the Manifesto seemed to contain a contradiction which in fact reflected the distinction made between noblemen and others. On the one hand,

[1] PSZ, 1762, N. 11445.

"the hateful expresssion" must henceforth mean nothing, and people were forbidden to use it. On the other, soldiers, domestics, boatmen, factory workers, and all lowborn (*podlye*) people who used it against their superiors, landowners, or enemies were to be arrested and questioned as to whether they understood the meaning of the word. If they did not, they were to be released. If they did, they were asked to state their case, then placed for two days in prison without food or drink to "think it over" (*na razmyshlenie*). If they still stood by their statements, the prisoners were to be sent to the Senate.

It is difficult to believe that this manifesto stemmed the flow of denunciations, although it is likely that the more tolerant attitude of the early years of Catherine's reign reduced their significance in the eyes of the government. We discover, for example, from a letter of Catherine to Governor General Saltykov, expressing doubt about the validity of a denunciation, that certain Old Believers made false denunciations during the holidays for the purpose of being subjected to torture and testing their ability to withstand it. There were many such denunciations in the former Secret Chancery, but, Catherine added, "I hope you will agree they deserve contempt."[2]

The best evidence, however, that denunciations remained welcome to the government was that they were rewarded, at least in nonpolitical cases. To fight contraband trade and speculation in Petersburg, custom officials called for outside help, and accusers were offered a percentage of the value of the seized goods. A certain Zotov received seven thousand rubles from the custom house for his assistance, and he used this money to register in the third guild of "outside merchants" (*inogorodnye gosti*) in the capital.[3] In fact, it was impossible to draw a line between political and other denunciations, to welcome some and condemn others, and the conclusion must be that the use of accusers remained a powerful tool of political control.

A second method of learning the existence of political deviations was the interception of mail. Here two considerations worked at crosspurposes. On the one hand, it was necessary to encourage the use of the mail as trade and industry developed and cultural progress made inroads into provincial and local towns. On the other, epistolary exchanges were such a valuable source of information on the mood of provincial society that the interest of the government in learning their contents was obvious. A circular letter sent by Prince Viazemskii to all governors in January 1782 forbidding any agency to open letters shows that confidence in the secrecy of the mail was lacking. At any

[2] "Pis'ma imp. Ekat. Velik.," 32-33.
[3] Kulakova, 188-189.

rate, this prohibition did not extend to the Moscow and Petersburg post offices, where letters were opened when necessary. Military censorship was also a source of information.[4] Once again the absence of assumptions guarding man's private world against the intrusion of public power made the interception of mail a natural activity whose intensity varied with the perception of danger.

Police control was also considerably facilitated by the universal use of passports. The social order required that all peasants be accounted for and tagged as the property of a landowner, the treasury, or the Court, because the labor of each peasant represented an irreplaceable financial contribution to the standard of living of the landed nobility and to the operation of the army. Police, fiscal and social considerations were closely intertwined to demand the creation of a rigorous instrument of control over the movement of the tax-paying population. This instrument was the internal passport.[5] Yet, not only the travelling peasant was required to possess a passport but also noblemen, churchmen, and townsmen. The passport was not merely a "bureaucratic" device to tie the lower orders to the ruling class; it was first and foremost the badge of an extremely strong sense of communal accountability.

Its origin goes back to the first census of 1719 and the *Plakat* of June 1724, which provided the following. If a peasant remained in the uezd within which he was registered and did not go farther than 32 km (30 *versta*) from his village, he had to get a handwritten pass (*otpusk*) signed by his master or the steward of the estate and the parish priest. If he wished to travel at a greater distance, he had to submit a *propusknoe pis'mo*, also called *pokormezhnaia*, stating how long he was authorized to leave, the maximum term not exceeding three years. No such document could be given to the wives and children, who in this fashion were considered hostages for their husbands and fathers. The peasant presented this document to the land captain (*zemskii komissar*) of the uezds, later the voevoda's clerk, and received a handwritten passport in return for a payment of two kopecks. Both the *pis'mo* and the passport contained the name of the peasant, his height, facial description, and any other characteristics (*primety*) serving to identify him. The ukase of May 1743 introduced the printed passport, following widespread forgeries by peasants who presented documents written by anyone willing to do this for a fee. Printed passports were issued over the signatures of the governor, the voevoda, or the officer assigned to the collection of the capitation, and peasants

[4] Piontkovskii, 96; "Pis'mo gen.-prokurora."

[5] For general information on the passport system, see Kazantsev.

caught at checkpoints like city gates, river crossings, and inns without passports for travel beyond 32 km were to be arrested and returned to their communities.[6]

This legislation remained in force for the remainder of the century. After the reform, passports continued to be sent from the Senate's press to the gubernia boards, which distributed them among the uezd treasurers. Serfs brought their passes from the landowner or his steward and state peasants from the lower *rasprava* to the treasurer, who filled out the form, inserted the date shown on the pass at which the peasant had to be back, and collected the fee. A distinction was made in December 1763 between one-, two-, and three-year passports for which the fee was raised from a flat 2 kopecks to 10, 50, and 100 kopecks (one ruble). By the end of the reign, passports cost one, three, and five rubles respectively.[7]

Nobles received their passports from the agency in which they served and, if they were not in the service, probably from the voevoda and later the upper land court. Churchmen received theirs from the Synod and the bishops. Passports for the townsmen, however, raised certain problems.

Merchants had their own corporate agent in the town, and this gave them a certain autonomy from the administration of the voevoda. It also created a certain duality of power which bred corruption. A merchant wishing to leave the town received a handwritten authorization on stamp paper over the seal of the *magistrat* if he intended to remain within the same uezd or within 32 kilometers of his residence. When he applied to the voevoda for a printed passport, however, he was not required to submit a *propusknoe pis'mo* from the *magistrat*. As a result, the voevoda felt no compulsion to grant a passport and, unless his good will was purchased, showed little concern for the business motives of the merchants. It also happened that certain merchants could not be allowed to leave the town because of unpaid debts or because it was their turn to contribute their services to the administration of the town. Only the *magistrat* could judge their credit and confirm the completion of their civic duties. Yet, without the need for a previous authorization, the voevoda felt free to act as he pleased, to the detriment of the interests of other merchants. Since *magistraty* were made independent of the voevodas in 1743, it was logical that merchants should receive their passports from their *magistrat*. New passport forms were printed in the Senate's press without reference to

[6] The *Plakat* is in PSZ, 1724, N. 4533; the regulations on passports are in part II, art. 12-16; see also 1726, N. 4827; 1743, N. 8738; 1762, N. 11708.

[7] PSZ, 1771, N. 13635; 1774, N. 14231, pt. 4 and 10; on the fees see 1763, N. 11988, pt. 10; 1782, N. 15580; 1794, N. 17226.

the authorization of the voevoda and were sent to the *magistraty* through their central agency, the Central *Magistrat*. After the local government reform, the *magistraty* received their forms from the uezd treasurers.[8]

Passports also contained an individual's criminal record. Since the 1730s those whipped in public for theft, loiterers, and "suspicious" persons were forbidden to reside in Petersburg, but they could still obtain passports. In the 1770s the Senate accepted a request of the Policemaster General that individuals who had been publicly whipped were to be forbidden to enter any town and could no longer receive printed passports. If they applied for a written one, it would contain a similar prohibition, and the guard would refuse them entry at the gates.[9] Anyone without a passport was considered a fugitive and subject to banishment by administrative order.

The passport system, originally a fiscal measure designed to trace payers of the capitation already listed on the rolls during the preceding census, developed into a method of controlling the movement of the entire population, and became in the towns a means of elaborate spying into private dwellings. The supervisor had to know everyone in his ward, and one purpose of turnpikes established at the end of the streets was to stop suspicious persons and require them to produce their passports. The Instruction (*punkty*) of the Policemaster General stated that the owner of every house had to declare within twenty-four hours anyone who came to stay and anyone who left. Even if there were always people willing to take the risk, if it was in their interest to do so, of not declaring who was staying in the house, such a law appealed to a widespread readiness to inform on neighbors in a system where the command relationships were strong but deviant behavior immediately aroused suspicion. This law was reaffirmed in the Police Code, and reminders were published in the newspapers from time to time when circumstances required greater vigilance.[10]

The police also sought to keep track of the population by appointing an employment agent (*makler slug i rabochikh liudei*) when the sheriff and the *magistrat* felt that too many people were coming to the town. Anyone seeking work had to register with the agent, giving his name, residence, and the type of work he was looking for; employers were

[8] PSZ, 1744, N. 8889; 1791, N. 16971; 1792, N. 17031; 1792, N. 17057. False passports could be obtained at the Preobrazhenskii cemetery in Moscow, the center of a large colony of Old Believers: Piontkovskii, 97.

[9] PSZ, 1770, N. 13545.

[10] PSZ, 1718, N. 3203, pt. 11; see also 1728, N. 5333, art. 47; 1763, N. 11974; OL, art. 229, 252; Police Code, art. 35, 120, 157.

encouraged to register their employees with the agent. The sheriff retained the right to expel from the town anyone not registered.[11]

POWERS OF EXECUTIVE POLICE

These powers did not come into existence until after the reform created separate judicial and fiscal agencies. Then police powers became a social force exercised by representatives of the ruling class for the protection and enhancement of their interests as well as the integrating element in administrative action, providing the unity which the reform had seemingly destroyed.

The breakup of the pre-reform local administration along functional lines did not in fact destroy its unity because it was not followed by a similar development in the central government, where concentration of domestic administration in the hands of the Procurator General remained the rule until the end of the reign. Without such separation of functions vested in mutually independent colleges or ministries, each seeking to develop a network of subordinate local agencies, local administration was bound to remain unified under the authority of the governor and the governor general. The separation of judicial administration and tax collection from the single trunk of general administration was not done for the purpose of limiting arbitrary power, but for technical reasons. Neither the governor nor the voevoda had the time or the ability to examine and decide a multitude of technical problems requiring constant application and follow-up by trained individuals. Efficiency required that technical matters be separated, but the imperatives of power required that the execution of technical decisions remain a political prerogative.

At both ends of the judicial process the police played a crucial role. The delivery of summons, the collection of evidence, the execution of court decisions remained their responsibility. The execution of civil decisions was by no means the simple operation it seems to be. It happened that the police, in real-estate cases primarily, would carry out a decision in such a way that the winner of the case would find himself the loser and would be compelled to take legal action, if he had the means and the patience, to get the original decision properly executed. The police in such cases was not only the tool of strong landowners against their less fortunate brethren but also an instrument to maintain the social and economic primacy of the nobility against the state peasantry or the townsmen. The Morshansk sheriff, for example, refusing in the 1780s to let the inhabitants of the town take

[11] Police Code, art. 181, 189.

possession of the plots they had been given free of charge in return for rebuilding the town, spilled pitch in the shop of a merchant who refused to accommodate him with a bribe.[12]

In criminal justice the role of the police was fundamental. Investigations, not only of crimes but also of "events" (*proizshedstviia*), gave it a powerful leverage. An "event" was simply an unusual occurrence arousing suspicion of foul play, such as a drowning, a suicide, a fire, or the discovery of a corpse. An innocent event could be transformed into a serious case if the police had ulterior motives. Investigations were conducted by the land captain or an assessor in the countryside, and by the *pristav* in each district of the town. If the police were convinced that no crime was committed—and this might require payment of a bribe—a report was sent to the police board or to the uezd court.[13]

During an investigation, not only in the Secret Expedition but in other police agencies as well, it was customary to resort to the assistance of a priest, a practice illustrating most clearly the association of politics and religion in the repression of crime and the religious implication in the violation of secular norms. A ukase of November 1762 provided that prisoners should not be put to the torture without first being subject to an "admonition" (*uveshchanie*) to confess to a "learned priest" (*uchenyi sviashchenik*). The bishop of Rostov and Iaroslavl, Afanasii, was instructed to prepare a booklet with quotations (*dovody*) from the Scriptures to guide the priests because in "certain towns" there were no learned priests, and a ukase of January 1763 emphasized the use of the admonition and compassion as preferable to torture in extracting confessions. The purpose of the admonition was not only to make a suspected criminal tell the truth— the presumption was of course one of guilt—but to bring him to make a confession of his sins and to repent. If he did, he would avoid torture. He also had to tell the priest whether he had gone to confession before being caught and where. Thus, the association of crime and sin was brought out with full force.[14] Repentance was not a mitigating circumstance—*ne kasaetsia do suda*—before the court, which was required to apply the letter of the law; it was only a manifestation of humble submission to the political leadership and the Church and an acceptance of punishment. This procedure was the most striking illustration of the lack of recognition by the ruling class of a private

[12] Dubasov, 34. A good illustration of a case in which the winner became the loser is in TsGVIA, f. 44, d. 50, II, fol. 19, 24 (Chernigov).

[13] Police Code, art. 99-102, 105-106; OL, art. 232; PSZ, 1782, N. 15568.

[14] PSZ, 1764, N. 12227.

world beyond its reach: for if there is no secret of the confessional, then man must render to Caesar alone his unconditional allegiance.

The search for suspects forced the land captain to travel in inclement weather, to brave snowstorms and the spring muds. If he could not find the suspect, he arrested the steward or the *starosty* and the *vybornye* and kept them as hostages (*poruchiteli*) until the suspect was found. An indictment was drawn up, backed if possible by a confession, and turned over to the uezd court or the lower *rasprava*—in the town to the *magistrat*—depending on whether the suspect was a nobleman or a state peasant. This indictment was the basic document, and it often settled the fate of the prisoner. Without open trials, adversary proceedings, or legal representation, investigations turned into repressive instruments of class justice. Preventive detention was another dreadful weapon in the hands of the police. Peasant witnesses were summoned from their fields to the town and detained at the pleasure of the police, despite the insistence of the Organic Law and the Police Code that this must not be done since it interfered with work in the fields. Preventive detention was aggravated by delays in obtaining documents from other agencies and by the requirements that in serious cases prisoners must be marched to the gubernia capital and detained until the final disposition of their case. All the while, a suspect who might be innocent was kept in infested prisons with real criminals. This certainly was one of the cruelest punishments that the police could inflict if it chose to misuse this power for personal ends.

The confusion between preliminary detention and imprisonment following a judicial sentence was also evident in the fact that the police ran the prisons. Eighteenth-century prisons, in Russia and elsewhere, were ghastly places where little attempt was made to separate prisoners according to age, sex, type of crimes, and even social class. Some prisoners were awaiting trial in preventive detention; others were on their way back to be whipped at the place of their crime, or were being sent to Orenburg or Siberia. The guard was often inadequate, and crowded conditions threatened to erupt into violence. Sometimes lesser criminals were sent to the workhouse or were placed on bail (*na poruki*), with reliable citizens to help with the housework, or in local shops like tanneries and slaughterhouses. They had to return to the prison in the evening. All prisoners, guilty and suspect alike, were under police jurisdiction, and their treatment depended on the good will of the police. The same Morshansk sheriff whipped prisoners to his heart's content, but in Tambov the prisoners were once invited to a drinking party and then released in the street.[15]

[15] Got'e, I, 345, Salias, 92-93, 105-106; PSZ, 1784, N. 16008; 1785, N. 15568; Dubasov, 35; Tarasov, 64, 73-79.

At the other end of the judicial process, the execution of criminal sentences was vested in the police. Since so many punishments were various forms of corporal punishment which, given an equal number of blows, can be applied with greater or lesser severity, the good will of the police could make a great deal of difference. In smaller towns corporal punishment was administered by the sheriff or the land captain. An executioner was included in the staff of the governor and the provincial voevoda in 1763, but there is no mention of him in later tables of organization. Even in Petersburg it is not certain that there was one: the ukase of 1768 ordered the Policemaster General to stop the practice of seizing persons at random among the spectators lining the streets and to choose instead other prisoners as executioners.[16]

Sheriffs and land captains were also the executive agents of the Treasury. Before the reform the capitation rolls were kept by the voevodas. If taxes were not paid on time, the uezd voevoda had to visit estates and villages and collect the arrears. Some, however, were not eager to trespass on the property of powerful landowners, who sometimes took up arms with their peasants against the representatives of the central government. The reform vested the keeping of the rolls and the collection of taxes in the uezd treasurers and the gubernia treasury chamber. If a tax was not paid within four weeks after the deadline fixed for its collection, the treasurer reported the delinquents to the chamber and to the land captain. The latter with one assessor and two soldiers repaired to the estate or the village and lived off the peasants for three days. Unfortunately, there were sometimes good reasons why taxes could not be paid, and this gave the police a license to behave as they pleased.

It is true that land captains were not always forceful in applying the letter of the law. Some, like their predecessors, the voevodas, were naturally not eager to force the issue against the large estates. Others, decent men, probably knew there was nothing to collect. But in uezds where a large percentage of state peasants resided, land captains could not miss the opportunity to line their pockets while enforcing the law. The horror stories reported by Dubasov from Tambov gubernia, where the land captains extorted ten times the amount they were authorized to collect, may have been caused by the fact that large numbers of peasants belonged to the treasury. If land captains were found too slow in collecting the arrears, the treasury chambers asked the gubernia board to compel them, but there was little the board could do unless willful negligence was involved. And if all measures were unsuccessful, the last resort was the stationing of troops in a village (*ekzekutsiia*),

[16] PSZ, 1763, N. 11991, vol. 44², 69; 1768, N. 13108; Trefolev, "Zaplechenyi master."

a form of systematic and vengeful exploitation.[17] Whatever could be had would pass into the hands of the troops, the treasury would collect nothing, and there would be nothing to collect in the years to come.

SUMMARY POWERS

Powers of executive police derived from the latitude given to the police to carry out the decisions of other agencies. Summary powers belonged to the police as agents of general and municipal administration. They were exercised without recourse to judicial review, at the highest level for political reasons, at the lower levels to maintain the integrity of the social order. Fedor Krechetov, already mentioned, was prosecuted at the initiative of Archbishop Gavril, who urged the Petersburg police board in January 1788 to investigate the publication of Krechetov's brochure. This was done by the local *pristav* on orders of the police board, and the case was brought before the Petersburg lower *nadvornyi* court, which accepted the objections of the prelate but imposed no punishment in August 1790. Less than three years later, however, a denunciation was sent to the Petersburg governor Peter Konovnitsyn, together with a petition addressed to the Empress (*proshenie na Vy-sochaishee imia*). Such petitions were either sent directly to one of the Empress's secretaries or to a high official, who forwarded them to the agency having jurisdiction on the matter unless it required the Empress's personal attention. The petition in this case was a formal ac-cusation that Krechetov had spoken "indecent words" against the Empress and the heir, insulted the Senate, called Orthodox believers idol worshippers, and favored the emancipation of the serfs. The blend of political, religious, and social heresy is indeed striking. In May 1793 the accuser and Krechetov were questioned in the Secret Expedition. A questionnaire (*doprosnye punkty*) was presented, and the answers to each question (*punkt*) were sent to the Procurator General, who ordered Sheshkovskii to find out whether Krechetov had any patrons (*pokroviteli*). Some witnesses were interrogated in the Expedition, others in the office of Prince Viazemskii. The latter then submitted a report to the Empress, summarizing the findings of the investigation and recommending the penalty.

Other cases were prosecuted on direct orders of the Empress if she took a personal interest. Radishchev's famous book, printed in his own press with passages added after a first copy had been cleared by the senior policemaster, was seized by a *pristav*. A copy was sent to

[17] OL, art. 141-142, 426; PSZ, 1782, N. 15405, par. 19, and 15357, Romanovich-Slavatinskii, 351.

Catherine, who reacted violently to its contents. From then on Shesh-kovskii could have done nothing to prevent the development of the case to its sad conclusion. The investigation was conducted in the Secret Expedition, orders concerning the detention of Radishchev were routed through Governor General Brius, and the indictment was dictated by Catherine herself to Bezborodko, who sent it to the criminal chamber. Novikov was investigated by Governor General Prozorovskii at the personal order of the Empress, who then sent him to Shlisselburg fortress for fifteen years without trial. Krechetov was also imprisoned there for eight years.

One practice distinguished the procedures of the Secret Expedition from those of other police agencies: the unabashed use of torture. An attempt to abolish torture altogether was made at the very beginning of the reign, and some contemporaries saw this as one of the greatest achievements of the reign. The claim that torture was abolished by Catherine rests on a misunderstanding which tells us a great deal about the coarseness of the age. Torture (*pytka*) was conducted in the presence of the judge and secretaries, who took down the answers of the prisoner. It was applied with a variety of instruments: the knout, the whip, with the prisoner bound by his hands and feet to a wooden pole; hot iron prongs pointed and threaded; cold water dropped on the head until the prisoner passed out; suspension by the hands. Voevodas were forbidden to use this type of torture in 1763: all prisoners to be tortured were to be sent to the governor. Catherine's Great Instruction condemned it, and subsequent legislation indicated that the Empress opposed its application. Yet, it is known that Sheshkovskii applied the knout in the Secret Expedition, at the residence of the Procurator General himself. Moreover, the abolition of torture did not exclude the application of "forceful questioning" (*pristrastnyi dopros*) with a whip or sticks (*batogi*). Prince Viazemskii, in his report to the Empress on the Tsaritsyn soldier Dmitriev, was well aware of the difference when he wrote that the soldier had confessed to saying that Peter III was in the Crimea after being subjected to "*pristrastnyi dopros* with sticks but not to *pytka*." The soldier was released without additional punishment since the interrogation was considered sufficient punishment. Sheshkovskii's favorite method was to stun the prisoner with a blow of a stick applied under the chin which sometimes broke the teeth. Some investigations were conducted without any record being kept (*keleino*), in such a way that people who managed to survive the ordeal were too ashamed to talk about what had taken place or went mad. Obviously, forceful methods were still used despite the abolition of torture. Procurator General Samoilov's remark to Sheshkovskii that he "knew by what means to get at the truth" had a sinister ring. Yet, to contemporaries who lived in a world where corporal punishment was liberally used in all walks of life, beating with a stick or a whip was nothing unusual.[18]

The penalties imposed by administrative order were usually banishment, including drafting into the army and the garrisons, and imprisonment in a fortress, and they were meted out at various levels of the hierarchy, from the Empress, who confirmed the recommendations of the Secret Expedition and the Procurator General, on down to the landowners and peasant communities. The satirist Fedor Emin, who poked fun at the Academy of Sciences and the Academy of Arts in his "Dream Seen in the Year 1765," was imprisoned for two weeks on Catherine's order in the Peter and Paul fortress. The Dedilovo voevoda was sent to Shlisselburg, and his wife and two daughters were banished to Siberia. Arsenii Matseevich died in solitary confinement in Revel fortress. Sukin and the two Pushkins who forged assignats were banished, one to reside in Orenburg for life, another to settlement in Siberia, the third to detention in a distant fortress for life. Radishchev's death sentence (imposed by a court) was commuted to exile to Eastern Siberia for ten years. Bogdanov was sent to hard labor for life in Taganrog, and the unfortunate Kravkov, for a much lesser offense, followed Archbishop Arsenii in the Revel fortress. The secretary of the Skopin land court who reported abuses committed by local officials was declared insane and incarcerated in the dreaded Spaso-Efimev monastery in Suzdal.[19]

The Empress, who had a not undeserved reputation for "liberalism," was not alone in dealing harshly with the opposition. The ruling class which supported her was even more intolerant of resistance among its own "subjects." Landowners possessed the right to banish peasants without the benefit of a trial. The offenses for which they could be so punished were clearly moral, social, and political. The interrelation of these three grounds is evident from the use of the words insolence (*proderzost'*) and harmful (*vrednyi*). The ukase of January 1765 empowered landowners to banish their serfs for insolence to no less than hard labor "for as long as they wish," and that of August 1767 forbade peasants to complain to the Empress against their masters and threatened those who did with hard labor in the Nerchinsk silver mines. These orders contained no empty threat, and it is estimated that be-

[18] Kulakova, 237-238; Chechulin, *Nakaz*, ch. X, par. 192, 197; "Obriad," 58-59. Catherine did not know or did not want to know that torture was being applied in the Expedition: see de Madariaga, 249; Gernet, "Politicheskii sysk," 27-29.

[19] Kulakova, 26-27; *Krest'ianskaia voina*, 359; Sivkov, 259, "Son," and "Pis'mo k Konovnitsynu."

tween 1768 and 1772, 20,515 serfs were banished to Tobolsk gubernia
and Eniseisk uezd for violating them. Countless others were drafted
into the army, another form of banishment for life.[20]

All these offenders, whether satirists or peasants, exhibited in common a lack of respect for the established order, a sinful pride negating
the precepts of the Orthodox Church, which taught humility and
rejected criticism as a solvent of authority; and an inability to submit
to the often despotic rule of the community. Their expulsion was not
expulsion from the community of believers, but it was an act of pur-
gation by which the community rid itself of harmful elements and
banished them to the ends of the Empire or to the darkness of a prison,
and thus restored its balance, its self-satisfaction, and the undisturbed
contemplation of its traditional ignorance.

In the towns efforts were made to define and thereby circumscribe
the arbitrary powers of the police. The 1768 Supplement to the Great
Instruction sketched a line of demarcation between the jurisdiction of
the courts and that of the police. Courts took up cases submitted to
them and reached their decision in accordance with established procedures. Judicial cases were defined by reference to the severity of
punishment. Within this framework the task of judges was to find the
law and apply it without letting their conscience sway their judgment.
Thus the powers of the courts were enumerated and their proceedings
became technical operations. By contrast, the jurisdiction of the police
was residual: the suppression of crimes not included by law in the
jurisdiction of the courts remained its responsibility. It did not punish
and cut off (retranche) from society; it "corrected" and compelled
violators to live in accordance with rules. Its action was constant and
pervasive and its penalties less severe. "To curb license and maintain
in order the things entrusted to it, it is enough if its penalties consist
in corrections, fines, and other punishments which shame and degrade
(couvrent d'infamie) those who misbehave."[21]

The early distinction between crimes as violations of the laws and
other infractions as violations of rules of good behavior under police
jurisdiction was not made in practice until the Police Code of 1782.
Articles 191 to 274 contained a short penal code for the use of the
police boards.[22] If the violation was a crime, the board placed the
suspect in preventive detention, and sent him to the court, where he

[20] PSZ, 1765, N. 12311; 1766, N. 12556; 1767, N. 12966; Eroshkin, 125; Alexandrov, 273-277, 280-281. De Madariaga has made a convincing case for the possibility
that this power to banish serfs was suspended after 1773: "Catherine II," 39-47.

[21] PSZ, 1768, N. 13075, art. 531-565.

[22] Police Code, art. 70-72, 155; art. 191-232 (offenses), 233-274 (penalties).

would be punished in accordance with his guilt and the nature of his crime, as stated in the law—such is the formula repeated paragraph after paragraph. Other violations were to be punished by the police. They included disturbing the service in church, selling liquor and providing entertainment before the end of the liturgy; building, selling, mortgaging, or renting houses without informing the *makler*; carrying arms without authorization; drunkenness, playing cards for money, selling lottery tickets, and performing plays without the authorization of the board; prostitution; swearing in public; petty theft if the value did not exceed twenty rubles and the theft was not committed for the fourth time, willful damage, escaping arrest; trade in forbidden goods and deception in trading.

The penalties were interesting because they embodied the intent of the Instruction to "correct" and to "shame." Some were fines assessed against the cost of maintaining a soldier or a hospital patient for half a day or more. Fines were usually combined with a provision to keep the culprit under arrest until he could pay them. Certain penalties were meant to shame him. Prisoners detained in the workhouse—one of those "enterprises" under police jurisdiction—had to work away the fine following a whipping or detention on bread and water, depending on the nature of the offense, usually theft. The amount of the fine determined the number of days in the workhouse—where an inmate received three kopecks a day—and was paid to the police, plus up to eighteen percent payable in part to the police, in part to the person who was defrauded or robbed. The police also imposed a variety of other fines. It granted permits to cab drivers (*izvozshchiki*) and fined them for violations. If a complaint was made to the oral court that not enough liquor was available at the local bar run by the treasury, the sheriff imposed a fine equal to six percent of the value of the undelivered amount, twelve percent for a second complaint.[23]

Some offenders for whom the law intended a more shameful punishment were sent to the house of correction (*smiritel'nyi dom*). Detention there was reserved for card players, those who played for money or games of chance, who opened a house for such games and made a living from it. The punishment varied from detention for twenty-four to seventy-two hours and was followed by detention in the workhouse until the fine was paid. It was also reserved for prostitutes and procurers (up to half a year), for the use of offensive (*brannye*) words in public before the well-born and those of higher

²³ PSZ, 1781, N. 15231, art. 81.

ranks, and for the hapless males or females over the age of seven who visited the public bath reserved for members of the other sex.

REMEDIES

Despite the fact that abuses of police power, as we understand them today, were built into the system, the question must still be asked whether remedies were available against them. The answer to this difficult question is hardly to be found in the law but depended upon personal behavior and the public mood in various uezds. Power is limited not by statutory prohibition alone, but above all by the mutual claims of social groups capable of mobilizing resistance and thereby protecting themselves against the intrusion of outside pressures. The nature and scope of administrative discretion is very much a reflection of the nature of social relationships at any given time. The coarseness of social manners is not conducive at first glance to the elaboration of remedies against violence by public authorities. On the other hand, no society can operate without some mechanism to protect individuals against public abuse. A privileged group at least must be able to obtain redress, for the insecurity of all threatens in the long run the very security of the collectivity itself. In the reign of Catherine we are in the presence of two complementary trends: a powerful yearning for definition, privilege, and protection on the part of the nobility and to a lesser extent the townsmen as well, and an insistence by the nobility upon social primacy and the consequent degradation of the peasantry.

Certainly the assumption behind the convocation of the Legislative Commission, the publication of the Organic Law, and the grant of charters to the nobility and the townsmen pointed to a desire to define and protect social relationships and to guarantee the observance of "legality" by public authorities. Roughly, there were three avenues of redress. One might be called the legal, and consisted in the review of investigations by the courts. The second was a social one and depended on the influence which the marshals of the nobility individually or as a body could exercise over the land captains. Finally, redress could also be obtained against abuses by both land captains and sheriffs by appealing to the gubernia board and even to the governor general in person.

The law allowed appeals of the land court's decisions to the uezd court or the *rasprava*. If the defendant could prove that a land court had acted unlawfully, he had four weeks to notify the land court and his case had to be removed to either court. In addition, all investigations, including those where no criminal act had been discovered, had to be sent to the uezd court, *rasprava*, or *magistrat*, in order to determine whether the police had been negligent. If it should find against the police, the court could order a new investigation or refer the case to the criminal chamber, where action might be taken to ask the gubernia board to proceed against the police board or the land court.[24]

How effective were these legal remedies? If the extensive jurisdiction of the police in the countryside reflected the cruelty of serfdom, legal remedies were also a function of the social order. An order based on inequality cannot afford equal remedies to all. The *magistrat*, except perhaps in the gubernia capitals, was not influential enough to challenge a sheriff who was at least a colonel not used to bargaining with townsmen unless the community had some funds at its disposal to bribe him. Similarly, the state peasants were a large and unprotected "fund" to be raided often with impunity. Their only protector was the "director of economy," an official who was not on the staff of the governor but merely a member of the treasury chamber and most likely a landowner himself. Legal conflicts that might develop between state peasants and nobles were likely to be settled by force, and the uezd judge was no less interested than the land captain in trampling upon the peasants' rights unless he chose, for personal reasons, to stand by them. The serfs had no legal remedies open to them since they possessed no juridical personality and, having taken no oath to the ruler, stood somewhat outside legal society, despite their numbers.

This leaves the nobles. If a noble were to seek redress against injustices suffered at the hands of a land captain, he might indeed seek it before the uezd judge, who ranked higher than the land captain and need not fear the latter's arrogance. He might also seek it by turning to the gubernia and uezd marshals, who represented the nobility, often important and well-connected nobles who could put pressure on the captain. Such peer pressure was probably the most effective restraint on a land captain who wished to retain his lucrative position.

The third method of seeking redress or checking the abuses of the land captains or the sheriff was to appeal to the gubernia board. Before the reform, the only recourse was to go to the gubernia capital and plead before the governor. Mertvago describes how at the age of fourteen, after his father was hanged by the Pugachev rebels, he was threatened with a beating by the provincial voevoda of Alatyr. The boy retorted that he could not be whipped because he was a nobleman, and he intentionally insulted the voevoda by calling him a soldier's son. The voevoda then made his life and that of his friends unbearable

---

[24] PSZ, 1798, N. 18386; 1821, N. 28852.

in the town, and when troops arrived he billeted soldiers in the quarters where he and his mother lived. Kazan, the gubernia capital, was too far away, and the roads were unsafe. His only recourse was to call on the regimental commander and to tell the story of his eviction. The commander took a liking to the boy, removed the soldiers, and his friendship neutralized the spite of the voevoda.[25] The reform made a distinction between disciplinary sanctions and judicial trial. Officials appointed by the gubernia board were dismissed by administrative order. The dismissal of the sheriff required the Senate's sanction. The governor also had the power to commit to trial in the criminal chamber all officials in the gubernia (except those appointed by the Empress), and the sentences of the chamber, once approved by the governor, took effect immediately unless the penalty was death, whipping with the knout, or loss of "honor."[26] Very much here depended on the energy and commitment of the governor, who was an outsider and could set the tone of official behavior during his tenure.

Yet, it is also evident that the nobility knew how to protect its land captains if it chose to and that the latter knew how to blunt the intervention of the governor. Dubasov tells the story of the Spassk land captain in Tambov gubernia, the scourge of the state peasants in the uezd. When the peasants of a village refused to give him the usual gifts to which he had grown accustomed (honey, fresh fish, etc.), he had the headman (*golova*) beaten by soldiers and dragged around the village. Then he asked for a recommendation (*odobrenie*) by the peasants that they were satisfied with him. In another village, the *sotskii* was flogged a hundred times for not giving him one hundred dried carp on time. But, on a neighboring estate, probably belonging to Alexis Orlov, there was a steward who complained to Governor Derzhavin in Tambov. Asked to explain his actions, the captain accused the steward of seizing state land from the peasants, using them to work on his land with the result that they were unable to pay their taxes, and of sheltering vagrants (*bespasportnye*) on the estates. When Derzhavin arrived, the elders (*stariki*), who had been thoroughly frightened by warnings of reprisals if they cooperated with the governor, stated that they were satisfied with the land captain. And this would have been the end of the investigation if a retired sergeant and tax farmer, who had also been beaten and imprisoned by the captain, had not gone to Riazan to complain to Gudovich, Governor General of Riazan and Tambov. Gudovich ordered the captain tried in the Tambov criminal chamber, but for reasons that are not quite clear Der-

[25] "Zapiski Mertvago," 25-26, 30-34.
[26] Police Code, art. 125; OL, art. 229, 233, 245, 254, 268; PSZ, 1784, N. 16022.

zhavin stood up for him, and the captain was forced to retire. Then
the Spassk nobility stood up for its own. Under the next governor the
former captain was elected uezd judge and began to so harass the
steward that the frightened peasants stopped paying their debts to
him. He finally went to Moscow, where Alexis Orlov brought the
matter before Prince Viazemskii, and the Senate ordered the Tambov
governor to see to it that the steward's debts were paid to him. The
captain's vendetta, however, apparently continued. What a long process, and what energy and persistence were needed to bring the administration to proceed against a simple land captain, and with what
meager results![27]

The police reform created an apparatus which brought the ruling
class closer to the townsmen and peasants, a device by which that
class could work out its relationships with the socially dependent. Its
most original innovation was to establish on a systematic basis, at the
very periphery of the ruling class, an association between landowners
and the "best men" of the state peasantry and merchantry, who now
were to sit together in land courts and police boards to discuss matters
of immediate interest to their respective communities. Placing the sheriff in class VIII, already in the very core of the ruling class, while the
land captain remained in class IX, resulted from a conscious discrim-
ination in favor of the towns, whose population was thus ranked below
the ruling class but above the state peasantry, while the serfs remained
under the patriarchal jurisdiction of their owners. Because the police
forces at its disposal were rudimentary, the efficiency of the new organization must not be overestimated, but in a peasant world still so
little affected by the forces of change, it may have been adequate for
its purpose.

The preferential status given the towns was also noticeable in the
attempt to define the summary powers of the police, i.e., to recognize
a form of social contract between the ruling class and the elite of the
townsmen, among whom one must mention the tax farmers and other
merchants who were prime candidates for cooptation into the secretarial ranks of the ruling class. Such an agreement provides a fine
illustration of Obrebski's finding that social antagonism abetted by
membership in two different cultural worlds did not exclude the adoption of members of the folk-groups, provided they were relegated to
very subordinate positions within the ruling class.

The social aspects of the reform were thus much more important
than the political. To see the police reform—and this applies to the
judicial reform as well, as we shall see presently—as a bureaucratic

[27] Dubasov, 30-33.

reform would be a mistake, unless one persists in seeing in the ruling class a "bureaucracy." Although the post of sheriff was a full-time position, that of land captain was not, and its incumbent in fact drew a full salary for part-time work. The clerical staff came from townsmen and even peasants—although this was forbidden—who did not belong to any national corporation with its own rules and privileges but were hired and dismissed at will by their employers.

What, then, was the purpose of this reform? If we follow Harold Lasswell's definition of politics as the "story of who gets what, when, and how,"[28] the police reform was a systematic attempt to create spoils in the form of paid administrative positions for the purpose of securing the maximum exploitation by the ruling class of the socially dependent in the towns and countryside. Exploitation can be reconciled with a social contract if it is concealed behind a higher purpose. The 1760s seem to have been marked by a widespread breakdown of order in central Russia, especially in its border provinces like Pskov, Orel, Voronezh, and along the Volga. Banditry kept villages and estates insecure, and made travel difficult for noblemen, for merchants, and for peasants; and arson was one of the most terrible calamities to afflict a Russian town. Therefore the reform met a need strongly felt by all classes, and the association of their representatives to fight a common danger secured the legitimacy of the reform. In the towns specifically, the new apparatus was designed to provide services which could not function without the widespread cooperation of the population. But greater exploitation also came in the wake of organization, as the collection of taxes also became more efficient. It is likely that bribery increased with the number of posts. The various "re-educational" enterprises (workhouses, etc.) run by the police with the fines it collected certainly led to misappropriation of funds. Consequences were similar in the countryside, but on a wider scale. The repression of banditry, at the very time serfdom was reaching its apogee, reflected the maximization of the possibilities offered by that social order; such maximization was a profitable activity in the short run, but one fraught with danger as the legitimacy of serfdom began to be questioned at the very end of the century.

[28] Quoted in M. Fried, "State: The Institution," in IESS, XV, 147.

PART III
THE JUDICIARY

JUDICIAL ORGANIZATION

CENTRAL AGENCIES

To approach a study of the Russian judiciary in the light of our discussion of the ruling class and the police requires a word of caution. The satisfaction of a multitude of claims arising among individuals and between individuals and agencies in the pursuit of their activities remains the fundamental test of the viability of a political system. If titles to property cannot be enforced, if wills are not recognized, if contracts are not honored, and abuses cannot be corrected, and if there is no authority to give satisfaction to aggrieved parties, violence becomes the only resort and destroys the foundations and the hopes of any civil society. To this dual function of the judiciary—providing a peaceful resolution of private claims and checking abuses—is added another, more active and repressive. The judicial power, "so terrible to mankind," as Montesquieu put it,[1] becomes here an instrument of class rule by which the foundations of the social and political order are protected against any threat, actual or potential, and exploitation is given a legitimacy which sanctions all but its worst abuses.

These judicial functions were naturally vested, not in separate courts, but in administrative agencies staffed with individuals who belonged to the managerial level of the ruling class. A separate judiciary, therefore, did not exist, and administrative agencies were often called judicial (*sudeiskie*) as if to emphasize their primary function of administering the law.

But what was the law? It was a body of normative acts, indispensable in any human collectivity, governing relationships between individuals and groups and establishing procedures for the settlement of disputes. But these acts did not issue from the conflict of political forces, from a legislature embodying the idea of the state, nor were they the reflection of an unacceptable natural law. They were no more than internal regulations of the ruling class, technical devices with which that class governed its internal affairs and its relationships with the socially dependent; as such, they were adequate instruments in the hands of the political leadership, used when suitable, overlooked when irrelevant. The Russian ruling class has often been accused of arbitrary

[1] Montesquieu, I, 153.

behavior; this should mean no more than recognition that it was a political class, imbued with an ethnic self-righteousness and religious intolerance that acknowledged no limit on the exercise of its political mission.

The reforms, as we shall see, did establish separate courts but shied away from introducing systematic rules of judicial procedure. Likewise, little progress was made in the work of codification, and for good reasons. The new courts, like the new financial agencies, served a technical function. They provided a forum for the settlement of disputes, but the execution of their decisions remained a political prerogative: either the stronger members of the ruling class were able to obtain settlements that favored their case, or they appealed to the political leadership for a final ruling; and separate courts established for townsmen and state peasants were strictly subordinated to the managers of the ruling class. For these men there existed no restrictions based on law. If they violated the norms considered indispensible at a given time and caused local opposition by junior members of the class to their continuance in office, they were recalled and perhaps disciplined, but seldom disgraced. Arbitrariness was a fact of life because the ruling class encountered at the time no outside resistance forceful enough to compel it to abide by abstract rules driving their universal validity and binding force from a mutually acceptable compromise among competing forces.

Two Senate departments were originally invested with a chiefly judicial responsibility, the Second in Petersburg and the Sixth in Moscow. The Second Department usually consisted of four or five senators in the 1760s and 1770s, seven or eight during the remainder of the reign. Appointments were made by the Empress for an indefinite period. A total of twenty-seven senators were appointed, nine of whom constituted the core of the department over a thirty-four-year period. Some were purely court figures, like Martin Skavronskii, nephew of Catherine I, and Alexei Naryshkin. Others belonged to the Trubetskoi-Saltykov clan, like Peter Trubetskoi (1764-1781), Pavel Mansurov, and Ivan Kozlov. Four should be included in the military establishment: Fedor Glebov, Andrei Shcherbatov, Nikita Murav'ev, and Lukian Kamynin, all related by marriage. The senior procurator headed a chancery of thirty-eight clerks.[2]

The department received appeals against the decisions of agencies based in Petersburg: the branches of the Colleges of Justice and Landed Estates, the Land Survey Expedition, and the Criminal (*rozysknaia*) Expedition. It also received appeals from the Moscow, Novgorod, and

---

[2] PSZ, 1763, N. 11991, vol. 44², 59-60; 1767, N. 13029; Kulakova, 245.

Arkhangelsk gubernia chanceries. When the colleges were abolished in the wake of the provincial reform, the department received appeals against the decisions of both the civil and criminal chambers. It was also responsible for the trial of officials, including governors, for crimes committed in office. The investigations were usually conducted in the Petersburg branch of the College of Justice and, after the reform, in the criminal chambers. The jurisdiction of the Second Department extended even to the Baltic provinces and Little Russia, despite the existence of a Third Department for the territories in which Russian law did not apply.[3]

The Sixth Department was a bit smaller. Its membership did not exceed four or five senators, and there were six in 1796. It was also steadier than that of the Second Department. Eleven of the twenty-six senators appointed between 1764 and 1796 served for several years. At least four were closely related to the Trubetskois: Sergei Gagarin, Ivan Viazemskii, Peter Volkonskii, and Matvei Rzhevskii; two were former members of the Second Department (Kozlov and Kamynin); and the senators with the longest tenure in this department all belonged to what I have called, for want of a better term, the foreign-policy-military establishment (Vsevolod Vsevolozhskii, Mikhail Shcherbatov, Fedor Osterman, Nikolai Durnovo). Thus, the leadership of the judicial establishment was a closely knit group bound by marriage and other family ties with the two great clans. It is not quite true that the emergence of a powerful procurator general resulted in the downgrading of the Senate, unless we look at it in purely organizational terms. It would be more accurate to say that the Senate judicial establishment and the Procurator General, especially during the second half of the reign, formed a small committee of the political leadership controlling the sources of patronage and operating as the ultimate arbiter, under the Empress, of litigation, feuds, and disorders among the ruling class and dependent social groups.

The jurisdiction of the Sixth Department was identical with that of the Second Department. It received appeals against the decisions of the colleges of Justice and Landed Estates, the *Sudnyi Prikaz*, and the Moscow Criminal Expedition, and from the gubernia chanceries south of the Volga. Like the Second Department, it was a trial court for governors and voevodas and other officials whose investigations were conducted in the College of Justice. Its territorial jurisdiction was much

---

[3] PSZ, 1763, N. 11989, pt. 1; 1764, N. 12046; 1768, N. 13170. I have not found any list of gubernias assigned to each Senate department. It has been said that none existed: *Istoriia Prav. Senata*, III, 277. Yet it is obvious, from 1771, N. 13559, that it did exist. I assume here that the gubernias and provinces reporting to the Petersburg colleges or their branches were in the jurisdiction of the Second Department.

larger than that of the Second and, not surprisingly, it soon was unable
to cope with a huge backlog of cases. By late 1770 there were 1,050
cases awaiting decision, and no increase in staff would be sufficient
to process them. The solution was found in transforming the Fifth
Department into a second appellate department in Moscow. This department, which had only thirty-seven cases on its docket, never grew
into more than a pale copy of the First Department. It had become a
mere administrative body for certain important investigations, but
financial matters were sent from the Moscow-based colleges directly
to Petersburg. As a result, it was free to take up additional cases, and
it was made to share the appellate jurisdiction of the Sixth Department:
cases which the latter could not handle were turned over to it, presumably after obtaining the approval of the Procurator General.[4]

The Second Department nevertheless remained the more important.
Its location near the centers of power made it the favorite court of
appeal. Despite the de facto existence of a territorial jurisdiction, the
appellants were given the choice of appeal to either department. It
was also natural to give preference to the Second Department because
Senate procedures favored the appellant willing to defray the additional cost of an appeal in the northern capital. If the decision was
not unanimous in the Sixth Department, the case went before the
general assembly of the Moscow departments, and there was always
the possibility that it might then be referred to the Petersburg Senate.
At the end of 1796 some 4,290 cases remained undecided in the Second
Department against 773 in the Sixth.[5] Unless we assume that the
Muscovites worked much harder than the Petersburg senators, it is
obvious that the Second Department had become the most important
and the most congested court of appeal in the Empire.

Another office, that of *General Reketmeister*, was established in
1720. Patterned after the French *maitre de requetes*, it examined complaints, delays, and "unjust" decisions in agencies and brought the
matter before the Senate or referred it to the Empress. Some "petitions
addressed to Her Majesty" were also routed through this office, and
in such cases the *General Reketmeister* functioned not unlike a state
secretary. The table of organization of 1763 placed it in Petersburg;
it was a small office of six persons. A branch of five persons under
his deputy operated in Moscow. With a salary of two thousand rubles
the *General Reketmeister* was placed on the same level as the senior
procurator of a Senate Department. Two of the four holders of the
post later became senators: Ivan Kozlov (1762-1768) and Nikolai

4 PSZ, 1771, N. 13559; 1765, N. 12512.
5 PSZ, 1805, N. 21605.

Maslov (1771-1780). Arkadii Terskii (1781-1796), a former senior secretary in the First Department, was a product of the Senate establishment who enjoyed considerable influence because the Empress greatly valued his judgment.[6]

Two colleges were specifically responsible for judicial administration, although other colleges also possessed judicial functions, notably those of Commerce and Mining and the Central *Magistrat*. The Colleges of Justice and Landed Estates (*Votchinnaia*) were based in Moscow and kept a branch office in Petersburg. The former was a court of appeal against the decisions of governors and voevodas and a tribunal of first instance for officers of the Guard and foreigners residing in Petersburg and for the inhabitants of Petersburg gubernia, Vyborg, and Narva. It fined local chanceries for delays in processing cases and investigated crimes when it received denunciations or ordered local chanceries to do so. It alone, however, was responsible for the investigation of all officials accused of violating the law and their oath of office.

In criminal matters the college had no jurisdiction over death sentences; such sentences coming up from the gubernia chanceries were sent directly to the Senate. Other sentences, opinions, investigations—the terms are often interchangeable in eighteenth-century procedure—referred to the college by governors, provincial voevodas and the Criminal Expeditions in Moscow and Petersburg were decided in the college both in point of law and of fact. Its jurisdiction in civil matters seems to have been restricted to the notarization (*svidetel'stvo*) of wills and various deeds (*kreposti*), and to the collection of fees for these services. We have, for example, the case of retired Colonel Liubistkov, old and blind, who asked the Empress's permission to make two Court ladies the heirs to his estate. Catherine ordered the college through the Governor General of Moscow to visit the colonel to ascertain that he had no lawful heirs and that these were his real wishes. In another case, a division of property between a major and his daughter was challenged by a third party. The case was heard in the college, and, despite the confusion of claims and the emotions they aroused, the Empress refused to intervene.[7]

The table of organization of 1763 divided the college into three departments. The president, in class III or IV, sat in the first depart-

[6] PSZ, 1763, N. 11989 and 11991; Dmitriev, *Istoriia*, 512; *Istoriia Prav, Senata*, II, 343-344, 481-483, 600-601. On the *General Reketmeister*, see 416-421.

[7] PSZ, 1763, N. 11989, pt. 13; 1767, N. 12943; "Pis'ma imp. Ekat. Velik.," 20, 78-79; *SIRIO*, II (1868), 419-424; Gribovskii, *Materialy*, 2-3, 7-8, 12, 14-15. No statute was published for the College of Justice, but there is much information in TsGADA, f. 16, d. 334 and f. 370, d. 57, fol. 39-52.

ment, the vice-president in the second, and a state councillor headed the third. Each department had two additional members. The chancery was very large, consisting of 9 secretaries, 106 clerks, and 27 guards, a total of 142. The Petersburg branch was much smaller (30 persons) and was not divided into departments.[8] The two presidents of the college between 1764 and 1781 (Ivan Divov and Alexei Iakovlev) were closely associated with the Trubetskoi family and the post of *General Reketmeister*.

The College of Landed Estates was divided into four departments. There were 12 members (*prisutstvuiushchie*) and a procurator, 12 secretaries, 171 clerks, and 36 guards. It also contained a large archive run by 27 persons and an additional member, bringing the total staff of the college to 260. Its Petersburg branch contained another 39.[9] The president of the college was for many years (1760-1776) Mikhail Lunin, who married the sister of Senator Nikolai Nepliuev, nephew of the Panin brothers. It should not escape our notice that the leadership of the judicial colleges was shared, like the membership of the Senate departments, among the candidates of the two great clans.

The college was threatened with impotence in the 1760s as it attempted to provide centralized record-keeping, accounting for all transactions (sales, purchases, mortgages, and the execution of wills) in a period of increased real-estate activity. Transactions acquired legal force only after presentation in Moscow for verification (*spravka*) and registration (*zapiska*) in the college. Buyers and sellers of land from Petersburg gubernia, Novgorod, Belozersk, Pskov, and Velikie Luki provinces went to the Petersburg branch. This branch also had jurisdiction over all lands and villages granted by Imperial or Senate decision in Ingermanlandia and over litigation affecting these properties. The archive of the college remained the repository of all completed transactions in all the provinces of the Empire where Russian law applied, and it supplied copies of the original documents to the branch and to litigants. It also kept genealogies for reference in inheritance cases. Its condition, however, negated many of the advantages of centralization. The old reference books were made of ordinary paper, and many were in a stage of decomposition from age and dampness. In transfers to Petersburg and back they were often damaged, and clerical errors rendered many a reference unreliable. In the 1760s the purchase of new books made of parchment must have improved the condition of the archive, yet even the upper floors of the building, where the

[8] PSZ, 1763, N. 11422; 1763, N. 11991, vol. 44², 61-62, 70.
[9] *Ibid.*, and 1786, N. 16307.

members met, were in such a dilapidated state twenty years later that they threatened to collapse.

The insistence on centralization and poor record-keeping bred corruption and worked great hardship on people of small means. At a time when roads were bad and unsafe and distances often insuperable, many could not afford to leave their homes and travel to Moscow or Petersburg, bear the cost of living in these capitals, and wait weeks and months for documentation or for legal title. A nephew who had received ten souls from his aunt might not consider the game worth the candle. Thus many owned property without title to it and sold it to others without any registration ever taking place. Unscrupulous landowners would sell property to someone who could not afford to go to Moscow, then sell it a second time to someone else who did go to the capital and obtained legal title.[10] The possibilities for mischief were many and tempting to imaginative speculators, and the Chichikovs must already have been well-known figures, especially in distant uezds where the machinery of government—if, indeed, it existed—had broken down.

The land survey of the central provinces carried out over some twenty years beginning in the mid-1760s was a major step toward the reduction of these abuses. Properties were surveyed and bounded, maps were drawn up, and an enormous documentation became available for reference in litigation. Land survey was naturally closely related to "landed estates." When it began in 1755, a central chancery was set up in Petersburg and a gubernia chancery in Moscow. In 1762 the two were merged, and in 1763 land survey became the responsibility of one of the departments of the College of Landed Estates. In 1765 a commission was created to examine the paltry results of a decade of activity, and it was decided to place overall responsibility in a new Expedition of Land Survey in Petersburg. Although it was not called a Senate department (unnumbered) until 1795, it was nevertheless a committee of three or four senators under the de facto chairmanship of the Procurator General. Among its members we find here again representatives of the two clans (Andrei Shuvalov and Ivan Kozlov, Nikolai Nepliuev) and state secretary Teplov. Its chancery of seventeen clerks was headed by a senior secretary of the Second Department. Its archive, together with that of the College of Landed Estates, was in Moscow; both were placed in the 1790s under Senator Matvei Dmitriev-Mamonov, father of the former favorite. The Expedition received appeals against decisions of the Moscow chancery,

[10] PSZ, 1745, N. 9100; 1740, N. 8145; 1773, N. 14056; see also 1765, N. 12371; 1786, N. 16307; B-va, 71-73.

and its own decisions were appealed to either the First or the Second
Department, and, after the Expedition became a department, to the
general assembly of the Petersburg Senate departments.[11]

LOCAL AGENCIES AND THE REFORM

Until the reform, the voevoda—whether provincial or other, since there
was no established hierarchy among them—was a trial judge. His
decisions could be appealed to the governor and the latter's decision
to the College of Justice. There were thus four instances, including
the relevant Senate department. But the voevoda was not the first court
in all criminal and civil cases. In the towns and the countryside there
were "courts" organized along class lines: courts for townsmen, for
state peasants, and for peasants of the Imperial family. In the towns
there were *magistraty* and *ratushi*, already mentioned. There were also
oral (*slovesnye*) courts, established in 1727 with a simplified procedure
to speed up the handling of business litigation. They consisted of two
judges (*vybornye*), elected for one year by merchants, who sat together
with a burgomaster, received their instructions from the *magistrat*,
and reported to it at the end of their term. The peasants of the Imperial
family sued before their administrators; the former peasants of the
Church sued before their treasurers and were punished by them. Appeals went to the Chancery for Court Peasants (*Dvortsovaia Kantseliariia*) and to the College of Economy. State peasants came under
their elected officials (*starosty* and *sotskie*), but since there was no
central agency responsible for them their last resort was the provincial
voevoda or the governor. As for the serfs, they were at the mercy of
the bailiff and ultimately of their owner. In other words, except for
the oral courts, the judicial and the administrative structure were one.
The jurisdiction of this administrative personnel, however, was restricted to cases to which peasants or townsmen of the same class
(*soslovie*) were parties and those in which they were sued by outsiders.
If *they* sued outsiders, and in all felonies, the case went before the
voevoda.[12]

The administration of justice in Moscow and its gubernia presented
special problems. The city was the most populous in the Empire;
countless merchants, peddlers, and workmen made a living in the
largest market of the nation; and escaped prisoners could hope to find
there better than anywhere else the anonymity they needed. Since the

[11] PSZ, 1763, N. 11989, pt. 14-15; 1765, N. 12541; 1796, N. 17445; 1765, N.
12448, pt. 16; 1773, N. 14069; 1775, N. 14332.
[12] Got'e in *Sudebnaia Reforma*, 193-195, and Got'e, I, 390-391; Dmitriev, *Istoriia*,
494; PSZ, 1732, N. 6068, pt. 2, 13.

1730s there existed in the city a *Sudnyi Prikaz* with jurisdiction over anyone (*liudi vsiakogo china*) bringing suit in Moscow, whether or not he resided in the city; and a *Sysknoi Prikaz* for felons caught in Moscow. The gubernia chancery was freed of judicial administration since appeals against the decisions of the *prikazy* and those of the provincial and other voevodas were sent to the College of Justice and from it, if need be, to the Senate. In 1763 the *Sudnyi Prikaz* was divided into four departments under a "chief judge." The post was occupied by state councillor (class V) Afanasii Afrosimov from 1765 to 1782. Each department decided cases by unanimous vote, and the general assembly met only to discuss matters for which no law was found and on which members could not agree. It was not a very large agency of 12 members—3 per department—a procurator, 12 secretaries, 149 clerks, 25 guards and couriers, a total of 200 persons, larger than that of the College of Justice itself.[13]

The *Sysknoi Prikaz*, renamed Criminal Expedition (*rozysknaia ekspeditsiia*) in 1763, was a much smaller body, and it did not have the autonomy of the *Sudnyi Prikaz*. Its staff was included in the table of organization of the Moscow gubernia chancery, and consisted of only twenty-six persons. Its one member was court councillor (class VII) Sergei Davydov in the 1760s and Prince Nikolai Bariatinskii in the 1770s. It investigated, tried, and punished prisoners. The expedition was also the central transit prison for those banished to Orenburg and Siberia. Its jurisdiction was much enlarged in 1763, when voevodas were forbidden to apply torture without the approval of the governor. As a result, all felons caught in Moscow gubernia were referred to it. The situation in the northern capital was similar. A Criminal Expedition was created in the chancery of the Petersburg governor identical to that of Moscow and with the same kind of jurisdiction for the northern provinces. It was headed in the 1770s by college councillor Egor Naumov (1768-1778). Civil cases were tried, as in other gubernias, in the chancery and were appealed to the branch of the College of Justice, and then to the Second Department.[14]

The structure of the pre-reform judiciary, both central and local, remained tolerably efficient as long as the bulk of the population remained concentrated in the central region. The gradual extension of private landownership in the south and mid-Volga region generated

---

[13] Dmitriev, *Istoriia*, 464-465; PSZ, 1763, N. 11989, pt. 9, 11991, vol. 44^2, 65-66, 71.

[14] Lipinskii, 1-3; *S.-Peter. stolichn. politsiia*, 51, 285-286; PSZ, 1768, N. 13134; Gribovskii, *Materialy*, 1-3, 7-8, 11-12; for the Petersburg expedition, see PSZ, 1763, N. 11871, 11981, vol. 44^2, 69. A very full survey of the Moscow expedition's activities is in Lazovskii.

centrifugal tendencies which put pressure on the government to decentralize the administration of justice. The instructions (*nakazy*) sent
by the provincial nobles to the Legislative Commission are full of
complaints about the inadequacy of the judicial structure and about
the difficulty of obtaining redress in claims over property and inheritance. Their suggestions vary, but they agree in their assumption that
the provincial nobility should be given a large share in the administration of justice, both in order to facilitate access to judges by mul-
tiplying their number and to confer on local landowners the authority
to settle disputes with due regard for their interests. Indeed, the local
landowner was less favored at the time than the townsman, who could
turn to his *magistrat* and receive satisfaction within the patriarchal
structure of his class.

Some nobles leaned toward the establishment of separate courts.
Those of Ostrov uezd (Pskov province), for example, proposed a court
of two or three landowners to decide quickly land disputes and minor
offenses (*derevenskie obidy*). The judges would summon the respondent, examine the documents, and decide the case in all fairness (*po
spravedlivosti*). The emphasis on fairness and not on the law is characteristic. The desire for a court of landowners below the voevoda
reflected a desire for a private jurisdiction that could work out norms
embodying the common interest of the landowners. In misdemeanors
such as theft of grain or hay or house possessions and timber, the
subject caught red-handed or against whom there were strong suspi-
cions would be brought before these judges and if found guilty would
be flogged as an example to others and then released. In felonies this
court would examine only the facts and refer them with its opinion
to the voevoda. It would have a small staff with *sotskie* and *desiatskie*
serving as couriers.

Other nobles were less ambitious and leaned toward a mixed court.
Those of Voronezh wanted civil cases to begin at the provincial level
only. The nobility of the province would elect three judges for two
years who would form a "civil" (*sudnaia*) expedition" attached to the
voevoda's or the governor's chancery and would be called his assistants
(*tovarishchi*) with the equivalent salary. Those of Arzamas wanted a
"trustee" (*opekun*) elected for two years, but they too leaned toward
a mixed court. Small suits between landowners and their peasants
would be settled in it without the intervention of the voevoda. Dissatisfied parties could appeal to the full court with the voevoda. These
nobles would protect illiterate nobles, widows, and children, and the
serfs of absent landowners. If they performed well, they would receive
a recommendation from the nobility. As a kind of afterthought the
nobles suggested that voevoda and procurator might just as well be

abolished so that the administration of justice would be in the hands of persons delegated (*poverennye*) by the entire nobility.[15]

The reform went a long way to satisfy the interests of the land-owners. A new court was created in each uezd, consisting formally of a judge in class VIII and two assessors (*zasedateli*) in class IX. Uezd courts were established in all gubernias except Arkhangelsk. In two others (Olonets and Viatka) there was only one. Translating these ranks into military ranks gives us a better idea of the relationship between judge and assessors. In the Valdai court, opened in 1777, the judge was a lieutenant colonel, one assessor was a captain, and the other was a second lieutenant. This court combined civil and criminal jurisdiction. When matters concerning widows and minors were brought before it, the uezd marshal took part in the proceedings and the uezd court became a trusteeship court (*opeka*).

Judges and assessors were elected for three years by the gubernia assembly of the nobility and confirmed by the governor. The court was maintained by the state budget. The judge received 300 rubles, each assessor 250, and a secretary in class XIV 200. The clerks were all appointed by the gubernia board. We know, for example, that the son of a merchant, Stoliarov, submitted in 1790 an application to the Novgorod board for the post of copyist in the Valdai uezd court. He included four recommendations and a certificate from the Valdai public school that he had entered the school in 1787, knew how to read and write (*pravopisanie*), had been reasonably good in arithmetic, and knew his catechism (*zakon*). He was of good conduct and under article 62 of the statute of public schools he deserved to be given preference over other candidates. He was accepted.[16]

What kind of people were the judges and assessors? Opinions vary. P. Arsen'ev, for example, formerly a land captain, uezd judge in Novyi Oskol in 1788, had property in this and other uezds of Kursk gubernia, and was praised for his integrity. At the other extreme, the previously mentioned Spassk land captain of Tambov gubernia, who had been forced to retire for committing acts of violence against state peasants, was reelected by the nobility as uezd judge. And a manuscript satire ridiculed the nobility for passing over an educated and respected noble and electing an ignoramus and Mr. Deaf and Mr. Blind as assessors whom the secretary was sure to lead by the nose. Dubrovin tells us they were of two kinds, the ignorant ones and the connoisseurs (*doki*). The former served for a single term and sought to carry out their duties

[15] SIRIO, XIV (1875), 279-281; LXVIII (1889), 359, 107-108.

[16] OL, art. 18-19, 51-52, 196, 420; 1796, N. 17494, vol. 44², 256; Grigor'ev, *Reforma*, 323; Pardalotskii, 776, 781-782, 787. For the *opeka*, see OL, art. 20-21, 209-211, 421, 220.

in good conscience, but since they did not know the law and had no code to guide them they only incurred the wrath of the landowners for trying to please everyone and ended up the prisoners of their secretaries. The others were the true politicians of the uezds. They knew how to guarantee their reelection and how to tip the scales toward the party that paid most. Even those secure in their uezds, however, had to remain on good terms with the gubernia board: it had the power to commit them to trial in the criminal chamber, to fine them for improper decisions, and to sequester their property for non-observance of procedural forms.[17] But to remain on good terms with the board was only an extension of the uezd politics at which these men were so successful.

The principle embodied in the creation of the uezd court—that the nobility as first estate, must have its own court—was extended to the other two social groups, the state peasants, including those of the Imperial family, and the townsmen. For these peasants, separate lower courts called *raspravy* were established in various uezds on recommendation of the governors general. In only five gubernias—Arkhangelsk and Olonets, whose population consisted largely of state peasants, and in Kazan, Viatka, and Simbirsk gubernias, which had, in addition, a large population of non-Russian nationalities—do we find a *rasprava* in each uezd, but some were present in each gubernia, even in that of Petersburg, which had only one. Each court consisted of a judge in class IX of higher, appointed by the gubernia board, and four assessors elected by the villages for three years; their election required the confirmation of the governor. There was no requirement that they be peasants: they could also be landowners or retired officials, and they were certainly local people. It met, like the uezd court, three times a year: from January 8 to Passion week; from Trinity Sunday to June 27; and from October 2 to December 18, or at other times with the approval of the governor.[18]

In the towns the new *magistrat*, like the old one, consisted of two burgomasters and four *ratmany*, elected in all gubernia capitals and uezd centers for three years by the assembly of townsmen. Confirmation by the governor was implied. The burgomaster was in class XI or XII (in uezd centers) and the *ratmany* were one class below. These ranks permit us to see the place of these courts in the judicial hierarchy, which reflected the internal hierarchy of Russian society. The uezd court, the lower *rasprava*, and the *magistrat* were on an

[17] "Sumerechnye raskazy," "Razgovor," 489-490; Dubasov, 33, 36; Dubrovin, II (1899), 63-64.

[18] OL, art. 34-35, 52, 58, 74. For the background of the *raspravy*, see Pavlova-Sil'vanskaia, "Sozdanie."

equal footing as courts of first instance, but the uezd judge was in class VIII, the *raspravnyi* judge in class IX. The burgomasters obviously ranked much lower. The uezd judge was the highest elected official in the uezd, but the burgomasters were outranked by the sheriff, who was also in class VIII but was appointed by the Senate. Like the other courts, the *magistrat* was subordinated ultimately to the gubernia board.

Burgomasters and *ratmany* were also paid from the state budget but received less than other officials in similar classes; and the *magistrat* was the only one of the three courts that had no appointed secretary. It usually hired one, together with clerks, "at a high price" we are told in a decision of 1801; but these secretaries, who came from among the *raznochintsy*, were not allowed to seal (*krepit'*) the minutes and the extracts from decisions because they had not taken the civil service oath and thus could not be called to account for errors or mischief. Uezd centers also had an orphan court (*sirotskii sud*) to handle litigation affecting the widows and children of townsmen. It was the equivalent of the trusteeship court of the uezd, but its composition was somewhat different. Its chairman was the town head, and it consisted of two members of the *magistrat* and the town *starosta*. The oral courts were retained but were separated from the *magistrat* by replacing the burgomaster with a judge in class XIV elected for one year and apparently unpaid.[19]

THE NEW GUBERNIA JUDICIARY

The establishment of three trial courts to replace the jurisdiction of the voevoda necessitated the creation of an appellate court in the

---

[19] OL, art, 28-29, 54-57, 72, 279, 422; PSZ, 1781, N. 15202; 1796, N. 17494, vol. 44², 257; 1801, N. 19763. On the oral courts, see Dmitriev, *Istoriia*, 489-490; PSZ, 1754, N. 10222; 1831, N. 4281; 1766, N. 12721; OL, art. 26, 57, 72, 277.

The *nadvornye* courts provided the separate organization required by the motley population of the two capitals. Each consisted of a judge in class VIII and two assessors in class IX, all three appointed by the Senate. These courts were thus the only courts of first instance entirely appointed by the government. Their jurisdiction was left rather vague, and the reference in the Organic Law to the "capital of Her Majesty" seems to mean that only one was at first intended for the northern capital. A second was later created in Moscow and a third in Arkhangelsk. The court tried people who resided (*prebyvaiut*) in the city in the military, court, and civil service, and *raznochintsy* who did not have real property in Petersburg; in other words, people who did not fit into the new structure of courts organized along class lines. See OL, art. 472-489; Dmitriev, *Istoriia*, 529. For Petersburg see PSZ, 1780, N. 15035; 1783, N. 15650 and 15652; 1796, N. 17428; and the case of the pastry-cook apprentice of the Court and a soldier of the Preobrazhenskii regiment in 1795, N. 17387; for Moscow, see 1785, N. 16272; for Arkhangelsk, 1784, N. 16059.

gubernia capital. In addition, three intermediate courts were created between the gubernia and the uezd. They operated in the gubernia capital, and, although their purpose seems clear, there is some confusion as to their origin.[20]

The first was the upper land court (*verkhnyi zemskii sud*), consisting of two departments, one criminal and one civil. Each department had a chairman in class VI appointed by the Empress from two candidates submitted by the Senate, and five assessors in class VII elected for three years. There was also a procurator and two *striapchie*. The court met in the usual three sessions, but two members of each department were required to remain available between sessions to accept requests and cases. They had no authority to decide cases.

This court fulfilled at least two functions. It received appeals against the decisions of the uezd courts, the trusteeship courts, and the lower land courts. Its jurisdiction included "complaints of noble against noble, civil and criminal cases concerning estates (*votchiny*), privileges of nobility, wills, rights of inheritance, doubtful possession, *bezchest'e*," and the so-called *dela do prava striapchikh kasaiushchiesia*, i.e., suits brought by the procuracy on behalf of the government.[21] In this mostly judicial capacity, however, the upper land court was not truly a court but a sort of jury.

It may seem incongruous at first glance to detect such an institution in the Russian provincial judiciary of the 1780s. But if a jury permits a man to be tried by his peers and if we accept its definition as "a certain number of men, selected according to law and *sworn* to inquire of certain matters of fact, and to declare the truth upon evidence to be laid before them,"[22] then this "court" was a jury, even if it did not sit with a judge. And this is all the more true since in serious criminal cases—most likely in civil cases as well—the upper land court did not decide a case but "examined the circumstances," passed sentence but then referred the case to the criminal chamber for "decision." Indeed, the very concept of jury was inherent to the organization of the judiciary along class lines. There is an interesting comment in one of the *nakazy* to the Legislative Commission, which may have served as a model for the upper land court. If one of the parties was dissatisfied with the decision of the judges elected by the nobility in the uezd, he should state his objection to them and they would gather several nobles from the uezd to decide whether the case was decided fairly. If they found against the judges, they would send their finding to the agency

[20] Grigor'ev, *Reforma*, 237-238; Dmitriev, *Istoriia*, 527.
[21] OL, art. 13-14, 49-50, 60, 65, 112, 166-173; PSZ, 1796, N. 17494, vol. 44², 255.
[22] Black's Law *Dictionary*, St. Paul, Minn., rev. ed., 1968, 993-994.

having jurisdiction over them, meaning, in the context of the 1760s, the voevoda or the governor.[23] Thus the idea of a body of elected nobles accepting evidence and passing advisory judgment, which they then referred to a regular court for final decision, was in the air, and the upper land court was not simply an unwanted court left over from an abandoned plan, but had a positive role to fulfill.

A second purpose of the land court was to serve as an administrative agency for the gubernia nobility. Service matters seem to have gone through it. When a Tambov nobleman pleaded illness to account for his failure to join a delegation sent to meet the Empress on her way to the Crimea in 1787, the gubernia board had him investigated by the land captain, who rejected his explanation. Thereupon the nobleman filed for retirement with the upper land court, and the request was passed on to the board. Perhaps these courts also served as local bodies for the Heraldry, helping it to keep track of appointments and retirement in the elective service of the gubernia. In general, the court seems to have been looked upon as the corporate representative of the nobility in the gubernia, a role which paralleled that of the marshal. After an uprising of peasants on the estates of Count Apraksin in Pskov gubernia in 1776, the Empress ordered Governor General Sievers to conduct an investigation and advised him that if excessive taxation by the count was the cause of the revolt the upper land court must appoint a trustee over his property. In 1795 we find the upper land court of Petersburg examining jointly with the gubernia *magistrat* reports that distilleries had been illegally established in the city itself.[24] In this capacity the court acted as an advisory body to the gubernia board in matters concerning the nobility.

Similar courts were created for the townsmen and state peasants, the gubernia *magistrat* and the upper *rasprava*; they too were supported by state funds. Their chairmen were in class VII, appointed not by the Empress but by the Senate on recommendation of the gubernia board; the assessors were elected by townsmen of the gubernia capitals or by the villages of state peasants forming the jurisdiction of the court. Each of these intermediate courts had the usual complement of one procurator and two *striapchie*.[25]

[23] *SIRIO*, XIV (1875), 279-281. The model for the upper land court, however, was probably the Oberlandgericht of Estland: Pavlova-Sil'vanskaia, "Uchrezhdenie," 309; see also Jones, *Emancipation*, 228.

[24] Salias, 115-116, *SIRIO*, XXVII (1880), 122; PSZ, 1795, N. 17367.

[25] OL, art. 32-33, 36-37, 50, 53, 58, 62, 66, 73, 75, 309-314, 353-359, 417, 433-434, 449-465; PSZ, 1794, N. 17494, vol. 44², 225; 1795, N. 16188, art. 176. See TsGVIA, f. 44, d. 50, II, fol. 186-193, for a case where the lower and upper *rasprava* falsified a document in order to let a local nobleman enserf a village of Cossacks.

This new gubernia judiciary was capped by a criminal and a civil chamber. Each consisted of a chairman in class V appointed by the Empress from two candidates submitted by the Senate, two councillors in class VI, and two assessors in class VIII chosen by the Senate, and a secretary in class XI. The two chambers were closely integrated with the gubernia board that appointed and assigned the clerks, granted leave to the members, and recommended for promotion and other rewards. They were not truly independent courts but committees of the gubernia administration to which, in accordance with the principle of division of labor, litigation and criminal cases were submitted for consideration and disposal, subject to the review of the governor.

Two peculiarities of these courts should be noted. Each chamber was considered to be the equivalent of a department of the Colleges of Justice and Landed Estates whose functions were now deconcentrated at the gubernia level. They received cases from the intermediate courts, and their decisions were appealed directly to the departments of the Senate in Moscow and Petersburg. They were thus more responsive to proddings to operate more expeditiously and to pressures by the landed nobility to protect its interests against those of other social groups. The other peculiarity of the chambers was that none of their members was elected, as if to serve notice that final decisions at the gubernia level must be made by officials belonging to the core of the ruling class and responsible to its leadership.

This, however, in no way invalidates the contention that these men also belonged to well-established families in the provinces, with their own interests to defend. Most of the 154 chairmen of judicial chambers in the twenty-six central gubernias between 1775 and 1796 were former provincial voevodas, governors' deputies or councillors of gubernia boards, gubernia or central procurators, and officials of various central agencies. More than half (81) stayed fewer than three years, but the figure is misleading because it includes appointments made during the great shakeup of 1793 and 1794, most of which were terminated by the death of the Empress in 1796. But the long tenures of the others are very significant and illustrate the influential role played by powerful families in the life of their gubernias. About forty-four served seven years or more, including five who served thirteen years and two who served seventeen years in the same gubernia. Vasilii Chicherin, who had been provincial voevoda in Pereslavl-Zalesskii (Vladimir gubernia), became chairman of the Vladimir civil chamber in 1778 and then served seventeen years in the Tambov civil chamber. We know that the Chicherin family was extremely influential in Tambov gubernia, as Governor Derzhavin found out to his sorrow. Andrei Saburov, the chairman of the criminal chamber, remained in his post eleven years. Alexei Vorontsov culminated his unusually long tenure as voevoda in Vladimir with the chairmanship of the civil chamber. The Urusovs were strongly represented in Vologda gubernia, and the Khrapovitskiis gave several uezd marshals and a gubernia marshal in Smolensk gubernia. There was even a tendency to elect a chairman gubernia marshal, but it was forbidden to combine the two posts at the same time.[26] Since the ten members of the judicial chambers were all hereditary nobles and most certainly owned property in a gubernia and there were no representatives of the towns and state peasants, the gubernia court structure was controlled by a small committee of influential nobles who administered justice in the interests not only of their class but also of the dominant families of the gubernia.

There was another new court, one that did not quite fit in with the chambers or the other courts. It was the court of equity (*sovestnyi sud*), consisting of a judge in class VI chosen by the governor general from a list of candidates selected by "each judicial agency of the gubernia," by which was probably meant the two judicial chambers and the three intermediate courts. When the court took up cases brought by nobles or townsmen or state peasants, the judge sat with two noble assessors in class VII or two assessors from the towns in class X or two peasant assessors with the usual immunity from corporal punishment without trial. These assessors, like those of the other courts, were elected for three years and were confirmed by the governor. The selection of the judge in the two capitals seems to have required the confirmation of the Empress.

This court combined the functions of an arbitration court in civil cases and those of a humanitarian court for juveniles and the insane. It was instructed not to apply the law in all its severity—therefore it had no procurator—but to exercise restraint, show compassion and understanding. The court referred its decisions to the governor, who forwarded them to the Empress. A higher (*vysshii*) court of equity was planned but was never established, and gradually the decisions of the

[26] Based on Turkestanov; Salias, 608, refers to the two Chicherins as chairmen of the two chambers, but Turkestanov lists only one Chicherin as chairman; same in *Mesiatseslov*. Dolgorukov, "Zapiski," mentions the Vrasskiis in Penza gubernia (1914, N. 2-3), where the best known family of landowners were the Kurakins; see also PSZ, 1784, N. 15913. It is true that not all chairmen and assessors were landowners and that many officials were very poor, like the assessor of the Olonets civil chamber—hardly a good case, perhaps—who was growing blind at age 63 and asked to be retired on half his salary because he had five small daughters and no place to go. But was not the contrast between the power to decide many local cases and poverty a powerful incentive to try to join the local nobility, who, however poor, still had a place to retire and a fairly secure source of basic necessities? See TsGADA, f. 16, d. 804, II, fol. 80-81 and 92-96, 119 (for chairman Arends).

gubernia courts were sent to the Second Department. The court of
equity was severely criticized by Ivan Lopukhin, former chairman of
the Moscow criminal chamber, and himself elected judge in Moscow
in 1802. It could not truly function as a humanitarian court because
there was not enough human empathy (*pronitsatel'nost'*) in the highly
conservative Russia of his day, and a discriminating understanding of
various degrees of guilt was still limited to the few who had judicial
experience or training. As an arbitration court it was useless since
litigants could also resort to private arbitration, and it was abused by
dishonest parties. Whatever its faults, the court of equity was an interesting experiment that recognized the importance of customary law
in a system where the exclusive validity of statute law was repeatedly
emphasized.[27]

The judicial reform reached completion when the colleges, which
had become superfluous, were closed. The new courts opened in Petersburg in May 1780, in Moscow in October 1782, and the central
agencies ceased receiving new cases. Civil appeals against the decisions
of the gubernia chanceries were referred to the civil chambers, and
criminal cases not yet decided by the governor went to the criminal
chambers. The Criminal Expeditions were immediately closed. The
Petersburg branches of the Colleges of Justice and Landed Estates were
ordered in October 1780 to close within a year, but this remained a
pious wish; both were not closed until 1783, and the branch of the
Central *Magistrat* remained open until 1785. In Moscow the *Sudnyi
Prikaz* and the Central *Magistrat* ceased operations some time in 1784,
the College of Justice in July 1786. In October 1785 it was decided
to separate the archive of the College of Landed Estates from the
college itself, to terminate all outstanding claims as soon as possible,
and the college closed in January 1786. Three members were made
responsible for the archive. It was in such poor condition that an
enormous amount of work still had to be done to establish reliable
records, copies of which would be sent on request to the civil chambers
in the gubernias. Its staff consisted of 3 secretaries, 136 clerks, and
19 guards, a total of 158 persons at the cost of 21,236 rubles a year.[28]

Some of the conclusions made in preceding chapters are even more
relevant here. The judicial reform in its organizational aspect was an
extremely far-reaching division of the spoils. In each uezd center where

[27] OL, art. 40-41, 49-50, 53, 58, 63, 65, 73, 395-401, 430; Bantysh-Kamenskii, I
(1836), 350; RBS, XVI (1913), 149; "Zapiski Vinskago," 194; Grigor'ev, 246-251;
Korkunov, "Proekt," 135-138; Lopukhin, Zapiski, 141-144.

[28] PSZ, 1780, N. 15056, 15074; 1782, N. 15347, 15530; 1783, N. 15660; 1784,
N. 16110; 1785, N. 16222, 16273; 1786, N. 16307, 16419; 1787, N. 16555. The
Central *Magistrat* itself was closed earlier in 1782: Ditiatin, 389-390.

there had been a single voevoda—let us assume that his deputy took care of other, non-judicial, matters—there were now two judges and six assessors, and this in 321 uezds of central Russia instead of the 177 in existence before the reform. The provincial voevoda disappeared, but intermediate courts were created, consisting of six judges (chairmen) and twenty-six assessors. A single governor's deputy in ten gubernia capitals who perhaps had responsibility for judicial administration had been replaced by two chambers of ten judges and assessors in twenty-six gubernia capitals. Thus in central Russia alone the size of the judicial personnel rose from approximately 217 to 4,060, including the personnel of the courts of equity. Almost 1,986 of these were noblemen, most of them local landowners elected in their gubernias, since the membership of the twenty-six judicial chambers did not exceed 260 officials. The new rural and urban judges, who must have been in most cases former officers demobilized after the Turkish war, were not truly officials, even if they were all listed in the *Mesiatseslovy*. They received a salary from the state treasury, but most served for only a few months of the year, were elected for only three years, and were not transferable from one gubernia to another. The offices which they—except the peasant assessors—filled were classified in accordance with the Table of Ranks, but the rank of the office attached to the holder only so long as he served in it (*za uriad*), and promotions do not seem to have taken place within this provincial "civil service," except perhaps as a special favor.[29] These new judges were the true delegates of their communities; their sense of justice was perforce colored by their class interests. The hierarchy of the intermediate courts and the association of noblemen and townmen in the upper *magistrat* and with state peasants on the upper *rasprava* reflected the social hierarchy, and the exclusively noble membership of the chambers guaranteed that the interests of the nobility would be protected in the final disposition of cases.

The anti-bureaucratic thrust of the reform is nowhere more evident than here. A vast central apparatus of more than five hundred officials and clerks was dismantled, and although many were retained to run the archives of the former colleges, most clerks were dispersed among the gubernia capitals and uezd centers and must have been reluctant to go if they equated their transfer with a demotion. While the landless nobles were given a chance to acquire an estate in their new assignment, it is likely that these disgruntled clerks formed one of the pressure

[29] Tim uezd judge Shumakov asked Governor General Prozorovskii for a promotion (*dacha china*) after serving his three years. Procurator Stromilov reported to Prince Viazemskii that there was no law on this: TsGADA, f. 248, d. 6560, I, fol. 48-49.

groups pushing for the restoration of the colleges at the end of the reign. An unwieldy mechanism incapable of providing the services most needed by the rank-and-file nobility was replaced by twenty-six provincial court systems more responsive to local pressures. Thus the reform represented a partial decentralization because it shifted the decision of a vast number of cases from appointed officials to elected representatives, and a significant deconcentration from the center to the provinces.

As a result of the reform the division between civil litigation and criminal cases became a more modern one than the old division between the jurisdiction of the two colleges. The notarization of wills, the registration of deeds, and all trusteeship cases were removed from the jurisdiction of the College of Justice to the civil chambers, and the trial of officials for crimes committed in the exercise of their duties was made to begin in the criminal chambers. The deconcentration was felt more strongly in litigation bearing upon landed property. Copies of survey books, old and new, were deposited in the civil chambers, and additional documentation, including genealogies, could now be obtained from the archive of the College of Landed Estates. All litigation over landed properties and land survey had to begin in the uezd courts or the chamber—when the court was not in session. Orders granting title to land (*otkazy*) previously issued by the college now came from the uezd courts. Appeals from the provincial *magistrat* which used to go to Moscow were now lodged in the civil chamber of each gubernia capital.[30] The benefits of such a deconcentration become even more obvious if we take into consideration the geographical aspect. Kursk was 541 km from Moscow, and the distance from Tambov was 502 km, from Kazan 871 km, and from Saratov 954 km. After the reform, interminable trips to Moscow, let alone Petersburg, were no longer necessary in the vast majority of cases since uezd centers were often within a 100-km radius of the gubernia capitals. Even more than the reform of the police, the judicial reform helped create an environment which reduced the level of violence and naked extortion among members of each social group by producing an adequate framework to settle differences. In social terms, the reform represented an extensive territorial redistribution of the elite, and within each gubernia it brought about a formalization of control by the landed nobility over the fate of townsmen and state peasants.

The reform indeed recreated in the provincial administration the military hierarchy with which the elite always had been familiar: lieu-

[30] OL, art. 173, 197, 199; PSZ, 1775, N. 14400; 1778, N. 14829; 1784, N. 16098, 16110; 1786, N. 16307.

tenant generals as governors general, major generals as governors, colonels in the upper land court, majors in the uezd courts, and captains in the land courts. It retained the hierarchy of the ruling class and preserved its unity. If Potemkin, now the leading figure in the dispensing of military patronage, was probably the guiding force behind the creation of governors general, the Procurator General's authority in matters of civilian patronage emerged considerably broadened in the 1780s. In this sense, the reform was a political compact between the two most powerful leaders of the Empire between 1775 and 1792.

In another sense, the judicial reform, even more than that of the police, was a social compact between the nobility, on the one hand, and the merchants and state peasants, on the other. It formalized the hierarchical relationship until then taken for granted and strengthened the hands of the nobility by giving it at the gubernia level the final say in most matters affecting the socially dependent classes. In return for such recognition, their representatives were associated with those of the nobility in the decision of cases to which either merchants or peasants were a party. At the same time, this new relationship contained the seeds of conflict, because the recognition of the nobility's leadership in the judicial system tended to legitimize its exploitative policies, a conflict which in the long run would destroy the credibility of the pre-reform judiciary.

JUDICIAL PROCEDURE

IN THE LOWER COURTS

Judicial procedure is the heart of any judicial system, for it provides the very methods by which grievances are redressed. If the ends are often clear, the means to reach them are not, because their value is the source of inevitable disagreements and reflects the perennial dispute over the meaning of "justice." If we agree with Richard Wortman that the tsarist state "held the judicial function in disdain,"[1] and sympathize with the many noblemen who complained to the Legislative Commission about the difficulties of obtaining satisfaction, certain general causes must be found to explain such an attitude, causes going beyond those common to other European states, where the accretion of precedents over the centuries had also created considerable chaos by the middle of the eighteenth century.

Rational and binding rules of social and political behavior, of which procedural rules are but a subspecies, are the product of a compromise between contending groups, of a modus vivendi recognizing the equality of the contenders, the autonomy of their internal constitution, and the mutual danger inherent in the destruction of the compromise. Russian society was a command structure in which the dominant principle at all levels, reinforced by Orthodox teaching, was submission and unity, i.e., the very denial of the autonomy and conflict conducive to the establishment of legal rules. The result, paradoxical perhaps at first glance, was a society closely approaching the Hobbesian model of a war of every man upon every man, in which order was maintained, for order there must be in any society, by forcing the weaker to submit and to recognize their submission. In return, considerable mobility was accepted within the ruling class, in which the weak of one day might very well become the strong of the next, and vice versa, a situation typical of a non-bureaucratic society "lacking the concept of law in the sense of relatively stable impersonal and nonpolitical norms and procedures."[2] Thus, a permanent but diffuse upward and downward dynamism animated the ruling class, fostering a respect for the strong rather than for the law and accepting degra-

[1] Wortman, 3.
[2] Bendix, "Bureaucracy," in IESS, II, 212.

dation rather than protection in the name of abstract rules. Such an attitude among members of the nobility was considerably reinforced in their relationships with the socially dependent groups. Therefore, it was a natural and pervasive assumption at all levels of Russia's vertically integrated society that recourse was to be found not in the law but in persons, and that procedures were merely designed to protect the hegemony of the strong.

The first stage in judicial procedure was the filing of a complaint (*proshenie, chelobitnaia*) with the voevoda, who did not necessarily welcome new litigation because it was standard practice to fine him if his judgment was overturned. Plaintiffs were required to pay a fee of three rubles (raised to six rubles in 1794), irrespective of the value and nature of the suit, be it for trespassing of cattle, seizure of land or woodland, illegal cutting of timber, theft of grain or hay or a pair of peasant *lapti*, personal insults, refusal to pay a debt, etc. Such complaints were called *iskovye chelobitnye*.[3]

Once the complaint had been accepted, the next stage was to summon the respondent before the voevoda. This second step was the most difficult, and this was generally recognized at the time. Respondents might be far away in the service, strong enough to refuse a summons from an old soldier of the *shtatnaia komanda*, or clever enough to disappear in time. Some of the delegates to the Legislative Commission brought instruction from their electors demanding tougher measures against the harassment of summon servers and even the use of force against recalcitrant respondents, evidence enough of the chaos pervading the countryside.[4]

The third step was the examination of the evidence and the decision of the voevoda. The evidence, the counter-claims of the respondent, and all documentation were attached to the separate paragraphs (*punkty*) into which the original complaint was divided. When both parties were satisfied with the presentation of their case, they signed (*ruki prikladyvat'*) each separate paragraph. Then an abstract (*vypiska, ekstrakt*) was made from the original proceedings, which could cover hundreds, even thousands, of pages, and it was read to the litigants, who stated their objections to bias or lack of clarity, requested cor-

---

[3] B-va, 73-74; PSZ, 1763, N. 11988, pt. 6. On the paralyzing effect of the fear of fines, see TsGADA, f. 16, d. 334, fol. 20. Other complaints, of a non-judicial nature, were called *iavochnye chelobitnye*. The charge for these was only 25 kopecks, unless the request was for state money and affected *interesnye dela*. There was no charge for these, and they were written on simple paper; PSZ, 1764, N. 12210 and 1763, N. 11988, pt. 6.

[4] PSZ, 1723, N. 4344, pt. 5-6; Fonliarliarskii in TsGADA, f. 16, d. 190, fol. 11-12. See also *SIRIO*, XIV (1875), 255, 260-261; LXVIII (1889), 355-356.

rections, and signed it. Finally, the secretary appended under each paragraph the relevant laws, and the voevoda, together with his deputy, decided each paragraph separately. Their decision was then announced to the litigants.[5]

No formal distinction existed at the time between civil and criminal procedure, and there has been some controversy over whether this outline applied equally to the trial of criminal cases.[6] To answer this question it seems best to divide criminal cases into three major categories. The first included crimes against the "first two points," i.e., attempts on the person of the ruler, insult to his person, treason, and rebellion (*bunt*). Such crimes were highly sensitive, and their prosecution was outside the law. Even the procedural ukase of 1723 (*o forme suda*),[7] which purported to establish rules of procedure for all civil and criminal cases, specifically exempted them from these rules. They belonged to the jurisdiction of the Secret Expedition. Their investigation was conducted in Moscow or Petersburg, torture was freely used, and the fate of the defendant was entirely in the hands of the Empress.

The second category included felonies under the general heading of *razboinye, tatinnye i ubiistvennye dela*: highway robbery, larceny, and murder. Each of these crimes carried the death penalty. Others, especially vagrancy and various forms of fraud, were punished by hard labor or banishment, with or without whipping. These crimes were prosecuted under the rules of inquisitorial procedure (*rozysk*), and we saw that there was in Moscow an "expedition" to handle them, separate from that (*Sudnyi Prikaz*) established for civil litigation.[8] The heart of inquisitorial procedure was the application of torture and the confession, proclaimed by the Military Articles of Peter the Great to be the best form of proof. The use of torture, however, was gradually restricted. In January 1763 uezd voevodas were first forbidden to apply it, and later that year the prohibition was extended to provincial voevodas. As a result, all criminals subject to torture were sent to the gubernia capitals, and its application was made to depend upon the authorization of the governor. In 1773 the Senate was ordered to send to the governors a copy of Catherine's Great Instruction (*Nakaz*), chapter X, articles 192-197. The *Nakaz* did not abolish torture, but only tried to show that it was useless. At any rate, it had a certain deterrent effect, so much so that in 1769 Governor Maslov found it

[5] *SIRIO*, XIV (1875), xv; PSZ, 1723, N. 4344, pt. 2-4, 8.

[6] See Peterson, 345-355.

[7] PSZ, 1723, N. 4344.

[8] Lipinskii, 42-47, 50-52; PSZ, 1763, N. 11750; 1764, N. 12227; 1767, N. 12941; Lopukhin, *Zapiski*, 69.

necessary to obtain the Empress's approval before ordering the torture of a serf girl accused of killing her landowner. The ambiguity, however, persisted, and in November 1774 Catherine ordered the Procurator General to explain to the governors that there was no difference— except in the Secret Expedition of course—between torture (*pytka*) and "forceful questioning" (*pristrastnye rasprosy*), and that all corporal violence (*istiazaniia*) must be stopped in pursuance with Chapter X. As a result, one must assume that, legally at least, torture was abolished on the eve of the reform. This was the opinion of Lopukhin, chairman of the Moscow criminal chamber, who claimed that this made Catherine's name immortal among the beneficiaries of mankind.[9] Yet, even without torture, procedure remained inquisitorial, assumed the guilt of the defendant, retained preventive detention, and insisted on a confession.

Finally, there were all the other offenses, which we can simply call misdemeanors. They included theft for small amounts, injuries suffered in scuffles, etc. Here a man had to sue a suspect before the voevoda to obtain redress and with the help of witnesses and material evidence seek to have the defendant declared liable for damages and subject to a fine or corporal punishment. These were the most common offenses, but the resort to "civil procedure" merely brought to the fore its failure to provide for redress against the strong and the well connected. It is true, however, that forms of civil procedure continued to intrude in the prosecution of felonies, and the conclusion must be that in practice at least no precise line of demarcation was recognized between a private suit and official prosecution, even in a murder case.[10]

The reform drastically altered judicial organization but made relatively few changes in procedural law. No equivalent of the Police Code or the several important statutes on financial procedures of 1781-1782 was ever published. The closing of the colleges, however, was in itself an important procedural reform; and several innovations broadened the use of conciliatory procedures, emphasized the importance of mitigating circumstances, and placed a ceiling upon the jurisdiction of courts at each level.

Resort to the court of equity in civil cases depended on the consent of both parties. If they could not reconcile their differences, the court asked each party to send mediators (*posredniki*) to examine the case

---

[9] PSZ, 1781, N. 15313; *S.-Peter. stol. politsiia*, 51; PSZ, 1779, N. 14870; Semevskii, "Volneniia," 199; Korolenko, 133-142; Lopukhin, *Zapiski*, 69. The classic criticism of torture is in Beccaria, ch. XII, 30-36. In retrospect, however, it is not certain that torture was abolished in the reign of Catherine: see Chichagov, 86 (editor's note); Levenstim, 57; Trefolev, "Razskazy," 314-324, 328.

[10] See for example PSZ, 1767, N. 12986.

together with the court. If these mediators could not agree, the court made the final proposal. If it was rejection, both parties were summoned and given a reasoned opinion (*primiritel'nye sposoby*). Its rejection ended the jurisdiction of the court. There were at least two flaws in this procedure. One was that a party, most likely the innocent one who shied away from prolonged litigation, could not force a clever and more resourceful opponent to accept conciliation. The other, very typical of Russian legislation in the light of our previous discussion, was that conciliation was not only a pre-judicial stage, but that resort could be made to it even after formal proceedings had begun. Thus an unscrupulous litigant would announce in the middle of formal proceedings that he was ready to settle out of court (*po miroliubiu*), follow all procedural steps before the court of equity, and at the last moment refuse to settle. The case would then return to the uezd court, the upper land court, or the civil chamber. The absence of fines to punish such abuses only encouraged the practice.[11]

A second innovation in civil procedure, probably the most important and the most durable borrowing from Baltic court procedures, was to restrict the jurisdiction of the lower courts to suits of a certain value and to impose a ten-year limitation (*davnost'*) in both civil and criminal cases. No appeals were allowed from the lower to the intermediate courts if the value of the suit was under twenty-five rubles.[12] It was the first time that the jurisdiction of a court was defined by the value of the claim it could entertain, and the effect was a tighter definition of the hierarchy of courts.

In criminal procedure three innovations are interesting. One was in the jurisdiction of the courts of equity. Article 399 of the Organic Law applied to crimes committed by the insane, minors, and witches because of "stupidity, fraud, and ignorance"; and those committed "out of some misfortune or as a result of some convergence of circumstances aggravating their punishments beyond the lawful measure." In other words, the article excluded three categories of individuals from the ordinary severity of the law and opened the way for the recognition of mitigating circumstances. Another provision—that prisoners should be kept in prison no more than three days and must be released on

---

[11] *SIRIO*, LXVIII (1889), 103-104. Perhaps that is the meaning of OL, art. 233, allowing a plaintiff to turn to the uezd court if he was not satisfied with the decision of the land captain, but not by way of appeal. See also OL, art 400; PSZ, 1778, N. 14829, pt. 8; "Zapiski Vinskago," 101-102; Lopukhin, *Zapiski*, 143-144; *RBS*, VII (1916), 510 (A. Zubov).

[12] PSZ, 1775, N. 14275, pt. 41 and 44; 1787, N. 16551, pt. 4. But deeds of purchase made public by the *magistrat* or the uezd court could not be challenged after two years: OL, art. 290. On the 25-ruble limit, see art. 201.

order of the court until the case was tried—has been compared with the habeas corpus only to be ridiculed as out of step with Russian reality. But the division of criminal violations into three large categories helps us again place this provision in its proper perspective. Article 401 stated specifically that it did not extend to state crimes and felonies. Thus, it is not so unrealistic to assume that the court of equity could play a valuable role in protecting the small offender against the full force of the penal law, inasmuch as it was also an important responsibility of the procuracy to correct the abuses committed by the widespread use of preventive detention. The point, of course, is that the jurisdiction of this court can have been effective only in the gubernia capital, since it is difficult to imagine that a man who had stolen a hat would be brought up from an uezd center merely for the purpose of being released from jail.[13]

In a third innovation, the criminal jurisdiction of the lower courts was defined negatively as all crimes for which the penalty was neither death, nor public whipping (*torgovaia kazn'*), nor infamy (*lishenie chesti*),[14] and thus restricted to misdemeanors. The term *torgovaia kazn'* originally meant the knout, but it was enlarged to include whipping in 1775, so that the jurisdiction of the new courts was narrower than it would have been otherwise. Similarly, the important ukase of April 1781 broke up the old felony of larceny (*vorovstvo* or *tat'ba*) into three categories and provided penalties for first offenders and recidivists. Larceny up to three times if the items stolen each time were valued at less than twenty rubles was no longer a felony but was punished by detention in the workhouse by decision of the land court or the police board. No appeals were allowed.[15] In other cases lower courts completed the investigation, cited the relevant laws, and forwarded the case to the appropriate intermediate court.

APPELLATE PROCEDURE

The efficiency of an appellate structure depends on the existence of a hierarchy of courts with jurisdiction clearly defined at each level, on procedures distinguishing sharply those of the first instance from those of the appellate court, on precise deadlines for appealing lower-court decisions, and on penalties for failure to observe them. The lack of

[13] OL, art. 395, 399, 401; "Zapiski Vinskago," 101; Lopukhin, *Zapiski*, 142-143; Tarasov, II, 396; for the two cases, see PSZ, 1776, N. 14539, 1780, N. 15000.

[14] Infamy referred to the loss of social status, of membership in a legally recognized social class, like the nobility or the merchants.

[15] PSZ, 1775, N. 14275, pt. 2; 1781, N. 15147; OL, art. 110-111; Police Code, art. 70.

all four attributes in the pre-reform "judiciary," hardly worthy of the name since separate local courts did not exist, was the major reason for the confusion and delays which marred the operation of the system.

The ukase of July 1762 was an important attempt to establish appeal deadlines. Until then the practice had been to send a petition stating the intention to appeal and then to await the authorization of the college to send up the case. Now, upon receipt of the voevoda's or the governor's decision, both parties were to state in writing within a week whether they intended to appeal. If they did, the voevoda, automatically and without any charge for stamp paper, had to send the case within ten days to the college, where it remained sealed until a petition was received from either party. If none was received within a year, the case was returned for execution of the voevoda's decision. In 1763 a fee of six rubles was imposed on the appellant when he filed his notice of appeal. As no limit was yet placed on the value of suits subject to appeal, the new fee was an attempt to discourage those who appealed without cause. It also placed a heavy burden upon those who felt they had not received their due before the voevoda. At any rate, it forced litigants to think twice before turning to a higher instance unless the suit was of such value that the fee was a nominal one.[16]

Fees and fines were two sides of the same attempt to regulate the number of appeals. Procedural fines imposed on judges for erroneous judgments and delays are found in the General'nyi Reglament of 1720, the procedural ukase of 1723, and the ukase of July 1766. It is quite possible that these fines were not rigidly enforced, at least until after the governors and voevodas were given a regular salary in 1763, because we find many references in the nakazy to the need to enforce the legislation and even to impose effective penalties on judges whose decisions were so flawed that they needed to be appealed. A consequence of the fear of fines, however, may have been that the voevodas sought less to apply the law as they were required to do than to conciliate the claims of the two parties so that neither would appeal.[17] But appeals resulted not only from the erroneous judgment of the voevodas. In order to dampen the ardor of malicious litigants (iabedniki) who appealed for the sake of it, it was proposed that the appellant be fined if the higher court decided against him.

More was needed to improve the appellate process, which remained encumbered by the traditional absence of training in logical discourse

---

[16] PSZ, 1762, N. 11629; 1763, N. 11988; 1764, N. 12298.

[17] See for example SIRIO, LXVIII (1889), 356. On fines, see below. This is what led Got'e to call the court of the governor and voevoda "mirovoi sud": 390-391.

and of a rational distinction between the examination of evidence in the lower courts and the review of their decisions. Appellants, for example, were allowed to bring new evidence before the higher court so that the latter functioned both as a court of appeal over the case received from a lower court and as court of first instance over the new evidence which had to be investigated, documented, presented to the other party, etc. A case was not looked upon as a whole, and it happened that only some parts of it would be appealed while others were not. No doubt there must have been cases received in the colleges that were so disfigured that the determination of what exactly was at stake was extremely difficult and time-consuming. Even if additional evidence had been barred from the higher instance, the very meaning of appellate review was not clearly defined. All official agencies were required to enforce the words of the law and were forbidden to interpret its meaning. If any agency could not find the law or had doubts (*somnitel'stva*)—and who would not in such a system?—it was required to forward the case to a higher instance. Thus, whenever a case exhibited some complexity, no final decision (*reshitel'noe opredelenie*) was possible, and the case then moved in purely formal fashion all the way to the Senate. The most likely bottlenecks were the two judicial colleges, to which cases converged from all over the Empire, except from some borderlands.

In criminal cases procedures were simpler. In accordance with the Instruction of 1728, governors were empowered to confirm death sentences, excepting those over noblemen, which required Imperial confirmation. After 1753 this enormous power was considerably restricted when the confirmation of the death penalty became the exclusive prerogative of the ruler. All such sentences were forwarded by the governor to the Senate, and further action was suspended until final decision there. The provincial voevoda and the governor in his province remained, however, the final judges in all but a few other criminal cases. Appeals were not allowed, and the only recourse was a petition to the College of Justice for review on grounds of violation of the law.

After the reform, appeals to the intermediate courts were limited to suits valued at between 25 and 100 rubles, and the appellant had to leave 25 rubles with the lower court and state that he truthfully thought that his appeal was justified (*chto on pravoe delo imeet*). If the intermediate court upheld his claim, the deposit was returned; if it decided against the appellant, the money was deposited with the Board of Welfare, which paid interest that could be used by the lower court "at discretion." In other words, the deposit turned into a fine. In addition, the old fee of 6 rubles was retained—it was raised to 12 rubles in

1794—so that an appellant whose claim was valued at 30 rubles had to take a chance that he might lose 31. These deposits were clearly intended to discourage the appellant if the value of his suit was not far above the minimum or if he appealed without cause. The Organic Law, however, sought to leave the door open to poor litigants by waiving the requirement for a deposit if they took an oath that they were indigent. Failure to announce the intention to appeal within one week of the lower court's decision rendered the decision final.[18]

Appeals to the civil chamber from any of the three intermediate courts followed similar rules. The appellant had to deposit 100 rubles, which also turned into a fine if the chamber decided against him, and he had to pay once again the fee of 6 rubles. The notice of intention to appeal had to be filed within a week, and the decision of the chamber was final if the value of the claim did not exceed 500 rubles.[19]

Russian law recognized two different procedures of reviewing criminal cases. As a rule, formal appeals (*appeliatsiia*) were not recognized, but a defendant was allowed to file a complaint (*zhaloba*) or request (*pros'ba*) asking for a review. The difference seems to have been that an appeal set into motion a series of procedural steps and the removal of the case to a higher court, while a complaint was accepted or rejected at discretion, was not necessarily followed by a review of the case in a higher court, and did not suspend the execution of the sentence. If the case remained in the lower court, an order would be sent to correct the procedural irregularities and to retry the case. After the reform, sentences to punishments less severe than death, infamy, or public whippings (*kazn'*) did not go higher than the criminal chamber. A ukase of May 1796, however, allowed defendants to file formal appeals called *otzyvy* in the Senate and required a deposit of 200 rubles.[20]

If the sentence was death, infamy, or public whipping, it was not carried out but was forwarded to the relevant intermediate court: such transfer was called *perenos* and was automatic. The defendant, already

---

[18] Grigor'ev, *Reforma*, 235, 244; OL, art. 200-202, 285-288, 341-343; PSZ, 1778, N. 14829, pt. 4. To say that the deposit turned into a fine seems justified from a comparison of articles 200, 285, 341, and articles 179, 321, and 365 of the Organic Law. The first three state that if the intermediate courts find that the appeal was lodged without any ground (*pravost'*) the 25 rubles remain with the court and are deposited to collect interest which may be used at the discretion of the lower court at the end of each year. The last three state that if the intermediate court finds the appellant filed his claim (*vchinal delo*) in the lower court without any ground it will impose a 25-ruble fine, which may be used to support the schools of the uezd. Two different things are seemingly involved here, but the six articles probably refer in fact to the same thing.

[19] OL, art. 174-178, 316-320, 360-364.

[20] SZ (*Svod Zakonov*) 1832, XV, art. 1074-1080; PSZ, 1796, N. 17465; 1802, N. 20561.

in custody since his arrest unless he had found bail (*poruki*), was sent with the case to the gubernia capital. The intermediate court had no authority to pass final judgment. It reviewed the circumstances of the case, could interrogate the defendant and include additional evidence, and it passed sentence (*prigovor*). Then, the case was sent with an abstract (*opisanie*) to the criminal chamber.[21]

The chamber, seen as the equivalent of a department of the College of Justice, had no more authority than the intermediate courts. It reviewed the investigation conducted by the land court, the proceedings in the lower and intermediate courts, confirmed or reduced the penalty suggested by these courts, and then referred the case to the governor or governor general, whose decision was final unless he disagreed with the chamber or unless the defendant was a nobleman or an official.[22] The prisoner was sent back to the place where he had committed his crime in order to be whipped and branded as an example to evildoers (*v strakh zlym*). If the sentence contained the usual double punishment of whipping followed by banishment to hard labor, he was then taken back to the gubernia capital to await transportation to Siberia or to a fortress.

THE APPELLATE JURISDICTION
OF THE SENATE

Litigants turned to the judicial departments of the Senate with either formal appeals to review the decisions of colleges, voevodas, or governors before the reform, of judicial chambers thereafter, or with complaints against delays in the lower courts. In the latter case it was the responsibility of the *General Reketmeister*'s office to pass judgment on the validity of the complaints before they could be considered by a department. Two examples will illustrate his activity. In 1775, a clerk, Ivan Smirnov, sentenced in 1769 by the Astrakhan *magistrat* to whipping with the knout, appealed the refusal of the Central *Magistrat* to review the decision and release him from detention. The *Magistrat*

---

[21] OL, art. 111-112, 180, 322, 366; PSZ, 1782, N. 15539.

[22] OL, art. 106-108, 110-113; PSZ, 1795, N. 17387; 1789, N. 16763; 1799, N. 18933. Crimes committed by officials followed a separate procedure. Officials were sent to the criminal chamber for investigation and trial by order of the governor or governor general, who also confirmed the verdict of the chamber in last instance unless he disagreed with it. Objections were made that this procedure placed officials at a disadvantage vis-à-vis other criminals whose case was reviewed twice in the intermediate court and the chamber. After 1784 *all* sentences to death, infamy, and public whipping, even if the criminal had no rank and was not a nobleman, had to be forwarded to the Senate. Lesser sentences were confirmed by the governor in last instance: PSZ, 1784, N. 16022.

was requested to explain why this was not done. In 1785 the widow
of an Orel merchant asked that her case be heard by the Senate and
that the execution of the decision of the civil chamber be suspended.
This was refused on the ground that the Senate had no jurisdiction
and that the petition contained offensive language and errors of form.
The petition was returned, together with the six rubles. (In 1795 the
petition of four *odnodvortsy* of Kursk was rejected on similar grounds).[23]

Once a case reached a department, the procedures described in
Chapter I were followed. The case was placed on the agenda by the
senior secretary, and a day was appointed for its presentation. An
abstract of the entire case was prepared by the chancery of the department. This was the crucial document on which the senators would
base their decision. It should contain all the key elements of the case,
the dates on which it was decided by a governor or a college, the
decision of these agencies, supporting documents (*spravki*), and the
relevant laws. This was no easy task at a time when legal terminology
was still so imprecise and quotations were often inaccurate paraphrases
of unclear passages. The need for exact documents was very real since
they constituted most of the material evidence. As late as 1775 senior
procurator Volkonskii complained that genealogies sent by the College
of Landed Estates did not contain references to deceased members of
the family and were thus useless in the decision of inheritance cases.
Such cases had to be returned to the college for corrections (*vypravki*),
a practice causing endless delays,[24] and showed how the work of the
Senate was hampered by the inadequate education of officials serving
in subordinate agencies.

The litigants were then summoned to read and sign the abstract.
The appellant appeared in person or was represented by his counsel
(*poverennyi*), and the college whose decision was appealed was represented by one of its members. If a party did not appear and his
opponent requested a decision, an announcement was published three
times in the newspapers at intervals of two weeks, summoning the
delinquent to appear. If he did not appear within five months of the
last announcement, the case was brought up for decision without him.
The decision of the senators had to be unanimous and had to be
acceptable to the senior procurator. Otherwise it was referred to the
general assembly of the Petersburg or Moscow departments. The judgment of the department, however, was executed pending the final
decision of the general assembly, which might not come for months;
this could have strange consequences, as we learn from the ukase of

[23] PSZ, 1767, N. 12946; TsGADA, f. 393, d. 731, 1011, 1049.
[24] PSZ, 1767, N. 13030; 1775, N. 14246; *Ist. Prav. Senata*, II, 464-467.

1798. If a department's decision ordered the transfer of real property from one party to another, it happened, for instance, that the latter ruined, mortgaged, or sold it before the general assembly reversed the decision, and the original owner then found himself the loser. And, of course, if for the same reasons the general assembly could not make a final decision, the case was sent to the Empress by the Procurator General. No appeal to the Empress was allowed to the litigants. The decision of the department was returned to the college for execution either directly or through the local govenor or voevoda.[25]

The reform introduced few changes in the procedures of appeal to the Senate and virtually none in the internal procedures of the Senate. The colleges were abolished, and much of their jurisdiction was vested in the judicial chambers. Appeals to the Senate against the decisions of the civil chambers were forbidden unless the value of the claim exceeded 500 rubles. In such cases the appellant was required to leave 200 rubles with the chamber. As in the lower courts this deposit was returned to the appellant if he won his suit but turned into a fine if the Senate decided against him.[26] However, litigants were permitted to file a request (*proshenie*) with the governor general or the Senate, asking a review of the case on grounds of procedural irregularity. Such requests had no binding force and were accepted or rejected at discretion.

The scope of the Senate's jurisdiction over criminal cases remained much narrower. These cases could reach the Senate in three ways. Some were death sentences imposed by the governors, the *Sysknoi Prikaz*, and the College of Justice, which after 1753 required the confirmation of the Empress on the recommendation of the Senate. With the de-facto replacement of the death penalty by hard labor and whipping with the knout, however, most sentences no longer required senatorial confirmation. The only exceptions were sentences passed on noblemen, clergy, and converts to Orthodoxy sentenced for felonies, and cases in which the death sentence was mandatory, such as crimes against the "first two points," violations of certain quarantine regulations, and perhaps murder. The reform made few changes. Governors and governors general retained the authority to confirm all but death sentences. However, the execution of criminal sentences was suspended if they deprived a nobleman or a merchant of the first two guilds of his privileged status, or if the governor disagreed with the sentence of the chamber: the entire case together with an abstract had to be sent to the Senate. Much remained to be done to improve procedural standards. Complaints were made that the abstracts were too

[25] PSZ, 1762, N. 11726; 1764, N. 12040, 12189; 1765, N. 12350; 1798, N. 18347.
[26] OL, art, 131-133; PSZ, 1775, N. 14400, pt. 19.

long, more like descriptions of the case than outlines of the major circumstances and of what remained for the Senate to decide.[27]

Criminal cases in which the defendants were civil servants were usually referred to as *sledstvennye dela*. Officials appointed by the Empress—down to class VI (colonel)—were removed, investigated in the College of Justice, and tried by order of the Empress in the Senate, and the latter's sentence required her confirmation. Those appointed by the Senate—down to class XIV—were placed under investigation by governors or presidents of colleges, and their cases were referred to the College of Justice and the Senate. As to the clerks, their fate was in the hands of governors and presidents of colleges. After the reform, the role of the College of Justice devolved upon the criminal chambers. All officials were investigated by the chamber—lower courts were explicitly excluded from this—and its findings were forwarded through the governor to the Moscow Senate or to Petersburg. For example, in 1789 the Novgorod criminal chamber investigated the Staraia Rusa salt-and-liquor store manager, a lieutenant Skudin, for misuse of his post resulting in a shortage of these two taxable commodities. It forwarded its opinion to the Senate, which submitted a report to the Empress, asking for degradation to the ranks and the sale of all his property to compensate for the losses to the treasury. The Empress imposed her own sentence: degradation and loss of nobility, banishment to a Siberian garrison, and, if the proceeds from the sale were not enough, the balance should come from a fine on the members of the treasury chamber who had appointed the manager.[28]

Finally, brief mention should be made of the Senate's sitting, together with the Synod, as a High Court to try major crimes against the state. It happened three times in the reign of Catherine: in 1764 to try Captain Mirovich; in 1771 to try the mutineers who rose in Moscow during the plague and murdered Archbishop Ambrose; and in late 1774 to try Pugachev and some of his accomplices.

Although the Senate was the last instance in most cases, the Empress also possessed considerable judicial powers. These were the most sensitive of her powers and the most difficult to evaluate. The power to appoint, however extensive it might be, still affected relatively few people in a fixed number of posts. The ruler's financial power influenced in the most intimate fashion all the operations of government

[27] SZ, 1832, XV², art. 1133; PSZ, 1800, N. 19622.

[28] *Ist. Prav. Senata*, II, 587-593. The point is made here that both the Senate and the Empress did not as a rule take stern measures against crimes committed by members of the ruling class; see also PSZ, 1766, N. 12781; 1763, N. 11869, and *SIRIO*, III (1868), 226-227; 1782, N. 15360; 1789, N. 16799; 1786, N. 16456; and Salias, 619-622; 1793, N. 17166.

but seldom determined the fate of individuals. But the exercise of the judicial power in its many forms, without appeal, could seal the fate of individuals, high and low, or erase the infamy to which they had been subjected and return them to their families.

The theory underlying this great power was that of "justice reserved," and was common to most of the ancien regime states. It assumed, on the one hand, that judgments of the supreme courts were final and on principle could not be attacked; on the other, that all justice resided in the king and emanated from him. While delegating its exercise to his officers he nonetheless retained the plenitude himself and could quash any decisions.[29] In Russia this assumption was strengthened by a deep conviction that the ruler was the ultimate authority for the Russian Orthodox community and that his or her final pronouncements were in the nature of a divine command. By the middle of the eighteenth century it seems that a solution to the intractable contradictions between the claim of universal jurisdiction and the impossibility of examining all cases was being sought in the definition of an explicit statutory restriction of the Empress's role in civil and criminal justice while "justice reserved" was at the same time implicitly recognized.

As a rule, no appeals were allowed against the Senate's decision, on pain of severe punishment. Thus the civil decisions of the departments and the general assembly had the force of law and did not require Imperial confirmation. However, in the three situations with which we are now familiar—lack of unanimity, inability to find the law, and the objections of the Procurator General—this official submitted a report to the Empress with his own opinion. This naturally applied to criminal cases as well. In addition, sentences on nobles and officials to death and infamy and on certain converts to Orthodoxy also required the confirmation of the Empress. Finally, the Empress received, but directly from the governors, the sentences of the courts of equity, but these were gradually turned over to the Second Department, possibly with the instructions to resubmit the case for final confirmation.[30]

The ruler also possessed the power of pardon, which was a humanitarian gesture, an act of divine mercy restoring a criminal to the community of believers, but one also derived from the exclusive power to legislate. Since every court, including the Senate, was required to apply the letter of the law, the pardon created an exception to its

[29] Esmein, 242-243.

[30] *Ist. Prav. Senata*, II, 600-601. For examples see PSZ, 1776, N. 14539; 1780, N. 15000; 1785, N. 16154; 1786, N. 16308. The context of these last two documents is not clear, but they were codified in 1832 under articles 1343 of SZ, XV² (jurisdiction of the courts of equity).

application. In the form of an acquittal or a reduction of sentence, it was either individual or collective. Collective pardons were included in the manifestoes issued on the occasion of the anniversary of major events, such as the coup of June 28, 1762, Catherine's coronation, the signing of a peace treaty (viz., Kuchuk Kainardji), the unveiling of the monument dedicated to Peter the Great, etc.[31]

The non-statutory, extra-legal jurisdiction of the ruler was much more extensive. Here, at the risk of over-simplifying a very fluid situation, one can distinguish three roles performed by the Empress. She could intervene directly in the judicial process by inspiring the Procurator General's objection to a Senate decision, or simply request that a case be brought before her. We know, for example, that Catherine asked *General Reketmeister* Maslov to examine the Senate decision of an inheritance case involving a house bought by the deceased, a Mme Verre, with a gift from the Empress. But Maslov contended that the decision was proper, and after a stormy scene with the Empress submitted to her the drafts of two orders, one based on the law, the other on her discretion (*po vole tsarskoi*). Catherine agreed not to push her claim, but it is obvious that she could have. In sensitive cases, like that of Radischev, for example, the Empress dictated the indictment to her secretary Bezborodko; the Petersburg criminal chamber and the Senate knew what remained for them to do, although in this particular case the Senate turned out to be less pliant than might have been expected.[32]

The Empress also responded to petitions (*chelobitnye, prosheniia*), of which two kinds are relevant here. Some were in fact real appeals seeking to overturn a Senate decision; others were petitions asking for permission to act in a legal capacity.

The petitions for review were sent to the state secretaries, who forwarded them, with the approval of the Empress, to the relevant Senate departments. The ukase of December 1762 forbade petitioners to turn to the Empress unless they were dissatisfied with the decision of the Senate and considered their case entirely just (*sovsem spravedlivo*), or had received no satisfaction to the complaint addressed to the *General Reketmeister*. The assumption, however, remained that the petitioners took a chance if the decision of the Senate was upheld. Thus we have the case of three peasants of the Court who appealed the decision of the Chancery for Court Peasants. The Senate confirmed

---

[31] The manifestoes are in PSZ, 1762, N. 11667; 1782, N. 15488; and others. See for example 1763, N. 11869; 1766, N. 12781.

[32] Bantysh-Kamenskii, III (1836), 284-285 (Maslov).

the decision, but the peasants sent a petition to the Empress. The Senate ordered them flogged on the public square.

The case of Major Bukharov's wife, who appealed a decision of the Second Department, was another example of the high risk inherent to any attempt to overrule the Senate. The petitioner had sued over the inheritance of some real property. The Empress ordered the department to prepare an abstract for her consideration, and she found the decision to be in accordance with the laws. As a result, she placed Bukharova at the disposal of the Senate for daring to challenge its decision (*v udovolstvie Nashego Senata otdaem v polnuiu onago voliu*). Bukharova was summoned before the general assembly, the Imperial order was read to her, she fell on her knees and begged with tears for forgiveness of her crime. The Senate magnanimously, in emulation of "Her Majesty's compassion and humanity," exempted her from criminal penalties, and sent a report to the Empress expressing its gratitude for her protection against "unfair petitioners" (*nespravedlivye chelobitchiki*). Such dramatic ceremonial may have been exceptional, but it served to remind litigants that they should look upon the Senate as a court of last instance. In another inheritance case, however, three petitioners appealed different parts of the decision of the Sixth Department. Again an abstract was prepared, but the Empress rejected the appeal on ground that the deadlines had expired.[33]

Petitions were also sent against delays in the Senate and its refusal to come to a decision. We learn from the case of a widow Veimarn, who eighteen years earlier had obtained an Imperial ukase to the Senate to examine her case, that it still had not been decided in 1794, indeed that the Senate had sent it back to the lower court. The Procurator General was ordered to have the case examined immediately in the Second Department, and all parties and senators were forbidden to leave the capital until it was settled.[34] A similar category of petitioners included those who sought an Imperial order compelling government agencies to give lawful satisfaction. It seems that the implication of such an order was that the offending party was required to inform the Secretariat—the Veimarn case notwithstanding—of whatever action was taken. They also underscored the personal, "maternal," bond between the Empress and her subjects.

Other petitions were of a different kind, in which the petitioners turned to the ruler to obtain permission to perform a legal act. Thus the Empress confirmed in 1767 the division of property proposed by

[33] PSZ, 1767, N. 12881; 1769, N. 13354. A volume of petitions submitted to the Empress in 1775 and received by Secretary Kozmin is in TsGADA, f. 10. d. 545. A petition written in the remarkable style of the late seventeenth century is in "Iz proshlago."
[34] PSZ, 1794, N. 17210.

Peter Sheremetev and his wife, née Cherkasskaia, among their son and two daughters. Their marriage in 1743 had formed the largest private fortune in Russia. Certain property settlements required Imperial approval, but it is not clear beyond what point this was no longer necessary. Princess Obolenskaia complained to the Empress that her mother-in-law had not returned her dowry and refused to let her see her son. Another example was that of Princess Gruzinskaia, who complained that the trustees of her sequestered estate gave her only 350 rubles for support and that she had had to sell a dress to support herself. The Governor General of Moscow was ordered to investigate. We also have the interesting case of Lieutenant General Danil Zhuravlev, the son of Church peasants, who served in the famous grenadier company of the Guard in 1741 and was given a hereditary estate of 543 souls. He sent a petition to secretary Teplov, saying that he was old, had no children, and wanted the Empress's permission to name a nephew as his heir, since his two brothers were still peasants and could not inherit real property. The Empress agreed, "in view of his services."[35]

To evaluate the impact of these procedural reforms, not only on the administration of justice but on people's lives as well, is extremely difficult because we do not have any monographs on the subject. The word "reform" calls to mind change and improvement, but Catherine's reform took place in a very conservative society, and most of the procedural changes derived simply from the need to determine the relationships between the three levels of courts in the gubernia. As Isabel de Madariaga had pointed out, the attitude of Russian society to law and justice did not change, and the very idea of legality remained alien to it at all levels.[36] Legal standards certainly did not improve in the provinces, although more people—the litigants and those who served in the courts as elected representatives—were made aware of the need for consistency in presenting evidence. But written procedure and the secrecy of deliberations only spread corruption among more judges and continued to favor those in leadership positions.

It would be useful to know, for example, how many cases a voevoda decided before the reform, and how many came before the three lower courts in approximately the same uezd after the reform. Without even this information we can still obtain a general view of judicial activity in Nizhnii Novgorod gubernia (thirteen uezds) in 1787. A total of 3,286 cases was decided in that year: 2,058 in the three lower courts, 921 in the three intermediate courts, and 307 in the two chambers and the court of equity. At all levels the overwhelming majority of

[35] RBS, XXII (1911), 189; "Pis'ma imp Ekat. Vel.," 26-28, 39, 53.
[36] Madariaga, 586.

cases consisted of civil suits. There were as many noble litigants as urban and peasant ones together. Very few cases were appealed to the civil chamber: only two, while 132 were examined following a complaint (*po pros'bam*) of one of the parties. The share of the court of equity was 83 cases.[37] To judge from these few statistics it appears that the intermediate courts were very active and that most cases stopped there, i.e., did not involve more than 100 rubles or neither party wanted to appeal. Thus the reform may have considerably reduced the amount of frivolous appeals and must have compelled a decision of cases locally, by elected representatives of the social classes to which the litigants belonged. This alone certainly marked a considerable improvement that made justice more accessible and more responsive to the needs of the parties.

On the other hand, the success of the reform was threatened by forces which the reformers did not anticipate. The second Turkish war that began in 1787 and the irresponsible resort to the printing press fostered inflation and depreciated the value of property, goods, and services. The criterion chosen to limit the jurisdiction of the three levels (25, 100, 500 rubles) gradually lost its original meaning. The result should have been to siphon off more and more civil cases, especially those involving promissory notes (*vekseli*), toward the civil chamber; this, however, cannot be proved without statistical evidence, which should also take into consideration whether the very success of the lower courts did not also cause more litigants to bring their cases before them.

[37] TsGADA, f. 16, d. 778, fol. 232-234.

CHAPTER III

PUNISHMENTS

We observed in the preceding chapter that Great Russia was not only a political community but also a community of Orthodox believers. The consequence of the suffusion of social and political life with precepts of Orthodox morality was an identification of secular and divine justice, of law and morality; and the observance of morality required adherence to standards and beliefs of which the Church was the guardian because they were the guarantee of man's salvation.[1] Thus the positive law acquired the nature of a moral precept sanctioned by the authority of the ruler, and its violation was not only a secular misdeed but also an immoral act and a sin (*pogreshenie*).

Hence the importance of the confession of a crime and of repentance. To confess was to admit that a wrong had been committed, and repentance was inconceivable until that admission had first been made. Repentance in turn entailed the acceptance of punishment, submission to the "admonition" of the priest, a promise to bridle the pride that had led to the commission of a sin. Even if repentance was not a mitigating circumstance, the lack of it was likely to aggravate the punishment. In such a context punishment was retribution in the name of a stern and demanding ideal, a purification of the community's hallowed soil, and a humiliation of the offender before the members of his own community. This retribution served as deterrent, to frighten others, to frighten evildoers (*v strakh drugim* or *v strakh zlym*).[2] What other purpose could be served by the practice of returning the condemned criminal to the place where he had committed his crime, there to be whipped in front of the assembled villagers? Punishment also had a second purpose, to reform the offender, and sentences often contained a dual penalty. Banishment for life to hard labor or to settlement was the usual punishment after whipping. It was a substitute for the taking of life, seen as morally reprehensible. It expelled an offender from a community, forced him to expiate his crime in distant and inhospitable Siberia, from which there was no return. If he was sentenced to settlement there, he was permitted eventually to become a full member of that other community.

[1] von Bar, *History*, 55, 79, 81-82, 90-94, 229, 392, 467.
[2] OL, art. 113; von Bar, 6, 81. On crimes as disease, see PSZ, 1770, N. 13478: a criminal "infested" (*zarazivshiesia*) with bootlegging.

The *nakazy* given to the deputies elected to the Legislative Commission were very suggestive of popular attitudes in town and countryside alike toward punishment. Many considered torture necessary as a deterrent to crime and to obtain confessions. While the nobility sought to obtain immunity from torture and corporal punishment for itself, it did not look favorably upon the extension of this privilege to others, and if anything it asked for harsher penalties, even a policy of terror to eliminate brigandage.[3] Some townsmen asked for draconian punishment for trivial offenses. By contrast, Catherine's Great Instruction (*Nakaz*), replete with paraphrases of pronouncements by the best philosophers of the European Enlightenment, only bears testimony to bookish utopianism—although the Lutheran background of the Empress must have made her receptive to the repressive implications of the fusion of morality with positive law. Yet, the very impulses drawing the nobility toward the acceptance of the French language and European civilization in order to rationalize its privileged status created a climate favorable to the mitigation of penalties, at least among the more educated circles. The use of torture was ultimately discontinued. The Liquor Code of 1765 replaced corporal punishment for violations of its provisions with modest fines. The ukase of 1781 abandoned the blanket application of the knout for larceny and restricted it to recidivists and to those who stole objects valued at more than twenty rubles.[4]

The Empress's secular outlook, so different from that of her predecessors, was also responsible for a dramatic change of tone. The words "compassion" (*miloserdie*) and "humanitarianism" (*chelovekoliubie*) recur again and again in manifestoes and Imperial orders. It is as if she understood that attitudes in the provinces and towns would not change unless the Autocrat abandoned that stern and unbending glare of the Christ Pantokrator and the Orthodox saints looking down upon parishioners from the iconostasis. Perhaps some of her charm, self-respect, and decency filtered down to the governors' offices where severe sentences came for final confirmation, but one cannot be too sure. If her reign appears in retrospect less harsh than Anna's and even Elizabeth's, less disciplined than those of her son and grandsons, social relationships still remained so coarse that little progress could be made in improving the penal law. The triumph of serfdom and the creation of courts dominated by the nobility pervaded the administration of justice in gubernias and uezds with a spirit intolerant of dissent among social inferiors and of "insolence" (*proderzost'*) against superiors.

[3] Brückner, *Katharina*, 490-491; Papmehl, "Problem," 285-286.
[4] PSZ, 1765, N. 12448; 1770, N. 13748; 1781, N. 15147.

The importance of moral precepts in the penal law explains the simplicity of punishments. The ultimate penalty remained death, rarely applied *de jure* but often resulting from corporal punishment and exposure to inclement weather during resettlement to places of exile. The second most important penalty was knouting, usually followed by hard labor in mines and fortresses. The third was whipping, often followed by banishment to a settlement. These penalties—death, knouting, and whipping—were classified as *kazn'* to distinguish them from corrective punishments (*ispravitel'nye nakazaniia*), and only higher courts could order their application: governors and provincial voevodas before the reform, criminal chambers after it, unless the case was referred to the Senate.[5] If the last two are combined with banishment, which complemented them, it appears that the three major punishments were death, corporal punishment, and banishment.

THE DEATH PENALTY

Every student of Russian history has read that the death penalty was abolished in the reign of Empress Elizabeth and was replaced by banishment to hard labor. This is not quite true, and the issue needs clarification. The death penalty was the ultimate means by which a serious offender was expelled from the community, an act of purification for the shedding of blood or for the gravest attempts against the values of the community. It was prescribed in sixty-three separate cases in the *Ulozhenie* of 1649, and it found its apogee in the reign of Peter the Great, marked by so much reform and so much tension, both domestic and international.[6] But this penalty, awesome in the hands of builders of states, becomes a hated instrument in the hands of lesser rulers and their favorites, whose insecurity fosters in their executive agents cruelty and morbid fear. The sad period between the death of Peter the Great and the accession of Elizabeth is an eloquent testimony to the degradation of the death penalty into an instrument of misrule.

Death sentences were imposed by governors and voevodas alike, but voevodas were required to send theirs to the governor, who alone had the power to confirm them. To give a measure of the extent of this gubernatorial power to confirm such sentences, it will be enough to say that the death penalty was mandatory not only for state crimes, such as those against the person of the ruler and his family, and

---

[5] PSZ, 1774, N. 14275, pt. 2; 1787, N. 16513.

[6] Vitkorskii, 60-66, 91-94. The Military Code of 1716 imposed the death penalty in 122 cases: *ibid.*, 132.

rebellion, treason, and espionage, but also for felonies understood in the widest possible sense, such as murder, rape, arson, counterfeiting, embezzlement of state funds, collecting illegal taxes, cutting down trees intended for Navy use, non-execution of Imperial orders, not reporting taxable individuals to census takers, failure to send account books on time, highway robbery, and theft for the fourth time.[7] With such powers a governor was the true master of all individuals in his gubernia except the most privileged. Death sentences for converting Russians to another faith and those imposed on noblemen required the approval of the ruler.

The Empress Elizabeth, a deeply religious person, who brought to the throne a generosity that was in marked contrast to the vengeful spite of her predecessor, Anna Ioanovna, had promised on the eve of the coup of November 1741 that she would never shed blood, and her reign indeed marked a definite trend away from the widespread use of the death penalty. On August 2, 1743, shortly before the peace with Sweden, Marshal Lacy, the commander-in-chief in Finland, was ordered not to confirm death sentences for the murder of Swedish subjects and for marauding (grabezh), and to replace death with mutilation by cutting off the right hand and slitting the nose, and with hard labor for life. In May 1744 the Senate reported to the Empress that in gubernias, provinces, and towns the death penalty was being imposed indiscriminately (ne po nadlezhashchim vinam), and that even innocent people were being executed. It ordered all agencies, governors, and voevodas to send detailed abstracts on those death sentences and to suspend all executions until the Empress's confirmation was received. Nine years later the Senate reported that there were 110 death sentences for murder, 169 for larceny and brigandage and other offenses, and 151 sentences to hard labor, or 430 sentences awaiting the confirmation of the Empress. In addition, there were 3,579 criminals whose cases were not yet terminated, and it was expected that the sentences of many of them would also have to be sent to the Empress. All this would take time, and meanwhile prisoners ran away, and the Empress was very busy with other matters. The Senate also objected to cutting off the hands of criminals since they would no longer be able to do useful work. It asked the Empress to replace this mutilation with whipping with the knout (but retained the slitting of the nose), followed by hard labor for life. The report was accepted on March 29, 1753, the date usually adopted to mark the "abolition" of the death penalty.[8]

[7] PSZ, 1728, N. 5333, pt. 15-16, 19, 38; Viktorskii, 148-172, 196-214.
[8] PSZ, 1744, N. 8944; 1753, N. 10086; Viktorskii, 215-232.

The considerations adduced by the Senate are strong evidence that much more was involved than the humanitarian impulse of an Empress who had pledged not to shed blood. The large number of capital crimes resulted in the perversion of justice in the provinces, while the proposed automatic referral of death sentences to the Empress threatened to create an impossible situation. In fact, the death penalty was never abolished, but it remained mandatory for a large number of offences, and the "courts" continued to impose it as a matter of course in accordance with the *Ulozhenie*, the Military Articles of Peter the Great, and other laws.[9] The former voevoda of Kaluga, Miasoedov, for example, was sentenced to death for bribery and embezzling funds intended for the purchase of food and hay for the army. His case reached Catherine, who pardoned him although "he deserved death" and banished him to his estate under police surveillance. Not only did legislation on capital crimes remain in force under Catherine, but the death penalty was imposed in 1766 for interference (presumably with the use of force) with the activities of land surveyors and in 1771, during the epidemic of plague in Moscow, for stealing the belongings of the dead from their houses; indeed the claim has been made that Catherine did not have the same qualms as her predecessor about confirming death sentences.[10]

Such sentences were carried out in various fashion. Some criminals were shot, others hanged. Mirovich was beheaded. The old practice of quartering—cutting off the arms and the legs, then the head—was still used. Pugachev was quartered, although the Empress sent orders that his head should be cut off first, a small consolation perhaps, but a sign that public opinion was growing more hostile to these barbarous exhibitions, at least in the capitals. Peter Panin, who crushed the Pugachev rebellion, did not share this repugnance. In September 1774 he had a certain Mosiakin, who also called himself Peter III, sentenced to be quartered in Voronezh, his head, hands, and legs to be sent to his village. Only premature death in prison saved the man from such horror.[11]

[9] In England, where the death penalty was imposed for a wide variety of offenses, a similar trend was noticeable: many offenders were given benefit of clergy and sent to the colonies: R. Hofstadter, *America at 1750*, New York, 1973, 47-48.

[10] PSZ, 1754, N. 10306. Several cases described in Korsakov, "Dela" (179-183, 187-188) illustrate the imposition of the death penalty followed by a declaration that the defendant would be subjected to the knout and banishment, on the ground that the death penalty was "suspended" (*uderzhana*) or would be imposed upon receiving confirmation (*do posledovaniia o takovykh podlezhashchikh smertnoi kazne ukaza*): the formula is very revealing. On Miasoedov see PSZ, 1763, N. 11869. See also PSZ, 1771, N. 13676; 1766, N. 12570. Shcherbatov's opinion on the death penalty is in *Sochineniia*, I, 427-455.

[11] Piontkovskii, 98-99.

Mention should also be made of another punishment called "political death." The same ukase of 1743 stated that this punishment should ultimately replace physical death, but the Empress herself was not sure what it meant, and asked the Senate to tell her for what crimes it was imposed. The Senate answered that the ukase of 1699 imposed it on custom-and-liquor tax-collectors who defrauded the government. The criminals were sentenced to physical death, were exposed publicly on a block or gallows, and their sentence was commuted to whipping with the knout, followed by banishment to hard labor or settlement. Such sentences were also imposed for hiding serfs from the authorities during census-taking; committing violent acts in the Senate, Synod, and other agencies; perjury, etc. Thus the distinguishing feature was public exposure, a public humiliation of the criminal designed to emphasize the particularly obnoxious nature of his crime. The Senate took pains to emphasize this feature and added that while governors and voevodas (with the approval of the governor) could confirm sentences to hard labor they had no authority to confirm those to political death, which should be treated like sentences to physical death. The most famous case was probably that of Daria Saltykova, a perverted landowner who took sadistic pleasure in torturing her serfs. The Empress herself ordered full publicity. On October 18, 1768 she was taken to a platform (eshafot) surrounded by grenadiers with drawn swords, chained to a pillar for one hour, wearing around her neck a sign saying "torturer and murderer." All Moscow came to see the "maneater" (liudoed), who was then imprisoned in a monastery, where she died twenty-three years later.[12] The combined effect of the ukase of 1743 and the report of 1753 was to replace the death penalty with whipping, usually followed by banishment, unless the Senate chose to recommend its application in a particular case to the Empress.

CORPORAL PUNISHMENT

The de-facto abolition of the death penalty after 1753 resulted in the massive application of the harsher forms of corporal punishment for state crimes and all sorts of felonies, and to many observers corporal punishment became the distinguishing feature of the Russian penal law. These punishments came into use during the ascendancy of the Muscovite state, and by 1649 had become so widespread that the Ulozhenie sanctioned the application of the knout in some 140 cases. But the knout, the very symbol of Russia in the early nineteenth cen-

---

[12] PSZ, 1753, N. 10086 and 10087; "Saltychikha," 543; "Sovremennoe pis'mo," 94-95. Daria Saltykova ("Saltychikha") was the aunt by marriage of Nikolai Saltykov, president of the College of War. She was responsible for the death of some 138 serfs, all women.

tury, was only the most severe form of corporal punishment. Flogging with a whip was another form, so was beating with sticks (*batogi, palki, pruti*) and running the gauntlet in the army. These punishments, which cause intense pain, were not intended to damage the body permanently. In fact, of course, one could die under the knout or after running the gauntlet, and the health of many must have been permanently impaired despite the greater physical endurance of past generations. But there were also punishments intended to maim, which remind us of the code of Hammurabi and the *lex talionis*: cutting off the tongue for insulting the ruler and the Church, cutting off the hand for attempts by a serf to kill his lord and for larceny and fraud, cutting off the fingers of some thieves. Other maiming punishments were intended to leave the criminal recognizable for the rest of his life if he should flee from his place of banishment: such was the purpose of cutting off the ears, gradually replaced in the eighteenth century by slitting the nose "to the bone," as the ukase of 1724 put it.[13]

Whatever the nature of all these punishments, the humiliation of the criminal was their common purpose. The execution of a death sentence was a solemn act, and a criminal who went bravely to the scaffold and died with dignity assumed a certain stature. But beating or whipping destroyed the dignity of any man, reducing him to a bundle of crushed flesh begging for mercy; and running the gauntlet was the most degrading of these public spectacles, since it meant the systematic destruction of a man at the hands of his peers.

The ukase of September 1754 set out to determine how the decision of the previous year to substitute "cruel punishment" with the knout for the death penalty should be carried out. All sentences to physical and political death imposed by voevodas were to be submitted to the governors or the *Sysknoi Prikaz* (in Moscow) or the Policemaster's chancery (in Petersburg). If these agencies confirmed the sentences, their execution was suspended until final confirmation was received from the Empress. In the meantime, "so that the criminals do not avoid punishment in the long interval until the abstracts are examined," those sentenced to physical death were to be whipped with the knout, have their nose cut off, and be branded with the Russian letters VOR (thief), and sent to hard labor. All other sentences for felonies to the knout, mutilation, branding, and banishment for life were confirmed by the governors. The decision, no doubt, was inspired by the concept of "reserved justice." The sentence was commuted to a presumably milder one and was carried out; there was always the possibility, however, that the Empress would choose to exercise her dis-

[13] Timofeev, 290-294, Tankov, 192.

cretion and have the original penalty reinstated. Whether this ever took place is unknown.[14]

Whipping with the knout was called *torgovaia kazn'* because it had traditionally been administered on the public market (*torg*) square. In March 1775 flogging with an ordinary whip was also called *kazn'*, and as a result sentences to the whip required the confirmation of the governor. Birching (*rozgi*) was confirmed by the voevodas or belonged to the jurisdiction of the landowners over their serfs. Seldom used in Russia proper in the eighteenth century, but applied extensively in Little Russia and the Baltic provinces, it was usually reserved for minors or employed as a form of mitigation of the more severe punishments. Corporal punishments administered publicly were not always followed by banishment, especially after 1775, but the criminal continued to suffer certain disabilities. Individuals whipped with the knout could not become soldiers, and soldiers thus punished could not become officers. After 1787 these offenders were forbidden to come to the gubernia capitals and were restricted to the uezd centers.[15]

Corporal punishment applied to all classes of Russian society until late in the eighteenth century. Even the aristocracy was not immune from the knout, as the Lopukhina and Bestuzheva cases of the 1740s illustrate. But the spread of enlightened ideas and the gradual emergence of a civil society founded on the recognition of some elementary rights reinforced the humiliating nature of corporal punishment, and privileged groups sought immunity from it. Progress was extremely slow because corporal punishment was not merely an instrument of repression in the hands of governmental authority, but also a favorite tool in the hands of the stronger at all levels of society. It was the symbol of the hierarchical nature of Russian society, the instrument to enforce obedience and conformity, confession and repentance within the great community of believers. Thus attacks on corporal punishment were equated with attacks on the very foundation of the social and political order. Significantly, the clergy was the first social group to receive immunity. The ukase of June 1767 noted that in dioceses and monasteries priests and monks were beaten and tortured by their ecclesiastical superiors as if they were common people (*podlyi narod*), and concluded that this was a major cause of the contempt in which they were held by their parishioners. It forbade such practices and ordered that priests should be put to work or deprived of their revenues instead. The replacement of corporal punishment by fines and labor

---

[14] PSZ, 1753, N. 10086; 1754, N. 10306.

[15] PSZ, 1775, N. 14275, pt. 2; 1799, N. 18898. On the physical damage resulting from corporal punishment and the revulsion it sometimes caused among spectators, see Bezrodnyi, 296; also Timofeev, 293-294; PSZ, 1787, N. 16566.

was extended in 1771 to deacons as well. Fourteen years later, by the Charters of 1785, nobles, merchants of the first two guilds, and "honored citizens" (*imenitye grazhdane*) were also granted immunity, as members of a social group. The way had been paved by collective exemptions like those granted to deputies to the Legislative Commission, to state peasant assessors elected to the lower and intermediate courts for the duration of their commission.[16] Thus the penal reform of the latter half of the eighteenth century affirmed the privileged status of the ruling class, which exemption from the capitation and the adoption of western dress, language, and mores had already considerably strengthened. On the other hand, this trend toward the formalization of privileged status broke the "democratic" uniformity of the penal law and threatened the consensus binding high and low in a single community of believers.

BANISHMENT

Corporal punishment was followed in most cases by the removal of the prisoner from the community. Some prisoners were banished to hard labor,[17] others were simply resettled in areas desperately short of manpower. The purpose of banishment, apart from colonization, was to make the criminal expiate his crime in a hostile environment and to give him a chance, in certain circumstances, to start a new life and redeem himself.

The ukase of 1753 ordered the banishment of convicts to Rogervik (Baltiiskii Port), on the coast of Estland, where the Navy was trying without success to build a major naval base. Convicts were also used on Kotlin Island, where the fortress of Kronshtadt guarded the approaches to Petersburg, and in the 1780s we also find them building piers (*vodianye raboty*) in Riga.[18] The army, of course, made much greater use of convict labor, especially in the east and south, where the frontier remained insecure until the very end of the reign. When the administration of the Nerchinsk mines sent word in 1773 that it had enough convicts, the Senate sent two thousand to Orenburg, where Governor Reinsdorp was busy repairing the fortifications—a wise precaution that saved the city when Pugachev laid siege to it in the fall

[16] PSZ, 1767, N. 12909, 12948, XV; 1771, N. 13609; 1785, N. 16187, art. 6, 15, 16188, art. 107, 113, 135; Timofeev, 293-294.

[17] Hard labor was still known throughout most of the eighteenth century under the general name *katorga*, but the word gradually came to be used to distinguish work in mines from construction and repair work in fortresses (*krepostnye raboty*).

[18] PSZ, 1753, N. 10086; 1784, N. 16065; 1788, N. 16174. Some were also sent to Astrakhan: Iudin, "K delu Mirovicha."

of that year. During that rebellion communications with Siberia through Kazan, Ekaterinburg, and Orenburg were virtually cut off, and there could be no thought of sending convicts to the area. They were sent instead to work in various fortresses, depending on their place of origin: some 5,500 convicts were thus redistributed. The Senate, however, was usually apprehensive about sending convicts to border outposts from which they could easily flee, and refused a request of the College of War to send some to Kiev to relieve civilians. In March 1775 the despatch of convicts to fortifications was suspended, and they were again sent to Orenburg and Siberia. Interrupted again during the second Turkish war in 1788, it was resumed four years later.[19] Only young and able-bodied men could do fortress work. Carrying heavy stones, building high walls, working in cold water (in ports) was not only physically exhausting but carried the danger of being crushed or drowned. Conditions were even more difficult in the mines— the gold mines of Ekaterinburg, the silver mines of Kolyvan, and the silver and lead mines of Nerchinsk—where exposure of toxic fumes doomed the convicts to rapid death.

Banishment to hard labor was for life (vechno), and there were no provisions for adapting the sentence to the crime. A common criminal convicted for stealing a horse valued at twenty-five rubles might find himself doing the same work for life as a murderer or a state criminal. Men over forty-five were not sent to the mines, but even those in their seventies were sent to other forms of hard labor. Thus banishment meant the inexorable uprooting of an individual, his final expulsion from the community. A hard-labor convict lost whatever privileged status he may have enjoyed. His property was placed under trusteeship for the benefit of his children. If he had no children, it was confiscated; his wife in either case received the share of the estate to which she would have been entitled in her husband's death. The convict in fact was considered dead (podobno iakoby umre) before the civil law, and the only remaining bond between him and his family was the sacrament of marriage, which only the Synod could annul. With the Synod's permission, a wife could follow her husband to hard labor.[20]

Banishment to settlement was a punishment of a very different order, and served three purposes. On the one hand, it was a punishment imposed for a wide variety of crimes such as illicit trade in vodka, fraud, theft, sending unlawful petitions to the Empress, circulating anonymous letters. It followed a public whipping and was one of the

[19] PSZ, 1773, N. 13975, 14077; 1774, N. 14126, 14158; 1775, N. 14286; 1780, N. 15020; 1785, N. 16159; 1788, N. 16634.
[20] PSZ, 1720, N. 3628; 1753, N. 10086, 10101.

punishments requiring the approval of the governor. On the other hand, it was a favorite means of getting rid of undesirables by administrative order without subjecting them first to corporal punishment. A governor would banish a clerk to settlement, and landowners since 1760 would deliver to the governors their peasants and domestics whom they found guilty of "insolence"; they were automatically despatched to Siberia without trial.[21] Finally, it served a non-penal purpose when state peasants were resettled in frontier regions, a policy to which the Russian government resorted with equanimity whenever it considered it necessary to speed up a "natural process." The settlement of Siberia had been going on for some time, but the support of a military and administrative superstructure required the development of agriculture, the multiplication of settlements along the strategic route from Tobolsk to Kiakhta on the Chinese border, and their extension to other areas of Siberia that were not attractive to ordinary settlers.

Usually, exiles were distributed among established communities, where they could easily be watched; they took part in the work of peasants; and they paid the poll tax. Those who were too old to do any work or were in poor health, including those whose hands and legs had been damaged by the chains they had worn for so long, posed a problem. It had been government policy to give them a passport for the richer regions (*khlebnye mesta*), where they could support themselves by begging, but the governor of Tobolsk opposed this in 1768 as a contribution to vagrancy. To avoid having to support them with state funds he recommended that they be placed with individuals in the towns who were willing to pay the poll tax for them in return for work; they could also marry "serf girls" (*krepostnye devki*). But the Senate strongly opposed this on the grounds that it would only lead to the introduction of serfdom (*kholopstvo*) in Siberia.[22]

A form of banishment to settlement was banishment to residence (*na zhit'e*), usually but not exclusively to the Orenburg Territory. In January 1763 the Senate banished to residence for life in Nerchinsk a woman who seems to have had a long history of false denunciations and who had sent a petition to the Empress containing false accusations. This may have been an unusual case, the odder because banishment followed whipping with the knout. There were other cases in the early 1760s, however, showing that even this mild form of pun-

---

[21] PSZ, 1720, N. 11166. See above p. 134. Beccaria (53) voiced strong support for banishing those who disturbed the public peace and did not obey the laws. He also believed that a life sentence of servitude should replace the death penalty as a sufficient deterrent to "any determined spirit" (48).

[22] PSZ, 1768, N. 15053.

ishment followed severe corporal punishment. The ukase of February 1763, which sought to restrict the application of torture and the use of preventive detention, ordered the banishment to residence in Siberia of individuals implicated (*ogovornye*) by a criminal, who did not confess after being subjected to torture and for whom no one wanted to put up bail.[23] These were essentially suspects against whom nothing had been found but who were considered undesirable by reason of the fact that they had been accused of something.

Those banished to residence were required to live in towns, while those banished to settlement lived in rural communities. Perhaps there existed a scale of towns for different categories of prisoners. Obviously, living in Orenburg must have been more pleasant than living in Nerchinsk or Iakutsk. Fedor Sukin, former president of the College of Manufactures, was stripped of his civil-service rank and banished to Orenburg for life for failure to denounce colleagues in the agency who had conspired to issue counterfeit assignats. He was on friendly terms with the governor and the commandant, and kept up his correspondence with friends in Moscow and Petersburg. Grigorii Vinskii was banished to Orenburg in 1780 for a similar offense. He was well received by the vice-governor and enjoyed freedom of movement in the Orenburg Territory, a huge area which also included Bashkiria at the time. Dmitrii Mertvago tells us how his brother-in-law, just retired from the service, had tampered with his orders to show that he had been promoted from lieutenant to captain. He was degraded to the ranks, expelled from the nobility, and sent to Ufa.[24] To judge from available cases, it seems that banishment to residence was a standard punishment for various kinds of fraud, and it may have been more or less reserved for members—or former members—of privileged groups.

For those banished either to settlement or to residence there was a possibility of redemption not open to hard-labor convicts. In 1781 the government ordered prisoners sentenced to settlement from Iaroslavl and Vologda gubernias sent instead of Siberia to Kola, above the Artic Circle, to populate the "town" and develop the cod fisheries. Those of good conduct and accepted by the community were allowed to register as townsmen (*meshchane*) after three years; and their children were also allowed to become state peasants. The decision must have applied to similar situations elsewhere, as we can see from the case of Koz'ma Peredovshchikov. Banished to settlement in 1788, he joined the local community (*obshchestvo*) of peasants and later became a

[23] Gribovskii, *Materialy*, 1-2, PSZ, 1763, N. 11750, pt. 3.

[24] *Krest'ianskaia voina v Rossii*, 359, "Zapiski Vinskago," 164, 173-174, "Zapiski Mertvago," 71, 77-81.

second guild merchant in Turukhansk. These changes, it seems, took place by simple agreement with the local community, or perhaps with the approval of the governor.[25]

There is no doubt that in the eyes of the government banishment of the fit to the army and the unfit to settlement were two equal punishments. At the very beginning of the reign two manifestoes summoned Russian fugitive peasants to return from Poland and Lithuania and promised amnesty to those who returned willingly. Those who refused to return and were captured by Russian military detachments were divided into two groups. Fugitives, healthy but unfit for service, were banished to settlement. Those fit for military service were banished to Siberia to staff the cavalry and infantry regiments stationed there. A fit man was 1.5 meters tall (two *arshin* and three *vershki*), healthy, and without physical disabilities (*uvech'e*). As a rule, however, this form of banishment seems to have meant banishment to units stationed in Siberia and to "distant garrisons," and not to the regular army. It may have been a favorite punishment for clerks: the Tambov clerks who took bribes, the Kaluga clerks who defrauded the government, or the Borovichi mailman who stole sixty rubles from the mails. It may or may not have followed corporal punishment. Thus, in the case of a Rzhev merchant and his father who did not fulfill their contract to transport salt to Moscow and Velikie Luki, the Senate ordered both whipped and banished to army ranks if they were fit or to settlement if they were not.[26] Military service was for life, or as long as a man was fit; it subjected him to harsh discipline and cut him off forever from his native village. For those who lived to old age it probably ended as banishment to settlement or to residence.

OTHER PENALTIES

Corporal punishment and banishment were the most dramatic and widely used penalties for a great variety of offenses, but they were not the only ones. Among the penalties imposed by the Church on laymen that of penance (*pokaianie*) was the most common. It was imposed usually as a supplementary penalty following a criminal sentence for such offenses as blasphemy, theft of religious objects, murder, and manslaughter. Penance was done in a monastery; it entailed the denial of communion unless death was imminent. Monasteries were also used as places of detention for murderers when there was a suspicion of

[25] PSZ, 1767, N. 12397; 1781, N. 15124; 1783, N. 15672; 1785, N. 16227; 1798, N. 18362.

[26] PSZ, 1765, N. 12396; 1766, N. 12556; 1773, N. 14071; Dubasov, 34-35; PSZ, 1763, N. 11869; Pardalotskii, 786-787.

insanity.[27] The attempt to build separate madhouses during the reign of Catherine—its success is unknown—sought to "secularize" insanity and view it as a medical problem. However, the continued resort to monasteries was nowhere better illustrated than in the selection of the formidable Spaso-Efimiev monastery in Suzdal as a place of detention for certain individuals declared insane "due to circumstances known only to Her Majesty,"[28] in other words, individuals declared insane on social or political grounds.

Such a declaration of insanity is one of the most curious aspects of the Russian penal law, and certain contemporary developments show that the practice remains very much alive. It was, however, clouded in secrecy, and very little is known about it. In 1786 one ensign Ganrider sent a report describing abuses committed in Ufa gubernia which threatened in his opinion to lead to bloodshed unless legality was soon restored. He was investigated, accused of freethinking, then declared insane and expelled from the country. Professor Melman, mentioned earlier, was likewise declared mentally disturbed before being deported. In 1795 the secretary of the Skopin lower *rasprava* who reported abuses committed by local officials was investigated by the Secret Expedition, declared insane, and incarcerated in the Suzdal monastery.[29]

Perhaps the oddest of these cases, because it showed that such declarations of insanity were not only measures of repression imposed by agencies of the political police but were found acceptable within a much broader circle, was that of one Gavrilov, a customs official. In the service in various places since 1761, he was appointed finally to the Sorokoshichi customs house on the Drieper in Chernigov gubernia. If his own statements are reliable, he had worked diligently and received good recommendations (*attestaty*). In 1782 he denounced the director of the customs house to the councillor of the treasury chamber responsible for customs administration. Instead of investigating the alleged embezzlement of customs revenue, the councillor ordered Gavrilov's arrest. The unfortunate official was kept in detention, an attempt was made to poison him, and he was starved until he signed a confession that he had written his denunciation in a state of insanity

[27] Gribovskii, *Materialy*, 3-4, Kostomarov, 481-488; see also PSZ, 1799, N. 18977, Lebedev, "O brachnykh razvodakh," 7-8. On church penance, see PSZ, 1770, N. 13500; 1785, N. 16168; 1797, N. 18212; 1780, N. 15029; 1769, N. 13262; 1777, N. 14597; 1780, N. 14996. On individual cases see PSZ, 1770, N. 13508; 1766, N. 12600; 1776, N. 14539; 1780, N. 15000.

[28] TsGVIA, f. VUA, d. 50, fol. 246-247; on the Suzdal monastery, see Gernet, I (1960), 280-286.

[29] Kulsharipov, 151, Sivkov, Ocherki, 259.

(*v bezumie*). Thereafter, he was dismissed from his post, publicly declared insane, and ostracized by his fellow noblemen and officials. The
letters VP (*vor i plut*—thief and swindler) were stamped on his file,
and Gavrilov found himself without any prospects of employment. He
turned to Marshal Rumiantsev, Governor General of Little Russia,
and asked that his name be cleared, but Rumiantsev's secretary answered that he should come to Kiev and find a doctor willing to give
him a statement that he was indeed sick and insane when he wrote
the denunciation and that he had now recovered. In despair Gavrilov
asked the First Department of the Senate to declare him sane (*sniat'
ego bezumstvo*), but the department could find nothing better than to
order the governor general to investigate the case, determine whether
the denunciation was justified, and punish the embezzlers if any were
found.[30]

The implications of these three cases are extremely interesting. To
complain outside the authorized channels of the procuracy against
abuses, especially financial ones, committed by noble officials could
be dangerous business. One finds very little concern in the Gavrilov
case for the defense of the state's fiscal interest against noblemen who
used their official positions to help themselves to a source of public
funds whose accounts were particularly difficult to audit. The fact that
"well-born society" ostracized him points to widespread collusion
between officials and the local nobility, who shared a common ignorance of the boundary between the private and the public interest.
A declaration of an informant's insanity in such cases was a form of
"internal" banishment, imposed not in accordance with the positive
law, which seems not to have recognized it, but for the purpose of
self-defense on the part of the ruling class.

There were four major kinds of financial penalties. The first might
be called procedural fines because they were imposed on subordinate
agencies whose decisions were overruled on various grounds, as, for
example, when a provincial chancery claimed that there was no law
to decide a particular case, while the College of Justice decided that
there was, or even when a decision was based on presumably relevant
laws but the superior agency chose others. This bizarre procedure
derived from a theoretical model in which it was assumed that the
laws were well known and that they had been codified. The colleges
were often placed in an impossible situation. On the one hand, they
had to request a Senate decision if they could not find the law and
were fined if it was found that the law existed; on the other, they were

30 TsGVIA, f. 44, d. 50, II, fol. 144-149.

also fined if they applied the law but were overruled on the ground that they had chosen the wrong one.

Ivan Divov, the president of the College of Justice, complained in a report of 1766 to the Empress that these fines, together with the absence of codified law and the difficulty of getting defendants to obey summonses to appear in court, were the three major causes of the intolerable delays paralyzing the administration of justice. The fines were heavy: a provincial chancery was fined twenty percent (twenty kopecks per ruble) of the value of the suit, the gubernia chancery forty percent, and the College of Justice eighty percent. Since the College of Justice was called upon to decide claims sometimes exceeding 10,000 rubles, the enormity of the fine was the strongest deterrent to action, and judges at all levels preferred to bury the case in the hope that the parties would settle out of court. Fines were also imposed for violating procedural rules set in the ukase of November 1723, 500 rubles for the first offense, 1,000 rubles for the second time. The only relief against such paralysis was an Imperial pardon, either individual or collective in the form of an Imperial manifesto.[31]

A second category of fines included those imposed for violations of various administrative procedures and came under the provisions of the ukase of July 1766 and several others. They ranged from ten to fifty rubles (for recidivists) for such offenses as failure to acknowledge receipt of Senate orders, tardiness in reporting, asking the Senate to examine matters not included in the agency's jurisdiction, writing unlawful petitions on behalf of private individuals, unauthorized absences from work, etc. These fines, like the procedural fines, were imposed on the entire personnel of the agency except the clerks, who did not have civil-service rank.[32]

A third kind of fines included those imposed for criminal violations such as bribery. Governor Shakhovskoi was fined 2,630 rubles in 1766 for taking bribes and tolerating widespread corruption in Kursk province. Such fines were also imposed for failure to go to confession once a year. Finally, there were the so-called *vzyskaniia* or *nachëty*, i.e., usually compensations for losses incurred by the Treasury following the default of a tax-farmer or other individuals bound by contract to deliver goods to the state, such as provisions and fodder to the army. In accordance with the general rules on contracts of December 1776, a tax-farmer who did not pay or deliver on time was charged the loss of an additional half percent per month beyond that date, if negligence

---

[31] TsGADA, f. 16, d. 334, fol. 20; PSZ, 1723, N. 4344; 1762, N. 11667; Gribovskii, *Materialy*, 24-26.

[32] PSZ, 1765, N. 12483; 1766, N. 12710; 1762, N. 11706; 1766, N. 12648; 1782, N. 15357; 1765, N. 12417.

was proved. Those who sold salt and liquor illegally were fined twice the amount of their profit, etc.[33]

This presentation of the essentials of the penal law serves to illustrate some of the themes discussed in the preceding pages. The "abolition" of the death penalty by Elizabeth must be seen as an element in the compact between the ruling class and the folk-society, reluctant to shed blood by formal legal process and inclined instead to inflict a public humiliation upon a defendant and expel him from his community to another, on the fringes of the Orthodox world, where he could start a new life. It is a fact that most laws are obeyed as if they were customs, and it is difficult to enforce those that are remote from customary assumptions. To retain them nonetheless is to call forth a challenge to their legitimacy. Within the ruling class itself the indiscriminate resort to the death penalty to punish crimes of unequal gravity, a legacy of the tension characteristic of Peter the Great's reign, raised likewise the question of legitimacy. Out of this convergence of views there was born a profound reaction against the death penalty that would continue well into the nineteenth century.

This, however, did not affect the power of the core of the ruling class to settle the fate of the socially dependent as it saw fit, but it brought it into line with the expectations of townsmen and peasants who transgressed the written law or norms of social relationships. Even if the governor lost some of his arbitrary power after the reforms, since he merely confirmed the sentences of the criminal chamber, he still remained the ultimate guardian of the social order in the provinces. The power of a gubernia board to banish by administrative order was not different from the customary practice of peasant communities to select recruits or expel undesirables. Here was a congruence of styles that made even exploitation acceptable, although, as was pointed out, the exemption of the nobility, clergy, and merchants from corporal punishment had the opposite effect.

On the other hand, increased resort to banishment and hard labor strengthened the power of the judicial departments of the Senate to decide cases in the last resort. Reserved justice referred to the power of the Empress to intervene at any time in the administration of the judiciary; it also, by implication, restricted her power to pass final judgment to cases in which she had a personal interest. The Senate departments (or their general assembly) became supreme courts for most cases which the governors chose to refer to their political lead-

[33] PSZ, 1766, N. 12781; 1765, N. 12483; 1767, N. 12909; Gur'ev, "Ispovednyi shtraf," 11-24; Semevskii, "Sel'skii sviashchennik," 505-506; Tankov, "K istorii." On the *vzyskaniia*, see PSZ, 1766, n. 12781; 1773, N. 14086; 1776, N. 14544, pt. 13-14; 1781, N. 15174, art. 89, 95-97, 101-103; N. 15231, art. 112, 117, 127-129.

ership. In a system marked by the absence of a bureaucracy governed by stable, legal, and impersonal norms, the confirmation of sentences was a political act inspired by the need to defend the social order and the privileges of the ruling class.

Punishments did not only cause physical and emotional suffering. In some cases they also cancelled the privileged status of an individual. If the senators were the final judge over a priest or a merchant, the Empress alone could expel a nobleman from the ruling class. This was consistent with the assumption accepted at all levels of that class that any changes in the status quo required the confirmation of the Empress, as the arbiter of disputes among the ruling families. To say that Russian justice was political is to say that its application to members of the ruling class had to take place within the patronage contexts existing at a particular time. In expelling a merchant the senators were exercising their social and political leadership; in expelling a member of their own class they required the assent of their leader, whose legitimacy they had previously sanctioned.

PART IV

FINANCIAL
ADMINISTRATION

CHAPTER I

FINANCIAL AGENCIES

CENTRAL AGENCIES

The emphasis in the preceding pages has been on the class content of the police and judicial reform, governed by rationalist considerations but anti-bureaucratic in nature because its result was chiefly to enable the landed nobility to strengthen its hold over the entire peasant population and the towns. The background of the financial reform, however, was more complex. To facilitate the extraction of resources from the population in an economy of scarcity, precisely in order to make possible a program of decentralization in police and judicial administration and to sustain the momentum of a foreign policy designed to open up new lands for the ruling class, it became imperative to raise the level of administrative performance. Efficiency here meant not simply breaking the stranglehold of a central bureaucracy, bringing the ruling class closer to the dependent population, and creating local agencies to facilitate its operations; it meant above all training clerks and selected members of the ruling class, both at the center and in the provinces, to process complex statistical material and to become familiar with elaborate accounting and auditing procedures. Thus the reform of financial administration marked a recognition by the leadership that improved bureaucratic procedures were necessary to guarantee the success of its program.

The importance of financial administration was nowhere so evident as in the size of the central government machinery and the complexity of its procedures. The heart of the Senate, after its division into departments in 1763, was the First Department in Petersburg. It was larger than the judicial departments, and its membership of four or five senators in the 1760s had doubled by the 1780s and included eleven senators in 1796. The most reliable index of its status was the participation of two members of the Cabinet in its deliberations, and these were among the most trusted advisers of the Empress (Elagin, Olsuf'ev, later Zavadovskii). The Policemaster General and the Governor General of Petersburg were virtually ex officio members. In addition, the three political families were permanently represented in it: the Trubetskoi-Saltykov clan by Ivan Viazemskii, Alexei Mel'gunov, and Andrei Shuvalov, all three related by marriage; the military-foreign-policy establishment by Marshal Golitsyn and his brother-in-law

Nikolai Iusupov; and the party of the borderlands by Nikolai Samoilov, Potemkin's brother-in-law, Mikhail Krechetnikov, one of the
favorite's protégés, and Peter Passek. Thus the First Department was
clearly the central committee of the elite to which all financial problems
which could not be settled in the colleges were automatically referred.

The Fourth Department was less important, although it was the
appellate instance for the Colleges of War and Navy, the Commissary,
the Provision (*Proviantskaia*) Chancery, the Chancery of Artillery and
Fortifications, and some other military bodies. The two military colleges were not truly subordinated to the Senate; they operated inde-
pendently under the personal authority of the Empress, but the Fourth
Department was the conduit through which they assisted other colleges, governors, and voevodas or directed them to desist from practices which interfered with their operations.[1] It was a much smaller
department, usually of three or four senators, slightly larger in the
1780s and 1790s. Its most important members were Kirill Razumovskii (1764-1796) and his cousin Alexander Naryshkin (1769-1795);
others were their protégés or relatives. There were also two Vorontsovs—Roman, brother-in-law of Martyn Skavronskii, and his nephew
Artemii. This membership suggests a close connection with the Court,
reflecting the importance of military contracts as a source of revenue
for well-placed members of the elite.

A trend not toward an expansion of the central bureaucracy, but
toward the creation of a bureaucratic core of financial specialists entirely devoted to Prince Viazemskii began with the creation of the
Expedition of State Revenues in February 1773, when it was recognized that the First Department, as a committee of great lords and
generals, was not suitable for the backbreaking work necessary to
modernize the tax structure and carry through the budgetary reform
about to be launched. Its director was Alexei Vasil'ev (1774-1780), a
man of modest origins and the son of a former Senate secretary. He
had been Prince Viazemskii's personal secretary (*u General Proku-
rorskikh del*) for four years. The Expedition became the chief budget
office of the Imperial government to which all financial reports previously sent to the two departments had now to be sent.[2]

There is no better way to gauge the importance of public finance
in state administration than to observe that, while there hardly existed
a national police agency, and only two judicial colleges, one can easily
identify ten or twelve central agencies responsible for various aspects
of financial administration. Some functioned as collecting agencies for

[1] PSZ, 1763, N. 11989, pt. 1; 1775, N. 14395; 1796, N. 17648.
[2] PSZ, 1773, N. 13962; 1774, N. 14192; 1775, N. 14339; 1776, N. 14501; Iasnopol'skii, 79-80.

certain types of revenue; others functioned as treasuries as well; and there was a College of Audit.

The most important financial agency was the Commissary. It collected the capitation which was still the largest single source of revenue at the beginning of the reign, and received additional revenue collected by other agencies but earmarked for the maintenance of the army. It was the central treasury for army funds, and all disbursements were made by order of the Chief of the Commissary (*General Krigs-Kommisar*). This high official (lieutenant general) had often been in the past the procurator general himself, but Alexander Glebov was the last one to combine both posts. The Commissary was located in Moscow, and consisted of a major general, three commissioners, one procurator, and ninety-nine clerks—a total staff of 126, including the Petersburg branch. There was also a company of 130 musketeers for guard and convoy duties. Only three men served in the post of *General Krigs-Kommisar*: Glebov until 1775 and Nikolai Durnovo, who was probably forced out by Mikhail Potemkin (1783-1791), a distant relative and strong supporter of the favorite. Both Potemkins died in 1791, and Mikhail's widow later married Senator Iusupov. Durnovo was then restored to his post for the remainder of the reign.

The Provision Chancery was no less important. Its status had been gradually upgraded since 1720, when its chief, the *General Proviantmeister*, was a mere colonel; he was now a major general. The Chancery was based in Petersburg and consisted of a brigadier general, one colonel, one lieutenant colonel, a procurator, and 91 clerks—a total staff of 121, including the Moscow branch. This rather lopsided arrangement, which placed the Commissary in Moscow and the Provision Chancery in Petersburg, was explained by the different functions of these two agencies. The central region was the heart of the textile industry, and it was much easier to transport funds to Moscow than to the northern capital. The Commissary in Moscow functioned in a natural environment. But there were large concentrations of troops on the shores of the Gulf of Finland—three military regions were spread out between the Estonian coast and the Finnish border—and the Petersburg grain store was of vital importance, both as a price regulator and a permanent supplier of grain, groats, oats, and hay. There was a much greater turnover among the leadership of the Provision Chancery than in the Commissary, and six generals were appointed *General Proviantmeister* during the reign, one of whom was the same Durnovo (1771-1775).[3]

There were four major civilian collecting agencies, each responsible

³ PSZ, 1764, N. 12245; 1766, N. 12612.

for a certain type of revenue. The most important was the College of Revenue, which collected the proceeds from the sale of vodka.⁴ The college had a checkered history since its creation in 1719, when Peter intended it to be the major, if not the only, collecting agency in the Empire, capable at the same time of preparing a general revenue budget. Its sorry state in 1764 convinced the Empress that budgetary work had to be assigned to the office of the procurator general. Yet Catherine continued to rely on the president of the college as a major adviser and appointed to this post, after the short tenure of Boris Kurakin, Alexei Mel'gunov (1765-1777), brother-in-law of Nikolai Saltykov, who later became governor general in Iaroslavl'. The College of Revenue was the largest of the specialized agencies, with a total staff, in both capitals, of 249 persons. The Central Salt Board in Moscow was smaller. Its major function was not only to collect the salt revenue but also to develop production and to transport the salt from the eastern and southern borderlands across the country to the deficient areas in the south and west. It was headed by a chief judge, like the president of a college in class III or IV, and consisted of 2 councillors, 2 assessors, a procurator, and another 121 persons. The Board was poorly managed and unable to keep proper accounting of its far-flung operations, despite the reform carried out in 1772 by Mikhail Maslov.

Three agencies shared responsibility for foreign trade: the College of Commerce, whose function seems to have been a purely clerical one of collecting statistics and preparing an annual statement of the balance of trade; the influential Commission of Commerce, which discussed the state of Russian foreign trade and recommended measures to improve it; and the Customs Chancery. All three operated in Petersburg. Ernst von Münnich was director of the Chancery (1763-1784), president of the college (1763-1773), and head of the Commission (1763-1779), but never a senator. He was succeeded as president of the college by Alexander Vorontsov, the son of Roman, and a former ambassador to Great Britain and Holland. Among the members of the Commission we find two state secretaries (Teplov and Soimonov), four senators (Shcherbatov, Alexander, Artemii Vorontsov, and Iusupov) and two more "Germans" (Khristofor von Münnich and Timofei von Klingstedt). Vorontsov was succeeded in 1794 as president of the college by the poet Gavril Derzhavin. The fourth agency, after the Customs Chancery, was the College of Economy, another Moscow-based large college of 271 persons with a branch in Petersburg. Its responsibilities included the management of the former peasants and other properties of the Church, secularized in 1764.

⁴ PSZ, 1763, N. 11991, kn. sht., vol. 44², 61-71. For the origin of the College of Revenue, see Peterson, 140-179.

Alexander Romanovich Vorontsov

Following short tenures by Alexander Kurakin and Sergei Gagarin, the college was headed by Peter Khitrovo until its closing in 1786.[5]

Finally, there was a small group of three important agencies responsible for the finances of the Court. One was the Cabinet, described

[5] PSZ, 1763, N. 11985; 1764, N. 12122, 12087. Khitrovo was related to the Shuvalovs.

in Chapter I. The second was the Chancery of Court Peasants (*Dvor-tsovaia Kantseliariia*), responsible for the management of the Imperial family's peasants. It collected the quitrent paid to the local treasurers appointed by the Chancery, and it paid the salary and pensions of present and past Court personnel. It was a large agency numbering 300 persons in Petersburg and 169 in the Moscow branch, headed by the *Ober Hofmeister*—the equivalent of a full general or class II official. Martyn Skavronskii held that post from 1760 to 1776 and was followed by State Secretary Elagin, who had probably run the agency since 1763 and continued to administer it until 1786. The third was the managing office of the Court (*Pridvornaia Kontora*), chiefly a disbursing agency, responsible for the procurement of provisions and other supplies. It was headed by the *Ober Hofmarschall*. When its establishment was published in 1786 it consisted of 26 persons in Petersburg and 4 in Moscow.[6]

There was as yet no single central treasury, despite Peter's attempt to establish the *Stats-Kontora* in that capacity, but there were at least four treasuries: the Cabinet and the Chancery for Court Peasants, which may be considered one; the Commissary; the Navy (*Admiral-teistvo*); and the *Stats-Kontora*, which might be called the civilian treasury. Because certain sources of revenue were earmarked for certain definite categories of expenditures, there were four separate budgets, each requiring a central agency to receive, hold, and reassign funds received from various sources among other disbursing agencies. The civilian treasury consisted of two agencies, one in Petersburg, the other in Moscow, each headed by a chief judge, but one in class VI, i.e., two or three classes below the president of a college.[7] Their leadership was remarkably stable. The chief judges were colonels Semen Ashitkov in Petersburg (1765-1780) and Alexei Gagarin in Moscow (1765-1780).

Other financial institutions included three banks and the Mint. The Bank of the Nobility, created in 1754, together with the Commercial Bank, which remained of secondary importance, was the usual two-headed agency with directors in both capitals, among whom relatives of Prince Viazemskii and Kirill Razumovskii were prominent. The Assignat Bank, created in 1768 to help finance the Turkish war, was of crucial importance as a bank of issue through which an increasing amount of paper money was put in circulation with less and less regard for the virtue of restraint. The bank was headed by a board (*pravlenie*) operating through two branches, one in Petersburg under a single

⁶ PSZ, 1773, N. 14003, vol. 44², *kn. sht.*, 134-136; 1774, N. 14133.
⁷ PSZ, 1765, N. 12416; 1770, N. 13406.

director, the other in Moscow under two, and each with a staff of 27 persons. The importance given to this bank can be seen from the fact that the Chief Director was Andrei Shuvalov (1768-1789), who also sat in the First Department. The Mint included the Chief Expedition for the reconversion (*peredel*) of copper coins established in 1756 on the recommendation of Peter Shuvalov for the purpose of putting into circulation lighter copper coins and the *Monetnyi Department*, which was part of the College of Mining. It produced coins from copper and silver bought by the government and melted down the *efimki* (Joachimsthalers) collected in the Baltic customs houses into Russian silver coins. Its staff numbered 120 persons in Petersburg and 91 in Moscow.[8]

The College of Audit possessed two unusual features. It was divided into several departments based in Moscow, and it was headed simultaneously, as if to emphasize the sensitiveness of auditing, by a president—Mikhail Maslov (1765-1771) and Alexander Kheraskov (1772-1788)—and a "chief director," who obviously enjoyed higher status:[9] Iakov Shakhovskoi (1762-1766), Roman Vorontsov (1766-1778), and Alexander Golitsyn (1779-1780).

This central apparatus of financial administration formed the largest cluster of agencies in the Imperial government. Some 900 officials, clerks, and couriers and guards served in Moscow, another 800 in Petersburg, and were it not for the unusually large staff of the Chancery for Court Peasants, the importance of Moscow would be even more evident. This top-heavy bureaucracy was not efficient and, as we shall see later in this chapter, had developed autonomous tendencies resistant to pressures for integration and coordination. Its hold had to be broken before substantial progress could be made toward budgetary reform, of which the creation of the Expedition of State Revenues marked the first round.

LOCAL AGENCIES

The fiscal agents of the government in the provinces were the governors and voevodas. No separate agencies existed for tax collection except those established to manage the salt monopoly. The practice of appointing a staff officer in each gubernia and provincial capital to collect the capitation and dispatch it to military units was discontinued in

[8] On banks in general, see Borovoi; PSZ, 1754, N. 10235; 1764, N. 12127; 1765, N. 12602; 1766, N. 12702; 1768, N. 13219; 1771, N. 13702. The Foundling Home also operated as a bank: see Filiminov and de Madariaga, 477-478. For the Mint, see PSZ, 1756, N. 16023; 1762, N. 11439; 1768, N. 13044, 13117; 1788, N. 16622.

[9] Amburger, *Geschichte*, 219; PSZ, 1773, N. 14010.

1764, and the functions of these officers were assumed by one of the two deputies of the governor and by the deputy of each voevoda.[10]

Governors and voevodas, however, were not truly tax collectors. Rather, they were treasurers who received the funds collected in towns and villages. Many uezds before the reform had populations ranging from 40,000 to 60,000 souls, and not a few were even much larger. The network of intermediaries between the voevoda and the peasant taxpayer grew with the size of the uezd, and the success of tax collection depended on the cooperation of a vast network of men elected by their communities to help in the equitable distribution of the tax burden. These men provided the channels by which taxation was legitimized, by which the demands of the leadership expressed in lump sums for each gubernia and uezd were translated into an acceptable method of obtaining resources from a hard-pressed population.

It was the assembly of heads of families which adjusted the arbitrary demands of the voevoda to the community's capacity to pay by applying its own extra-legal criteria. Russian tax law, at least insofar as personal taxes were concerned, was a compendium of two bodies of law: the positive law, which set the rate of taxation per registered soul, fixed and equal for all, the amount to be paid by each community, the deadlines to bring it to the voevoda, and the penalties for non-compliance; and the communal law, which took into consideration the capacity to pay of each soul and distributed the burden accordingly. The positive law proclaimed the equality of all registered souls; the communal shifted a heavier burden onto the shoulders of the more prosperous and enterprising peasants, who assumed fiscal responsibility for those who could not pay or had left the community for one reason or another.[11]

As in much else, the town was the nodal point in fiscal administration. Taxes were paid in the office of the voevoda by both townsmen and peasants; and it was from the town that tax-farmers and salesmen elected by their communities or the *magistrat* conveyed the salt and the vodka for sale to the peasant masses. In each town a *starosta* was responsible for the collection of the capitation. He had a staff of assessors (*okladshchiki*) and collectors (*sborshchiki*) whose size depended on the importance of the town. The collection of indirect taxes required a more elaborate organization. The sale of vodka and salt—to take only two important sources of indirect revenue—took place in three different ways, by no means mutually exclusive. In one case the *magistrat* assumed responsibility for selecting the *larechnye* (who

[10] PSZ, 1764, N. 12138; Iasnopol'skii, 82; Got'e, I, 99-101.
[11] Alexandrov, 114.

kept the keys to the stores) and the *tseloval'niki* (who kissed the cross swearing to collect the revenue honestly), together with *golovy, burmistry*, and *vybornye*, who pledged to sell the same amount as during the preceding years, and by implication to make up for the arrears as well if the entire sum was not paid to the voevoda. In poorer towns without any merchants or *magistrat*, salt and vodka were sold "on faith" (*na vere*) by people chosen by the entire community, which assumed responsibility for the arrears. These two systems were favored until the 1750s because they were suitable to an economy where money was scarce and the only security against default was the property of a collective lessee. The fact that sworn collectors were not supposed to make a profit eliminated the incentive to sell. Merchants or state peasants sometimes chosen against their will were forced to leave their homes for long periods of time and suffered losses in their trade. The resulting resentment was not conducive to aggressive salesmanship, and persistent arrears were the natural consequence.

The third procedure was tax-farming. A tax-farmer was not elected by either *magistrat* or town. He offered on his own free will to sell at least the same amount as the average pledged during the past four years, plus a certain amount to induce the governor to give him the contract. In return for this pledge to deposit a definite sum for a certain period, usually four consecutive years, the tax-farmer was allowed to keep the proceeds from all additional sales. This was an attractive proposition for the government since the unpredictability of the revenue was one of the major obstacles to the preparation of a comprehensive national budget. It was also attractive to the townsmen because the tax-farmer employed his own staff and the town no longer had to elect reluctant fiscal agents save those still necessary to watch over the stores. But the advantage was largely nullified in the eyes of the population by the abuses inherent to tax-farming, especially of vodka. The tax-farmer was an aggressive man seeking to maximize his profit at any cost, and the sale of vodka beyond reasonable limits was offensive to public morality.

The number of fiscal agents elected by the towns was very large. In 1766 the town of Kashin elected 118 people to serve in various posts, of whom 59 were engaged in the sale of vodka, 35 in the sale of salt, and only 2 were responsible for the collection of the capitation. Tula elected 76, of whom 44 sold vodka, 16 salt, and 3 collected the capitation. And several of the others engaged in some form of fiscal activity. Kizevetter has given us a total number of 14,564 elected officials in 175 towns of central Russia.[12] If we assume that at least

[12] Kizevetter, *Posadskaia obshchina*, 172-183, 211, 217-223, 231-232.

eighty percent engaged in the collection of revenue (and this should be a conservative estimate) it appears that some 11,350 individuals constituted the real backbone of Russian fiscal administration, while there were no more than about 220 governors and voevodas in the territory of the twenty-six post-reform gubernias. These men were the extension of the official hierarchy into the communities that elected them, active agents undertaking to increase the profit of the treasury by selling salt and vodka together with their wares in widely scattered hamlets and villages that were beyond the reach of official agents. Conversely, voevodas could not operate without their tacit consent, without their willingness to mediate between the noble officials who demanded funds and the communities that agreed to part with them on their own terms. Nowhere else was the symbiosis between the ruling class and the socially dependent so continuous and so pervasive as here.

As a result of the excessive emphasis placed upon the dichotomy between state and society and on the repressive nature of state authority, the importance of consent as the very prerequisite of a tolerably efficient system of tax collection has often been overlooked. No one, of course, will deny the importance of coercion as the expression of sovereignty, but coercion can be effective only within the context of a broad consensus. It is thanks to Paul Bushkovitch that the attention of modern readers has been drawn to this oversight by traditional historians. It is tempting to harp upon the complaints of merchants that the sale of vodka and salt interfered with their business and to see them as the victims of an oppressive fiscal administration. But these complaints seem to reflect the restlessness of men on the make, intent upon shaking off the fetters of a communal world, much more than opposition to the fiscal constraints imposed from above. The sale of vodka was for the merchant what the sale of grain was for the landowner, a welcome source of cash in an economy which in so many ways was still close to a natural one. The spread of tax-farming in the reign of Catherine went hand in hand with the development of an upper stratum of townsmen given privileged status in 1775, for whom the collection of revenue became "a mechanism for the production of profit for the merchants as well as for the state."[13]

The symbiosis was no less evident in the annual extraction of large sums in the form of capitation and quitrent. The serfs paid the capitation to the voevoda and the quitrent to their masters. Other peasants paid both to the central treasuries, the "black" peasants through their *starosty*, the former peasants of the Church through their treasurers,

[13] Bushkovich, 395-398.

the peasants of the Court through their "administrators." The collection of the capitation by the lords or their stewards was not unlike tax-farming. A tax-farmer, we recall, had to pledge to pay a definite amount for a certain number of years and was free to keep whatever he collected above that amount. The lords were required to pay seventy kopecks per registered soul, but the amount of the quitrent was left to their discretion. The difference, of course, was that the amount pledged by the tax-farmer was expected to go up each time a new contract was negotiated, while the rate of the capitation remained fixed. Landowner and voevoda distributed the yield of these personal taxes in such a way as to benefit the interests of their class. The capitation went to support the army of noble officers and peasant conscripts. The quitrent was split into roughly two equal parts since the serfs still constituted about half of the population. The sums paid to the landowners went to gratify their private needs. The rest went to support the Court and the civil establishment of landed and landless noblemen. Thus voevoda and landowner, even if they were rivals at times in the competition for scarce resources, worked hand in hand as the agents of the dominant class, which used the revenue from the peasant masses as the source of its private support and the underpinning of its political power.

Governors, voevodas, townsmen, and peasants who collected the revenue were found everywhere and constituted in fact a single yet amorphous body of fiscal officials. In addition, there existed in a selected number of towns certain agencies standing apart from this organic chain of appointed and elected agents. Their relationship with the governor varied. Some were altogether independent, others were doubly subordinated to him and to their central agency in Petersburg or Moscow. Some were disbursing, others were collecting agencies. But all played an important role in the management of state funds, and no study of financial administration before the reform can afford to ignore them.

A first group consisted of the local agencies of the Commissary and the Provision Chancery. There were usually four commissary commissions in central Russia headed by a "senior commissioner" in the rank of brigadier general (Petersburg and Moscow) or colonel (Smolensk and Kazan). Each commission received the capitation and other funds assigned to it by the central Commissary from neighboring provinces for salaries and the purchase of equipment. The network of provision commissions was much more extensive because it followed closely the territorial distribution of the army. In the 1780s there were five commissions under a "provision-master general" (lieutenant colonel) in Petersburg, Moscow, Novgorod, Kazan, Nizhnii Novgorod, and

another four headed by a "senior provision-master" (major) in Vladimir, Smolensk, Voronezh, and Tambov. The task of these commissions was to purchase provisions and fodder with funds supplied by
the commissary commissions and to run some sixty-four stores in
central Russia alone.[14]

A second group of specialized agencies included the local branches
of the Assignat Bank. The first branch was opened in Iaroslavl' in
1772; four more were opened in Smolensk, Velikii Ustiug, Vyshnii
Volochek, and Nizhnii Novgorod in 1777; another seven in Novgorod,
Pskov, Tver, Tula, Orel, Kursk, and Tambov in 1781; and two in
Kazan and Arkhangelsk in 1782—i.e., in twelve of the twenty-six new
gubernia capitals. The purpose of these branches was to facilitate the
conversion of coins into assignats and vice versa without the need to
travel to Petersburg or Moscow. By the 1780s, however, only seven
remained. Three local banks called loan (zaemnye, ssudnye) "expeditions" were opened in Nizhnii Novgorod, Kazan, and Orenburg,
with a capital of 500,000 rubles each from a credit of 1.5 million
granted by the Assignat Bank to the Moscow Noble Bank to help
noblemen who had suffered during the Pugachev rebellion.[15]

Other specialized agencies were the custom houses where export
and import taxes were collected. The Petersburg custom house towered
above all others, as befitted the role of the port in Russian foreign
trade. In 1772, 37 percent of the export trade passed through the port,
and 46 percent of its import trade; by 1795 the share of Petersburg
had grown to 59 percent and 63 percent, respectively. The custom
house was a large agency of 244 persons in 1764, 338 in 1776. Its
personnel was in part appointed, in part elected by the Petersburg
merchants. It had two satellites, one in Narva, the other in Kronshtadt
with staffs of 31 and 15 respectively in 1776. The second largest
custom house, in Arkhangelsk, accounted for 39 percent of all imports,
17 percent of the exports. It had four little satellites at Kola, Onega,
Novodvinsk, and Mezen with a total staff of only 29 in 1776.[16]

Finally, there were three salt boards (kontory) in central Russia: in
Petersburg for the supply of the northern capital; in Nizhnii Novgorod,
where large stores were built for the salt brought from the upper Kama
in large river boats; and in Saratov, the headquarters for the exploi-

[14] PSZ, 1764, N. 12245; 1766, N. 12612; 1768, N. 13189; Dvukhsotletie Intendantstva, 36-39.
[15] PSZ, 1772, N. 13833; 1781, N. 15275; 1782, N. 15508; 1788, N. 16626; 1786,
N. 16479, par. 39; 1775, N. 14285, 14333; SIRIO, XXVII (1880), 180.
[16] Klokman, Sotsial'no-ekon. istoriia, 249, 308; PSZ, 1764, N. 12043; 1765, N.
12310; 1771, N. 13710. The combined shtaty are in PSZ, 1795, N. 17419, vol. 44²,
kn. sht., 224-251.

tation of the Elton salt lake. Smaller agencies called *kommisarstva* existed in Arkhangelsk, Olonets, and Pskov.[17] All these agencies, like the custom houses, were outside the control of the governor and depended directly upon their central headquarters, the Custom Chancery in Petersburg and the Central Salt Board in Moscow.

THE REFORM

The reform rejected the elective principle and carried out a radical deconcentration from the center to the provinces, where uezd treasurers took over the financial responsibilites of the voevodas and joined the land captains and the uezd judges to form the leadership of the uezd. A treasury chamber (*kazennaia palata*) shared with the two judicial chambers the specialized responsibilities which the reform removed from the direct jurisdiction of the governor. At the same time, both at the center and in the provinces, the reform concentrated financial administration in the office of the Procurator General and the treasury chambers, respectively, thus ending the fragmentation of responsibilities which had been so detrimental to orderly budgetary procedure.[18]

The care with which legislation defined the jurisdiction, responsibilities, and procedures of the treasury chambers illustrated their importance in the eyes of the government. The Organic Law called each chamber a joint department of the Colleges of Revenue and Audit. In fact, its jurisdiction was much wider than that of two colleges. Not only was the chamber required to keep the tax rolls and the statistics on the population of the gubernia, to negotiate contracts with tax farmers up to the value of 10,000 rubles—the pre-reform governor's power had been limited to 3,000—and to audit (*revizovat'*) local accounts. It was also given jurisdiction over salt sales and procurement, the construction and maintenance of public buildings, the protection of state peasants, the management of state lands and forests (activities that came under the general term of *domostroitel'nye dela*), and the defense of the fiscal interests of the treasury in litigation among agencies or with private individuals. In 1779 the custom houses passed under its jurisdiction; so did all factories and mines, private and state-owned, in 1781. Thus the chamber was much more than a local "treasury"; it was also an agency of economic management with power to exploit enterprises, procure supplies, store and ship goods. The

[17] PSZ, 1763, N. 11991, vol. 44², *kn. sht.*, 65-67.
[18] The major documents are the Organic Law (PSZ, 1775, N. 14392), the Instruction to the treasury chambers (1781, N. 15141), and the Instruction to the uezd treasurers (1782, N. 15405).

chamber, however, was not given the judicial powers of a college to hand down its own decisions and order their execution. It had to refer its uncontested (*bezspornye*) findings to the gubernia board for execution, either directly or through the land captains in the uezds, and it was represented as a party before either judicial chamber by the deputy procurator for fiscal affairs (*striapchii kazennykh del*). Its powers were strictly limited to the application of the letter of the law. It could not impose new taxes or remove existing ones from the books or cancel arrears; all its disbursements had to be authorized by Imperial or Senate ukases or orders (*assignatsii*) of the Expedition of State Revenues.

To carry out its many responsibilities the chamber was given an extensive staff. Each chamber was headed by a vice-governor in class V who received 1,200 rubles a year, or 360 rubles more than the chairmen of the judicial chambers who were in the same class. He was appointed by the Empress. The second-ranking official in the chamber was the "director of economy" in class VI, who received the high salary of 1,000 rubles, no doubt with the intention of protecting him against temptations, and who was appointed by the Senate on recommendation of the gubernia board. There were four other regular members of the chamber. A councillor in class VI was in charge of the "expedition" responsible for state, Court, and former Church peasants and leases of state property; for keeping records of transactions affecting them; and statistics on fairs and grain stores. The gubernia treasurer in class VIII was the supervisor within the chamber of all uezd treasurers in the gubernia. Of the two assessors, both in class VIII, one headed another "expedition" responsible for public buildings, bridges, and ferries; the other was sent out from time to time on inspection tours. All these officials were appointed by the Senate. The clerks came from a common pool run by the gubernia board which had at its disposal the sum of 6,980 rubles.[19]

The full extent of the deconcentration does not appear until the additional functions of the chambers are taken into consideration. An audit "expedition" was added in 1781, a vodka and salt "expedition" in 1782, an industrial (*gornaia*) "expedition" (in Olonets, Viatka, and Perm only), and even a custom "expedition" (in Petersburg and Arkhangelsk). Thus the entire fiscal and industrial apparatus in the two capitals was dismantled, and its functions—management, accounting,

[19] OL, art. 118-121; PSZ, 1779, N. 14957, pt. 6; 1781, N. 15127, 15141, art. 7-8, 10-15, 26-27, 32-33, 91-92; see also 1784, N. 15996, pt. 2, and 1786, N. 16358. For a list of officials, their ranks and salaries see OL, art. 11-12, 48-49, 51, 59, 61-62, 117 and PSZ, 1796, N. 17494, vol. 44², *kn. sht.*, 254-257; see also Slezkinskii, "Bytovye cherty," for an inventory of the property of the Novgorod gubernia treasurer (1791); Grigor'ev, 226.

and audit—were turned over to provincial officials appointed by the Senate. Another innovation was the "Board of Public Welfare" (*prikaz obshchestvennago prizreniia*), chaired by the governor and consisting of two representatives each from the upper land court, the gubernia *magistrat* and the upper *rasprava*. It could also hold joint meetings with uezd marshals and town *glavy*, and met once a year between January 8 and Passion week. The committee should be considered another financial agency because it operated much like a bank: given a basic capital of 15,000 rubles, it collected fines and donations, and either loaned these monies at interest or spent them for the construction of schools, theaters, and workhouses and for other philanthropic and cultural purposes.[20]

In each uezd the reform placed a treasurer in class IX, appointed for three years by the Procurator General (as State Treasurer) on the recommendation of the chamber. As their title implies, these treasurers received the revenue, disbursed funds on orders of the chamber, and kept accounts of all their operations. They were subordinated to the gubernia treasurer, and an effort was made to remove them entirely from the jurisdiction of the gubernia board: even their leaves of absence granted by the board required the approval of the chamber, which also passed final judgment on their official activities at the end of their three-year terms.[21]

The concentration of financial administration in the chambers was preceded by a reform of the treasury in 1780. Before the reform, as we have seen, separate treasuries existed for different types of revenues. The type of expenditure, ordinary or extraordinary, became the criterion when two new treasuries were set up in Petersburg. One was the Treasury for Ordinary Expenditures (*kaznacheistvo dlia shtatnykh summ*), headed by a state councillor (class V) appointed by the Empress. It consisted of a deputy in class VI, a treasurer (VIII), a secretary, and an undetermined staff of bookkeepers and clerks. The other was the Treasury for Extraordinary Expenditures (*kaznacheistvo dlia ostatochnykh summ*). The two treasuries and their branches in Moscow were larger than the *Stats-Kontora* and of higher rank. They were directly subordinated to the Expedition of State Revenues, specifically to the Procurator General.[22]

The major beneficiary of the reform was the Expedition of State

[20] PSZ, 1782, N. 15318, 15350, 15353; 1789, N. 16795; 1796, N. 17494, vol. 44², *kn. sht.*, 265, pt. 15; 1781, N. 15141, art. 36-43; 1782, N. 15409; 1784, N. 15968; 1790, N. 16915, 1782, N. 15348, 15554; 1784, N. 16101; Grigor'ev, 357. For the committee of public welfare, see OL, art. 38-39, 380, 383, 392, 429; Salias, 93, 109; PSZ, 1783, N. 15657.

[21] OL, art. 52, 122-123, 134-137, 163; PSZ, 1781, N. 15301.

[22] PSZ, 1779, N. 14957; 1780, N. 15039, 15075; 1784, N. 15927.

Revenues, broken up in October 1780 into four expeditions: the first
to keep accounts on the revenue, the second to keep accounts on
expeditures, the third to audit these accounts, and the fourth to collect
arrears. Each expedition consisted of a real state councillor (class IV)
and two state councillors; all three were appointed by the Empress.
There were a secretary and an unspecified number of clerks.

Each expedition was run like a college, with the real state councillor
carrying out the functions of the president under the *General'nyi Reglament*. The difference was in his subordination, not to the Senate
but directly to the Procurator General, who was now referred to either
as the "Administrator of the Expeditions and the Treasuries" or simply
as the interim State Treasurer. His control over the expeditions was
very tight. He received daily memoranda from each expedition on the
course of its activities, requested explanations, took disciplinary measures, and in serious cases referred the matter to the Senate or the
Empress. The four expeditions were of equal standing but worked in
unison. Joint meetings may have taken place, and the fiction seems to
have been retained that each acted in the name of the "Expedition of
State Revenues." These agencies were run by men close to the Procurator General.[23] Prince Sergei Viazemskii headed the first expedition
for many years (1782-1793). Vasilii Khlebnikov (whose name suggests
a non-noble origin, not unlike that of Alexei Vasil'ev, with whom he
was closely associated) was responsible for the second from 1787 to
1794. Vasil'ev, who headed the entire Expedition before the reorganization of 1780, became head of the third expedition (1781-1793) and
was followed by Prince Alexei Kurakin, son of the former president
of the College of Revenue and future Procurator General under Paul.
The fourth expedition was run by Vasil'ev's brother Andreian (1781-
1785) and Mikhail Buturlin (1786-1796), a relative of Kurakin.

The reform also affected the audit system. To facilitate its time-
consuming work, the new Audit Expedition created its own satellite
expeditions—the terminology is extremely confusing—for the auditing
of liquor and salt accounts of the local expeditions of the treasury
chambers and for those of the industrial expeditions. Its jurisdiction,
however, did not extend to the accounts of the Cabinet, whose director
was instructed to set up under his own administration a separate audit
expedition consisting of two college councillors and two clerks.[24]

The auditing of military accounts was similarly concentrated in the
College of War and its president, Potemkin. The same ukase of De-

²³ PSZ, 1779, N. 14957; 1780, N. 15040 and 15076; 1781, N. 15120 and 15140,
pt. 16; 1783, N. 15742; Iasnopol'skii, 84-85.

²⁴ PSZ, 1779, N. 14888; 1786, N. 16415; for the industrial expeditions see 1783,
N. 15739 and 15740.

cember 1779 created an audit expedition headed by a comptroller general in the rank of major general who was an ex officio member of the College of War. The new agency consisted of a senior controller (brigadier general) responsible for the auditing of the accounts of the Commissary as the central budgetary agency of the army, two controllers (colonels) responsible, one for the accounts of the Artillery and Engineers department, the other for those of the Provision Chancery. The Comptroller General, not unlike Prince Viazemskii in this capacity, received daily memoranda from the other members, brought before the assembly of the college any matters requiring additional consideration, as well as proposals of sanctions for inadequate performance. Similar provisions were made for the auditing of the accounts of the College of the Navy, its local agencies, and the Baltic Fleet; while the accounts of the Black Sea Fleet remained under Potemkin as its commander and Governor General of New Russia.[25]

The reform created no institutional link between the audit expedition under the Procurator General, the military and naval expeditions, and the audit expedition of the Court: it was a faithful reflection of the distribution of power in the middle years of the reign among Olsuf'ev and Bezborodko, Potemkin, and Prince Viazemski. Each controlled a very extensive jurisdiction, but, although the Procurator General had now brought under his wing almost the entire machinery of revenue collection as well as the treasuries, the ultimate control over expenditures escaped him, not only because he had to contend before the Empress against powerful rivals for the allocation of funds, but also because he lacked the institutional means to look into the propriety of expenditures and to check the insatiable demands of a wasteful military establishment.

The reform considerably enlarged the size of the provincial staff, a prerequisite to any improvement in tax collection and budgetary procedure. Until 1775 there was only the deputy of the governor or the voevoda to keep the accounts. This gives us about forty officials in class V and VI and some 180 deputies of uezd voevodas, perhaps in class IX, altogether about 220 officials to college the revenue in central Russia alone. After the reform, assuming each treasury chamber with its liquor and salt expedition consisted of 4 officials in class V and VI, and 5 in class VIII, we find 234 officials in these three classes, plus more than 300 uezd treasurers in class IX, not including some 400 retired non-commissioned officers from the Guard appointed to local

---

[25] PSZ, 1779, N. 14957; 1780, N. 15041; 1781, N. 15292. It seems that a separate auditing (*shchetnaia*) expedition was retained in the Chancery of Artillery, but subordinated to the Auditing Expedition: see PSZ, 1780, N. 15041, pt. 2.

treasuries—the so-called *prisiazhnye*—and several hundred clerks. This massive transfer of officials, all appointed by the Senate except the vice-governor, must have given the Procurator General extraordinary influence in dispensing patronage, and it was certainly one of the most extensive carpetbagging operations in Russian history.

But what are we to think about this apparent bureaucratization of financial administration? The comments made in the preceding chapter about the personnel of the judicial chambers apply here as well. The case of the director of economy (whether he was a local landowner or an outsider) is evidence that the interests of the landed nobility had not been overlooked when it was decided to appoint rather than to elect the new fiscal agents. In Smolensk gubernia, for example, the governor general recommended a former marshal of the nobility. In Petersburg gubernia the director in the 1780s was Anton von Engelhardr, former "general director of economy" in Lifland, and another Engelhardr served in the same post in Moscow. Although they were outsiders, Baltic nobles were known for the passion with which they defended their class interests. It is reasonable to believe that the manager of state properties was a landowner who took the interests of his class very much to heart. If we remember that the director of economy had jurisdiction over all state and Court peasants, the surveying of lands and forests, and the leasing of state properties (mills, forests, meadows—the so-called *obrochnye stat'i*), this appointment was a major patronage plum for the local nobility, giving it a free hand to exploit the peasants and domains of the treasury. The remarks of Prince Viazemskii and Bezborodko that the treasury was not getting a fair share of the revenue from its properties because the directors of economy were venal seem to confirm this.[26] As to the uezd treasurers who tapped the wealth of the nation at its very source, they were but

[26] TsGADA, f. 16, d. 632, fol. 3 (Smolensk); *SIRIO*, XXVIII (1880), 260, 276. Not all directors of economy, it is true, were local landowners: see Bolotov, IV, 751-752, 1091-1094. In Kursk gubernia, Prozorovskii, the governor general, had no confidence in the directors of economy: TsGADA, f. 248, d. 6560, fol. 35-36. In Viatka the director (together with the governor and the vice-governor) was accused of despoiling state peasants and collecting unauthorized taxes: "Podmetnoe pis'mo." On the Penza directors, see Dolgorukov, "Zapiski," 1914, N. 2 (Feb.), 73, 83; N. 3 (March), 68; N. 5 (Sept.), 60-61; N. 6 (Oct.), 57-59. Dolgorukov, vice-governor in Penza, was himself a local landowner. When he was physically assaulted by another landowner for allegedly seducing his wife, Dolgorukov found little support from the governor and had to appeal to the Empress herself to obtain satisfaction. The scandal was treated as a family affair, not as a case in which a private individual had raised his hand against a representative of the "state": "Zapiski," 1914, N. 6, 29-31. In Smolensk (and probably elsewhere) an exception was made to the 1714 law barring officials from contracting for the supply of goods to the government so that the vice-governor (a Potemkin) and the director of economy (related to the procurator) may not be "deprived of their rights as landowners": TsGADA, f. 16, d. 200, fol. 7.

nominally appointed by the Procurator General, and their incumbency was a second major source of patronage for the provincial nobility. What complicity we must assume between the land captain and the uezd judge, on the one hand, and the uezd treasurer, on the other, respectively elected and confirmed by the governor, and appointed from among the local nobles!

In one respect, however, these fiscal officials did have to keep in mind the interest of the "state." The ruler collected revenue from the peasants of the Court; the ruling class collected revenue from its own serfs and exploited natural resources to raise its income. But a substantial part of the funds collected locally went to support the army that represented a cross-section of society; it was assigned to purchase construction materials, food, and equipment from other segments of society. It is in this sense that fiscal administration served the higher interest of the collectivity, an interest distinct from the personal interest of the autocrat and the collective interest of the ruling class.

The creation of the treasury chambers, the expansion of the Expedition of State Revenues, and the creation of the two Treasuries for nearly all revenue collected in the entire country made the colleges no longer necessary. They were closed one by one in a most far-reaching dismantling operation. The *Stats-Kontora* was closed in 1783, the College of Revenue and the Salt Board in 1785, the College of Economy on January 1, 1786, and the Chancery for Court Peasants in November. The College of Audit, which had been trying to dispose of its backlog of cases since 1781, closed in 1788. Even the Custom Chancery was closed (1780), although the College of Commerce and the Commerce Commission continued to operate until 1796. The Assignat Bank remained, of course, but the Noble Bank was dissolved in 1786, when a new Loan Bank combining its functions with those of an insurance company and a bank for the financing of municipal construction was opened under a chief director, State Secretary Zavadovskii (1787-1796). When we add that the closing also affected the College of Mining—its managerial functions were transferred to the industrial expeditions of the treasury chambers—in 1785 and the College of Manufactures in 1780, it appears that the entire executive machinery of domestic administration had been dismantled by the late 1780s, and that Moscow had indeed ceased to be the administrative capital of the Empire.[27]

What, then, remained? The Cabinet, reorganized in 1786 into the

[27] For the *Stats-Kontora*, see PSZ, 1780, N. 15074; 1782, N. 15347; 1783, N. 15660; for the College of Revenue, 1784, N. 16096; the College of Economy, 1785, N. 16273; the Chancery of Court Peasants, 1786, N. 16451; the College of Audit, 1782, N. 15347; 1785, N. 16273; 1788, N. 16629; the Salt Board, 1783, N. 15880; the Customs Chancery and the College of Commerce, 1780, N. 15074; 1796, N. 17510.

chief economic and budgetary office of the Court; the College of War with the Commissary, the Provision Chancery, and the Chancery of Artillery, more than ever closely integrated into a single directing agency for the entire land army; and the Procurator General/State Treasurer, the undisputed master of the four expeditions. The abolition of the colleges removed several centers of influence whose presidents had enough authority to be given access to the throne. The managerial and administrative responsibilities of the colleges were either annulled by legislation, as in the case of the authorization to open new factories, or were turned over to the new treasury chambers, and their financial responsibilities were given to the Expedition of State Revenues. The leading figures of the Expedition, although still appointed by the Empress, were subordinated to the Procurator General.

Thus the effect of the reform was to reduce the size of the central government, to eliminate the direct links that had existed between the First Department and the executive agencies, and to establish the Procurator General as the prototype of a minister of finance through whom all communications addressed to the Senate had to pass. He was not only the "president" of the four expeditions. He also became the director of the Mint in 1788 and the chief director of the Assignat Bank in 1789, following the death of his relative Shuvalov. If we add that the treasury chambers reported to the Expedition of State Revenues and the procurator in each gubernia board was an agent of the Procurator General, the full extent of Prince Viazemskii's influence can easily be measured. And yet, as in a Greek tragedy, there was a fatal flaw. The Prince reached the zenith of his power in the late 1780s. But in 1789 he suffered his first stroke, and by 1791, the year of the death of his great counterpart Potemkin, he had become hopelessly crippled.[28] Long years of hard work and the ambition to assume ever greater responsibility than was humanly possible had taken their toll. After his death in January 1793 the posts of procurator general and state treasurer were no longer held by the same person. Alexander Samoilov became Procurator General and Director of the Mint, Senator Peter Miatlev (First Department) headed the Assignat Bank, and Fedor Golubtsov, a former personal secretary of Prince Viazemskii (1786-1792) and the son-in-law of Alexei Vasil'ev, became State Treasurer.

As we look back upon the reform, it appears that its lasting value was the creation of a simpler and well-integrated machinery for the

---

[28] On the sad condition of Prince Viazemskii in 1791, paralyzed, carried in a wheelchair, and unable sometimes to recognize other officials, see Dolgorukov, "Zapiski," 1914, N. 2 (Feb.), 64.

collection of the revenue and the maintenance of a regular cash flow, so that revenue and expenditure, at least in peacetime, would be known at any time and kept in relative balance. This was no mean achievement in the eighteenth century, and the reform of financial organization remains one of the most important components of the great reform.

THE EXPENDITURE BUDGET

THE THREE BUDGETS

It is customary to begin an examination of the national budget with a survey of the sources of revenue. The dynamic part of a budget, however, is not the revenue but the expenditure. The nearly permanent discrepancy between these two elements reflects the tensions between political ambitions and limited capabilities, between the ministers of finance, who seek to balance expenditures against the revenue, and the more enterprising leaders, for whom financial considerations are subordinated to the wider objectives of fame and power. The revenue increases slowly because it is usually close to the maximum amount which can be extracted or which it is politically expedient to extract at any given time. Expenditure levels can be raised by a stroke of the pen; greater political commitments abroad, army buildup, military campaigns, ambitious construction programs are always attractive. The second half of Catherine's reign provided a very graphic illustration of the tensions between political aggressiveness and inadequate resources, between a procurator general who felt that growing expenditures should be defrayed by taxation and limited borrowing and the leaders of the foreign policy and military establishment, who did not hesitate to court financial disaster if this guaranteed that Russia would become a great power on the Black Sea and in Central Europe.

One of the major problems faced by the political leadership before the reform was the inability to determine with reliable accuracy both the amount of the revenue and the level of expenditures. The often repeated contention that public finance was a state secret in Russia did not necessarily imply that exact figures were known even to the leadership. Rather, the conspiracy of silence over financial statistics served the interests of all agencies in the Court, the army, and the provinces in keeping vast sums unaccounted for. Class interest and the underdeveloped state of accounting reinforced each other to create a chaotic situation ripe for the application of the creed of the Enlightenment that reason and logic must guide action.

An expenditure budget can be simply a complex of departmental budgets, each of which has the advantage of locating responsibility and facilitating auditing. It can also be functional when funds are assigned for the performance of certain activities, whether or not these belong to the jurisdiction of one or more agencies. It may consist in part of special funds serving to finance specific activities but fed by specific sources of revenue which do not go into the general fund. It may finally consist of ordinary and extraordinary expenditures, the definition of each type remaining unstable. The pre-reform Imperial budget—if one can be said to have existed—rested above all on departmental budgets. After the reform, it became chiefly a functional budget, in combination with the use of special funds, especially for the financing of the vodka and salt monopolies as well as state industries. In both cases, however, the overriding principle was the distinction between ordinary and extraordinary expenditures.

There were compelling reasons at the time for relying on this least effective criterion. No one knew how much was collected and how much was spent. The emphasis therefore had to be placed on identifying a core of permanent expenditures, subject to few and easily monitored changes. An ordinary expenditure was one authorized by a table of organization (*shtat*) approved by the Empress, and automatically renewed from year to year unless changes were made. These expenditures were chiefly salaries and a lump sum for the hiring of clerks and for office supplies. Extraordinary expenditures were those that either could not be fitted into a table or resulted from the operation of market forces which distorted the projection of the original estimates. Naturally, the preparation of an ordinary budget required the existence of a table of organization of all agencies—precisely what was lacking at the beginning of the reign. This deplorable situation helps us to understand the importance of the nearly complete table published in December 1763, showing in detail the title and salary of all personnel employed by each agency in Moscow and Petersburg, in the gubernias and uezds. At the same time a military commission was engaged in preparing a similar table for the field army, the garrisons, and the artillery. Therefore it was not until at least 1765 that the Russian government possessed for the first time the basic documents necessary for the compilation of an ordinary expenditure budget.

The size of the extraordinary budget reflected a number of circumstances: the accuracy of the ordinary budget, whether all permanent expenditures had truly been included; the political and military situation requiring short-term expenditures; and various domestic programs increasingly defined in functional terms after the closing of the colleges. The following table (in millions of rubles) shows the growing share of extraordinary expenditures in the total budget:[1]

[1] Kulomzin in *SIRIO*, XXVII (1880), xxxii-xxxiv. I follow Kulomzin here because of the distinction made between ordinary and extraordinary expenditures. Chechulin

	Ordin. Exp.	Extra. Exp.	Total	% of Extra. Exp.
1765	19.7	.6	20.3	3
1773	25.9	2.5	28.4	9
1785	43.8	14.4	58.2	24
1794	49.5	15.6	65.1	27

The sharp increase in the percentage of extraordinary expenditures in the 1780s was due to a combination of factors, including the financing of the national debt and larger appropriations for the military and naval establishments. In addition, the general rise of prices for commodities purchased by the government upset the permanence of the ordinary budget predicted upon stable prices. To a large extent the rise of extraordinary expenditures simply meant that the assumptions upon which the ordinary budget was built in the 1760s were no longer valid.

Before the reform there were four separate budgets: for the Court, for the army, for the navy, and for the civilian administration. Each had its source of revenue, its own expenditures, and received additional sums from whatever source was available. After the reform which brought about a concentration of treasury operations, ordinary expenditures in the four budgets were financed from one treasury, while the other functioned as a reserve from which funds were withdrawn to cover extraordinary expenditures. When funds were inadequate, the government resorted to the printing press.

The level of ordinary expenditures in the military budget was fixed by the tables of organization for infantry and cavalry regiments and for battalions of garrison troops, as well as by separate tables for all agencies constituting the military establishment. In the 1770s, for example, a regiment of musketeers (2,093 men) cost 52,567 rubles, of which 28,239 were for salary; a regiment of cuirassiers (1,124 men) cost 59,124 rubles, and one of dragoons (1,872 men) 76,456 rubles. Salaries for the so-called *generalitet* (310,300 rubles) were paid separately among three marshals, eight full generals, twenty lieutenant generals, and fifty-one major generals.[2]

---

gives the following total expenditures (*Ocherki*), 313-317: 1765, 22.6; 1773, 38.9; 1785, 56.5; 1795, 79.1.

[2] These figures come from a large sheet (fol. 161) inserted in the Commissary's report of September 1776 to the College of War: TsGVIA, f. 12, d. 46. It will be noted that the total allowance for each of these superior officers does not match the figures given in Appendix B. The reason is that the figures entered here include, beside basic salary, additional allowances for provisions (*ratsiony*) and domestic help and the same for their adjutants. Accordingly, the total allowance of a marshal was 14,905 rubles, that of a

This ordinary budget formed the core, relatively permanent, of the expenditure budget. If salaries were stable, the prices of cloth, provisions, and fodder were not, and their increase was reflected in the rising size of the extraordinary budget. The Military Commission, for example, chose to retain in 1765 the existing base prices of 1.20 rubles for a *chetvert* (two hectoliters) of rye flour, 1.50 for one of groats, 75 kopecks for one of oats, and 10 kopecks for a *pud* (16.4 kg) of hay, even though it recognized that they were no longer realistic. In so doing the Commission paved the way for a major distortion of the expenditure budget as larger and larger sums had to be classified as extraordinary expenditures. By 1790 food prices had skyrocketed beyond recognition. In the south, for example, the price of flour and groats ranged from 1 to 8 rubles (in the Crimea), that of oats from 2 to 3.40 rubles. Hay, however, was everywhere cheaper than the official price. The impact of rising costs on the ordinary budget can be measured by the fact that sixty-five regiments of infantry consumed 396,435 *chetverti* of rye flour, and a difference of, say, 3 rubles per *chetvert* entailed an extraordinary expenditure of 1.3 million rubles. A table for 1785 shows an appropriation of almost 2 million rubles from the Treasury for Extraordinary Expenditures to the Provision Chancery, including 1.2 million for the purchase of provisions and forage due to increased costs. In 1790 the additional cost had risen to 4.9 million and was already the largest single item in the extraordinary budget.[3]

A second type of extraordinary expenditure no longer depended upon obsolete price scales but consisted of outlays considered temporary or extraordinary in the sense that they were unforeseen or could not be included in a table of organization.[4] Within this category one finds later in the reign a distinction between "permanent" (*obyknovennye*) and other expenditures. Such semantic confusion shows that the attachment to the old division was becoming purely sentimental. It was comforting to think that ordinary expenditures were fully covered by revenue from taxation, while forgetting the unpleasant truth that the extraordinary budget was getting out of hand. Self-

---

full general 7,086 rubles, of a lieutenant general 3,598, and that of a major general 2,685 rubles.

[3] PSZ, 1766, N. 12612, pt. 4; TsGVIA, f. 18, d. 3/196, fol. 10-12; *SIRIO*, XXVIII (1880), 264, 336-338.

[4] Such expenditures included, for example, 180,000 rubles sent to Potemkin to pay the carpenters employed in the construction of the Kherson shipyards, 30,000 rubles to Vice-Admiral Pushchin for the construction of Kronstadt harbor, 227,631 rubles for the repair of fortresses; and large wartime expenditures such as 2 million rubles for the fleet in the Mediterranean in 1772 and 3.2 million for the Baltic fleet in 1789: see *SIRIO, ibid.*, 174-185, 335-339.

deception became the rule among the close collaborators of the Empress during and after the second Turkish war, with disastrous results.

A similar division between ordinary and extraordinary expenditures was found in the civilian budget. The combined cost of maintaining the major agencies of the Imperial government listed on the table of 1763 was about 1.2 million rubles, of which about 700,000 went for central agencies. Kulomzin's table gives figures ranging from 1.7 to 2.9 million between 1764 and 1773, but the absence of a breakdown makes it impossible to use these figures for purpose of comparison.[5]

The reform at first altered radically the relationship between central and local spending. While central government spending increased slightly, largely because the expansion of the Expedition of State Revenues cancelled some of the savings derived from the closing of the colleges, local government expenditures now took the lion's share of the ordinary budget. The ordinary budget for 1783—if outlays for the clergy, the schools, pensions, and public construction, not considered in 1763, are now included—totalled 13.7 million rubles, of which 5 million were disbursed directly by the treasuries in Petersburg and Moscow, and 8.7 million was spent directly in the provinces. By 1795, however, the share of central government spending was on the rise—14.6 million against 10.1 spent in forty-two gubernias—largely because more and more funds were being channelled to the Cabinet and the banks. In the 1790s separate funds, not included here, for the operations of the vodka and salt monopolies were also incorporated into the ordinary budget, probably because their level of expenditures depended on the number of stores and taverns and the provisions of contracts made usually for four years.[6]

This ordinary budget was more stable than that of the Commissary because the bulk of its outlays was for fixed salaries which were not subject to price fluctuations. Its growth depended on additional appointments and pay increases, two variables subject to few changes, while the fluctuation of the price of food followed market forces beyond government control. However, for the very reason that the budget was so compact a large number of items could not be fitted into it and required financing from the Treasury for Extraordinary Expenditures.

The table for 1785, already mentioned, lists a number of such expenditures, which may be classified under five headings of very unequal importance. Some items were permanent; others were temporary outlays. Foreign debt repayment (2.1 million) was the largest item among

[5] PSZ, 1763, N. 11991, vol. 44², 59-71; see also SIRIO, V (1870), 228-229.
[6] SIRIO, XXVIII (1880), 249-253, 475-479.

extraordinary expenditures in the purely civilian budget; another constituted loans to the Assignat Bank to help it finance the operations of its local branches; a third consisted of pensions, one to the former khan of the Crimea, the other to Baron Dimsdale (who inoculated the Empress against smallpox), although one would think that such expenditures should have been defrayed by the Cabinet; a fourth included lump sums placed at the disposal of the Procurator General and Ivan Betskoi for paving the streets of the capital and completing the construction of the Neva embankment, etc.; and a fifth included monies used to settle claims against the treasury.[7]

The budget of the Court can likewise be divided into ordinary and extraordinary expenditures, although the very nature of Court expenditures, much of which was in the form of gifts of objects and properties, makes it impossible to tabulate even an approximate amount. Kulomzin gives an ordinary budget of 1.7 million for 1764, 2.2 million for 1773 and two million for 1782, but Chechulin lists total expenditures of 2.4, 2.9, and 4.7 million for these three years. The 1786 table totalled 1.7 million and enables us to identify the major items of expenditure:[8]

Permanent Expend.	694,943	Salaries	168,922
Temporary Expend.	685,595		
Pensions	189,376	Total	1,738,836

Permanent expenditures (okladnye nepremennye—the terms are synonymous) included expenditures for the Guard regiments, upkeep and repairs of palaces, and allocations for the Imperial theaters. Temporary expenditures, combined here with miscellaneous expenditures (netochno polozhennye), included the repayment of loans to the Assignat Bank and appropriations for construction, and two large items (290,000 rubles) representing settlement of claims between the Cabinet and the Orlov and Lanskoi families. The third largest item consisted of pensions to individuals close to the Court and to medical personnel. The budget did not include the salaries of high Court officials, including those who served at the Court of Paul. Estimates for 1786 totalled 3.8 million, but Chechulin gives total expenditures of 6.6 million. The difference of 2.8 million may have represented extraordinary expenditures. Some of the confusion in these Court expenditures resulted from the fact that a rigid distinction between the Court and the civilian budget did not yet clearly exist. The construction of

[7] Ibid., 263-270, 323-330.
[8] SIRIO, V (1870), 228-229; Dvukhsotletie Kabineta, 327-386, 389.

boats in 1772, subsidies to soldiers retired in Kazan, and funds for the restoration of the Glukhov cathedral, as well as the salaries of foreign doctors, were not expenditures properly belonging to the jurisdiction of the Cabinet. Some construction expenditures likewise belonged to the civilian budget.[9]

This brief outline can only suggest an approach to a study of the Imperial budget. The distinction between ordinary and extraordinary expenditures was a useful one, but the terms did not lend themselves to an accurate definition. Once ordinary expenditures were subdivided into permanent and temporary ones, it became difficult to distinguish temporary from extraordinary expenditures, and the latter in turn contained several subdivisions. The confusion was aggravated, paradoxically enough, by the abolition of the colleges. The positive features of the reform were reduced by the resulting disappearance of departmental budgets (except for the army and navy), which provided the institutional props of a national budget. The triumph of the territorial principle of administration was reflected in the structure of the civilian budget, consisting after the reform of some fifty territorial budgets and a central government budget, in other words two horizontal budgets without any vertical prop connecting and sustaining them. The central government budget became the budget of the two treasuries supplemented by contributions of the Assignat Bank.

BUDGETARY PROCEDURE:
THE CIVILIAN BUDGET

The weakness of the College of Revenue, which never grew into the budget office it was intended to be, resulted in a permanently lopsided relationship between revenue and expenditure. A single budget, whether balanced or not, assumes an exact correlation between total expenditures and total revenue from taxation and other sources, including borrowing. The non-military departmental budgets, on the one hand, showed a surplus in most cases, since expenditures were chiefly military outlays, while those of the military departments showed a permanent deficit which had to be covered by dipping into the surplus of this or that college. The result was that any new expenditure was not simply a draft upon a central treasury but required that a new source of revenue be found among surpluses accumulated in some other agency, and a surplus sufficiently permanent to guarantee that the new expenditure would be financed without interruption. Such fragmentation, aggravated by permanent arrears and the absence of a revenue

[9] *Dvukhsotletie Kabineta*, 362-368; TsGVIA, f. 44, d. 50, II, 305.

budget, created an unreal atmosphere in financial administration and resulted in considerable delays in paying the troops and civil officials, whose salaries formed the single largest item in departmental budgets. Therefore, the reform of the budgetary process, undertaken by the Empress from the very beginning of her reign, had to settle two major problems. The fragmentation of the expenditure budget had to be ended and replaced by a single table of expenditure for civilian administration; such achievement assumed the elimination of the financial autonomy of the colleges. The second task was the creation of an annual revenue budget. After much effort, tables of expenditures were drawn up in the Expedition of State Revenues for 1769, 1773, and 1776-1777, and after the completion of the administrative-territorial reform, were prepared annually until the end of the reign.[10]

Any expenditure, no matter how small, required the approval of the Empress. Requests were submitted directly by colleges in the reports of their presidents when these possessed enough authority to have direct access to the throne, or through the Senate. The payment of salaries was considerably simplified by the unification of salary scales in the 1763 table of organization. A general authorization (*assignatsiia*) was now issued by the *Stats-Kontora* for every four-month period (*tret'*), and every agency was required to send it reports on the use made of these funds and on its cash balance, the amount of which was automatically deducted from the allocation for the following period.[11] The table of organization became, so to speak, a new law, and the disbursement of lump sums was authorized in pursuance thereof (*po shtatam*) three times a year without further Imperial approval.

Other expenditures not authorized by the table required initially a separate Imperial authorization (*po osoblivym ukazam*). They were either expenditures made necessary by amendments to the table of organization (*sverkh-shtatnye*) which, once approved, were treated as ordinary expenditures; or temporary ones made for specific projects or periods of time and whose renewal required approval each time. These became part of the extraordinary expenditures. Their financing was the most complicated element in pre-reform budgetary procedure. There was as yet no truly central treasury because the concept of "general (*obshchie*) state revenues" was incompatible with the specialization of revenue collecting. There was the custom revenue, the revenue from the sale of vodka and of salt, the capitation, the quitrent, etc., each type of revenue associated with a different agency, and a multitude of other sources were lumped together as "treasury (*stats-*

[10] Troitskii, *Fin. politika*, 262-265; see also the general survey in Duran.
[11] PSZ, 1764, N. 12209; 1765, N. 12343.

kontorskie) revenues." Thus, for every item of extraordinary expenditure that could not be covered from the disbursing agency's own funds,
a source had to be found in some other "treasury" where other revenues were collected. Moreover, the funds collected by each of these
agencies sometimes never reached the center. They were often paid
irregularly and with considerable arrears. Allocations were made on
the basis of anticipated receipts that might never materialize, so that
the arrears in the money room of a given voevoda were reflected in
the inability to pay some official's pension or to build a new building
somewhere else because such expenditure had been pegged to a particular revenue. The system obviously generated such complicated accounts that it must have been simply impossible to audit them.

As work progressed on the consolidation of all types of revenue into
a general fund, the financial autonomy of the colleges was undermined
and the treasury assumed a central importance for the financing of
both ordinary and extraordinary expenditures. The bottlenecks created by the exceedingly rigid dependence of specific items of expenditure on a definite source of revenue tended to disappear. The fragmentation of the expenditure budget along departmental lines gave
way to a more modern budget structure organized around categories
of expenditures—salaries, pensions, education, communications. Thus
the colleges as fiscal agencies simply became superfluous. Meanwhile,
the territorial reform made it possible for the first time to prepare
territorial budgets supported by funds collected locally and to abandon
the cumbersome practice of departmental budgets put together inde-
pendently from a variety of sources.

The preparation of an annual national budget became the responsibility of the second department of the Expedition of State Revenues
after the Expedition's division in October 1780. It was prepared in
detail for the entire civil administration and in lump sums for the
army, the navy, and the Court. This department had to keep a record
of all tables of organization and of all Imperial commands on extraordinary expenditures, including pensions, additional salary granted to
individual officials, entertainment (*stolovye*) allowances, and lump-
sum grants (*edinovremennye vydachi*). The concentration of treasury
operations under the Procurator General had at last made possible a
comprehensive expenditure budget.[12]

The second step was the translation of this budget into some twenty-
six territorial budgets for central Russia alone. Strict rules of accounting were introduced to help the treasury chambers keep track of all

[12] Kulomzin in *SIRIO*, XXVIII (1880), xxiv-xxviii; PSZ, 1780, N. 15075, 15076, pt.
10-12; 1781, N. 15120, par. 31-33, 42-51.

revenue collected in the gubernias, and these amounts were made
known to the first department in periodic reports from the chambers.
The expenditure budget of each gubernia consisted of five parts: local
expenditures, contributions to the Commissary and to the Navy, and
transfers to the Treasuries for Ordinary and Extraordinary Expenditures. The following table (for 1793) provides a clear example of such
distribution:[13]

	Vladimir	Smolensk	Tver
Expend. in Gubernia	200,521	164,089	221,051
Transfers:			
to Commissary	400,000	250,000	410,000
to Navy	110,000	50,000	100,000
to Tr. Ord. Expd.	220,000	235,000	280,000
to Tr. Extra. Expd.	32,938	53,426	65,774
Total outlay	963,459	752,515	1,076,825
Total collection	992,319	752,515	1,101,931

Local expenditures consisted of four blocks: permanent (*vsegdash-
nye*) outlays, extraordinary ("temporary") ones, and expenditures attending the operation of the liquor and salt monopolies. Permanent
expenditures included salaries and pensions paid under the table of
organization of the gubernia to the civil administration and the clergy,
1,000 or 2,000 rubles for unforeseen needs (the so-called *ekstra-
ordinarnaia summa*), and a separate sum for the maintenance of prisoners and for the shipment of funds from the uezd centers to the
gubernia capital and on to Moscow and Petersburg. "Temporary"
expenditures represented a small part of the gubernia budget, and they
too were essentially additional salary or pension, with only small sums
allocated to education, road or canal building, and other investments
in the economy of the gubernia. A glance at tables of expenditures for
1792-1795 clearly shows that the overwhelming share of these expenditures went into the pay of officials, all nobles, appointed or

[13] Kulomzin in *SIRIO*, V (1870), 222; PSZ, 1784, N. 15950. Funds from Vladimir
went to the Moscow treasuries, those from Smolensk and Tver to the Petersburg treasuries. The difference between total outlays and total collection (28,860 rubles in Vladimir, 25,106 in Tver) represent the amount collected by separate agencies, such as postal
revenues, withholdings for medical care, receipts from the sale of powder and saltpeter,
and revenues from properties sequestered for default in repaying loans. The source gives
no explanation for the missing 28,860 in Vladimir, and I have assumed that their source
was the same as that of the 25,106 rubles in Tver.

elected. To take only the case of Vladimir gubernia in 1793, 168,006 rubles out of the 200,521 remaining in the gubernia for local expenditures were allocated to pay the salary and pensions of officials, and another 26,596 to support the clergy.[14]

Once these territorial budgets (*rospisaniia*) were completed they were submitted to the Procurator General for approval, then sent to the treasury chambers some time in November. They were binding documents for the chambers during the coming year, and no changes were allowed without the approval of the Procurator General. A crucial change was introduced by the provision that all Imperial commands authorizing new expenditures at the discretion of the Empress would henceforth be addressed to him (*na ego imia*).[15] Thus, it became feasible for a single official to concentrate in his office both the knowledge of all documents authorizing expenditures and the authority to make the necessary adjustments in the process of executing the expenditure budget. The centralization of budget making was nearly complete, and it was now possible to submit to the Empress at the end of each year tables of anticipated expenditures for the coming year.

The territorial budget also determined how much each gubernia had to deposit in the Treasury for Ordinary Expenditures. These funds were used to defray the expenditures of the Court and the Guard, of the College of Foreign Affairs, of various central agencies such as the Senate, the Church, and the staffs of various commissions, for pensions and construction programs included in the various tables of organization. And once the share of the Commissary and the Navy had been apportioned, the balance of the revenue was sent to the Treasury for Extraordinary Expenditures, which served as a reserve fund for all other "extraordinary" expenditures covered by taxation. In addition, all balances remaining at the end of each four-month period from the non-payment of salaries to people who did not actually occupy the position to which they had been appointed or of pensions of deceased pensioners were deposited in the account of this treasury. The financial role of the colleges came to an end with the order of December 3, 1780, directing them to deposit in it all available balances and cease holding any funds.[16]

The civilian expenditure budget, however, was only one of three

[14] *SIRIO*, XXVIII (1880), 406-407.

[15] PSZ, 1780, N. 15076, pt. 11-12; 1781, N. 15120, par. 31; 1781, N. 15140, pt. 11; 1782, N. 15266; 1784, N. 16040; *SIRIO*, XXVIII (1880), 249-253, 388-393, 402-407.

[16] PSZ, 1780, N. 15076, pt. 10-11. The College of Audit acknowledged receipt of the order: TsGADA, f. 16, d. 340, fol. 234.

such budgets. Military budget procedure will be examined presently, but a few comments may be made here about the Court budget. Until the reorganization of 1786 this budget was largely autonomous in an administrative and political sense. The Chancery of Court Peasants collected substantial sums, and the gold and silver of the Kolyvan and Nerchinsk mines as well as a share of the revenue from the sale of salt passed into the revenue of the Cabinet. The expenditure budget was that of the Chancery, the Cabinet, and the *Pridvornaia Kontora*. It was yet another autonomous budget, but one much larger than that of any one of the civilian colleges. The chief budgetary officer was the Director of the Cabinet. But the growth of Court expenditures and the increasingly difficult financial situation brought the budgetary reform to bear upon the preparation of the Court budget as well. When the Chancery was abolished, the quitrent collected from Court peasants passed into the general fund. The gradual shrinking of the salt revenue also assisted the process of integrating a substantial share of the Court budget into the general budget. This in turn necessitated the preparation of a comprehensive table of organization for the entire Court, a task that was not completed until after the death of Catherine.[17] Politically, this budget remained autonomous under the ultimate direction of the Empress herself; its operation, however, was coming under the scrutiny of the Procurator General.

Much progress was also achieved by the reform of audit procedures. Hitherto the operations of the College of Audit had been regulated by the Instruction of May 1733. All colleges collecting state revenue, including the Commissary, the Chancery of Artillery, and the Navy, as well as the Guard regiments, were required to send their accounts, usually within ten months following the end of the year, to the College of Audit. Local accounts from the gubernia and provincial chanceries were used to audit the activities of the voevodas when they came up for a transfer or a promotion. The result was an incredible confusion as tens of thousands of accounts received over the years from all over the country accumulated in the quarters of the college and remained unattended for lack of staff. The Director of the College, Roman Vorontsov, reported to the Empress in 1769 that 53,170 accounts remained on the agenda and gave a long list of 408 agencies showing how much cash still remained in their store rooms, in accordance with the ukase of 1766 requiring all agencies to report the amount of their cash balances. This does not seem to have applied to the Salt Board, which had not sent its accounts to the College since 1735 and was by its own admission unable to cope with accounts coming from some

[17] PSZ, 1786, N. 16415.

six hundred places where the sale of salt was taking place. Yet, the Senate had recommended in 1764 that all these accounts should be sent directly to the College of Audit![18] The absence of a preliminary audit at some stage between the local voevoda and the central college reflected the persistence of Muscovite practices, linking the most humble local agent directly with the central government, but it was a major flaw creating an administrative nightmare from which there was no escape short of radical change.

The reform introduced basic modifications in auditing procedures but did nothing to guarantee the independence of so essential a mechanism of control over the execution of the budget. Following the dismantling of the central colleges, the focus now shifted to the new treasury chambers, which functioned not only as collecting and disbursing agencies and local treasuries but also as agencies auditing their own operations and those of the uezd treasurers. A preliminary audit was made in each gubernia capital at the end of each year, and a final audit followed in the Audit Expedition in the early months of the following year. The central agency no longer received several hundred different accounts but only about fifty from the chambers, and these accounts already represented a consolidated audit of the operations of several hundred uezd treasurers. The task of auditing local accounts had become much simpler.

Another novelty was the insistence on keeping accounts up to date at all levels. The practice before the reform was to wait until the end of the year to draw up a general statement of receipts and expenditures, which was then submitted to the College of Audit. Such documents drawn up after the event, and in some cases probably from memory, must have been designed primarily to present to the auditors of the college a picture acceptable to their essentially formal conception of what an audit should be. But treasurers were now required not only to keep a record of their daily transactions but also to "check themselves" (*poveriat' sebia*) by what must have been a form of double-entry bookkeeping, showing at the end of each day accumulated receipts and disbursements. At the end of each month they were expected to send to the treasury chambers an abstract (*vypiska*) from their accounts. These monthly abstracts were used to prepare tables of receipts and expenditures for the entire gubernia during the preceding four months (*tretnye vedomosti*), and a consolidated annual balance for

[18] PSZ, 1733, N. 6391 and 1735, N. 6855; TsGADA, f. 16, d. 340, fol. 179-190 and 90-133.

the entire gubernia had to be sent to the Audit Expedition by January 10.[19]

Budgetary Procedure:
The Civilian Budget

The expenditure budget of the land army consisted of three departmental budgets.[20] That of the Commissary was the largest; it included expenditures for the payment of salaries and the purchase of cloth and equipment. The Provision Chancery and its local commissions were responsible for the procurement of grain and groats for the troops, oats and hay for the horses. And the Chancery of Artillery, with the smallest of the three budgets, had to meet expenditures for both the payment of salaries to garrison troops and their provisioning. The distribution of these tasks, which were part of a single function— clothing and feeding the troops—served to maintain a certain equality among the three agencies, yet required the creation of a single budget office and treasury for the concentration of decision-making and of funds as the prerequisite of any attempt to prepare a consolidated budget for the entire army: the Commissary alone collected funds allocated to the military establishment, and decisions of any questions exceeding the competence of the three agencies were made in the College of War.

Ordinary expenditure budgets, drawn up in the three agencies, were consolidated by the Commissary into a single budget for the coming year. This budget had to show not only the expenditures but also the source of the revenue and the gubernias of origin. It was then submitted to the College of War not later than October, and it was probably approved in routine fashion since these ordinary expenditures had already received Imperial sanction. For example, Durnovo submitted a budget of 9.3 million rubles for 1780 on October 25, 1779, and the college announced its confirmation on December 3 in orders sent separately to Durnovo, the Commissary, and the two chanceries.

The capitation was the major source of revenue (seven out of 9.3 million) followed by the sale of vodka (1.8 million), the proceeds of which belonged to the jurisdiction of the College of Revenue. In each province and gubernia two elements were known in advance: the anticipated revenue from the capitation and local expenditures for

[19] PSZ, 1781, N. 15118, 15141, art. 4, 15194; 1782, N. 15405, art. 88-89.
[20] PSZ, 1766, N. 12612, pt. 22. This section on military procedures is based on two major documents: TsGVIA, f. 12, d. 235 (budget of 1780) and d. 48 (budget of 1796).

military personnel. Whenever these expenditures were large and exceeded the revenue (chiefly in the borderlands), the balance between expenditures and revenue was apportioned among neighboring gubernias, usually on the basis of territorial propinquity. If, in turn, the total sum of expenditures assigned to each of these gubernias should exceed the revenue from the capitation, the difference was made up by adding to it a share of the revenue from the sale of vodka. What is not clear is how the share of the College of Revenue was determined. We must assume that whenever the level of ordinary expenditures was raised, provision was made automatically for an additional contribution, so that negotiations were necessary between the Commissary and the college about the annual share of the revenue from the sale of vodka.

Requests for extraordinary expenditures were submitted directly to the College of War and required the confirmation of the Empress. There were of course no deadlines for their submission. The Provision Chancery, for example, reported to the college on November 19, 1790 that its estimated expenditures for 1791 amounted to 7.6 million, while the ordinary allocation (*shtatnaia summa*) from the Commissary was only 3 million. A price list was appended as supporting evidence. The college accepted the Chancery's request for additional funds, and the approval of the Empress was obtained in December.[21] The next step was to find the funds to cover these extraordinary expenditures. Before the treasury reform of 1780, the Expedition of State Revenues kept tabs on the cash balances of various collecting agencies; an Imperial order was necessary to transfer them. In July and September 1778, for example, Kheraskov, the president of the College of Audit, reported to the Empress that he had received her order to put at Potemkin's disposal 105,000 rubles from the revenue collected in the college from fines imposed on delinquent agencies.[22] After the reform, the appropriations came from funds earmarked for extraordinary expenditures. To return to the same example for 1790, the Empress's confirmation of the request for 4.6 million rubles was announced to the Procurator General on December 24. The Expedition of State Revenues then authorized the immediate disbursement of 1.5 million, half from the Treasury for Extraordinary Expenditures, the other half from nineteen treasury chambers, which, instead of sending their balances to that Treasury, were to send them directly to the Chancery and its commissions. The Chancery then notified the College of War and the latter

21 TsGVIA, f. 18, d. 3/196, fol. 1-2.
22 TsGVIA, f. 16, d. 340.

the Senate's Fourth Department. Additional funds were released in the following fashion:[23]

Date	Amount	Nr of Gubs.
1791 Feb. 21	250,000	6
March 14	250,000	15
May 8	693,191	11
July 3	600,000	11
Dec. 2	761,758	9
1792 Feb. 11	531,433	4
Total	3,086,382	

The accounting and auditing of military expenditures and revenues was a very complex procedure. Accounts were kept on innumerable forms sent to the Commissary by voevodas and regiments. Until many of these forms were abolished in 1775, the voevodas sent weekly reports on their success in collecting the capitation and other items of revenue belonging to the Commissary, including the share of the proceeds from the sale of vodka, and separate reports on sums paid out for pensions, for the transportation of funds, and on those assigned for the expenditures of the Provision Chancery. After 1775 all these forms were consolidated into a single monthly form showing the total amount set aside for military expenditures, how much had been collected and the arrears.[24] From the commandants, commissary and provision commissions reports were sent showing how much had been spent and how much remained available. After the reform, consolidated reports were sent by the treasury chambers for each gubernia.

In the Commissary itself the utmost confusion seems to have prevailed, as Mikhail Potemkin reported to the College of War in December 1784. Instead of keeping a general ledger showing total revenue and expenditure, the agency kept fourteen account books for individual sources of revenue and items of expenditures and separate ones for carbineers and the Little Russian Cossacks. Some treasury chambers did not send their reports or, if they did, made no distinction between different sources of revenue. It was impossible to keep an up-to-date account of how much was actually received and available to defray expenditures for the Commissary as a whole. The confusion obviously resulted from the poor integration of two different princi-

[23] TsGVIA, f. 18, d. 3/196, fol. 17-38.
[24] PSZ, 1775, N. 14332, pt. 57-69 and p. 162-163.

ples: a functional principle seeking to keep track of separate blocks
of expenditures (for pensions, for hospitals, for salaries, for the purchase of cloth, etc.) and a territorial principle according to which a
consolidated table of expenditures for the entire Empire should match
the total contribution made by the treasury chambers to the Commissary and the total outlays made in the local commissions.

To remedy this situation Potemkin recommended the creation of a
separate accounting "expedition" in the Commissary and of its counterparts in every local commission to supervise and coordinate the
work of the treasurers; and he submitted new blank forms of weekly,
monthly, quarterly, and annual reports for all commissions similar to
those of the treasury chambers so that comparisons could easily be
made. These recommendations were accepted by the College of War
and incorporated into a report of the Fourth Department confirmed
by the Empress on February 22, 1785.[25] Whether accounting procedures actually improved is uncertain. Russia went to war against the
Turks in 1788 and remained in a state of cold or hot war until the
end of the reign. Wartime conditions are not favorable to the keeping
of accurate reports. Moreover, Potemkin's report seems to have been
concerned only with the accounting of Commissary funds and left
untouched accounting in the Provision Chancery. This agency received
monthly reports on grain and hay prices, but their reliability was
seriously open to question.[26] The execution of contracts seemed easier
to monitor, but if grain was not supplied on time it had to be purchased
at whatever prices were offered on local markets. Accordingly, funds
assigned for certain purposes were diverted for grain purchases, thus
creating additional confusion.

Reliable accounting was a prerequisite of accurate auditing. Since
1724 regimental commanders had sent their accounts (schëtnye spiski)
to the College of Audit, and the creation of the commissary and provision commissions in the 1760s did not interfere with this long-
standing procedure. It was in fact similar to the practice followed in
the civilian government, where all local agencies down to the local
voevodas and magistraty sent their accounts separately to the College.
A report of 1764 to Chief Director Shakhovskoi complained that eight
rooms were filled with unaudited accounts from various places "and
especially the army" and that millions in state funds remained unaccounted for. Since the college was incapable of auditing the more than
four thousand accounts it received every year, Shakhovskoi recom-

²⁵ PSZ, 1785, N. 16157. The original is in TsGVIA, f. 12, d. 46, fol. 14-19.
²⁶ PSZ, 1775, N. 14332, pt. 93-98 and p. 111; 1776, N. 14501; 1785, N. 16137;
1795, N. 17405; 1796, N. 17433.

mended that a separate expedition be established for the auditing of military accounts. The proposal was not accepted by the Empress until 1779, although one such expedition was created for the Navy in 1764.

The new Comptroller General received accounts from regiments, garrisons, and commandants, from the Commissary, Provision Chancery, and Chancery of Artillery, and their local agencies directly. At the end of each year, ledgers of revenue and expenditures kept by regimental treasurers were submitted to a commission of officers of the regiment for a preliminary audit and then sent with all original documents (orders to disburse, contracts, communications from treasury chambers) to the Audit Expedition of the College of War. In addition, civilian agencies releasing funds to a regiment or other army command on orders of the Expedition of State Revenues were required to inform the Audit Expedition, and all such commands were instructed to report to it every delivery of funds and their origin. As a result the expedition would be able to check the accounts from the field against the documentation already available and pass on the legality of expenditures. It would then determine how much money, clothing, and equipment remained available (*nalitso*) in the entire country, to establish what might be called a national cash balance—an elusive goal pursued until then with little success by eighteenth-century financial administrators.[27]

Thus the reform introduced major changes in military budget-making. The creation of two civilian treasuries considerably facilitated the release of funds to the army, especially those earmarked for extraordinary expenditures. The subordination of the Commissary to a powerful president of the College of War, and the creation of an Audit Expedition placed the preparation of the estimates and the auditing of the accounts squarely in the hands of the military leadership. The Commissary received its funds in lump sums from the Expedition of State Revenues and submitted to it merely an annual abstract (*kratkie vypiski*) from the audited accounts, showing the success achieved in the collection of arrears. By the late 1780s the military budget had indeed become autonomous.

The only integrating mechanism in budgetary procedure was the office of the Procurator General. Since all four expeditions reported to him directly, Prince Viazemskii alone could obtain a true and comprehensive picture of Russian financial conditions at any given time, and the Empress had to rely upon his documents, if not upon his advice. This exclusive position was certainly much resented. In 1783,

[27] TsGADA, f. 16, d. 340, fol. 90-133; PSZ, 1764, N. 12459; 1779, N. 14957, pt. 4; 1780, N. 15041; 1781, N. 15219.

1785, and at other times the materials used by Catherine's advisers as the basis for their discussion of financial reforms were supplied by him, and Bezborodko complained to the Empress that the Prince "keeps the tables to himself and no one, no matter how trusted by Your Majesty, can reach any conclusion or give explanations to Your Majesty."[28] Derzhavin's remark that he kept funds in a secret reserve in order to demonstrate his ability to find resources when it seemed that there were none rings true,[29] and can be justified by the operation of a system in which the appropriation of new funds always depended upon the caprice of the ruler. But such practices also demonstrated how personalized inter-agency relationships had become after the reform. The weakening of the bureaucratic hierarchy made way for the self-assertion of powerful clans which carved the administration of the realm among themselves and jealously guarded the sources of their power. Bezborodko found it intolerable not only that Prince Viazemskii kept financial documents to himself, but that, since the Audit Expedition also reported to him, he was in a position to "audit himself"—additional evidence, if more is needed, of the enormous power accumulated by this outstanding public figure, head of the secret police, minister of justice and finance, and state comptroller.

[28] TsGADA, f. 19, d. 344, fol. 55-61.
[29] Derzhavin, 603.

CHAPTER III

THE REVENUE BUDGET

PREPARATION

While tax policy is grounded in economic reality, it is also a statement of social policy. In an economy still close to the natural level, short of cash and credit, and geared to the export of raw materials, the number of taxable commodities capable of producing a respectable and expanding yield was very small. As a result, at least a third of the revenue came from heavy personal taxes collected from the peasantry; at least another third came from the sale of salt and above all vodka, produced by nobles exclusively and sold to other classes; and another ten percent consisted of customs duties, the only tax imposed on the consumption of the nobility, who paid no personal taxes. The remaining 20 percent of the revenue came from various fees, fines, leases of state properties, minting operations, and taxes on industrial production. Since about 36 percent of the expenditures (in 1785) went to the army and navy commanded by noblemen, another 36 percent to pay the civil administration, and about 10 percent to meet the needs of the Court, the benefits derived by the nobility from its dominant position are obvious.[1]

In the early 1760s there was no "tax code" to guide local voevodas; some taxes and fees were collected without legal authorization, while others had long been cancelled. There was no agreed-upon terminology, and the same taxes sometimes bore different names. Accounting and audit were in a chaotic state. In short, the Imperial government did not know how much was actually collected, and estimates varied from 16 to 28 million rubles. Rough estimates for 1764 gave a total revenue of 9.3 million rubles, but fuller data gave 19.9 million for 1769.[2] As long as such wide differences persisted, no reliable revenue budget was possible.

Steps were taken at the very beginning of the reign to correct this situation. In 1764 the new Procurator General requested all gubernia and provincial procurators to send tables showing all items of revenue collected in their towns and uezds. The results, however, were so miserable that they "could not be submitted to Her Majesty." Six

---

[1] Chechulin, *Ocherki*, 256-257, 314-317.
[2] Iasnopol'skii, 74-75.

years later, when the first Turkish war was in full swing, the Empress ordered Prince Viazemskii to collect once again data for the preparation of a revenue budget. An instruction was sent over his signature and that of Mel'gunov, requesting every voevoda chancery in Great Russia to fill out and send directly to the Procurator General's office a standard form itemizing all articles of revenue, the collection of which was authorized by existing legislation "to the best knowledge of the government." A major effort was made to simplify terminology, and all revenue was divided into two categories: direct revenue (*okladnye*, i.e., taxes collected from a definite number of people at a fixed rate—*oklad*) and indirect revenue (*neokladnye*), each divided in turn into permanent and fluctuating revenue. The instruction requested these data for three consecutive years (1768-1770) and invited the chanceries to continue compiling the information regularly and to send it to Petersburg twice a year. The response was extremely encouraging—only 54 agencies out of 330 did not answer—and the general table for 1769 based on the information received was the first revenue budget to cover virtually the entire Empire. It showed a total revenue of 20.9 million rubles, of which 19.9 million had effectively been collected. Direct taxes yielded 11.1 million, including 3.9 million from the capitation of seventy kopecks per registered soul, and 3.3 million from farming out the sale of vodka; indirect taxes yielded 5.8 million, including a custom revenue of 3.2 million, and 3 million were repayments to the treasury. The blank form listed some two hundred different items of revenue, and the proceeds from each were methodically recorded.[3] This first revenue budget was a solid achievement and would serve as the basis for subsequent budgets.

Organizational deficiencies had also handicapped the central government in determining the full extent of its revenue. The statute of the College of Revenue (June 1731) made it responsible for the preparation of a revenue budget (*okladnaia kniga*), but the ink was barely dry when new legislation rendered this impossible. In August the Salt Board was placed under the Cabinet, and in December the collection of the capitation was vested in the Commissary. Subsequent legislation further removed additional items of revenue from the jurisdiction of the College. The quitrent (*obrok*) on state peasants was deposited in the treasury (*Stats-Kontora*), as were several new taxes introduced in 1763 to help pay official salaries. Also in 1763 the new College of Economy assumed jurisdiction over the quitrent collected from the former peasants of the Church, and the Customs Chancery over cus-

[3] "Pervyi opyt," 23-50.

toms receipts. Taxes on the production of iron and copper were Channelled to the College of Mining; confiscated properties and those of persons dying intestate (*vymorochnye*) were assigned to the Chancery of Confiscation. As a result, the vast jurisdiction of the College of Revenue was restricted to the collection of revenue from the sale of vodka.[4] The concentrated management of central finances envisaged by Peter the Great had given way under weaker rulers, when cliques and clans fought for their share in the distribution of patronage, to a bloated system wasteful of public funds, in which individual bureaucracies collected each a certain share of the total revenue, used part of it for related expenditures, and held the remainder until Imperial orders were received releasing certain amounts for stated purposes. In such a system there were treasuries but no Treasury, departmental revenues but no general revenue. This is the context in which the reforming activity of Prince Viazemskii must be placed. We know almost nothing about the power struggle which must have accompanied the breakup of this financial bureaucracy, but credit must be given to an Empress who understood the importance of concentrating the collection of the revenue and to a Procurator General who was able to carry through to its successful conclusion a reform of such magnitude.

The trend toward a reconcentration of treasury operations began with the creation of the Expedition of State Revenues in February 1773. In June 1775 a major attempt at simplifying the accounting of the revenue was announced, and a large number of financial reports, now considered superfluous, were abandoned. The years 1776-1781 saw the establishment of a uniform territorial division, an additional prerequisite to the rational compilation of financial statistics. Meanwhile, national revenue budgets for 1773, 1776, and 1777 were drawn up in the Expedition,[5] and the experience derived from this encouraging development laid the ground for the first truly national revenue and expenditure budget for 1781. The reorganization of the Expedition in 1780 and the creation of satellite expeditions in the treasury chambers, together with the publication of a "code" of financial procedures in 1781, completed the setting up of a machinery capable of drawing up national budgets on an annual basis. Beginning in 1781, ten years after the elaboration of the first revenue budget for 1769, tables of revenues and expenditures were drawn up every year in the Expedition,

---

[4] TsGADA, f. 16, d. 664, 11-34; Troitskii, *Fin. politika*, 249-265; SIRIO, XXVIII (1880), 109-110.

[5] SIRIO, V (1870), 219-223.

and historical scholarship remains greatly indebted to Kulomzin for making them available in printed form.[6] They were submitted to the Empress at the end of each year by the Procurator General in his capacity as State Treasurer. Although these revenue tables were not truly complete—they included only "ordinary" revenues—they represented considerable progress in bringing order in the chaotic state of Russian finances. The following table illustrates the growth of the net revenue between 1765 and 1795. The major items of revenue, personal taxes, the proceeds from the sale of vodka, and the customs receipts will be examined separately.[7] The figures following are in millions of rubles.

1765	19.–	1785	40.–
1775	25.6	1795	55.1

The reform not only made possible the regular keeping of accounts showing anticipated revenue and actual receipts; it was also a major step toward the consolidation of the revenue budget and the creation, probably for the first time, of a general revenue fund.

The revenues of the Commissary were of two kinds: regular revenues, routinely assigned to it under existing legislation, and supplementary appropriations each year to cover the balance between the regular revenue and anticipated expenditures. An illustration may be found in the report of the Military Commission to the Fourth Department in 1765, asking for the confirmation of an annual revenue budget of 8.1 million rubles. The estimates of the Commission included 5,879,000 rubles from the capitation and a number of other personal taxes, 1 million rubles from the revenue collected by the College of Revenue, 424,000 rubles from the salt revenue, 248,921 rubles from the customs receipts, and 335,996 rubles from the revenues of the Stats-Kontora.[8]

The revenue budget for 1780 was perhaps the last one prepared along traditional lines. The creation of the two treasuries for ordinary and extraordinary expenditures put an end, or nearly so, to the specialization of revenue and established at last a general revenue fund

[6] SIRIO, V-VI (1870-1871).

[7] See SIRIO, XXVIII (1880), xxxii-xxxiv, and Chechulin, Ocherki, 257-262. I follow Chechulin's figures giving the net revenue, i.e., the total revenue less the costs of collection.

[8] PSZ, 1765, N. 12472; TsGVIA, f. 12, d. 235, 3-4.

into which all types of revenue were deposited. Henceforth, the revenue of the Commissary took the form of one large lump sum, reviewed and approved by the Expedition of State Revenues, and released by order of the Procurator General, together with a table showing the amounts to be contributed by each treasury chamber from its own general fund collected in the gubernia.[9]

We can conclude either that the revenue of the military establishment had been integrated into a general revenue tightly controlled by the Procurator General or that the military had obtained a free run on the treasury, since the Commissary, through the College of War, was authorized to petition the Empress for an order to release additional funds from a seemingly inexhaustible source if it was dissatisfied with the budget-cutting of the Expedition of State Revenues. At any rate, a much smoother mechanism had been found to make funds available to the Commissary commissions and to guarantee a relatively free cash flow despite the innumerable bottlenecks typical of eighteenth-century administration.

The evolution of the Court's revenue budget followed very much the same course, although it still remains difficult to determine its exact amount. It consisted of the ruler's personal income—the so-called *komnatnaia summa*—the amount and origin of which were matters of Imperial prerogative; and the revenue of the agencies which grew around the Sovereign with responsibilities for the provisioning and the entertainment of the Court and the administration of its properties.[10] Before the reform the internal sources were supplemented by transfers from other agencies. In 1781 the contribution from the salt "revenue" was replaced by an annual 1 million grant from the Treasury for Extraordinary Expenditures and another 1.2 million for current expenditures at the rate of 100,000 rubles a month. After 1785 these 2.2 million came from the Treasury for Ordinary Expenditures, which also contributed the 150,000 rubles formerly taken from customs receipts, following the closing of the Customs Chancery and the Chancery for Court Peasants. Additional expenditures were increasingly financed by the issue of paper money; we already find in the table for 1786 an item of nearly 300,000 rubles from the Assignat Bank. The total revenue budget in the 1780s seems to have been about 3.4 million rubles.[11]

---

[9] TsGVIA, f. 12, d. 48, 72-73.

[10] Zhidkov, 87.

[11] This composite budget is drawn from *Dvukhsotletie Kabineta*, 369-371, 387-389; PSZ, 1762, N. 11631; 1764, N. 12064; 1789, N. 16747; *SIRIO*, V (1870), 294; VI (1871), 229-239; XXVIII (1880), 263-264, 267.

The remainder of the revenue can conveniently be lumped together under the heading of civilian revenue. The specialization of revenue and the absence of a central treasury were just as much in evidence here. The College of Manufactures collected the proceeds from the sale of stamp paper; the Postal Administration had its own treasury for various postal fees; the College of Audit collected fines from innumerable agencies for delays in not sending their reports, etc. The more agencies, the greater the possibilities of fraud and the difficulties of keeping accurate accounts. As a rule, the revenue of each agency was intended to serve a dual purpose: to defay the administrative expenditures of the agency and to serve as a mini-treasury from which withholdings were made by Imperial orders to assist other agencies to defray their own expenditures. The reform, as we have seen, completed the process of reconcentration of treasury operations under the immediate supervision of the Procurator General.

Much remained to be done to improve the condition of accounting. The revenue tables for 1769 were such an important achievement because they brought to the fore the existence of a thicket of useless, overlapping, and highly particularized taxes yielding such small amounts that no justification could be found for their retention; several yielded only twenty rubles, others fewer than ten. Overlapping taxes were combined, and those for which no legal authorization existed were cancelled. Thereafter additional taxes were abolished by Imperial orders in the 1770s, and the instruction of 1782 established a definite list of legal taxes and fees for the guidance of uezd treasurers and treasury chambers.[12] Yet much more was involved than administrative reform, and rational assumptions were in danger of foundering against deeply ingrained prejudices. Given the widespread belief that service ought to be a source of enrichment, that the status of nobleman gave the right, albeit unsanctioned, to use public funds for private purposes, and the extravagance encouraged by the patriarchal psychology of the time, accurate accounting was faced with enormous difficulties; yet it was essential if an annual revenue budget was ever to be achieved.[13] The ukase of June 1775 and the statutes of 1781 were major steps in that direction:[14] they cancelled a large number of forms and made the treasury chamber responsible for the preparation of monthly and quar-

[12] "Pervyi opyt," 32-36, 42-48; PSZ, 1782, N. 15405.

[13] Iasnopol'skii, 80-82.

[14] PSZ, 1775, N. 14332; see also 1776, N. 14501; OL, art. 123, 140, 161; PSZ, 1778, N. 14772; 1781, N. 15141, par. 9, 67-68, 71, 75, N. 15144, 15248; 1782, N. 15405.

terly statements showing how much had been collected and how much remained in arrears.

MAJOR SOURCES OF REVENUE

The dominance of agriculture in the Russian economy, the limited development of towns, and the existence of serfdom imposed severe restrictions upon tax policy. Of the three major objects of taxation—property, sales, and income—property was the least likely to yield substantial sums. The landed nobility as ruling class paid no taxes on its properties, and those of the treasury were run by noble officials who had no interest in leasing them at high prices to fellow noblemen, even if they were in high demand. Consumption usually becomes the most important source of revenue as the spread of a money economy stimulates the growth of exchanges, but the number of taxable commodities remained limited in the eighteenth century to vodka for the lower classes and colonial products for the nobility. We shall see that the sale of these commodities did indeed produce the largest share of the revenue. Taxes on income, finally, were socially acceptable only for the lower classes and were in fact symbolic of their menial status. Such personal taxes were perfectly adapted to an agrarian economy and required no complex administrative machinery for their collection.[15] Their rate was fixed, the number of taxable units was known and declared to be permanent from census to census, the consent of the taxpayers was taken for granted because the tax was collected by their elected representatives, and coercion did the rest if cooperation was not forthcoming. That was why the capitation was allocated from the very beginning to the support of the land army, the most sensitive item of the expenditure budget.

The capitation was introduced by the so-called *Plakat* of June 1724 and fixed at seventy-four kopecks per registered soul, a figure obtained by dividing the projected costs of the army by the number of souls accounted for in the 1719 census. Immediately following the death of Peter, it was reduced to seventy kopecks in February 1725, and this rate remained unchanged until June 1794, when it was raised to one ruble. By then, of course, the original equivalence between the yields of the capitation and military expenditures had disappeared; we have seen that other sources were tapped to make up the difference. But the ukase of 1794 continued to maintain that the capitation was still a single-purpose tax, despite the existence of a general revenue fund,

[15] Ardant, 1, 413-416.

and noted that inflation, together with greater opportunities for the peasant to sell grain and his services, should make it easier to bear this additional burden. Since 1736 the costs of collecting the capitation were met by a surcharge of two kopecks per ruble, the so-called *nakladnye dengi*, raising the actual rate of the tax to 71 kopecks until 1794 and 1.02 rubles thereafter.[16]

The capitation, like corporal punishment (at least after 1785) was the great divider between the privileged classes and the remainder of society, the low-born (*podlye*) classes. Not only were all peasants required to pay it, but the townsmen as well, although the rates were different. The same *Plakat* of 1724 fixed its rate at 1.20 rubles per soul registered in the *kupechestvo* and the craft guilds (*tsekhi*). This tax was usually called the forty-*altyn*, after the *altyn*, worth three kopecks. In 1769, at the outset of the first Turkish war, the rate was raised to 2 rubles, reduced to 1.20 rubles in 1775, and raised again to 2 rubles by the same ukase of 1794. Meanwhile, the manifesto of March 1775 divided the *kupechestvo* into merchants organized into guilds (*gildii*) and shopkeepers. Only the latter were henceforth required to pay the capitation, whose socially discriminating role was thereby enhanced. The surtax applied also here, so that the actual rate was 1.22 rubles until 1794 and 2.04 rubles thereafter. Merchants, however, continued to pay a tax on income in the form of a one percent levy on the declared amount of their capital.[17]

Although usually considered a personal tax, the capitation was assessed in such a way that it became a territorial tax as well. The territorial unit was the estate, the village, the town, and the uezd. The landowner or his bailiff was responsible for the payment of the amount assessed against his peasants, as were the *starosty* and the "administrator;" of state peasants, and the *magistraty* in the towns. Taxpayers who left their communities with a lawful passport either paid at their place of work or arrangements were made for their community to pay their share. The capitation strengthened the patriarchal nature of the Russian peasantry. The share of those who could not pay because they were too young, too old, or too sick had to be assumed by the wealthier members of the community, thus creating a personal indebtedness that could probably never be repaid. Or it had to be spread among all other members of the community, thus reinforcing collective respon-

---

[16] PSZ, 1724, N. 4533, II-18; 1725, N. 4650; 1794, N. 17222; Peterson, 284-289; PSZ, 1736, N. 6872, pt. 8; 1763, N. 11988, pt. 16; 1776, N. 14516, pt. 12; 1781, N. 15287.

[17] PSZ, 1724, N. 4533, I-1; 1769, N. 13375; 1775, N. 14275, pt. 5; 1794, N. 17222, pt. 11-12.

sibility and deepening the crushing influence of the group over individual members.

The capitation was paid in two installments, the first between January 1 and March 1, the second between October 1 and December 15. These two terms were calculated to coincide with periods when both peasants and townsmen were expected to have ready cash: after the harvest, at the onset of winter when noblemen gathered in the towns for the elections or social activities, and in late winter, when peasants returned to their villages after a few months, carrying goods, felling trees, or working for money in the handicraft industries. The severe penalties for delinquency imposed by the 1731 statute were considerably mitigated in 1769 when the facile resort to dragonnades was replaced by fines on landlords and elected officials.[18]

The *Plakat* was also the original legislation for the collection of the quitrent. It imposed, in addition to the capitation, a forty-kopeck tax—the so-called four-*grivna* tax named after the *grivna*, worth ten kopecks—on all state peasants, a rate fixed to equal approximately the revenue collected by landowners from their serfs, the Court and the Church from their peasants. The ukase of October 1760 invoked the same argument, claiming that landowners were now collecting at least one ruble everywhere as a result of the growth of commerce and the rise of personal incomes, and raised the quitrent accordingly by sixty kopecks to one ruble. In November 1768, the rate was doubled, and the new two-ruble tax took effect retroactively on July 1, to be collected, like the capitation, in two installments. In the meantime, the properties of the Church had been secularized and its former peasants, now called "economic,"[19] were merged to form a separate category for accounting purposes. The quitrent collected from the state peasants proper, those living chiefly in the north, was assigned to meet the expenditures of the treasury (*Stats-Kontora*), while the funds received from the peasants of the Court and the Church belonged to the Chancery for Court Peasants and the College of Economy, respectively. A third increase took place in 1783 as part of a general attempt to help the revenue keep pace with the rising expenditures that threatened the fiscal autonomy of the borderlands in particular. Again, the justification was that the landowners were setting the pace and were now collecting about four rubles from their serfs. The treasury was now presented as a giant landowner placed at a competitive disadvantage

[18] PSZ, 1769, N. 13300; 1781, N. 15141, pt. 57, 60; 1783, N. 15871. Penalties in 1731, N. 5789, pt. 5-6; 1769, N. 13300; 1782, N. 15405, pt. 8, 34.

[19] A uniform quitrent of 1.50 rubles was imposed on those peasants as of January 1, 1764. It remained in effect until July 1, 1768: PSZ, 1764, N. 12060; 1781, N. 15253.

vis-à-vis the collectivity of landowners, and the quitrent it collected
as the treasury's own "landowner's revenue" (*pomeshchich'ii dokhod*)
was found to be so "incredibly small" that state peasants found no
incentive to work more, and serfs were taking the law into their hands
in the hope of changing their status to that of state or Court peasant.
In order to correct such imbalance, not only was the quitrent raised
to three rubles, but the surtax of two kopecks per ruble, which as late
as 1770 the Senate had ruled could not be collected, was added to it
as well.[20] Thus the quitrent rose from 1 ruble in 1761 to 3.06 rubles
in 1783, an increase so high that peasants in some areas fell into large
arrears, and no further attempt was made to raise it again during the
remainder of the reign. The following table illustrates the importance
of these two personal taxes, the capitation and the quitrent, and the
growth of their yields for the entire country after the censuses of 1782
and 1795.[21] The following figures are in millions of rubles.

	Capitation	Quitrent	Total
1765	7.–	2.–	9.–(9.3)
1775	7.1 (1773)	3.–	10.1 (12.2)
1785	8.7	10.8	19.5 (20.2)
1795	11.9	12.6	24.5 (26.–)

If we compare this table with the preceding one showing the total
revenue, it is clear that the share of personal taxes declined from about
half of the revenue budget in 1765 to less than a third in 1795. But
the share of the quitrent rose dramatically and surpassed that of the
capitation after the increase of 1783, and became the index of the
heavy burden imposed upon the peasantry by a treasury short of more
elastic sources of revenue in an agricultural economy dominated by
serfdom.

The importance of the quitrent raised in addition one of the most
fundamental questions of social policy. An interesting document found
among the reports of the Nizhnii Novgorod and Penza Governor
General (Rebinder)[22] illustrates the immense benefits derived by the

[20] PSZ, 1724, N. 4533, II-18; 1760, N. 11120; 1766, N. 12739; 1768, N. 13194;
1783, N. 15723; 1770, N. 13426; and SIRIO, I (1867), 298-300. See also Milov, 271-
274, 287-288, 308-310; PSZ, 1768, N. 13191; 1769, N. 13301, 13371.

[21] SIRIO, V (1870), 224-225, and tables in volumes V and VI. Figures in parentheses
are from Chechulin, Ocherki, 260-262.

[22] TsGADA, f. 16, d. 778, 229-231, 242-244. There are similar figures for 1791 on
365-366, 379-382.

local nobility from its privileged status. It tabulates the revenue collected from each category of taxpayers in 1787. It can be summarized for our purpose as follows:

	NIZHNII NOVGOROD		PENZA	
	souls	rubles	souls	rubles
state peasants	11,960	45,137	38,717	146,118
Court peasants	50,940	192,249	23,654	89,270
Church peasants	41,275	155,772	12,661	47,783
odnodvortsy	–	–	48,308	182,314
private serfs	267,422	190,947	184,840	131,976
others	31,157	77,188	13,089	36,029
Total	402,754	661,294	321,269	633,490

Thus, all peasants except serfs were taxed at the rate of 3.77 rubles—3.06 for the quitrent and 71 kopecks for the capitation—while the serfs who constituted in both gubernias more than half of the peasant population paid only the capitation. If the serfs had been taxed at the same rate as the state peasants, the revenue from those in Nizhnii Novgorod gubernia would have equalled 1,088,181 rubles. The difference between this sum and what was actually paid, or 817,234 rubles, equalled a sum which, instead of reaching state coffers, remained the private property of the landed nobility of the gubernia. If we add that the revenue from the sale of vodka amounted to 307,874 rubles, of which perhaps 88,231 rubles represented the amount paid by the treasury to the noble producers of vodka and about 45,000 for salary to noblemen elected to various gubernia posts, we obtain a sum of 950,465 rubles received by the landed nobility as a result of its privileged position. In other words, the landed nobility of one gubernia alone received from the treasury the equivalent of a subsidy of 1 million rubles a year, which happens to be the same amount as the entire revenue from that province for 1787. For Penza the total would be 662,248, or two-thirds of the annual revenue of 904,136 rubles.[23] If such considerations are extended to the whole of central Russia, where the census of 1782 listed 5,061,405 serfs in twenty-six gubernias,[24] the "gift" of a quitrent of 3.06 rubles represented the enormous sum of 15,487,900 rubles. These figures, more than any other evidence,

[23] I did not include 10,382 Court peasants attached to the Pochinki stud-farm taxed at a separate rate. I obtain the figures of 88,231 rubles by dividing 307,874 by three, giving 102,625 vedra of vodka and assuming that the state paid 85 kopecks a vedro for them.

[24] Kabuzan, Izmeneniia, 97-101.

are an eloquent testimony of the drain on the treasury represented by
the privileged position of the landed nobility, and the true measure of
its power in the administration of the Russian political order.

The revenue collected from the sale of salt and vodka constituted
the second most important source, although the salt monopoly gradually became a deficit operation as mounting transportation charges
began to cancel out what had been a substantial profit at the beginning
of the reign. Three factors determined the profitability of the monopoly: the sale price, production costs, including administrative overhead, and transportation charges. Fixed at forty kopecks a *pud* in July
1762 and reduced to thirty-five kopecks in 1775, the sale price was
raised again to forty kopecks in 1791. Against a background of high
inflation the real cost of salt to the consumer was thus much less than
it had been in 1762. Transportation costs, however, gradually cancelled the margin of profit. The net 1762 revenue—2.2 million rubles
of which 1 million was assigned to the *komnatnaia summa*—dropped
to 1.6 million as early as 1765. By 1785 it was only 1.2, while production and transportation costs went up from 1.2 to 2.9 million. By
1795 no profit was recorded, while costs skyrocketed to 5.4 million
rubles.

By contrast, the vodka monopoly was a handsome source of revenue,
although its profitability for the treasury was restricted by a notable
divergence between its interests and those of the landed nobility, who
had obtained a monopoly over vodka production in July 1754. Control
at the source was thus extremely difficult because there were many
producers and because the controlling agents, especially after the reform, were land captains elected by their fellow landowners. Control
at the other end was likewise difficult because of the abundance of
outlets. The answer was found, or was thought to be found, in channelling all production for the market to state-owned stores and farming
out the sale to individuals, preferably merchants, capable of putting
up adequate security against possible default. Producers were required
to sell their vodka to the store, not at cost but at a profit of over
twenty kopecks a *vedro* (12.3 liters), if we assume that the average
cost of production was sixty-two kopecks in the 1780s and the purchase price eighty-five kopecks. An enterprising nobleman selling 15,000
vedra could net a profit of at least 3,000 rubles, a larger income than
that of any appointed official in the gubernia, including the governor.
Tax farmers were invited to bid for contracts pledging to sell at least
as much vodka as had been sold under the previous contract at a
uniform price of 2.54 rubles a *vedro* in 1763, raised to 3 rubles in
1769 and 4 in 1794. Thus in the 1780s the net profit to the treasury
was about 2.15 rubles, less administrative overhead. Contracts were

confirmed before the reform by the governor if the amount did not exceed 3,000 rubles, by the treasury chambers after the reform for up to 10,000 rubles.

The most sensitive issue in the operation of the monopoly was the division of the profit among treasury, landed nobility, and tax-farmers. The system rested on the assumption that the tax-farmer had to sell his pledged amount at cost but would realize a profit from the sale of additional liquor purchased elsewhere, outside central Russia. The Code of 1781, however, sought to bind the tax-farmer to buy the additional amount from the store as well, thus reducing his profit to a mere margin. It also required him to obtain the approval of the land captain before he could bid for a tax-farm in the uezd. This was an invitation to fraud, as the only way to make a profit was to make an illegal deal with the local landowners to buy their vodka at a higher price than that offered by the treasury and sell it at three rubles a *vedro*. This probably explains the stability of the net revenue in the 1780s, between two periods of growth. Meanwhile, as the price of grain rose, so did production costs and the price at which the landowners agreed to sell their vodka.

This natural conspiracy of landowner and tax-farmer broke the monopoly. In 1795 local landowners were given the choice of dealing with tax-farmers or selling their vodka directly to the treasury. They themselves were now permitted to bid for tax farms, and tax-farmers could now keep their profits after selling the pledged amount. The registration of boilers—a requirement discontinued in 1766—was reinstated in a vain attempt to save face by tightening control at the source. As a result of these changes the net revenue rose sharply. In 1765 it was 4.2 million rubles, in 1775 and 1785 6.9 and 9 million rubles, respectively, but in 1795 it reached 17.7 million, while the costs of collection rose from 1 million in 1765 to 6.6 million rubles in 1795.[25]

Customs receipts were a third important source of indirect revenue and one which simultaneously was tailored to suit the interests of the landed nobility, despite the seemingly paradoxical assertion that the "customs revenue was in the Russian financial system the only important article of the revenue budget whose receipts were not collected directly from the lower taxable classes." These receipts, however, rose by only 138 percent between 1765 and 1795, while the yields of the personal taxes and the vodka monopoly rose by 242 percent.[26] Essentially, the customs revenue was to a large extent the difference

[25] I have discussed the salt and liquor monopoly in some detail in LeDonne, "Indirect Taxes."

[26] Chechulin, *Ocherki*, 221.

between the profit realized from the export of agricultural and related products grown on private estates and state properties and the costs of importing luxury and "colonial" goods to satisfy the tastes of the privileged class.

In 1763 the farming out of the customs revenue was discontinued. Collection became the responsibility of the Customs Chancery, and the Commerce Commission began work on a new tariff which took effect on March 1, 1767. A compromise between mercantilists and free traders, between the interests of the treasury and those of producer-importers, it retained high duties and competed with a separate tariff for the Baltic ports. A new tariff took effect on January 1, 1783, coinciding with the completion of the administrative-territorial reform and reflecting chiefly free-trade influences. The following table (in millions of rubles) illustrates the decline of the trade balance after this new tariff:[27]

	Imports	Exports	Balance
1768	8.2	12.1	+ 3.9
1778-1780	12.5	18.–	+ 5.5
1790-1792	25.6	26.–	+ .4

Imports rose by more than three times, while exports more than doubled, and by 1793 the balance was on the verge of turning negative, with disastrous consequences for the credit of the ruble on the foreign financial markets. To contemporaries the solution resided in sharply curtailing the import of luxury goods, developing native manufactures, and exporting native industrial products.[28] A breakdown of the major components of exports and imports clearly shows that Russia's foreign trade was the trade of the landed nobility and a few other privileged groups in the civil service and the upper layers of the merchant class.

Naval stores, which later played such a prominent part in the nobility's opposition to Alexander I's rapprochement with France after Tilsit, were the major staple of Russian exports. Hemp, flax, tallow, canvas, leather accounted for 11.5 million rubles in 1778-1780; timber and iron for 2.2 million; grain and caviar for 1 million—a total of

[27] Semenov, II, 39-45. Figures for 1778-1780 and 1790-1792 are averages for three years. See also Rubinshtein, "Vneshniaia torgovlia," 345, 348, 352.

[28] "Nachertanie o pooshchrenii poleznykh izobretenii" (1794) recommending granting patents to inventors in order to stimulate innovation; "Zamechaniia zdelannye kapitanom Elium po raznym predmetam na pol'zu gosudarstva otnoshchiesia" (undated but before 1792), recommending reduction of luxury imports and the development of national industries for export; both in TsGADA, f. 16, d. 189, ch. I, 39-85, 113-117. See also Klingshtet, 45-56; Bak, "Ekonomicheskie vozreniia," 132-134.

14.7 million out of 18 million rubles. For 1790-1792 the total was 21.9 million. On the import side, wines, champagne, rhum, sugar, coffee, dyes, silk and finer cloth accounted for 7.1 million in 1780-1782 and 16.5 million in 1790-1792. Chechulin estimated that 22 out of 32 million rubles worth of imports for 1790-1793 was paid out for textiles, gold and silver articles, precious stones, paintings, furniture and musical instruments, wines, sugar, coffee, chocolate, and various other gastronomical products. Restrictions placed on luxury goods in April 1793 were made palatable by the need to erect a barrier not only to the ideas of revolutionary France but also to its trade. Such temporary measures could not fundamentally alter the pattern of Russian foreign trade. Only the rising demand for naval stores explained the steady growth of revenue from 2.4 million in 1765 to 5.4 million in 1795.[29]

A comparison of the four major sources of revenue from taxation in the preceding pages has shown their overwhelming importance. In 1765 personal taxes (capitation and quitrent), proceeds from the sale of salt and vodka, and customs receipts yielded 17.5 out of 19.6 million; in 1785, 35.1 out of 40 million, and in 1795 49.1 out 56.1 million rubles. The remaining 1.5, 4.9, and 7 million may be briefly accounted for. This additional revenue came from taxes in kind or in money on iron and copper minting and from the mining of copper coins; and from an extremely broad spectrum of taxes called *kantseliarskie sbory* that included virtually everything else, such as revenue from the lease of state and Court properties (mills, lands, fisheries, stalls), fees charged for the performance of legal services such as charges for stamped paper, for filing suits and appeals, the printing of commissions, for passports, the registration of contracts, fines, etc.[30] While this additional revenue was certainly not negligible, it does not warrant separate consideration in this brief survey of the major sources of revenue.

FINANCING THE DEFICIT

It is now apparent from the foregoing discussion that the Imperial budget suffered from a structural imbalance between rising expenditures and insufficient revenues depending upon fixed personal contributions and the sale of vodka rather than upon an expanding gross national product. Except for a few temporary expedients to supplement the revenue obtained from taxation, only two additional sources of revenue were available to the Imperial government: foreign bor-

[29] Semenov, II, 418-434, 436-448; Chechulin, 221-223.
[30] Chechulin, 260-262.

rowing, which began with the first Turkish war, and increasing the money supply by printing assignats.[31]

The Manifesto of December 29, 1768, drafted by State Secretary Kozmin, was quite clear about the reasons for establishing an Assignat Bank and printing paper money. In a vast empire such as Russia, it was stated, distances alone were an obstacle to the improved circulation of money, on which the well-being of the people and the flourishing of trade depended, but an enlightened government must surmount natural obstacles in order to foster the general good. The weight of copper coins was another obstacle hindering their circulation. There were no local banks to facilitate the turnover of private capital and no central bank to issue obligations valid as legal tender. This would henceforth be the purpose of the two Assignat Banks in Petersburg and Moscow. In the 1770s local branches were opened all over the country to speed up the exchange of copper coins for assignats.

The assignats were issued at first in large denominations of 25, 50, 75, and 100 rubles. The seventy-five ruble assignat was discontinued in 1771 because counterfeiters found it easy to change the number twenty-five into seventy-five, but fifteen years later five- and ten-ruble assignats made their appearance, printed on blue and red paper respectively. The initial issue was for 1 million rubles, equally divided among the two banks, and the Procurator General anticipated that a total amount of 3.5 million rubles would ultimately be issued. By the beginning of 1774, however, 17.8 million rubles worth of assignats were already in circulation, but the Empress imposed a ceiling of 20 million in January.[32] Assignats were convertible into copper, and their enormous advantage was quickly recognized. The reforms of the 1770s took place against a background of fiscal stability; danger signals were but faintly heard.

The reforms were barely completed, however, when the preparation of the 1783 budget disclosed the alarming prospect of a major deficit. While ordinary expenditures were set at 19.2 million rubles, or about the same level as in 1767, overlooking fluctuations between 16.5 and 25.9 million in the intervening years, extraordinary expenditures jumped

[31] Foreign borrowing need not concern us here in a book devoted to internal administration.

[32] Gur'ev, 26-27, 32-36; PSZ, 1768, N. 13219, 13220; 1771, N. 13628-13629; 1773, N. 13945; 1786, N. 16484; 1787, N. 16523; 1774, N. 14096. Assignats were sent by mail for a charge depending on the weight (*vesovye dengi*) and, after 1785, an additional charge of half a percent of the value of the package (the so-called *poluprotsentnyi sbor*): PSZ, 1785, N. 16172. Kulomzin suggests that a memorandum by (possibly) Sievers was instrumental in convincing the Empress of the need to issue assignats: "Assignatsii," 217.

from 3.8 million in 1782 to 12.4 in the following year. Since the reserve available to the Treasury for Extraordinary Expenditures amounted to only 3.2 million, the government was suddenly faced with the task of finding 9.2 million rubles. A commission consisting of Prince Viazemskii, Shuvalov, Vorontsov, and Bezborodko, representing the three dominant political families, was instructed by the Empress to find means to plug this enormous deficit. The commission submitted its report in April 1783, and most of its recommendations were incorporated in the famous ukase of May 3, 1783.[33]

The commission took a conservative stance, reflecting the ideas of the Procurator General. It claimed that the resources from taxation were far from exhausted and drew up a program of tax reform consisting of two parts. The quitrent on state peasants should be raised from 2 to 3 rubles and that of the *odnodvortsy* from 1 to 3 rubles. In a separate document, not published by Kulomzin, Shuvalov expressed his approval of such a simple device—expected to yield 3.8 million rubles out of the anticipated 5.1 million in new revenue—on the grounds that this was a mere internal regulation (*ekonomicheskoe rasporiazhenie*) by Her Majesty as landowner (*v litse pomeshchitsy*), since any landowner could raise or reduce the quitrent from his peasants "at discretion."[34] Interesting reasoning, indeed, reflecting an awareness that the personal interest of the Empress could be balanced with the collective interest of the ruling class. The commission here was functioning as a committee of landowners advising the largest landowner in the realm to do what they and their brethren had been doing all along. The commission's report also proposed to raise the price of stamp paper; "did not dare" to recommend an increase in the price of salt; recommended that merchants exempted from recruit levies should pay, not 360 rubles per man as stated in the law of 1766, but 500 rubles; and that the 1782 law imposing a quitrent on industrialists who opened factories on state lands with a labor force of attached peasants should apply to those who opened such factories before 1782. Obviously, peasants and merchants were to be the major contributors of the new revenue.

The second part of the report sought to integrate the tax structure of the Baltic provinces, Bielorussia, and Little Russia with that of Great Russia by introducing the capitation and changing the method of collecting the vodka revenue. The administration of the borderlands

---

[33] The report was published in *SIRIO*, I (1867), 297-312. The original is in TsGADA, f. 16, d. 148, chast' 15, 190-217. Additional material is on 562-568. The ukase of May 3, 1783: N. 15724.

[34] This document is in TsGADA, *ibid.*, fol. 568v. It is unsigned and undated. I attribute it to Shuvalov on the ground of similarity in the handwriting.

belongs to the next chapter, and it will suffice here to say that although their integration was a goal of policy since the beginning of the reign and found powerful support among the nobility of both Russia and its borderlands, the actual process of integration seems to have been justified on fiscal grounds.[35]

The revenue did rise and kept oscillating between 40.5 and 44.8 million during the decade 1783-1793, but total expenditures rose to 76.4 million by 1793. Beginning in 1785 the Imperial budget showed a deficit every single year until the very end of the reign. New ways had to be found, and policy differences hardened in 1785 when Prince Viazemskii and Bezborodko took opposite stands in what must have been a heated controversy.[36]

The Procurator General expected a deficit of 9 million rubles for 1785, due not only to insufficient revenue as such but also to arrears amounting to about 2 million a year out of a total revenue of 42 million. To cover most of it, he suggested two sets of measures reminiscent of the recommendations of the commission of 1783. The tax on declared capital should be doubled, postal peasants (*iamskie*) should be merged into the body of state peasants and also taxed at 3.77 rubles per soul; state domains should be better known, surveyed, catalogued, and leased at reasonable prices to avoid scandalous situations such as that in Riazan province, where 48,292 *desiatins* of hayfields (52,638 hectares or 130,388 acres) were leased for four years at a paltry 17 rubles a year; private factories on state lands should be taxed; police boards should be financed by a new tax; and peasants should be required, over and above payment of their personal taxes, to supply flour, oats, and hay to the army at fixed prices. Prince Viazemskii expected this additional taxation to yield 3.8 million rubles. To obtain another 4.4 million he proposed raising the capitation on peasants to 1 ruble, on townsmen to 1.50; cancelling the annual appropriation of 20,000 rubles for public construction in each gubernia; raising taxes on mine owners and discontinuing the payment of salaries to elected officials because they lived at home on their estates and such payment was a favor (*milost'*) and not a compensation for services; this alone would save 1.4 million. Finally, the exemption from recruit levies in the borderlands should be purchased by a tax of twenty-five kopecks per soul, and towns and landlords there should no longer be permitted to sell vodka.

The Empress turned over these recommendations to Bezborodko

---

[35] Gabriel Ardant (I, 14-17) in his stimulating book on taxation has argued that fiscal pressures are often to be found behind political decisions.

[36] *SIRIO*, XXVIII (1880), 258-283; the original of Bezborodko's comments is in TsGADA, f. 19, d. 344, fol. 1-50. See also Kulomzin, "Assignatsii," 226.

and asked for his comments. The state secretary took a position which he knew would be pleasing to her, one which was economically sound but fiscally dubious. No one who knew the thoughts of Her Majesty would have dared make such recommendations, he told her. Nowhere in Europe were ordinary expenditures so far below the revenue, leaving a substantial surplus for extraordinary expenditures—an amazing statement on the part of such a high official who should have known that ordinary expenditures were kept artificially low. He agreed that the capitation could be raised, but not then, and that the treasury should get more out of its domains. But he strongly rejected Prince Viazemskii's other recommendations, as likely to hamper economic development. Taxes on mine owners would raise the price of iron and give an advantage to the Swedes. Additional taxes on the borderlands would not be in accord with the generous disposition of Her Majesty and would ruin many families. Local construction, on the other hand, attracted people, stimulated trade, developed the circulation of money, and created wealth. This in turn would make it possible to find the resources to pay local officials. Bezborodko then pleaded ignorance of the true financial situation, since the Procurator General kept the figures to himself, but felt confident that an increase in personal taxes, additional revenue from the new provinces annexed after the war, the development of foreign trade, and, of course, resort to the Assignat Bank would yield enough resources to cover the deficit. Catherine's grateful comment ("very, very good, with God's help") showed that she had been told what she wanted to hear.

Bezborodko assumed that economic expansion would yield ever greater revenue, while Prince Viazemskii, who held the purse strings, took a narrower and more pessimistic view of the situation. Repeatedly, until his retirement, he would ask the Empress to increase the revenue from taxation only to find himself isolated among the proponents of a vigorous foreign policy aiming at consolidating Russian gains against the Turks. By 1786 there were 45.3 million rubles worth of assignats in circulation, clear evidence that the ceiling imposed in January 1774 had not been observed. In 1786, against the strong opposition of Prince Viazemskii, the ceiling was raised to 100 million. Then came the second Turkish war, during which the Assignat Bank became the credit agency of the treasury, and by the end of the reign some 157 million rubles worth of assignats were in circulation, despite the solemn promise of the Empress made in June 1786 that the ceiling of 100 million would "never" be exceeded. As a result, the value of the assignat fell from 97 kopecks in 1787 to 68.5 kopecks in 1796, gold and silver coins left the country to cover expenditures for the army abroad, and traders began to hoard copper.[37] Prince Viazemskii did not live to witness the ruin of a fiscal policy made under the influence of adventurers from the borderlands, but it would have been a source of satisfaction to him to see that his recommendations of 1785 were finally carried out in 1794, when a tax program was announced calling for a new census—the first one to come so soon after the preceding one—an increase of the rate of the capitation, a grain tax, a double tax on declared capital and on Jews, new taxes on inheritance and industrial production; and state lands were offered for sale.[38] But the decision made in 1785 had set the course of fiscal policy for an entire decade. Inflation began to act like a magic potion. It encouraged the Empress and her close advisers from the Ukrainian and Smolensk nobility—the Potemkins, Khrapovitskiis, Bezborodkos, and Zavadovskiis—to avoid fundamental choices between an aggressive foreign policy which brought glory to Russian arms and a responsible fiscal policy unable to sustain such an expansionist program. It helped borrowers, chiefly noblemen who looked forward to a reduction of their debt burdens. It encouraged superficial economic development unsupported in the long run by technological innovation. It ruined retired officers and officials on pensions and fixed salaries paid in assignats, and it bred corruption on a gigantic scale. Inflation undermined the very success of the reform, and public opinion was ready by the end of 1796 to accept a radical change of course.

The financial reform serves as a kind of case study for the historian investigating the sources of power in Catherine's reign. The few changes made in fiscal legislation aimed at demarcating more clearly the ruling class from the socially dependent, as the increase of the quitrent brought into starker relief the fiscal exemption of the nobility. Granting privileges to the merchants in return for an increased contribution created an elite among the townsmen from which candidates could be recruited into the ruling class. Discussions over the direction of fiscal policy illustrated most vividly the duality so characteristic of the ancien regime state, between the ruling house and the aristocratic families[39] that sanctioned its legitimacy. It also confirmed their common interest in maintaining the status quo. Raising the quitrent paid by the peasants of the Court and those of the treasury was legitimized by the fact that landowners had already raised it on their estates and by the fear lest a lighter burden draw serfs away from their masters. On the other hand, the same concern for legitimacy may have explained the growing

[37] Gur'ev, 37-38; Chechulin, "Vypusk"; Kulomzin, "Assignatsii," 227-236; PSZ, 1786, N. 16407, pt. 1; 1789, N. 16744; Lappo-Danilevskii, "Sobranie," 371.
[38] PSZ, 1794, N. 17221-17228.
[39] Dorn, 18.

arrears. Inability to pay certainly played a role, but the question must be raised whether the refusal to pay a tax does not mark as well a rejection of its legitimacy.

The financial reform also raised fundamental questions about the relationships between the ruling class and the bureaucracy. If serfdom and an undeveloped economy severely limited the broadening of the fiscal base, maximizing resources to support the westernization of the ruling class and the expansion of the military establishment—thereby legitimizing the Romanov house in secular terms—required improving the efficiency of tax collection. Thus the ruling class had an interest in bringing order to the chaotic situation inherited from the 1730s. Prince Viazemskii's leadership in restructuring agencies and procedures was certainly one of the most remarkable achievements in the history of Russian administration. At the same time, it is almost certain that this very reform accelerated the development of a true bureaucracy which the police and judicial reform precisely sought to retard, a bureaucracy with its own claim to legitimacy, which two generations later would challenge the leadership of the ruling class. The rise of Vasil'ev was perhaps symptomatic of a new trend, and it would be interesting to determine how many of the men who entered the core of the ruling class after the death of Catherine came from families of clerks specializing in financial administration. Finance more than any other activity required a sense of order, application, and consistency. The demand for accountants, cashiers, and treasurers, in addition to the usual clerks and "subclerks," was bound to result in the development of a bureaucracy of non-noble origin, one of men with a conception of their role going beyond that of treasurers of the ruling class. Thus the financial reform contained two elements which perhaps strengthened each other in the minds of the reformers but which in the long run threatened to drive a deep wedge between the landed nobility and a rising bureaucracy. The one derived considerable resources from the exemption of its serfs from the quitrent payable to the treasury; the other was bound to view such exemption as incompatible with an efficient fiscal system. The bureaucratization of the ruling class is a phenomenon of the nineteenth century; and the attendant divergence of interests destroyed the unity of that class at the very time when the legitimacy of serfdom was being undermined by economic development and cultural progress.

PART V

THE ADMINISTRATION OF
THE BORDERLANDS

INTRODUCTION

By the 1770s, the territories acquired by conquests, peace treaties, and settlement formed an immense semicircle from the Gulf of Finland to the Urals, and each possessed an identity requiring an individual approach on the part of the Imperial government. Despite the recognition of the fundamental contrast between Great Russia and its borderlands, there has been little systematic analysis of their mutual contributions within the framework of the Empire as a whole, although in no other country (with the possible exception of China) has this relationship served as such a faithful barometer of the political climate.

Russian policy was essentially assimilative because the intensity and pervasiveness of its claim, based on a tradition opposed to diversity and dissent, could not permit the continued existence of institutions and practices fashioned by outside influences. But the translation of this claim into a coherent policy raised many thorny questions. In Siberia, where there could be but feeble resistance to the inroads of Russian civilization, there were two major problems: finding settlers for the development of an agricultural base to sustain the civil administration, the garrisons, and the operations of the mines; and maintaining a limited military presence to forestall nomadic raids into settled areas. Similar problems were found in the Orenburg Territory and the Northern Caucasus.

In the western borderlands the situation was much more complex. The stationing of large numbers of troops was a heavy burden, and the search for an acceptable fiscal policy to sustain it raised questions directly affecting the social constitution of those territories. Any tolerably efficient administration rests upon a large measure of consent on the part of those with local authority and power: the Polish and polonized nobility as well as the Baltic nobles had grown used to an extensive autonomy into which the public power of the Great Russian ruling class seldom intruded; they would look askance at any interference with their "privileges," which were defended by local courts using Polish and Swedish laws and procedures, among others. Moreover, as if to underscore the difference with Great Russia, the language was not Russian, and the religion was either Catholicism or Lutheranism. To baptize a Tungus prince was possible, but to convert an Ungern-Sternberg was inconceivable. The enmity between Catholicism and Orthodoxy, almost as old as medieval Christianity, reinforced the secular enmity between Poles and Russians. A policy of assimilation in these borderlands was counterproductive, as the Poles had discovered when they persecuted the Cossacks and the Orthodox; and Russian colonization was not the answer, since it would upset the social compact in force there.

Thus it would seem that a single assimilative policy toward the borderlands would flounder in a mass of contradictions, but this is true only if the social content of that policy is overlooked. The reign of Catherine witnessed a systematic attempt to introduce uniformity with Russian patterns in the administration of the borderlands; the explanation for this radical departure from the policy of her predecessors must be found in the convergence of the interests of the Great Russian ruling class with those of the established and aspiring land-owning class in the borderlands. This convergence was most noticeable in the Ukraine, where the Cossacks, having played out their historical role, were being downgraded to the condition of state peasants, while their *starshina* joined the ranks of the Russian nobility. The gradual integration of the Ukraine affected Lifland and Estland as well. The adoption by the Organic Law of 1775 of many institutions and procedures in operation in those two gubernias facilitated the rapprochement between the Baltic and the Russian nobles, although ethnic and religious tensions remained.

The profound differences between Great Russia and its borderlands had been reflected in a variety of institutional patterns. A number of agencies in the central government were responsible for the administration of Siberia and the Baltic provinces. One of them, the Siberian *Prikaz* created in 1730, was closed late in 1763, its responsibilities for the collection of furs given to the Pelt Expedition of the Cabinet. The administration of the Kolyvan mines had been subordinated to the Cabinet since the 1740s; that of the Nerchinsk mines was removed in 1764 from the jurisdiction of the College of Mining and placed under a "commanding officer" responsible directly to the Empress and the Senate. The Cabinet continued to exercise considerable responsibility for the administration of Siberia. Its director, Adam Olsuf'ev, who was also a member of the College of Foreign Affairs directly concerned with relations with China and the Kazakhs, was the Empress's closest adviser in Siberian affairs. Another important adviser (in the 1760s) was the former governor of Siberia, Fedor Soimonov, who sat in the Fifth Department; later in the reign, his nephew, State Secretary Peter Soimonov, was appointed Director of the Mining Expedition of the Cabinet when Bezborodko was emerging as the dominant figure among the Empress's secretaries.

Two agencies were responsible for Baltic administration, one judicial, the other financial, both created in the 1720s. The table of organization of 1763 provided for a College of Justice "for Lifland, Finland, and Estland Affairs" consisting of a president, a vice-president, three members, a procurator, two secretaries, and twenty-four clerks. The president was for many years (1741-1767) Fedor Emme, state councillor and judge advocate (*oberauditor*) of the Guard; after his death no successor was appointed until 1781, when the college had ceased to play an important role. Vice-President Timofei von Klingstedt (1765-1770) also sat on the influential Commerce Commission. The second agency, the Board (*Kontora*) of the College of Revenue "for Lifland, Finland, and Estland Affairs," was also based in Petersburg. It had three members and two secretaries but no procurator. The senior member (college councillor) was Ivan von Baumann (1765-1779), followed by Ivan Ludwig (1780-1796).[1]

The division of the Senate into four Petersburg departments placed the administration of the borderlands under both the First and Third Departments. The First Department had exclusive jurisdiction over fiscal matters, and the Branch of the College of Revenue was subordinated to it. The Third Department was a court of appeal in administrative and judicial matters for the southern and western borderlands. Among its most important members was State Secretary Teplov. Teplov wore many hats, two of them of interest here. He had been a protégé of the last hetman, Kirill Razumovskii, and was considered an expert on Ukrainian affairs. The report he submitted to the Empress in 1764 on the state of Little Russia presented a negative picture which influenced governmental policy. As a member of the Commerce Commission he was familiar with tariff questions. Tariff policy, predictably, affected the borderlands directly, and none more than the Baltic provinces, which had their separate tariff until 1782. The architect of the new tariff was Alexander Vorontsov, who succeeded Teplov in 1779 and remained in the department until 1793. And, of course, the key advisers of the Empress in matters of borderland administration included Bezborodko, a Ukrainian (with his compatriot Zavadovskii), and Potemkin, a product of the Smolensk nobility, whose administration of the south for sixteen years while president of the College of War places him in a class apart.

The local administration of the borderlands had little in common with that of Great Russia. There were voevodas in Siberia but none in the Ukraine or the Baltic provinces. Governors were not appointed

---

[1] PSZ, 1763, N. 11991, vol. 44², *kn. sht.*, 61-62. Names of the various members are listed in the *Mesiatseslov*. On the administration of Siberia, see Rafienko, 99-110.

in the Ukraine. There were governors general in Revel, Riga, and Kiev. There was a hetman in the Ukraine. Obviously, it was again in the Ukraine and the Baltic provinces that the contrast with the uniform pattern of centralized administration was the greatest. The local nobility had clearly established its mastery over the political and social life of these territories, and its corporate agencies represented a force with which the Imperial government had to reckon. In Lifland the knights—the descendants of the Teutonic invaders who established themselves in the Baltic provinces in the thirteenth century and developed into a closed aristocracy—were represented in a local assembly called the *Landtag*, which elected for life a marshal of the nobility and twelve *Landräte* who sat together to form a "college." This institution was created by the Swedes in 1643 as an advisory body to the governor general in Riga but was abolished by decree in 1694 at a time when Swedish policy was taking a sharp turn against the privileges of the Baltic landlords. The knights, however, took advantage of the confused situation created by the Northern War to ignore the decree, and their college remained in existence until 1786. It set the rules for admission into the nobility and constituted the de facto government of rural Lifland; the city of Riga and a few other towns had their own charters.[2]

In the Ukraine, where the historical, ethnic, and religious background was so different, the situation was oddly similar. The administration of the hetmanate was controlled by a council of *starshiny*, the superior officers of the Cossack Host who had in common with the Baltic knights their membership in a military elite ruling the territory in which they and their followers were a distinct minority and where the towns also enjoyed a separate legal existence. This council was an advisory body to the hetman, and its members were confirmed, if not chosen, by the Imperial government. It consisted of eight executive officers called General Quartermaster, Judges (two), Secretary, Treasurer, Adjutant, and two Standard Bearers. Russian interference, however, had gone much further in the Ukraine than in the Baltic provinces, and a second advisory body was created in the form of a Little Russian College composed of an equal number of Ukrainians and Russians. Its intermittent existence (1724-1727, 1734-1750) reflected the fluctuations of Russian policy toward the hetmanate. When Kirill Razumovskii was eased out of his post in 1764, the hetman was replaced by a governor general (in Glukhov) and the college was restored, consisting of four Russians and four Ukrainians.[3] An unusual

---

[2] Gradovskii, "Istor. ocherk," 331-332; Troshchinskii, "Zapiski," 131-133; Mocul'skii, 59-60; Levenstim, 81.

[3] Gajecky, I, 7-12. On the various ranks found in the Ukraine, see "Zapiski iz dela," 116-128.

feature, unknown in the Baltic provinces, was the appointment of a Russian procurator, Alexei Semenov (1765-1781), who was the "eye" of Prince Viazemskii in the Ukraine; the governor general, the future Marshal Rumiantsev, was his relative. Thus, from an institutional point of view, the borderlands were divided into two categories: the Baltic provinces and the Ukraine, on the one hand, and the others, whose local administration followed the Great Russian pattern. In those two western borderlands the innovation consisted in the establishment of either a central agency functioning as an appellate board and local body representing the elite of the landed nobility, or a local board of mixed membership representing both the Imperial government and the elite of the landed nobility.

Before we turn to an examination of the administration of each borderland and the consequences of the reform, there is need to consider briefly the mood prevailing in the 1760s, when so many questions were being raised about the role of the nobility, the inadequacy of the law, and the economic development which inevitably challenged some of the premises of recent policy toward the borderlands. The Empress, it is generally accepted, was a foe of local particularism.[4] There were several reasons for her attitude. A German herself, she had to appear more Russian than the Russians if she was to remain on the throne, as her husband's misfortune had shown. The sorry spectacle of the fragmentation of the "German Nation" was enough to convince the politically conscious of the paralyzing consequences of clinging to outmoded privileges in an age of territorial expansion. Her mind was a classical one, receptive to suggestions that perfection was found in uniform patterns and methodical rules and she strongly believed that if all men belonged to a common humanity they were also subordinated to their social superiors. The internationalism of the aristocratic age in which she lived had little patience with sprouting national claims that territory and language were the foundations of consciousness, and the rude shock she felt at the news of the French Revolution was as much the result of grasping its immediate political implications as of seeing in it a direct challenge to her most cherished philosophical assumptions.

Her position toward the special status enjoyed by the borderlands was clearly and forcefully stated in the concluding paragraph of her instruction to Prince Viazemskii upon his appointment in 1764. To cancel "all at once" the privileges of Little Russia, Lifland, and Finland would be "improper" and to treat them as foreign territories would be a mistake and even "stupidity." A way must be found to "russify"

[4] Nolde, II, 35; Brückner, *Katharina*, 518-520.

them—as well as Smolensk gubernia, whose endogamous gentry still kept to themselves—so that they would "stop longing like [caged] wolves for the forest"; and the simplest way was to find "sensible" people in these provinces who would look to the Imperial government for guidance.[5] The Empress was hardly original in depending on a method of Russian foreign policy, still used in our own day, that sought those among a territory's political and social leadership whose interests coincided with the Russian government's. Whatever the method, the intent was clear: the Empress had no sympathy for local privileges and would curtail them when the first opportunity presented itself.

The Empress had come to the throne at a time when a proud nation, flushed by recent victories in the Seven Years War, had decided to settle accounts with the Turks, and the great victories of the first Turkish war transformed this pride into a vanity which some contemporaries found hard to bear. In the Baltic provinces the fundamental Russian premise that political sovereignty, Orthodoxy, and ethnic unity combined to form a powerful synthesis was bound to collide with the arrogance blended with racial superiority of the Germanic nobility and Riga merchants, who invoked their privileges to keep Russians out of their provinces and towns. The opposition to the inclusion of Baltic and other local privileges in the new code of laws was obvious when the question came up before the Legislative Commission in November-December 1767.[6] One would like to know more about the exchanges, but even the few comments at our disposal enable us to determine the major issues. It is interesting to note that one of the opponents of Baltic privileges was the second-ranking member of the Board of Revenue for Lifland, Finland, and Estland Affairs and its delegate before the Commission, Artemi Shishkov. In a brief submitted in December he pointed out that Lifland had another name (Vidzemme) "before the Germans came," and was populated by native inhabitants; that the Swedish king Charles XI had curtailed the privileges of the knights on the eve of the annexation by Peter the Great; and that in 500 years of nearly constant strife and shifting allegiances the Baltic nobility had been unable to codify an abundance of laws written in Latin, thus showing how inadequte their civil law remained. The Baltic provinces, he concluded, had never lived better than since their annexation and should be governed by the same laws as the other subjects of the Empress.

Shishkov thus addressed himself to two fundamental questions. It

    [5] *Istoriia Prav. Senata*, II, 796. On the close family ties of the Smolensk nobility, see Rovinskii.
    [6] *SIRIO*, VIII (1871), 322, 330-331, 335-339, 348-351, 377-378; Shishkov, 83-95.

was too early to exploit the ethnic issue, as would be done in the nineteenth century, by emphasizing the minority status of the German element, and such a policy would have been unpalatable to a landed nobility for whom serfdom and the exploitation of the state peasantry were a normal way of life. Rather, an accommodation had to be found with the Baltic nobility, to remove barriers separating it from the Russian nobility. Hence the repeated emphasis on "equality" for the good of all. This could not of course be understood as equality between the nobles and their social inferiors, but equality among the various nobilities of the Empire and their integration, by their acceptance of the same laws, into a "single political body," even if allowance had to be made for religious tolerance. Such equality of the privileged under the laws assumed naturally the extension of serfdom everywhere (except in Siberia), and it would result in the "fame and might" of the entire Empire, conceived in typical Russian Orthodox terms as the triumph of the communal interest over the particularisms of "certain private persons" who by clinging to their old privileges sought only their own good and not that of "society." Diversity was seen as the source of discord, unity as the source of strength. With unity came order and peace—a second theme for which there was considerable historical justification. The history of the Ukraine and Bielorussia in the seventeenth and early eighteenth centuries—not to mention other periods—is a sorry tale of ravage and plunder which ruined both peasantry and townsmen. Annexation into the Empire resulted in misfortune for many but created long-term security, for which the Russians were already taking full credit.

Another argument, with ominous implications for the nobility if they refused to see where their true interest lay, was that the Baltic borderlands had been occupied in wartime and transferred to Russia by a peace treaty with Sweden. "Capitulation by force of arms," said Lev Shishkov of Novosil uezd, "is not a distinction earned by the conquered but depends on the magnanimity of the conqueror." Privileges were not immutable rights; they were tolerated. It was perhaps no coincidence that many deputies who spoke before the Commission or supported motions came from the uezds of Belgorod and Voronezh gubernias, along the Ukrainian border. A modus vivendi was being reached with the Cossack *starshina*, and the issue of Ukrainian privileges had already lost much of its passion. The deputies therefore looked upon the Baltic privileges as the last obstacle to the unity of which they dreamed. In a sarcastic question well designed to sting their Lutheran hearts, the Baltic nobles were asked how they could still recognize laws given by the Pope to a long-dead archbishop. The Orthodox deputy of Kiev was asked how the citizens of his city could claim to be satisfied with laws written in Polish and Latin, which they could not understand. There was not only spite in these questions; there was also an arrogant assertion that the existence of the Russian "sovereign as the source of all civil law (*vlast'*) terminates the need for rights (*iskliuchaet potrebnost' prav*) on the part of foreign peoples [living] under his dominion (*vladychestvo*)."

Yet another argument was raised as though in passing by the same Lev Shishkov, which turned out to be of crucial importance. The deputy declared that he wanted the "equality" of all state taxes and revenues. He was seconded by the deputy from Voronezh, who had discovered that Lifland and Estland did not carry the same burden as other Russian provinces. Despite its complexity the issue could be framed in simple terms. The effect of the privileged status of the western borderlands was to strengthen private and corporate interests against the claims of the public power. The nobility of Great Russia, it was shown in the preceding chapter, used its political organization to generate enormous sums not only for the purpose of sustaining its privileged position but also to carry out its imperial responsibilities. The borderlands, still poorly integrated into the fiscal machinery of the Empire, were not contributing their share to the common pool. The unification of tax legislation thus became the concomitant of the integration and the "equality" of the nobility. Against such massive arguments the Baltic deputies made a poor case, suggesting that there was something subversive in the fact that private subjects dared to propose the annulment of privileges upheld by every sovereign since Peter the Great. They merely proclaimed their trust in the Empress as the first and last resort. If they had known what she had written to Prince Viazemskii three years earlier, they would have been less confident.

CHAPTER II

THE EASTERN BORDERLANDS

SIBERIA

This enormous territory was a country in itself, so much so that it was commonly said that travellers to Moscow were returning to "Russia." Until 1727 "Siberia" began at Viatka, and until 1764 there was but a single gubernia for the whole territory. It was divided into three provinces: Tobolsk (the "capital of Siberia"), Eniseisk, and Irkutsk. A second gubernia was created in 1764 with Irkutsk as its capital, and a third in 1783 around Kolyvan to include the Altai mines. The Organic Law was introduced in the three gubernias in 1782-1783. Their total population of 1,059,850 was distributed among six oblasti and thirty-three uezds.[1]

The importance of Siberia was reflected in the appointment of capable and trusted administrators. Major General Denis Chicherin (promoted to lieutenant general in 1774) had an unusually long tenure of seventeen years (1763-1780) in Tobolsk. He was succeeded, as the territorial reform was about to take place, by Evgenii Kashkin (1781-1788), Governor General of Tobolsk and Perm, and then by Alexei Volkov (1789-1796), former Governor of Riazan. Both were lieutenant generals. Tobolsk gubernia was administered after the reform by Major Grigorii Osipov, a relative of Potemkin, and state councillors Sergei Protopopov and Alexander Aliab'ev. Chicherin and Kashkin rank among the most capable governors of Catherine's reign. Both were majors in the Guard and corresponded with the Empress. Chicherin, the brother of the Policemaster General, ruled Tobolsk with a patriarchal mixture of generosity and cruelty typical of the Russian barin of his day. He showed great energy in settling the steppes, developing communications, and raising the cultural level of a rough frontier territory. He kept an open house for thirty persons every day, but did not hesitate to order the whipping, knouting, and branding of offenders who crossed his path, especially those who did not report their visitors to the police. He even ordered all house owners to keep a loaded musket to shoot on sight the "enemies of humanity" (robbers) who terrorized the town. Slovtsov, the historian of Siberia, praised

[1] PSZ, 1764, N. 12259 and 12269; Arsen'ev, 97; PSZ, 1775, N. 14242; 1782, N. 15327, 15555; 1779, N. 14868; 1783, N. 15675; 1784, N. 15921.

the civilizing influence of this most popular governor in Siberian history. Kashkin too was energetic, loved suppers, masked balls, and the hunt, but he was also a modest man who left a reputation for honesty and moderation, particularly in the treatment of the Old Believers in the Urals. He went on to become Governor General of Iaroslavl and Vologda (1788-1793) and of Kaluga and Tula until his death in 1796.[2]

Another long tenure was found in Irkutsk, where Major General Karl von Frauendorf was appointed Vice-Governor in 1753 and Governor in 1764. He was succeeded in 1767 by Major General Adam Bril, Brigadier General Fedor Nemtsov (1775-1778), dismissed for taking bribes and embezzling state property; then by Major General Frants Klichka, who remained until the introduction of the reform and later became Kursk and Orel Governor General. The reform was carried out by Lt.-Gen. Ivan Iakobi, Governor General of Irkutsk and Kolyvan (1783-1788), followed by Lt.-Gen. Ivan Piel (1789-1795), former Governor of Lifland and Pskov.

General Iakobi stands out as one of the great administrators of the reign. The son of a Pole who had emigrated to Russia in 1711 and remained commandant in Selenginsk for twenty-eight years, he had first-hand experience of Siberian conditions and had even visited Peking. A brave officer in the first Turkish war, he became a protégé of Potemkin and had been before his appointment in Irkutsk Governor in Astrakhan, Saratov, then Governor General of Ufa and Simbirsk. His energy and spirit of independence unfortunately broke his career. Implicated in a sordid affair (if we are to believe Derzhavin) in which the sinister hand of Prince Viazemskii was noticeable, he was accused of planning to involve Russia in a war with China and showing disrespect to the Senate, and was dismissed. Investigated by Sheshkovskii, he was exonerated five years later, following the intervention of State Secretary Derzhavin, who convinced the Empress of his innocence.[3]

One of the most important problems on the agenda of Siberian administrators was the security of the frontier against the Manchu Empire, then at the apogee of its power, and the Kazakhs, who maintained a constant pressure against the advancing line of Russian colonization. Traditional Russian policy in insecure frontier regions had been to build fortified lines linking fortresses at strategic locations, usually the confluence of rivers or river crossings. Two lines defended the plain between the southern Urals and the Altai mountains, where

---

[2] On Chicherin, see O rasporiadkakh Chicherina; Dmitriev-Mamonov, 14-15; on Kashkin, see Petrov and Kashkin. See also Abramov, "O byvshem."

[3] On Iakobi, see Derzhavin, 633-634, 636-643; PSZ, 1784, N. 16075. On his father's views on relations with China, see Sychevskii, 135-140, 199-202, 238-242. See also Shteingel.

the Siberian Tatars, the Kalmucks, and the Kazakhs of the Middle
Horde had once freely roamed. One was called the Ishim or Bitter
(gor'kaia) Line because it ran in part through a territory studded with
salt lakes; it began at Zverinogolovsk, the terminal of the Orenburg
Line, crossed the Ishim at Petropavlovsk and ended at Omsk on the
Irtysh. It was about 580 km long and protected the rapidly growing
settlements in the Ishim steppe. The second line, called the Irtysh or
simply the Siberian Line, began at Omsk, followed the right bank of
the Irtysh, and ended at Ust-Kamenogorsk, a major fortress of great
strategic importance because it defended the Altai mines, including the
nearby silver mines of Zmeinaia Gora, in the midst of an otherwise
defenseless open plain.

These lines and the troops assigned to defend them formed a separate
command called the Siberian Corps under a high-ranking officer, usually a lieutenant general. Ivan Springer commanded the corps in 1763-
1771, and was followed by Clapier de Colongue, a French engineer
general (1771-1777). Ivan Bagration, cousin of the future hero of the
1812 war, Nikolai Ogarev (1779-1789), and Gustav Strandmann (1789-
1796). These commanders were doubly subordinated—to the College
of War and to Chicherin in Tobolsk, and after the reform to the
Governor General of Irkutsk and Kolyvan—so that the entire frontier
of Siberia, from the Orenburg Line to the Sea of Okhotsk formed a
unified command with headquarters in Irkutsk. There was no line,
however, between Kuznetsk and the Amur river—some 3,180 km—
because the barrier formed by the Saian mountains was impassable
and the Mongol frontier beyond it was secure against nomadic inroads,
but there may have existed an unofficial "Chinese" line between Irkutsk and Nerchinsk centered in Selenginsk.[4]

Very few regular troops were stationed in Siberia. In the 1770s there
was only one regiment of dragoons. This regiment consisted of ten
squadrons (1,380 men), each stationed in one of the nine major fortresses on the line and in Irkutsk. In October 1786 the Siberian Corps
consisted of two regiments of dragoons and one regiment of infantry.
The dragoons were supplemented by detachments of Siberian Cossacks
on the Ishim Line and of Irkutsk Cossacks—2,140 men on paper, 662
in reality—in Transbaikalia, together with native troops, a Tungus
host of 500 men, and a host of 2,400 Bratsk Tatars in four regiments.
Here was an example of the typical Russian policy of using natives
to patrol the borders. By 1796, however, Governor Nagel would express alarm that the scattering of the Cossacks along the border was

[4] Amburger, Geschichte, 405; PSZ, 1771, N. 13649; 1763, N. 11931. There is a fine
description of life on the Irtysh Line with a description of Semipalatinsk in Andreev.

a dangerous practice, leaving non-Orthodox (*inovertsy*), whose ancestors had been Chinese subjects, without any Russians to watch over them.[5]

The largest military force in Siberia consisted of garrison troops. Seven battalions were assigned in 1764, about 5,400 men, three in Tobolsk, one in Tomsk, another in Irkutsk, and two in Selenginsk, staffed with recruits or retired soldiers and their children. These garrisons were inadequate to protect such an enormous region. They were too widely scattered; heavy demands were made upon them to provide convoys for great distances; and they were incapable of repelling a mounted enemy relying on surprise. In 1771, as activity increased along the entire steppe frontier during the first Turkish war, the College of War expressed concern over the security of the Siberian frontier and ordered the creation of five additional garrison battalions, bringing the total to twelve, and seven "light field units," each consisting of five hundred infantry, cavalry, and artillery. Only one of these was stationed in Eastern Siberia (Selenginsk); five were combined with the dragoons and the new garrison troops, to constitute a substantial defensive force of about 14,000 men stationed in the nine major fortresses of the lines: Presnogorkovsk, Petropavlovsk and Omsk on the Irtysh Line; Zhelezinsk, Iamyshevsk, Semipalatinsk and Ust-Kamenogorsk on the Irtysh; Biisk and Kuznetsk; the sixth was stationed in Kranoiarsk. To this military force must be added the *shtatnye komandy* introduced after the reform and consisting of about 1,570 men.[6]

The police, judicial and fiscal agencies provided for in the Organic Law were also introduced in Siberia but with certain modifications necessitated by the size of the uezds and the absence of a landed nobility. Instead of a uezd court or upper land court, a lower and upper *nadvornyi* court were created in the three gubernias. Noble assessors were not elected but appointed. On the other hand, the natives and the peasants attached to the mines were placed together with state peasants under the jurisdiction of the lower and upper *raspravy*.[7] The effect of the reform in Siberia was to create an elaborate apparatus of territorial administration, considerably larger than that

---

[5] "Rospisanie (1763)"; TsVIA, f. 12. d. 234, 2-4; PSZ, 1766, N. 12738; Dmitriev-Mamonov, 141-142, gives a figure of 11,635 men for the Siberian Corps in 1774.

[6] PSZ, 1764, N. 12135; 1769, N. 13390; 1771, N. 13649; 1777, N. 14562; TsGVIA, f. 12, d. 234; PSZ, 1796, N. 17524; *SIRIO*, XXVII (1880), 387. The Kolyvan battalion was probably the successor of a similar battalion consisting of four companies of infantry and one of dragoons set up in 1761 to protect the Biisk-Kuznetsk section of the line and guard the Kolyvan mines. It was reorganized in 1764 into a battalion of 523 officers and men, PSZ, 1761, N. 11185, pt. 10; 1764, N. 12230.

[7] PSZ, 1779, N. 14868; 1782, N. 15355, 15548; 1784, N. 16052; 1796, N. 17494, vol. 44², *kn. sht.*, 262-264.

in existence before the reform but one entirely appointed, and staffed—
in the absence of landed nobility—with either local retired officials or
other officials from outside Siberia. Thus, a paradoxical situation resulted in which a reform intended to create uniformity everywhere
was realized in Siberia without one of its major components: the
staffing of key positions with members elected by the local landed
nobility.

Tax legislation in Siberia distinguished between two major categories of payers. Natives (Ostiaks, Samoeds, Buriats) paid the *iasak*,
a tax of Moslem origin which the Russians borrowed after the conquest
of the Kazan khanate. It was originally payable in furs but was later
commuted into a money payment in whole or in part, a practice made
increasingly necessary as the supply of furs began to decline in the
eighteenth century. In Kamchatka it was collected in "sweet grass"
used to make vodka.[8]

The taxation of state peasants was closely related to the progress
of settlement, the development of a money economy, and the needs
of the Provision Chancery. These peasants were required to clear and
sow an additional lot of state land (*desiatinnaia pashnia*) or to supply
grain in kind from their own allotment to feed the officials and above
all the troops on the lines. They were also required to transport the
grain to fortresses. By the late 1750s, however, government policy
was beginning to rely on market forces to guarantee the supply of the
garrisons, although not without some resistance from the army. In
1762 peasants were allowed to sell their grain at market prices, and
their quitrent of forty kopecks (in addition to the capitation of seventy
kopecks) was raised to one ruble. A similar rate was applied to the
Nerchinsk peasants in 1765. The ukase of May 3, 1783 imposed a
uniform rate of three rubles on all state peasants and that of June
1794 raised the capitation to one ruble in Siberia as well. Criminals
banished to hard labor worked in the mines if they were healthy
and were under forty-five years of age. Other convicts were distributed
among villagers who were required to pay the personal taxes for them;
their male children at the next census would join the mass of registered
peasants. In the Kolyvan and Nerchinsk mines administrative personnel (*sluzhiteli*), craftsmen (*masterovye*) and hired workers (*rabochie
liudi*) were exempted from personal taxes, as were their children. The
justification given when this exemption was extended to the Nerchinsk
mines in 1763—the high cost of living and the reluctance of bachelors
to marry—provides an interesting insight into the effect of these per-

[8] On the *iasak*, see Nolde, I, 61, 72; *SIRIO*, XXVIII, 131-135.

sonal taxes on the birthrate in the borderlands, where the need for large families must have been checked by fear of the next census.[9]

As in Great Russia the proceeds from the sale of vodka was the second most important source of revenue. Vodka was sold "on faith" (*na vere*) in Siberia until 1767 and then was farmed out everywhere except in Irkutsk gubernia, where sale *na vere* was reintroduced in 1783 when no one was found willing to take a farm. One reason may have been the competition of the natives, who made a fermented liquor from the milk of cows and mares (*kumyzhnoe vino*). When tax-farmer Savel'ev invoked the monopoly of the nobility to distill vodka and asked that it be enforced to prevent losses to the Treasury, the Senate agreed. But the Empress overruled its decision and upheld the contention of Irkutsk authorities that to create dissatisfaction among the ninety thousand *inovertsy* in Irkutsk gubernia was dangerous policy. Savel'ev was already in arrears and it is possible that his experience deterred prospective tax-farmers. Since there was no landed nobility in Eastern Siberia, his case was at any rate a weak one. Data show that 135,137 *vedra* were sold in 1795 and that three state-owned distilleries produced 130,000 *vedra* in 1789. The production of vodka in Eastern Siberia was obviously a state responsibility. In Tobolsk gubernia state production was also the largest single source of vodka, although some of it also came from across the Urals. Towns and "companies" were allowed to distill, as one learns from Prince Via-zemskii's objections to Senator Vorontsov's claim in 1770 that to give such privilege to merchants was a violation of the privileges of the nobility, and from his insistence four years later that state-owned distilleries should be built to secure adequate supply.[10]

The Altai mountains and the Iablonoi range were the richest source of revenue. Olsuf'ev reported to the Empress in 1761 that the profit from the operations of the Altai mines, bought by the Cabinet from Akinfia Demidov in 1747, amounted to 3.3 million rubles in eleven years, including 89 *pud* (one *pud*: 16.4 kg) of pure gold and 2,824 *pud* of silver valued at 962,372 and 2,231,087 rubles, respectively; the net profit was 2.6 million, less operating expenses of 660,000 rubles. These Kolyvan-Voskresensk mines, as they were usually called, employed a work force of 27,000 men. Those of Nerchinsk employed only 6,000 but produced half as much silver. The ores also contained lead in such quantity that Russia was expected to become self-sufficient in the 1780s, and there was enough copper to mint a separate Siberian

---

[9] PSZ, 1762, N. 11633; 1765, N. 12449; 1766, N. 12738; 1782, N. 15429; 1763, N. 11891.

[10] *Svedeniia o pit. sborakh*, 209; PSZ, 1773, N. 13944; *Arkhiv Gos. Soveta*, I, 291-292; PSZ, 1789, N. 16742; 1765, N. 12500; 1770, N. 13416; 1774, N. 14168.

coin between 1766 and 1781. As the richer seams were becoming
exhausted, efforts were made to encourage prospecting and to staff
the administration with trained personnel, especially the mining corps,
which at the time attracted no one from the nobility because its officers
were held in contempt even by garrison officers; the sentries refused
to present arms to them. The Kolyvan mines were administered on
the spot by a "commanding officer" (*glavnyi komandir*), usually a
major general (Andrei Poroshin in 1761-1769, succeeded by Andrei
Irman), responsible to the Director to the Cabinet and the Empress:
the territory of the mines was completely outside the jurisidiction of
the governor in Tobolsk. Kolyvan gubernia was created so that the
entire population of the territory, whether they belonged to the peasantry assigned to the mines or were independent settlers, would be
subordinated to the same agencies. The governor of Kolyvan was given
full authority (*glavnoe nachalstvo*) over the mines under the Cabinet,
but in matters of general administration he was also subordinated to
the governor general in Irkutsk, a rather awkward arrangement. The
Nerchinsk mines were administered by the College of Mining until
1764, when Major General Vasilii Suvorov—first cousin of the future
marshal—was appointed to the new post of commanding officer (1764-
1774). The mining district was carved out into a separate jurisdiction
placed only in part under the governor of Irkutsk. Suvorov and the
mines were subordinated directly to the Empress and the Senate, but
police and judicial matters not directly related to mining administration belonged to the governor's jurisdiction. The mines were placed
in 1786 under State Secretary Soimonov, head of the Mining Expedition of the Cabinet, and the immediate supervision over the operations was given to the Nerchinsk senior commandant, Major General
Karl Handtwig (Gantvig).[11]

THE ORENBURG TERRITORY

What is called here for the sake of simplicity the eastern borderlands
also included the Orenburg Territory bound by the valley of the upper
Tobol, the Kama, Volga, and Ural rivers. Before the Russian conquest,
much of this territory was called Bashkiria. Its inhabitants had received
Islam from Kazan, paid tribute to its khans, and served in their army.
Its axis was the serpentine Belaia river, a left-bank tributary of the
Kama, easily connected by portage with the Ural river, beyond which

[11] On the Altai mines, see PSZ, 1761, N. 11185, 1779, N. 14868; 1786, N. 16312;
1783, N. 15740. For the Nerchinsk mines, see PSZ, 1763, N. 11891; 1764, N. 12075;
1778, N. 14804; 1787, N. 16497; "O vyplavke." There is much interesting material
in Maksimovich, *Sibir'*, chast' 3, 283-351.

roamed the nomadic Tatars and the Kazakhs of the Small and Middle Hordes, the enemies of the Bashkirs. A string of forts manned by the Ural Cossacks, a restless crowd of expatriates from the Don Cossacks, linked Orenburg with the mouth of the river, thus forming a natural barrier across the corridor in the depression between the southern Urals and the Caspian, through which nomads from Central Asia usually reached the Volga.

These conditions required that particular care be given to the selection of the Orenburg governor. The Territory was often used as a place of exile for some well-connected individuals, and one of these was Dimitri Volkov, who, after falling briefly from favor when Catherine seized power, returned to the capital to become president of the College of Manufactures. In a remarkable document written in May 1763 he suggested to the Empress certain qualities necessary to enhance the authority of the governor, together with his considerations on trade and the policy to follow toward the nomads. It was enough for a governor to win praise elsewhere, wrote Volkov, if he were just, did not take bribes, reduced litigation, and were not a coward—a frank admission that the local nobility possessed great power to paralyze and corrupt local administration and neutralize a governor's excessive zeal. In Orenburg, however, the governor must impose his authority upon the natives by his physical appearance and his ability to dispense justice to them without hiding behind the formalities of the law (*skorym slovesnym sudom*); his personal intervention and his willingness to punish his erring subordinates would thus make Russia a magnet for all surrounding tribes. He ought to combine in his office military command with civil administration, to prevent misunderstandings and useless correspondence, because "there are only military people here." Without a military command the town and the Kazakhs would despise him and feel that he was the handmaiden (*pod rukoiu*) of someone else. He went on to outline a generous policy toward the Kazaks, whose depredations were a major obstacle "on the road to India." The young hostages (*amanaty*) delivered to the Russians should be taught military science and the humanities so that, instead of dreaming of revenge, they would remember their stay among the Russians as the best time of their lives and would learn "to love Russia for her own sake and little by little would become russified." Russian and foreign merchants should not be treated "worse than dogs": Bukharans, Khivans, and Armenians should be encouraged to establish their own quarters (*slobody*) in Orenburg.[12] There was unfortunately a world of difference between Volkov and the rabble who filled the

---

[12] "Zapiska Volkova," 49-60.

ranks of the Cossacks and justified their violence by the resistance of
the natives, frightened by the inroads of an alien civilization. Only an
unusual individual would have the authority and the power to impose
order among the Russian population and give a new direction to
Russian policy toward the nomads.

Prince Avram Putiatin (1764-1768) left no permanent mark in
Orenburg, but his high rank (privy councillor or lieutenant general,
class III) was unusual for a pre-reform governor. He was succeeded
by Lt.-Gen. Ivan Reinsdorp in 1768. The new governor was a mel-
ancholy, indecisive man who found himself in the middle of two serious
crises. The Kalmucks, who had moved their camp along the left bank
of the Volga in the 1630s, were enticed by Chinese agents to return
to their old pastures in 1771. They met no opposition when they
crossed the Ural river, and large areas between the lower Volga and
the Ural once again became a deserted steppe. Rampant unrest among
the Ural Cossacks touched off the Pugachev rebellion, and Orenburg
had to sustain a long siege during which Reinsdorp was at least able
to keep the loyalty of the population. The last six years of his governorship were spent recovering from the ghastly destruction created
by the rebellion.[13] His death in 1781 coincided with the beginning of
the reform, which took place under the leadership of Ivan Iakobi,
whom we have already encountered, the new Governor General of
Ufa and Simbirsk.

The proconsul Volkov had called for did not arrive until the beginning of 1785. Described by Mertvago as "a German with all the
qualities of an ancient knight and of a latter-day *petit maitre*," the
handsome Osip Igelstrom was the son of a Lifland *Landrat* and was
connected, although his nobility was of recent origin, with the Mün-
nichs, Mengdens, and Stackelbergs, all prominent families of the Baltic
aristocracy. A Baltic baron with a Swedish name bringing order and
Russian civilization to restless nomads at the gates of Asia and assisted
in his task by the senior commandant of Orenburg with the Tatar
name of Iakov Zembulatov, major general in the Russian army—this
was striking evidence of the ability of the Russians to integrate the
social elite of their borderlands into a military service that recognized
status and promised promotion, and to use these men to spread the
principles of Russian civilization among their own people or other
indigenous nationalities. One can speculate here about the impact
upon local societies of the arrival of governors general in provincial
capitals in the wake of the reform. Vinskii, otherwise seldom generous
in his comments, appreciated the intelligence, knowledge, and polite-

[13] *RBS*, XV (1910), 554-556.

ness of Iakobi and of the officials in his suite. Ufa, where a class VII official had until then represented the government, now had a lieutenant general who knew the prestigious Potemkin. Noble families came from far and wide to settle in Ufa. Vinskii, an exile, taught French, history, geography, and mathematics to the children of the customs councillor. Igelstrom could not write Russian, and Mertvago, whose father had been killed in the Pugachev rebellion, began his career as his secretary. There is no doubt that the presence of these delegates of the top stratum of the ruling class raised the cultural level of the provincial nobility, that many a marriage must have been contracted between a local belle and their adjutants and that they helped many a young man make his way to Petersburg. Igelstrom left his mark on the administration of Bashkiria by his sense of justice, his feeling for order, and his respect for local traditions, as part of a policy of making Russian rule accepted and praised by a native population cowed by the brutality of his predecessors. His instruction (after his departure from Ufa) on the need to improve the quality of evidence presented before courts-martial shows his insistence that procedures must be fair to protect the defendants. He showed his cunning in trying to enlist the Moslem clergy—twice the size of Russian officialdom—to bring the Kazakhs into the fold. He supported the construction of mosques and played down the conversion of natives. He began an educational program that seemed to embody Volkov's ideas, but his support of the popular element among the Kazakhs against their khans was much less successful.[14]

The vulnerability of the Orenburg Territory was responsible for lasting tension; the Empress wrote to Iakobi in July 1782 to warn local officials against using the word sedition (*bunt*) too lightly in their correspondence.[15] Pugachev had left a vivid memory, and there were rumors in 1786 that another usurper had appeared. Throughout the eighteenth century the Territory remained an important wedge in the endless frontier with the Moslem world, and the Turks were always ready to exploit any form of dissatisfaction with Russian rule. Its geography, however, lent itself ideally to the creation of a military

[14] "Zapiski Vinskago," 177-180. Another important figure in the administration of the Territory was Maj. Gen. Tevkelev, of Kazakh origin: "Svedeniia o rode Tevkelevykh." On Igelstrom, see *RBS*, VIII (1897), 43-44; Dolgorukov, III, 137-140. Comments on court martial procedures in TsGVIA, f. 410, op. 1, d. 14, 10-11; "Zapiski Mertvago," 39-40, 484-489; Kulsharipov, 103, 112-113. There is, however, a very negative assessment of his activity in Iudin, "Baron Igelstrom." See also "Kirgiz-Kaisaki," in *ES*, XV (1895), 97-99.

[15] Ignat'ev 512-515; "Zapiski Mertvago," 43-45, 48-49. On the three Kazakh Hordes, see "Raznye bumagi Tevkeleva."

line separating the Bashkirs from the Kazakhs and surrounding Bashkiria. The Orenburg Line consisted of three sections extending over
2,650 km. One followed the Ural river (called the Iaik till 1775)
downstream to Gurev, a fortress commanding the mouth of the river.
The other ran along the river to Verkhneuralsk. The third went overland from the latter fortress to the bank of the Ui, followed it to its
confluence with the Tobol, and ended at Zverinogolovsk, where it met
the Ishim Line.[16]

The Orenburg Corps, commanded at least until 1769 by Lt.-Gen.
Peter Mel'gunov and then possibly by Reinsdorp, was commanded by
the governor general himself between 1781 and 1790 and in 1796. It
consisted of five garrison battalions, four stationed in Orenburg and
the fifth divided between Gurev and Uralsk, two outposts on the Ural
supposedly blocking the corridor between the Volga and the Aral Sea.
Companies from the Orenburg battalions were assigned to Ufa, Troitsk,
and Iletsk, the latter planted in the Kazakh steppe, sixty km south of
Orenburg to protect the salt mines of Iletskaia Zashchita. A second
force consisted of four regiments of trans-Kama "landmilitia," created
in 1736 and staffed with *odnodvortsy*, descendants of *streltsy* and
various other people, including Poles, resettled along the eastern borders. They were stationed on the Orenburg Line in four fortresses:
Verkhneuralsk, Kizylsk, Ozernaia, and Zelair. A third force consisted
of Cossacks organized in two hosts. The Ural Cossacks, a restless band
divided (by Nepliuev) into seven regiments of five hundred men each,
were stationed along the Ural river between Iletsk gorodok and Gurev.
The 4,500 Orenburg Cossacks, who could supply more than 1,200
men, resulted from the merger by Nepliuev in 1755 of the Samara and
Ufa Cossacks, and were used for patrol duty along the line and within
the gubernia, where the *shtatnye komandy* did not yet exist.

The exodus of the Kalmucks in 1771 showed that these forces were
inadequate to cope with an emergency. It took three months to gather
five hundred dragoons in Orsk and another month to obtain two
squadrons from the Siberian Line, during which time the Kalmucks
had disappeared into the desert. As a result, the number of garrison
battalions was raised to ten and newly created field units were stationed
in Orenburg, Orsk, and Troitsk. The land militia was abolished. Later
the new garrison battalions and the units were reorganized into three
infantry regiments and six field battalions (in 1786), and their cavalry
was used to form the Orenburg regiment of dragoons. Only the
Orenburg Cossacks remained under the jurisdiction of Orenburg after
the reform, the Ural Cossacks and the defense of the border between

---

[16] Donnelly, 195-199; Amburger, *Geschichte*, 345, *ES*, XII (1894), 157.

Uralsk and Gurev becoming the responsibility of the Astrakhan authorities. In the mid-1780s the total number of troops in the gubernia
was about 15,520 men.[17]

The administrative reform brought to the Territory the police and
judicial institutions of Great Russia. A police board was created in
Orenburg—and perhaps in Ufa—but in the absence of civilian officials
police administration was staffed with personnel from the garrisons.
Only five uezd courts were created in twelve uezds, reflecting the
scarcity of Russian landed nobility. There were, however, ten lower
raspravy intended for the Bashkirs and other native peoples as well
as for state peasants, and the governor general was instructed in 1782
to introduce a third assessor in the land courts to be elected in Bashkir
villages and to make sure that the natives were represented on the
upper raspravy in Orenburg and Ufa and the courts of equity. The
establishment of these peasant courts, although the Bashkirs did not
officially become state peasants, was part of an effort to break the
power of the native starshiny, who until the reform had administered
the volosts, subject to the largely nominal control of the provincial
chanceries; and to integrate a broader spectrum of the social leadership
of the native population into the Russian administrative hierarchy. To
settle disputes between Russians and Kazakhs of the Small Horde a
border court (pogranichnyi sud) was created in Orenburg in 1784
under the chairmanship of the senior commandant. It consisted of two
Russian officers, two local merchants, and two state peasants representing the Russian side, one sultan and six starshiny representing the
Kazakhs. Its jurisdiction was left undetermined, but the reference to
the intermediate courts and the fact that raspravy were later created
in the Small Horde reflected an obvious intention to draw the Kazakhs
into the Russian judicial orbit. The border court functioned in accordance with the Organic Law and applied Russian law. Iakobi was
instructed, and this was repeated to him when he was in Irkutsk, that
the inclusion of the natives in the new courts must be combined with
a policy of good will (laskovoe obrashchenie) toward them, and that
the fidelity, good behavior, and service of their leaders should be
rewarded by their inclusion into the nobility, so that they and the
remainder of their people would join the Russian people in a common
bond.[18] In Orenburg and Siberia Russian policy was clearly assimi-

---

[17] "Rospisanie (1763)"; PSZ, 1765, N. 12135; 1769, N. 13390; 1766, N. 12553;
1771, N. 13649; 1784, N. 15991, pt. 11, 16111; SIRIO, XXVII (1880), 386-387; PSZ,
1782, N. 15324. On the Ural and Orenburg Cossacks, see ES, XVA (1895), 586-588;
total strength in PSZ, 1783, N. 15636; see also Dubrovin, "Pred nachalom" and Vitevskii.

[18] PSZ, 1796, N. 17494, vol. 44², kn. sht., 262-265; 1798, N. 18478.

lative, attempting to achieve union by finding first a common ground from which the natives could be gradually integrated into the social, political, and religious world of Great Russia.

In Bashkiria the fiscal regime reflected, as it did elsewhere, the social composition of the population. The largest group consisted of Bashkirs and Meshcheriaks who after 1754 did not have to pay the *iasak* and who constituted a privileged community not subjected to personal taxes. As Russian influence grew in the Territory and pressure mounted to guarantee the security of the Orenburg Line without using field troops from the regular army, fiscal privileges came to be seen as a favor to be purchased by some form of military service. These natives were required to give one man from every eight *dvory* (household)— censuses in Bashkiria were by *dvor* not by soul—and the ratio was raised to one man from every three *dvory* in 1786, who served chiefly on the Orenburg Line, although some were also sent to the Siberian Line. This type of service was onerous, but the alternative was worse. The Bashkirs were in danger of going the way of the *odnodvortsy*, of joining the ranks of the state peasantry. A nomadic people, they preferred to join the ranks of the Cossacks and to retain some freedom. Government policy hesitated, and it was not until 1798 that Igelstrom's recommendation to incorporate the Bashkirs into a separate Cossack host (*soslovie*) was carried out.[19]

A similar policy was followed toward the so-called teptiars and bobyli. When Bashkiria was annexed, Bashkirs' and Meshcheriaks' land ownership (*votchinnoe pravo*) was recognized, and they did not become state peasants. The teptiars were people of various nationalities (but not Russians) who tilled Bashkir lands on a contractual basis; the bobyli were squatters. The law of 1760, which raised the quitrent from forty kopecks to one ruble, did not apply to them, nor did that of 1783 raising it to three rubles, and they continued to pay the same eighty kopecks imposed upon them in 1747. The result was a shocking inequality between the teptiars and bobyli, on the one hand, and, on the other, the state peasants resettled from Great Russia on Bashkir lands, who after 1783 had to pay the three-ruble quitrent, the capitation of seventy kopecks and the surcharge, in addition to delivering recruits at every new levy. The Senate resolved in December 1789 to place them on the same footing as state peasants, but an Imperial order directed Igelstrom in February 1790 to suspend execution. It very soon became clear, however that this favor had a price. It is likely that the teptiars, like the Bashkirs, feared their conversion into state peasants and offered instead to staff and outfit a "Cossack" regiment of five

[19] PSZ, 1782, N. 15324; 1784, N. 15991; 1783, N. 15680; 1787, N. 16592.

companies (*sotni*): an order of April 1790 authorizing the formation of the regiment referred to such a proposal. The government reaffirmed in 1794 that they were to be charged no more than eighty kopecks and added that the increase in the rate of the capitation did not extend to them.[20]

Thus, despite the strong impulse toward uniformity, the administration of the Orenburg Territory exhibited several very characteristic features, some of which were even created by the reform, especially in the area of justice and taxation. A major step, however, had been taken toward its integration into an Imperial framework common to both Great Russia and borderland gubernias.

[20] Kulsharipov, 127-130, 157; PSZ, 1761, N. 11186; 1789, N. 16825; 1790, N. 16836, 16856; 1794, N. 17282; see also 1789, N. 16761; "Zemel'nye akty."

CHAPTER III

THE SOUTHERN BORDERLANDS

THE SOUTHEAST

If we should hesitate to combine under a single heading the desert of Astrakhan gubernia and the steppes of the Ukraine, both history and geography would remind us that the unity of these southern borderlands was taken for granted by Russian officials and Tatar nomads alike. The frontier between the forest and the open plain was the battleground for the two great forces whose interaction had shaped the course of Russian history, the nomad and the settler; and the restlessness of the Cossack world added to the permanent insecurity of the plain the unsettling element of shifting alliances.

One of the components of this vast region was the Southeast, including the Caspian depression from the Ural to the Sulak rivers, the valley of the lower Don and of its tributaries, the Khopër and the Medveditsa, and the steppe of the Northern Caucasus. Administratively, it consisted of two parts. One was the "Land of the Don Cossacks," not divided into uezds until 1802, with a population of about 200,000 in 1775. Its capital was Cherkassk on the Don, and its basic unit was the Cossack *stanitsa*, of which there were fifty. The other was Astrakhan gubernia, whose seven towns were surrounded by desert. There the Kalmucks, the Nogais, and the Kazakhs roamed in search of pasture. It extended as far as the Terek, where Kizliar was a strategic point in Russia's relations with Transcaucasia. The territorial reform of 1785 retained the separateness of the Cossack Land and transformed Astrakhan gubernia into a *namestnichestvo* of the Northern Caucasus, divided into two *oblasti* (Ekaterinograd and Astrakhan).[1]

The administration of the Land of the Don Cossacks remained completely different from the ordinary provincial administration with which we are now familiar. Each *stanitsa* had its general assembly (*krug*), which elected the *starshiny*, who administered its internal affairs. These general assemblies were subordinated to the general assembly of the Cossack host, which elected its own *starshiny* and the ataman for no specific length of time and invested him with unlimited power, including that of confirming death sentences. In the eighteenth

---

[1] Got'e, I, 103, 110, 124; Arsen'ev, 96, 131; Klokman, 288-289; PSZ, 1785, N. 16193; 1786, N. 16366; 1790, N. 16858.

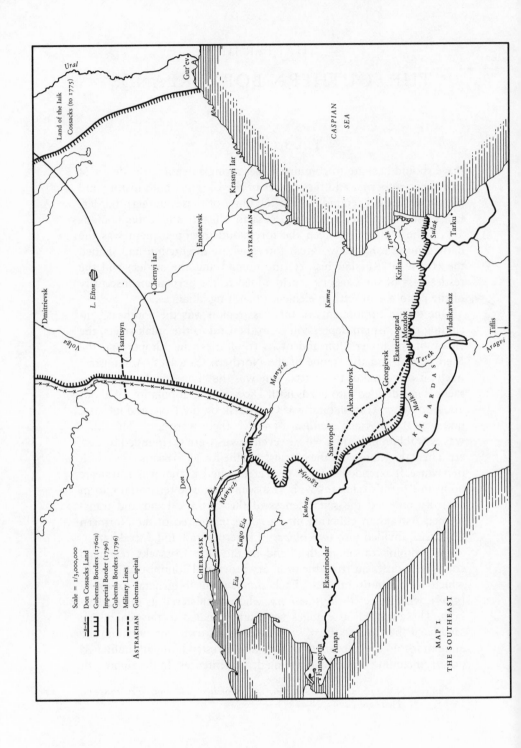

MAP I

THE SOUTHEAST

Scale = 1/3,000,000
Don Cossacks Land
Gubernia Borders (1760s)
Imperial Border (1796)
Gubernia Borders (1796)
Military Lines
ASTRAKHAN Gubernia Capital

Ural

Land of the Iaik
Cossacks (to 1775)

Gur'ev

CASPIAN
SEA

Krasnyi Iar

Enotaevsk

Dmitrievsk

Chernyi Iar

L. Elton

Tsaritsyn

Volga

ASTRAKHAN

Tarku

Suzak

Kizhar

Terek

Kuma

Ekaterinograd
Mozdok

Georgievsk

Vladikavkaz

Tiflis

Aragvi

Manych

Alexandrovsk

Malka

K A B A R D A S

Terek

Stavropol'

Egorlyk

Don

Manych

Kuban

Kugo Eia

CHERKASSK

Eia

Ekaterinodar

Anapa

Fanagoria

century the Imperial government gradually asserted its right to select
the ataman and to confer the rank of *starshina* upon those considered
favorable to the extension of Great Russian influence. The strengthening of this influence paralleled the growing social differentiation
among the Cossacks and the formation of an upper layer of well-to-
do (*domovitye*) Cossacks who needed the support of Russian authority
to assert their social claims in what still remained a "democratic" if
not an anarchic milieu. In 1775 Potemkin obtained from the Empress
the dismissal of ataman Sulin and his replacement with Alexei Ilovaiskii as part of a broader reform. The host remained under the
personal command of the ataman—Ilovaiskii was promoted to major
general—but the civil administration of the Territory was placed in a
collegial chancery declared to be the equal of a gubernia chancery,
and subject to the same regulations as those in force in Great Russia,
save where they conflicted with the privileges of the host. It consisted
of the ataman, two permanent members (*starshiny*) chosen by Potemkin, and four members elected for one year by a general assembly.
All six received a basic salary of 600 rubles. Both civil and military
administration were in turn subordinated to Potemkin, as Governor
General of New Russia and the Don.[2]

The administration of Astrakhan gubernia followed the regular pattern. The first governor appointed by the Empress was Major General
Nikita Beketov. Of Cherkess origin, he was the son of a former provincial voevoda in Simbirsk, and his mother was Swedish. He seems
to have been a very conscientious governor and did much to develop
the vineyards and fisheries of Astrakhan and trade relations with Persia. He was promoted to lieutenant general in 1773 and appointed
senator, but retired in 1780 to spend the last fourteen years of his life
on his properties near Tsaritsyn. His successor, Major General Peter
Krechetnikov, was the brother of the better-known Mikhail Krechetnikov, Governor General of Kaluga and Tula and protégé of Potemkin. Although the territorial reform did not take place until ten
years later, Astrakhan gubernia was placed in 1775 directly under
Potemkin, who turned over its administration to Major General Iakobi
in 1777 and to his distant cousin Pavel Potemkin in 1783. To the
difficult task of consolidating Russian authority in a nearly empty, yet
highly insecure, area was added the warfare in the mountains which
erupted under the leadership of Sheik Mansur in 1784 and demanded
Pavel Potemkin's full attention. In 1787, however, while remaining

---

[2] PSZ, 1775, N. 14251, 14330. The Don Cossacks still lived a life of their own: the
future ataman Denisov was advised by his uncle in the 1770s to take a bride "in Russia":
"Zapiski," 23.

governor general, he was sent to the army to fight the Turks before Ochakov.

If there is something uncertain about Potemkin's activity in the Caucasus, this is not the case with the fiery Lt.-Gen. Ivan Gudovich, son of the former treasurer (*podskarbii*) of Little Russia and son-in-law of Kirill Razumovskii, the last hetman. Gudovich is one of the finest examples of those whom posterity would call "Catherine's eagles." A brilliant officer in the first Turkish war, promoted to lieutenant general at thirty-three, he then remained in Little Russia until his appointment as Governor General of Riazan and Tambov. He succeeded Potemkin in 1792 as Governor General of the Northern Caucasus (but without Saratov), and the union of the latter with Riazan and Tambov brought together under a single administration the entire corridor from the lower Volga to the approaches of Moscow. In June 1791 he had stormed the Turkish fortress of Anapa, where he captured Sheik Mansur. He strengthened the Caucasian Line, accepting the submission of the Shamkhal of Tarku and the Khan of Derbent to Russia. He returned to the Caucasus in 1806 and won his marshal's baton for another brilliant victory over the Turks at the river Arpa in 1807. Known for his severity as well as for his courtesy, he was a highly educated man and a wealthy landowner who left his children nearly 13,000 souls.[3]

Since the military problems encountered in the Northern Caucasus had much in common with those found in Orenburg and Siberia—the continued restlessness of a highly mobile opponent counting on surprise—Russian tactics followed the usual practice of building fortified lines. The earliest in the region was the Tsaritsyn Line, linking the elbow of the Volga with the great bend of the Don and marked by four small fortresses. Its purpose was to bar the Nogai and the Kalmucks access to the Tambov-Riazan corridor. The other lines formed a semicircle along the frontier, to control the movement of mountain peoples into the plain whose axis was the Manych river, and were known simply as the Caucasian Line. A first section built in 1763 began at Kizliar, followed the left bank of the Terek, and ended at Mozdok. A second section, built between 1777 and 1780 under Iakobi, went northwest from Mozdok until it reached the Egorlyk, then followed the course of this river, of the Manych, and the Don to Cherkassk. It established a boundary between the pastures of the nomads and those of the Russians, enabled the latter to put pressure on the

[3] *RBS*, II (1900), 662-663, for Beketov and XIV (1905), 673-682, for Potemkin. On Beketov, who did not always distinguish between his official and private activities, see "Pis'ma k Krechetnikovu," 111-114. For Gudovich, see Bantysh-kamenskii, II, 165-179; genealogy in Dolgorukov, II, 192-193.

Crimean khanate, opened the way to the mineral resources of the mountains, and attempted to end the contraband traffic conducted by the nomads, who could cross the entire steppe to the Don and remain undetected. This second line superseded the Tsaritsyn Line, which was abandoned. The third line built in 1794 by Gudovich began at the then closed capital Ekaterinograd, reached the Kuban at approximately mid-point, followed its course almost to its mouth, and ended on the Strait of Kerch at Fanagoria.

Within this perimeter formed by the Caucasian Line, the Don and the Volga, troop concentrations were necessary in three areas: between Kizliar and Mozdok facing Chechnia, along the Kuban against the Circassians (*Zakubantsy*), and in Astrakhan. The garrisons here constituted the core of the force assigned to defend the frontier. Four battalions were stationed in Astrakhan, three companies of which were detailed to Chernyi Iar, Enotaevsk, and Krasnyi Iar; two additional battalions were stationed in Kizliar and one in Mozdak. There were no regular troops on the Tsaritsyn Line, which was defended by the Volga Cossacks, and no field-army regiments were permanently stationed in the region until the first Turkish war. In the late 1770s there were two regiments of infantry, two of dragoons, a Mozdok field battalion, and two battalions of Jaegers, in addition to irregular troops. All these units were subordinated to the governor general. Commandants in Chernyi Iar, Enotaevsk, and Krasnyi Iar reported to the senior commandant in Astrakhan, a major general; those in the fortresses on the line to the governor general.[4]

The role played by irregular troops, consisting of Cossacks and native detachments, was extremely important. By the mid-1770s the prestige of the Cossacks had sunk to an all-time low, and they were openly despised by army officers. It was the great merit of Grigorii Potemkin to have combined successfully two apparently contradictory policies. One was to integrate the Cossacks into a highly centralized structure with himself at the head, thus putting an end to whatever remained of Cossack autonomy; the other was to give them greater responsibilities, even in wartime, thus boosting their pride and self-esteem. At his recommendation a *sotnia* of Don Cossacks was even included into the Guard. The best example of this policy was the creation of the Black Sea Host with former Zaporozhians who distinguished themselves during the second Turkish war. They were settled between the Eia and the Kuban and given the defense of the line along

[4] PSZ, 1764, N. 12135; 1769, N. 13390; 1771, N. 13649; 1777, N. 14607; TsGVIA, f. 52, d. 124, fol. 194-196, 221-223, f. VUA, d. 234, fol. 2-4; PSZ, 1792, N. 17025, 1796, N. 17517; Samoilov, 1219; Iudin, "Iz Astrakhanskoi zhizni," Pishkevich, A., 48-49; Sakovich, 182-184.

the Kuban. The oldest Cossack host in the Caucasus was that of the Grebentsy, 373 men in 1776, who began to settle there in the sixteenth century and who built the Kizliar-Mozdok line. They had their own ataman, subordinated to the Kizliar commandant and the Astrakhan governor. The second host was that of the Terek (*Terskoe*), which had only 109 men settled in Kizliar. The Volga host was of recent origin. Created in the 1730s to defend the Tsaritsyn Line, its 540 men were settled in four *stanitsy* along the Volga between Tsaritsyn and Kamyshenka. After the closing of the line, part of it was sent to form the Mozdok regiment of 767 men to which 200 *kibitki* (1,000 males) of baptized Kalmucks were added in 1777, and the remainder was sent in the same year to defend the Ekaterinograd-Alexandrovsk section, where they formed a separate regiment. There was also an Astrakhan regiment of 500 Cossacks settled in seven *stanitsy* between Chernyi Iar and Astrakhan, and another 500 Cossacks between Kizliar and Kargalinskaia. In 1792 there were in addition six regiments of Don Cossacks on the Line.[5]

The creation of native regiments was in accord with traditional policy toward nomadic peoples absorbed into the Empire. In 1765, on the recommendation of the Kizliar commandant, Major General Potapov—whose brother was senior commandant in St. Dimitri and later became governor in Voronezh—mountaineers invited to settle within the Russian border around Mozdok were made into Cossacks and required to patrol the line under the command of a Kabardinian prince converted to Orthodoxy and made lieutenant colonel in the Russian army. The Kalmucks too were drawn into patrol duty. A small detachment guarded the shipments of salt from Lake Elton to Dmitrievsk against attacks by other Kalmucks, and those who remained after the exodus of 1771 were drafted to form a cordon from Astrakhan to the Ural river. In 1786, after the inclusion of the two Kabardas into the Empire, Grigorii Potemkin was ordered to form a "settled host" (*poselennoe voisko*), i.e., one that would not be used on distant campaigns, consisting of 900 men, 36 *uzdeny* (tribal leaders), and 18 princes receiving 12, 50, and 120 rubles, respectively. Twelve princes and twelve *uzdeny* were assigned to Potemkin's suite in order "to reduce and ultimately to eliminate their coarseness and savagery." In addition, 300 Ingush and 500 Osetins were to be hired at one ruble a month to police the Georgian Military Highway, linking Tiflis in Georgia with Vladikavkaz in the Northern Caucasus. And when the

⁵ Samoilov, 582, 1230-1231; PSZ, 1776, N. 14464; 1792, N. 17025, 17055; ES, XVᴬ (1895), 585-588; on the Grebentsy, see Bentkovskii; on the Volga Cossacks, Iudin "S Volgi na Terek."

Shamkhal of Tarku accepted Russian suzerainty he was sent by the Empress a feather to be worn in his cap and given the rank of state councillor (class III), a Russian honor guard, and 6,000 rubles "to maintain troops." In such a volatile region as the Caucasus this policy certainly reflected extraordinary confidence in the magnetic pull of Russian civilization and in the belief that the absorption of the native leadership into the Russian political order was enough to guarantee the loyalty of their peoples and the security of the frontier.[6] The Russians, however, were soon to suffer bitter disappointments.

The courts were also seen as channels to spread Russian influence and to create a community of interest between the Russian administration and local leadership groups. The Kabardinians, the only substantial native people from the mountains to be included in the Empire, were given lower *raspravy*, each *rasprava* to serve one or two clans, modelled after those already established in the Small Kazakh Horde, and without Russian officers. These courts were to follow local customs and to consist of the leading people (*lutshchie liudi*) in the clans. In addition, an "upper border court" was set up in Mozdok, consisting of Russian officials and of "the very best (*perveishie*) people" in the clans. This was a court of appeal against the decisions of the *raspravy* and a court of first instance to try cases of treason, murder, and robbery (*razboi*), the last crime being one of the most sensitive issues in Russian relations with the nomads. Its decisions were based on Russian law and required the confirmation of the governor general.

Russian policy toward the nomads mixed idealism with cynicism. Its ultimate purpose was the complete integration of the rank and file into the state peasantry, and of the leadership of baptized nobles into members of the ruling class, like Governor Beketov's ancestors. This direction of Russian policy was no less evident in Astrakhan, where a large community of Armenians, Tatars, and Indians enjoyed considerable autonomy. The Armenian colony had its own court and its own code, but its jurisdiction was naturally limited to cases to which Armenians were a party. Litigation between Armenians and Russians was brought before the *rathaus*, which operated like one of the oral courts created in central Russia in 1727, while Russians among themselves sued before the *magistrat*. Appeals went to the gubernia chancery and the Central *Magistrat* in Moscow. In 1765 a single court for all Astrakhan "Asiatics" was established, consisting of two or three judges chosen separately by the Armenians, the Tatars, and the Indians to try cases involving members of their own group, who sat together only when members of a different group were a party to the case. This

[6] PSZ, 1765, N. 12432; 1766, N. 12698; 1793, N. 17118; 1786, N. 16432.

court was placed under the supervision of a Russian official. Appeals went to the gubernia chancery, where Russian law applied. The court was abolished with the introduction of the reform and replaced by a lower and upper *nadvornyi* court subordinated to the judicial chambers; the "Asiatics" now had to plead before a regular Russian court following standard procedures.[7] Whether or not this represented an improvement is a moot point.

Tax legislation in the Southeast had to take into consideration certain privileges resulting from the peculiarities of settlement in the three constituent parts of the region, the Don Territory, Astrakhan gubernia, and the foothills of the Caucasus. The administrative reform did not take effect in the Don, and treasury chambers were not created; financial administration remained the responsibility of the chancery. The Don Cossacks did not pay the capitation or the quitrent, and there were no state peasants. There were, however, peasants from Great and Little Russia registered in the name of *starshiny* of the host and of individual *stanitsy* who were required to pay the capitation. In the Northern Caucasus, Cossacks and nomads were of course not subject to personal taxes. There were very few serfs; and state peasants resettled from central Russia and distributed by Pavel Potemkin along the road from Tsaritsyn to the line and around fortresses were so poor that they faced starvation upon their arrival. They were, however, subject to the capitation and the quitrent, on the same footing as their brethren in central Russia. As late as 1795, however, sixty-one percent of the population of Astrakhan-Northern Caucasus gubernia were not subject to personal taxes.[8]

In Astrakhan proper there was a treasury chamber after the closing of Ekaterinograd in 1790. The native (*aulnye*) Tatars in the city, descendants of those who remained after the annexation, did not pay taxes and only transported military freight (*tiagosti*) to Kizliar, after selling for 1,500 rubles a year their obligation to carry the mail to and from Tsaritsyn and Kizliar to the Cossacks settled along the Volga. Russian townsmen paid the capitation. Armenian and outside (*slobodskie*) Tatars were not required until 1785 to perform the services imposed on Russians such as selling vodka and salt, working as bookkeepers, supporting the night watch, etc., but the former paid a lump sum of 739 rubles deposited in the *magistrat* to help the Russians defray their expenditures (*v pomoshch kupechestvu*) and the latter 150 rubles, which belonged to the revenues of the *Stats-Kontora*. In ad-

[7] PSZ, 1785, N. 16194; 1792, N. 17025; 1764, N. 12174, pt. 8; 1765, N. 12307; 1799, N. 19028; Pogosian, *Sudebnik*.

[8] PSZ, 1795, N. 17302; 1786, N. 16429; Kabuzan, *Izmeneniia*, 110.

dition, both groups contributed 750 (or 900) rubles to maintain sol-diers' barracks; this sum was deposited in the chancery of the senior commandant. Despite the attempt by Beketov in 1764 and 1771 to extend personal taxes to non-Russians, the Senate refused lest the Armenians leave and the Tatars flee to Kizliar and across the border. The *raznochintsy*, descendants of fugitive peasants from central Rus-sia, were not so fortunate. To prevent their flight to Persia, where they turned Moslem (*busurmaniatsia*), they were required in 1745 to reg-ister as townsmen. By 1775, however, the Senate agreed with the Astrakhan *magistrat* that those who had never engaged in any trade should be made to pay 2.70 rubles, like other state peasants.[9] The legislation of 1783 seems to have applied to Astrakhan as well, but the capitation increase of 1794 did not.

NEW RUSSIA AND THE CRIMEA

The Kuban steppe was linked by geography and a common history with the khanate of Crimea and a crescent-shaped territory formed by the Gulf of Taganrog and the course of the rivers Northern Donets, Orel, Dniepr (to Kremenchug), Siniukha, Bug, Lower Dniepr, Kon-skaia, and Berda. The khanate, a vassal of the Ottoman Empire since 1478, was for the Russians the last barrier to the Black Sea and a source of permanent instability along their southern frontier where the interests of Russia, Poland, the Turks, and the Zaporozhian Cos-sacks had converged and diverged for more than two centuries with bewildering inconsistency. Insecurity was not favorable to settlement, and the region was still mainly an uninhabited steppe as late as the 1740s. In 1752 Serbs and Hungarians were settled south of the border

---

[9] PSZ, 1771, N. 13647; 1775, N. 14348, 14412; "Pervyi opyt," 39–42: the latter refers to 750, N. 13647 to 900 rubles. Another peculiarity of the financial regime of the southeast was the privilege possessed by the Cossacks to distill liquor for their own consumption. The Cossacks thus occupied in the administration of the vodka monopoly an intermediate position between the landed nobility and the peasants. There was, of course, a latent conflict between this privilege and the interest of the local tax farmer who sought to sell vodka to anyone willing to buy it. As long as the population of the region consisted largely of Cossacks, frictions were hardly noticeable. During the first Turkish war, however, when regular troops were sent to the Northern Caucasus, the tax farmer followed the flag—and stayed after the troops were withdrawn. It took an order of the College of War, to which the Cossacks complained, to "restore" the privilege. The Senate decision of 1777 did nothing to reduce the ambiguity of the situation. Cossacks were still allowed to produce and sell vodka and wine (from their own vineyards) in their villages, but tax farmers were also allowed to sell state vodka in Cossack *stanitsy*. Here as in much else, the Cossacks were faced with an insidious undermining of their historic privileges. See PSZ, 1767, N. 12818; 1770, N. 13505; 1777, N. 14606.

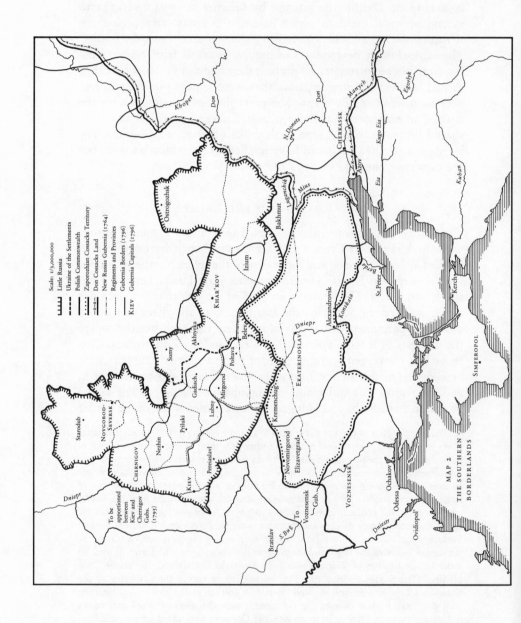

in a narrow zone bound by the Siniukha and a line running from its confluence with the Bug to the Dniepr. It was called New Serbia and its capital was Novomirgorod. The following year a colony of Serbs was settled along the Luganchik river, a right-bank tributary of the Northern Donets. Called Slavianoserbia, it was built around the fortress of Bakhmut, an observation point at the highest altitude in European Russia outside the Urals. These two colonies, organized as military settlements divided into "companies" (roty), constituted an extension into the steppe of the Ukrainian Line, which began at Izium on the Northern Donets, followed the course of the Bereka, the Orchik, and the Orel. Its administrative center was the important Belëv fortress on the Orchik. In 1764 the Ukrainian Line was closed, New Serbia became the gubernia of New Russia—Kremenchug was its capital—Slavianoserbia was renamed Ekaterininsk province, and the following year Elizavetgrad became the center of a second province.[10] It was placed under a "commanding officer" (glavnyi komandir) in the high rank of lieutenant general. Alexei Mel'gunov (1764-1765), not unlike Dimitri Volkov in Orenburg, was in semi-disgrace but soon bounced back to become president of the College of Revenue and later Governor General in Iaroslavl and Vologda. He was followed by Iakov Brant (1766-1767), who then became governor in Kazan. For the next six years, coinciding with the first Turkish war, the gubernia was placed under General Fedor Voeikov, Governor General in Kiev.

The Russian advance confirmed by the Treaty of Kuchuk Kainardji and the annexation of the Crimea changed dramatically the territorial configuration of the region. The elimination of the Zaporozhian Cossack Host in 1775 removed the last semi-independent community along the southern border with the khanate formed (until 1783) by the Dniepr and the Konskaia-Berda. The course of these two rivers dictated the layout of the "Dniepr Line" from Alexandrovsk on the Dniepr to St. Peter's fortress (the future Berdiansk) on the Gulf of Taganrog, built in 1770 to block once and for all Tatar access to Russian settlements in the steppe. The territory acquired in 1775 was divided into two gubernias, New Russia and Azov. Both were placed under Governor General Grigorii Potemkin, and "New Russia" was for the first time unified under a single administration. The third territorial reform of the region followed the annexation of the khanate in 1783. New Russia and Azov gubernias were merged into Ekaterinoslav gubernia, divided into fifteen uezds with a total population of

[10] "Novorossiiskii krai," in ES, XXI (1897), 290-291; PSZ, 1764, N. 12099; 1765, N. 12367, 12376. One of the Serbs left his memoirs: see Pishkevich, S; Pishkevich, A., was his son. See also Sakovich, 236-258, for a short history of the Ukrainian Line and the Serbian settlements.

744,550. The former khanate, i.e., the peninsula together with the steppe between the isthmus and the Dniepr and the Konskaia-Berda, became the *oblast* of Taurida (*Tavricheskaia*), the ancient name of Crimea, divided into seven uezds. It had a population of only 62,960 in 1789, of whom 45,855 were native Tatars. Finally, the so-called Ochakov steppe between the Bug and the Dniestr, acquired after the second Turkish war, was combined with four uezds of Ekaterinoslav gubernia to form Voskresensk gubernia, divided into twelve uezds.[11]

The Empress was fortunate in finding the forceful men needed to administer these new acquisitions. They included, among others, Ivan Sinelnikov, recommended to Potemkin for his energy, who became voevoda in 1778 in Slaviansk province (then Ekaterinoslav), and governor in 1783 until his death five years later from wounds suffered in the war; Vasilii Chertkov, former commandant in Elizavetgrad, governor of Azov gubernia (1776-1782), and Governor General of Voronezh and Saratov (1787-1793).[12] But the impulse, the vision, and the energy behind the development of New Russia belonged to Potemkin. His personal relationship with the Empress gave him access to the source of power; that was not enough, however. Neither Grigorii Orlov nor even Platon Zubov ever wielded the vast influence of Potemkin. He knew how to transform it into a program of action; and his administrative position and military commands gave him the means to translate his program into reality. The words "Potemkin villages" leave an impression of superficial and unfinished work, yet no one could have completed his task in the fifteen years he devoted to it. The settlement of the south, not only with Russians, but also with Wallachians and Moldavians, Bulgarians, Greeks, Georgians, Germans, Italians, Swedes, and Gypsies; the founding of a fleet; the building of towns and shipyards; the domestication of the Cossacks—all were durable achievements which outlived him and established foundations for the growth of Russian civilization on the Black Sea littoral. His authority rested on an unusual combination of functional and territorial commands. As president of the College of War and commanding general of all irregular troops his influence was felt as far as Orenburg and Irkutsk, where his two protégés, Igelstrom and Iakobi, were governors general. He was at one time Governor General of New Russia, Azov, Astrakhan, and Saratov gubernias; his cousin Pavel succeeded him in Astrakhan. If we remember that Pavel's brother was

---

[11] PSZ, 1775, N. 14380; 1770, N. 13504; 1783, N. 15696; 1784, N. 16028, 15908. Population figures for the Crimea are in TsGVIA, f. 52, d. 507, op. 1/194.

[12] On Sinelnikov, see Evarnitskii and Slavutinskii; on Chertkov, see *RBS*, XXII (1905), 351-352; on Kakhovskii, *RBS*, VIII (1897), 565-573. The *Mesiatseslov*, however, gives a state councillor Vasilii Kakhovskii as governor of the Crimea and Ekaterinoslav.

Chief of the Commissary, it is easy to appreciate the enormous hold of the Potemkin family over the military establishment in the middle years of the reign. The vacuousness of Platon Zubov, who followed him as governor general, a post he incongruously combined with that of Commanding General of the Artillery, could only enhance Potemkin's greatness in the eyes of his contemporaries.[13]

The occupation of the Black Sea littoral following the peace of Kuchuk Kainardji established a common border between the Russian and the Ottoman Empires, without the buffer zones created by the Zaporozhian Cossacks and the Crimean Tatars, and required permanent concentration of regular troops. A network of fourteen fortresses, some newly built, other restored, was established to support the distribution of the regular army.[14] The size of this army, excluding the detachments of Don and Chuguev Cossacks, fluctuated with military requirements, and only figures for peacetime years can give an idea of the force permanently stationed in New Russia. In the late 1770s troops stationed in New Russia, Azov and Astrakhan gubernias formed the Eleventh Military Region commanded by Potemkin. Eight regiments of infantry, two regiments of dragoons, and two battalions of Jaegers were stationed in New Russia gubernia; a regiment of dragoons and four regiments of infantry in Azov gubernia. Altogether this constituted a force of about 32,000 men, not including the hussars and lancers. The reform introduced the *shtatnye komandy* in Ekaterinoslav gubernia and the Crimea and later in Voznesensk gubernia, a total of three gubernia and thirty-two uezd *komandy* or about 1,325 men. It also introduced in five towns of Voznesensk gubernia which were not uezd centers the new position of town commander (*gradonachalnik*); like the sheriff, he was in class VIII. The new post was made necessary by the fact that settlers, especially foreigners, preferred the towns, which grew in importance without becoming natural centers of still sparsely settled areas. Two other towns (Odessa and Ovidiopol) were fortified, and their garrison and police were subordinated to a commandant. A separate police force called the customs guard (*strazha*) was created in the 1780s to patrol the coastline and the land border with the Ottoman Empire.[15]

---

[13] On Potemkin, see *RBS*, XIV (1905), 649-670; the Prince de Ligne's characterization is on pp. 666-667. The standard biography of Potemkin is still Soloveytchik's. On Potemkin's policies, see Raeff, "Style," 27-36.

[14] PSZ, 1764, N. 12180; 1770, N. 13460; 1779, N. 14838; 1769, N. 13351; 1777, N. 14654; TsGVIA, f. 52, d. 123; PSZ, 1784, N. 15929.

[15] PSZ, 1764, N. 12180; 1776, N. 14552; 1795, N. 17300; 1796, N. 17494, vol. 44², *kn. sht.*, 265. A censorship committee was created in Odessa in 1796: 17508. For the customs guard, see 1782, N. 15522; 1793, N. 17162; 1795, N. 17419.

Although New Russia had only recently been a nearly empty territory, its fiscal regime was complex, and the reform did not create the uniformity with Great Russian practices that might have been expected. The differences resulted largely from the peculiarities of the region's settlement and from the guidelines established by the statute of 1764 on the administration of New Russia gubernia. The area was divided into seventy districts (*okruga*), fifty-two of which were reserved for military settlers, two for urban inhabitants, and sixteen for foreigners, Old Believers and other Russians returning from abroad who were settled in villages (*slobody*). Districts were divided into lots (*uchastki*), and all inhabitants, military and others, were under the administration of a "company commander" who reported to the regimental commander in military matters and to the governor's chancery in civilian matters. Military settlers paid no personal taxes; state peasants and serfs were assessed not by soul but in accordance with the amount of land tilled (*s zemlei, a ne s liudei*). Serfs were to pay half (*vpoly*) the amount charged to state peasants because their owners were expected to bring them to New Russia at their own expense. These provisions remained unchanged until the end of the reign, with the additional provision after 1776 that non-military settlers were required to deliver recruits who were sent to staff two regiments of hussars. Peasants who had been the property of monasteries, chiefly Ukrainian ones which had not been secularized in 1764, paid the capitation in force in Little Russia and a quitrent (*chinshevye dengi*) of fifty kopecks assessed against a house (*khata, izba*) and a pair of oxen. In 1794 they were equated with state peasants of Little Russia and required to pay the capitation of seventy kopecks and a quitrent of one ruble, plus the surcharge of two kopecks per ruble. Little Russians belonging to the Poltava and Mirgorod regiments incorporated into Ekaterinoslav gubernia, who had remained in a privileged position, were now equated with their Little Russian brethren and required to pay 1.20 rubles if they were Cossacks, 1.70 rubles if they were state peasants, and 70 kopecks if they were serfs, in addition to the surtax. Finally, the Greeks, Armenians, and Wallachians were given tax exemptions ranging from three to thirty years, at the end of which they presumably were to be included in the pool of townsmen and would come under the provisions established for merchants and shopkeepers in Little Russia. In the Crimea the population was overwhelmingly native and personal taxes did not apply to it.[16]

Thus, the trend of Imperial tax legislation in New Russia pointed

[16] PSZ, 1764, N. 12099, II-3, IV-1, 12180; 1775, N. 14824; 1794, N. 17246; 1792, N. 17048, 17068.

to the extension in the region, not of laws in force in Great Russia, but of those recently introduced in Little Russia. The government could not fail to sense the natural affinity between Little and New Russia. Potemkin, Bezborodko, and even Rumiantsev were men with deep roots in the borderlands and understood that a large Cossack population, the extensive network of Greek communities, the variety of ethnic backgrounds, together with the physical unity of the Dniepr basin, created a greater solidarity between Little and New Russia than between New and Great Russia. The autonomy of Little Russia was indeed being curtailed, but a larger Ukraine was coming into being— one of those compromises out of which durable solutions are born.

A similar phenomenon was noticeable in the legislation governing the production and sale of vodka. The trade required two kinds of raw materials, both rare in the 1760s, grain and firewood. The statute of 1764 prohibited the distilling of vodka except by those willing to plant timber. Vodka was also imported from Poland, and the administration of New Russia gubernia collected revenue from a tax on vodka sold in taverns, called *shinki* in the Ukraine, after the expiration of the tax-exempt years. Imports from Poland were prohibited by the Tariff on August 1775 for Black Sea ports, yet they remained substantial, and Potemkin reported at the end of 1776 that the treasury had collected some 100,000 rubles from the sale of such imported vodka in three years. He also expressed fear that such prohibition would result in the destruction of the few forests of New Russia and raise the price of grain, and asked its repeal. The Senate agreed and restored the duty of sixty-six kopecks per *vedro* imposed by the Tariff of 1757.

The development of private landowning in New Russia outside the area of settlement governed by the statute of 1764 created a third source of vodka and introduced the contractual system in force in Great Russia, with an important qualification. In Great Russia contracts were confirmed in the treasury chamber and by the governor general if their value did not exceed 10,000 rubles. Potemkin, pointing out to the Senate that custom receipts were left at his disposal in order to limit as much as possible costly transfers of funds over great distances from internal provinces, asked in 1777 that revenue from the sale of vodka in New Russia and Azov gubernias be made "independent": this would allow him to confirm any contract, whatever the amount. His request was justified by the need to encourage settlement. Vodka sales were indeed the most valuable source of cash for landowners and Cossacks alike. If contracts had to be confirmed in Petersburg, 1,590 km from Ekaterinoslav, local people would never be able to go there in person. An outsider would make a better offer and would get the farm, and people of means would lose an incentive to come to New Russia. If the farmer went bankrupt, the two gubernias would never receive their badly needed funds. The arguments proved convincing to the Empress. After Potemkin's death, however, these contracts were negotiated in the capital.[17]

Thus, the production of vodka in New Russia was restricted to landowners, and in areas ruled by the 1764 statute, to settlers who agreed to plant trees. This production was supplemented by imports from Poland, from some borderlands, and from Voronezh gubernia. Vodka was sold by landowners, settlers, Cossacks, and tax-farmers at the market price, by Cossacks in their villages, by settlers in the original area of settlement, and by farmers elsewhere, except in some towns, but tax-farming and imports alone yielded revenue to the treasury. All in all, the fiscal administration of New Russia was closer to that of Little Russia than to that of Great Russia.

LITTLE RUSSIA

Although each borderland had its own history, its own separate pattern of settlement, and its own ethnic diversity—a combination of factors which made the formulation of a single policy toward the borderlands very difficult—the transition from one to the other was a gradual one, and this is nowhere more true than in crossing the Dniepr to enter Little Russia and the "Ukraine of the Settlements." The physical unity of the Dniepr basin tolerated only artificial barriers imposed by historical circumstances which changed dramatically during the reign of Catherine. The left-bank Ukraine, between the river and the approaches to the Central Russian Highlands, comprised two separate territories, historically and administratively. The hetmanate (*getmanshchina*), which joined Russia in 1654 under conditions which later became a constant source of misunderstandings, was divided into ten "regiments" (*polki*). The regiment was a territorial unit, and its population consisted of three major groups of uneven size. The Cossacks were divided into companies (*sotnii*) within districts (*povety*) including Cossack helpers, peasants, and townsmen. Some towns possessed a corporate identity granted to them by former Polish kings and by hetmans under the provisions of the so-called Magdeburg (Saxon) law. The ten regiments, with a male population of 1,024,460 in 1764, formed three clusters. Three regiments occupied the area between the southern tip of Smolensk gubernia and the Oster river, a

---

[17] PSZ, 1777, N. 14563, 14633; 1778, N. 14823; 1793, N. 17097; *Svedeniia o pit. sborakh*, 20-27, *Arkhiv Gos. Soveta*, I², 290-291.

tributary of the Desna (Starodub, Nezhin, and Chernigov). Another five formed a separate cluster between the Oster and the Sula rivers (Lubny, Priluki, Gadiach, Pereiaslavl, and Kiev). The last two were those of Mirgorod and Poltava, between the Sula and the Ukrainian Line.

The second territory was the Ukraine of the Settlements (*Slobodskaia Ukraina*), which formed a semicircle around the southern fringe of the Central Highlands, and a sort of buffer zone between the Belgorod Line and the wide open steppe exposed to Tatar raids. This zone of settlement was not unlike the Serbian settlements south of the Ukrainian Line, although it was of course much older. Its population consisted largely of Little Russians (*Cherkassy*—so named because the original settlers came from Cherkassy on the Dniepr), who found life unbearable in the first half of the seventeenth century in the right-bank Ukraine and moved northeast toward the Muscovite border into still empty territory, where they received certain privileges: the retention of their own form of Cossack self-government and the right to distill and sell vodka without limitations. In return for this recognition of their autonomy, they were required to defend their towns, thus advancing the perimeter of Russian defenses. The zone was divided in traditional fashion into five territorial regiments. The major town was Khar'kov, which by the middle of the eighteenth century had become the commercial center of the south for Russian, Polish, and "Turkish" goods.[18]

The chaotic situation into which the Cossack administration of the Ukraine of the Settlements had fallen prompted the dispatch of Guard Major Evdokim Shcherbinin on an inspection tour, and his recommendations led to the reform of 1764-1765. Khar'kov became the center of a new gubernia, and the other four regimental headquarters became first uezd centers, then provincial capitals headed by voevodas. An important innovation was the appointment of Great Russian procurators—to guarantee that Russian law would apply, despite the clear provision that the privileges of the Cossacks must remain in force. The provinces were not divided into uezds but into twenty-eight *kommisarstva* headed by *kommisary*, a post modelled after the *zemskie kommisary* of Peter the Great. The five Cossack regiments, not as territorial divisions but as military units, were reorganized into five regiments of hussars and integrated into the regular army. Shcherbinin

---

[18] For a description of the ten regiments, see Gajecky, I and II. On the Ukraine of the Settlements, see Hrushevskii and *Zapiski o slobodskikh polkakh*; see also "Bumagi, do upravleniia Malorossieiu," 144-146. For the reform, see PSZ, 1780, N. 15004, 15097; 1794, N. 17494, vol. 44², *kn. sht.*, 268; 1782, N. 15378; 1795, N. 17300. Aksakov, "Ukrainskiia iarmarki" contains valuable material on trade patterns, esp 100-109.

was appointed to administer the gubernia "with the authority of a governor" and remained the de facto governor until 1775.[19] The gubernia was then combined with Little Russia under Governor General Rumiantsev, then with Voronezh under Shcherbinin, Chertkov, and Potemkin. The Organic Law of November 1775 was introduced in 1780.

Little Russia proper had been ruled by the hetman since its annexation in 1654, except during the years 1724-1727 and 1734-1750, when the Little Russian College became the governing body of the territory. The hetman had long since become a mere appointee of the Imperial government, and the continued existence of the post depended on two considerations: as long as Moscow looked upon Little Russia as a client state whose very presence projected Russian power far beyond the Belgorod Line to the Dniepr, and as long as the nobility

Petr Alexandrovich Rumiantsev

[19] PSZ, 1764, N. 12293; 1765, N. 12397, 12430, 12440.

of Little Russia needed the hetman to help it consolidate its social power. The tenure of the last hetman, Kirill Razumovskii, brother of the Empress Elizabeth's morganatic husband, coincided with the creation of the Serbian settlements and the beginning of a steady pressure in the direction of the Black Sea, while a social process, to be examined presently, now created the "equality" of nobilities that some deputies of the Legislative Commission were calling for, i.e., a community of interests between Little and Great Russian nobilities. From client state the Ukraine was becoming another province of the Empire; the hetmanship was losing its raison d'être. To say, however, that it came to an end in 1764 is true only in the legal sense. The appointment of General Peter Rumiantsev, an illegitimate son of Peter the Great, as Governor General of Little Russia kept the hetmanship in being. Rumiantsev was no ordinary man. Soon to become one of the most famous generals in Russian military history, an excellent administrator, a man of commanding presence, and an irresistible seducer, he was one of the great aristocrats of the age and the ideal proconsul for the Ukraine. Much has been made of his rivalry with Potemkin; yet the two men were complementary. New Russia needed the vision and the dash of the parvenu from Smolensk; Little Russia, settling down to a life marked by the consolidation of serfdom, needed the presence of a leading figure of the establishment to guarantee that the emerging social order was secure.[20]

The "provincial" administration of Little Russia was vested in the colonels of the ten regiments, who combined all administrative and military functions and were assisted by a staff consisting of a quartermaster, a judge, a standard bearer, and a clerk. Companies were headed by an ataman and a staff of three. The regimental administration was largely appointed, but the lower levels were still elected at Cossack meetings. The appointment of three governors in 1782 showed that the reform meant not simply the introduction of Russian agencies. Lt.-Gen. Andrei Miloradovich was governor of Chernigov for fifteen years (1782-1796). The family, of Serbian descent, had property in the Gadiach regiment and gave at least three colonels in the eighteenth century. Two of the three governors of Novgorod-Seversk belonged to Little Russian families: real state councillor Ilia Zhurman had been General Judge of Little Russia, and Major General

---

[20] The governor general and president of the college resided in Glukhov until 1775, when the post of governor general of Kiev was abolished. He then moved to the old city, which became the capital of Little Russia until the end of the reign. On the administration of the hetmanate, see Hrushevskii. On Rumiantsev, see *RBS*, XVII (1918), 521-573, and Maksimovich, *Deiatel'nost'*; PSZ, 1775, N. 14381. For some comments on life in Glukhov, see "Zapiski Vinskago," 85.

Iakov Zavadovskii was the descendant of a colonel of the Starodub
regiment. Procurators and chairmen of judicial chambers bore Ukrainian names. In an assessment of a policy too often seen as a Great
Russian blow against Ukrainian autonomy, its social content must not
be overlooked; the intrusion of Russian administration went hand in
hand with the social integration of the Little Russian nobility into the
privileged class of the Empire: the phenomenal rise of Bezborodko,
Zavadovskii, and Troshchinskii, among others, provided the best evidence.

When we turn to a brief examination of the Russian military presence in the Ukraine, we note the relative unimportance of the garrisons
and the heavy concentration of regular troops. There were two reasons
for this. Little Russia contributed little to the Imperial treasury until
the reform, but the stationing of troops in a rich agricultural region
eliminated the costs of transporting provisions to the troops and compelled the population to billet the officers and the soldiers. It has been
estimated that every five *dvory* had to set aside two rooms (*kvartiry*)
for the army. The situation was in fact much worse, as the well-to-
do managed to avoid their obligations and increased, correspondingly,
the burden of poorer townsmen and peasants. The second reason was
the strategic location of the Ukraine vis-à-vis Poland and the Ottoman
Empire. A strong military presence was an immediate threat to the
right-bank possessions of Poland and beyond them to the Turkish
possessions in Moldavia. The Turkish and Polish problems were joined
here, and Russian military activity was bound to affect the solution
of both in decisive fashion. On the eve of the first Turkish war the
Ukrainian Military Region, commanded by Rumiantsev, consisted of
ten regiments of infantry, six regiments of carbineers, one regiment of
dragoons, and five regiments of hussars, a force of about 35,000 men.
After the war it was stripped of most of its cavalry. The five regiments
of hussars were still there; one regiment of cuirassiers was stationed
in Starodub; but there were now twelve regiments of infantry, four of
them stationed in Kursk and Orel gubernias. In the wake of the reform
the Little Russian Cossacks were reorganized into regiments of carbineers and became part of the regular army, and the *shtatnye komandy* were introduced in the three gubernias.[21]

Such was the framework within which the integration of the Ukraine
into the judicial and fiscal administration of the Empire took place.
This integration was motivated not only by Great Russian pressures

[21] PSZ, 1764, N. 12135; 1769, N. 13390; 1785, N. 16257 and 16306; "Rospisanie
(1763)"; Maksimovich, 95-97. On the poor conditions of the Cossacks before the
reform, see "Mnenie, na kakom," 77-78.

and by the fact that the extension of the perimeter of Imperial security along the Dniestr and the Black Sea littoral ended the historical role of Little Russia as a borderland. It also came about as a result of developments within the Ukraine tending to create, within an economic system common to both Great and Little Russia, similar social institutions, judicial agencies, and fiscal obligations.

In an extremely revealing report to the Senate, Kirill Razumovskii tried to explain in 1763 why a large number of land disputes should be settled by administrative decision (*sledstviem*) made in his office rather than by resort to the courts (*sudom*). When Polish landowners were forced out of Little Russia in the 1650s, their properties became the possession of the Cossack state (*voiskovye*), and their peasants became "state" peasants (*pospolitye*). Villages, mills, and other landed properties from the fund were given away by the hetman to reward the services of individual Cossacks for the duration of their lifelong service (*dozhivotnye, do laski*), while hereditary possessions (*votchiny*) required the confirmation of the tsar, on the recommendation of the hetman. After peace returned to Little Russia, irresistible pressures on the part of the Cossack leadership—whose social model was the very Polish nobility against whom they had just rebelled—to obtain estates at any price led to widespread abuses, of which two were outstanding. Requests for land grants or for title to land already acquired by whatever means were made directly to the tsar, who could only look favorably upon this new recognition of his authority by the Cossacks without the mediation of the hetman. Worse still, colonels of territorial regiments began to make such grants, title to which was or was not then obtained from the hetman chancery, and some colonels even resigned their office temporarily, with the understanding that the new colonel would grant them additional properties. What is relevant here is not the endless maze of legal claims, the fraud, and the violence accompanying this social revolution, but the breakdown of public authority abetted by the rising class of landowners, from whom the possession of land and the maximum exploitation of manual labor was the only source of wealth in an overwhelmingly agricultural economy. The example of neighboring Poland and Great Russia, where serfdom had already triumphed, was compelling. Razumovskii claimed in his report that he had refused to recognize grants made in doubtful circumstances, that some had been taken back, and that his decision to decide land disputes by administrative order was the only way to restore the legal procedure to acquire such grants, either by "universals" given by the hetman or "charters" given by the tsar. Such a decision was a grave threat to the landed nobility, and it reminds us of similar attempts by the Grand Duke of Kurland and Charles XI of

Sweden in Lifland. The removal of the hetman would eliminate the threat. The Empress was far away, and her representative would have no interest in opposing a trend with which he was familiar in Great Russia. This is to suggest that there was more to the abolition of the hetmanship than Russian fears that Razumovskii might want to make it hereditary in his family. There could be no effective hetmanship without the reversal of a trend in which 41,000 of the 45,000 homesteads (*dvory*) available in 1722 had been given away by 1750, and this the landed nobility could not tolerate.[22]

It is a common opinion among historians of the Ukraine that serfdom was proceeding at a rapid pace in the eighteenth century. The hetman state was a military state imposed upon a much larger mass of peasants by a Cossack minority.[23] A glance at the population of the regiments reveals the central fact in all its starkness. In the Starodub regiment—one extreme—there were 25,067 Cossacks in a population of 172,786; in the Gadiach regiment—the other extreme—there were still 39,988 Cossacks in a population of 69,802. This overall minority was divided among Cossacks who actually served and helpers (*podpomoshchniki*) who supplied the necessities of service and provisions during campaigns. The peasants forming the majority were called *vladelcheskie poddannye* and lived in villages owned by the *starshina*, the social and political elite of the Cossacks. It was in the interest of the landowners to keep the number of Cossacks small and to prevent the peasants from joining the ranks of the Cossacks while favoring transfers in the opposite direction, as was done by the hetman from the very end of the seventeenth century. Peasants had to be kept on the land, and the Lithuanian Statute of 1566 already required peasants wanting to move to obtain the authorization from the landowners, whose refusal could be challenged in court. But the courts were controlled by the colonels, and the right to move was not granted if it was a threat to the landed nobility. The so-called introduction of serfdom in the Ukraine by the law of May 3, 1783 marked in fact the recognition of a fait accompli.

Before the reform the judicial administration consisted of eighteen civil courts (*zemskie sudy*), seven of which were located in regimental capitals and another in Glukhov, consisting usually of a judge, an assessor (*podsudok*), and a clerk. Land disputes were brought before separate one-man courts called *podkomorskie sudy*, appointed by the regimental chanceries. The ten chanceries corresponded in some re-

[22] PSZ, 1763, N. 11812, esp. 240-243; on the right to move, see PSZ, 1763, N. 11987; see also "Nastavlenie vybornomu," 68.

[23] Hrushevskii, 418-419, 447-449, 460, 468; Gajecky, I, 1-12; Miakotin, I, part 2, 252-263.

spects to the provincial chanceries of Great Russia. There were also ten *magistraty*, of which six were in regimental capitals. Appeals against the decisions of these courts were taken to the Little Russian College, which functioned as a kind of gubernia chancery, whose decisions were appealed in turn to the Third Department of the Senate. The Greeks in Nezhin had their own separate court. In the Ukraine of the Settlements, small suits valued at no more than twelve rubles were handled by the *kommisary*, others went before the provincial chanceries.[24] The reform created four civil and four criminal chambers, the usual intermediate courts, and uezd courts as well as *magistraty* in some forty-six uezds.

If there was any doubt in central Russia that chairmen of chambers were the faithful servants of their class, there could be none in Little Russia. When Major General Peter Miloradovich, former colonel of the Chernigov regiment (1762-1783), became involved in a suit in 1785, it was discovered that the chairman of the Chernigov civil chamber, one councillor, and one assessor of the criminal chamber sent as a replacement were his relatives; so was the governor. The chairman of the Kiev civil chamber, Brig. Gen. Grigorii Ivanenko (of Wallachian ancestry), was a former colonel of the Pereiaslavl regiment (1766-1781); and the chairman of the Novgorod-Seversk chamber was Ivan Seletskii, whose family had headed the Divitsia company of the Nezhin regiment for over seventy years.[25] Not only was the *starshina* placed in full control over vital decisions affecting the distribution of wealth in Little Russia; the Cossacks were relegated to the status of state peasants. Only those who had acquired landed property could qualify as nobles; the others sued not in the uezd court but in the lower and upper *raspravy*. The jurisdiction of the *magistraty* was curtailed since their properties outside the town limits, sometimes considerable, were now considered "inappropriate" and placed under the directors of economy. A separate *magistrat* was created for the Nezhin Greeks.[26] The effect of the judicial reform was to consolidate the gains made by the landed nobility, to reduce the mass of Cossacks to the level of peasants, and to create a natural affinity between Ukrainian, Russian, and other landowners which made the separate status of the Ukraine a historical anachronism.

---

[24] The location of the courts may be found in the *Mesiatseslov* for 1773, among others; PSZ, 1762, N. 11541; 1763, N. 11812; 1765, N. 12430, pt. 7; 1768, N. 13340; 1781, N. 15224. See also "Nastavlenie vybornomu," 52-55; "Vozrazhdenie," 73-82; "Zapiski iz dela," 119-121.

[25] TsGVIA, f. 44, d. 50, II, 7-9, 13-20, 100-101; "Zamechaniia, do Malorosii," 2-5, 10-14.

[26] PSZ, 1781, N. 15265; 1785, N. 16250.

The fiscal reform had a similar effect. In the Ukraine of the Settlements a systematic census of Cherkassians took place in 1763 in order to determine their exact number not only in the Ukraine but elsewhere as well, especially in Belgorod, Voronezh, and Astrakhan gubernias, and to establish a rate of taxation commensurate with their status, which varied from place to place. Cossack helpers (*voiskovye obyvateli*, 154,808 souls) were required to pay 95 kopecks per soul beginning in 1765. Those living outside the territory of the regiments where the Cossack privilege of free distilling and free sale of vodka applied (22,329 souls) were assessed at 85 kopecks, but were allowed to move into regimental territory if they found the rate too high, a paradox which explains the importance of the sale of vodka in the revenue of the Cossacks. Non-Cossacks (*poddannye Cherkassy*) living on the properties of landowners and *starshina* (328,814 souls) in and outside the Ukraine of Settlements were taxed at 60 kopecks. This tax was difficult to collect because the right to move required that tax rolls be kept up to date. Since its proceeds were used to defray the cost of maintaining the five hussar regiments and some of the dragoons, the Commissary voiced concern lest this right to move interfere with the execution of this part of the military budget. To keep a close check upon the collection, villages were placed under supervisors (*smotriteli*), and fraud in reporting the number of souls was made punishable by confiscation of the estate and banishment of the stewards to Nerchinsk. The quitrent was not introduced, although the ukase of 1767 ordered the collection of such a tax (*chinsh*), equivalent to that collected by the landowners; its purpose, however, seems to have been merely to help pay the arrears of the capitation. Beginning in 1767 in Little Russia proper each homestead (*khata*) was taxed at the rate of one ruble, plus the surtax of two kopecks per ruble. This new tax yielded 240,744 rubles in 1783, while the revenue from the Cherkassians reached 459,265 rubles and represented the only direct contribution to the Imperial treasury, if one excludes the 600 rubles paid by the city of Kiev.[27]

It became even more obvious after the reform that revenue collected in the Ukraine (and other borderlands) was inadequate to support the new and larger administrative apparatus staffed largely by local landowners. There was no reason why the central treasury should assume the burden. The unprivileged should instead be made to pay the necessary sum, and this new fiscal policy would ultimately create the

[27] PSZ, 1763, N. 11773; 1764, N. 12293, IV-V; 1765, N. 12430, pt. 1-5; 1767, N. 12850; "Pervyi opyt," 39-42; SIRIO, I (1867), 309; PSZ, 1770, N. 13509; 1785, N. 16274.

"complete uniformity" between these borderlands and central Russia which would simplify accounting and remove the difficulties attending the "variety of situations" (*raznost veshchei*). The Commission of 1783 recommended a new consolidation of the urban population along Great Russian lines by requiring Cossacks and peasants wishing to engage in urban activities to register among the townsmen and in guilds. It also proposed the purchase from their noble owners of the peasants, lands, and buildings found in the towns, a phenomenon typical of former Polish territories, where towns were often the private property of landowners. Upon this new social division the government would graft the tax legislation in effect in Great Russia: the one-percent tax on the declared capital of the merchants and the 1.20 ruble capitation on shopkeepers. In the rural world, the capitation of seventy kopecks was extended to all peasants, whether serfs or peasants of the state or the church, and a quitrent of one ruble was imposed on the state peasants "until further notice" (*do ukaza*). The Cossacks too were taxed at 1.20 rubles per soul. In each case the surtax applied. Great Russian state peasants, chiefly in Novgorod-Seversk gubernia, had to pay the three-ruble quitrent in force in central Russia; so did the Cherkassians living outside Khar'kov gubernia. Within the gubernia the rates established in 1764 were raised by twenty-five kopecks to 1.20 rubles (or by fifteen kopecks to one ruble) for Cossack helpers, and by ten kopecks to seventy kopecks for serfs and peasants of the state and the church. The one-ruble quitrent and the 1.20 ruble capitation on shopkeepers also applied here. The reform was expected to double the total tax receipts from the Ukraine, even though the one-ruble tax on *khaty* was abolished. Since the capitation was intended to yield a fixed and reliable amount guaranteed by a census binding peasants to a definite place until the next census, the right to move outside the gubernia was automatically revoked, and this provision was at the root of the legend that the law of May 3, 1783 introduced serfdom in the Ukraine.[28] A considerable step had thus been taken by the mid-1780s to bring the fiscal regime of the Ukraine closer to that of Great Russia. The reform helped crystallize a new pattern of social relationships in which the landed nobility saw its status confirmed by exemption from direct taxation, while nearly everyone else joined the ranks of the "unprivileged" subjected to personal taxation.

[28] *SIRIO*, I (1867), 300-304; PSZ, 1783, N. 15724; TsGVIA, f. 44, d. 50, II, 41, 152-160; Glebov, 21-22; "Nastavlenie dannoe Rumiantsevu," 376.

CHAPTER IV

THE WESTERN BORDERLANDS

BIELORUSSIA

The importance of Bielorussia, a part of Lithuania within the greater Polish Commonwealth, derived from its strategic location on the watershed between the Western Dvina and the Dniepr, between Riga and Kiev, crossed in the east-west direction by the morainal ridge forming a natural invasion route via Smolensk to Moscow. Following the first partition of Poland in 1772 a large slice of Bielorussia was annexed to the Empire, whose border now ran along the Dvina from the confluence of the Evst to Beshenkovichi, then south overland to the middle course of the Drut', and along the Dniepr to the confluence of the Sozh'. This new territory was immediately divided into two gubernias, Pskov and Mogilev. Following a second territorial division (1777) in which Pskov was replaced by Polotsk as gubernia capital, the two gubernias had a total population of 1,283,100 in twenty-three uezds.[1]

Both gubernias were placed from the very beginning, i.e., three years before the reform, under a governor general who was none other than the president of the College of War, Zakhar Chernyshev. This was a novelty, as nowhere else was a governor general superimposed upon two governors, and it created a precedent to which reference was later made when the arrangement became the norm everywhere. The governors were placed *pod vedeniem*[2] of the governor general, that is, they possessed independent authority but were required to keep him informed of their actions. It was the governor general's function to supervise the execution in each gubernia of instructions received from Petersburg and to enforce unity in the administration of the newly annexed territory. These tasks were by no means complementary, but whatever contention may have developed was resolved by the fact that the first governor general was also the administrative superior of the two governors.

Three names stand out among the new political leadership of Bielorussia. Zakhar Chernyshev was one of the most important figures in the first part of Catherine's reign. The combination of the presidency of the College of War with a regional command anticipated a similar

[1] PSZ, 1772, N. 13803, 13808, 13888; 1773, N. 14014; 1776, N. 14499; 1777, N. 14603; 1778, N. 14762, 14774; "Plakat Chernysheva" and "Pis'ma k Krechetnikovu," 5.

[2] PSZ, 1772, N. 13807, 13808, pt. 7.

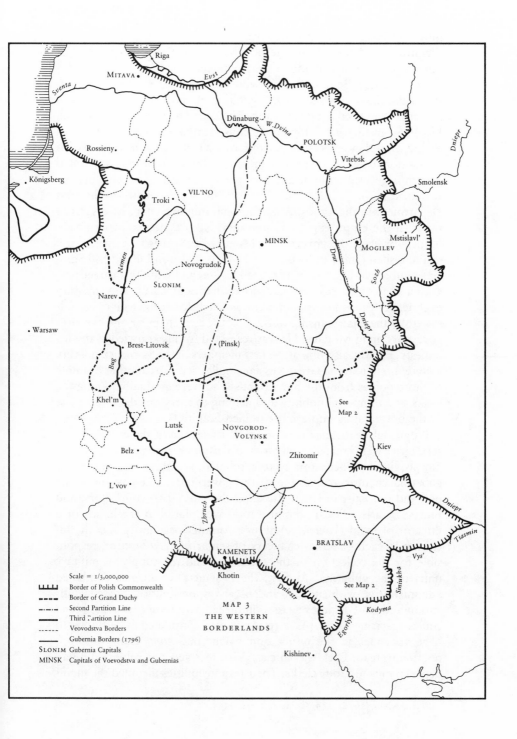

Riga

MITAVA •

Sventa

Evst

Dünaburg

W. Dvina

POLOTSK

Vitebsk

Dniepr

Rossieny •

Smolensk

Königsberg

Troki • VIL'NO •

Mstislavl'

Dnur

MOGILEV

• MINSK

Nemen

Novogrudok •

SLONIM

Sozh

Narev •

• Warsaw

Brest-Litovsk •

(Pinsk)

Dniepr

Bug

Khel'm •

See
Map 2

Lutsk •

NOVGOROD-
VOLYNSK

Belz •

Zhitomir •

Kiev

L'vov •

Zbruch

Dniepr

BRATSLAV •

Tiasmin

KAMENETS

Khotin

Vys'

See Map 2

Dniestr

Siniukha

Kodyma

Egorlyk

Kishinev •

Scale = 1/3,000,000
┗┻┻┻┛ Border of Polish Commonwealth
▬ ▬ ▬ Border of Grand Duchy
▬·▬·▬ Second Partition Line
▬▬▬ Third Partition Line
▭ ▭ ▭ Veovodstva Borders
▬▬▬ Gubernia Borders (1796)
SLONIM Gubernia Capitals
MINSK Capitals of Voevodstva and Gubernias

MAP 3
THE WESTERN
BORDERLANDS

move by Potemkin, but Chernyshev was a very different man, and Bielorussia did not afford the possibilities of New Russia. He was known for his unusual administrative talents, his hard work, and his sense of justice. Bogdan Passek, who succeeded Chernyshev in 1782, was a Ukrainian of Czech ancestry. His aunt married a Potemkin, and his father had been a judge in Little Russia and a voevoda in Belgorod. His arrest in June 1762 forced the conspirators to overthrow Peter III earlier than they expected, but this was hardly enough to justify his promotion to lieutenant general in 1766 at the age of thirty. Appointed governor general without any previous administrative experience, he remained in the post for fourteen years and was a senator in the First Department in the 1790s. A corrupt and immoral man, he disgraced the trust the Empress placed upon him. Nikolai Bogdanovich Engelhardt, however, the governor of Mogilev (1782-1791), came from a distinguished family of Swiss origin which settled in Lifland and Smolensk gubernia. He, too, was related to Potemkin, and his career paralleled that of Passek. He had no civilian and hardly any military experience before his appointment as Vitebsk voevoda in 1774, followed by the chairmanship of the Polotsk civil chamber and the vice-governorship in Mogilev. He was respected for his knowledge and his honesty. He was also one of the first members of the Smolensk nobility (*shliakhta*) to marry a Great Russian, and he serves as another example of those nobles from the borderlands who were gradually joining the ranks of an Imperial nobility and helping to carry out the integration of the borderlands into a more unified Empire.[3]

Provincial chanceries consisting of a voevoda, a deputy, and two secretaries were created in all provincial capitals in 1772 save Mogilev. No provincial procurators were appointed, but there was one in the gubernia chancery consisting of the governor, a vice-governor—the post did not exist in Great Russia at the time—two councillors, and four secretaries. Fiscal administration was placed in the hands of a director of fiscal (*kamernye*) affairs. Another peculiarity was the inclusion in each gubernia chancery of senior *krigs-kommisar*, responsible for the collection of the capitation and the supply of military units in the gubernia. At first, the provincial chanceries combined administrative with judicial and fiscal responsibilities, but civil litigation and land disputes were soon turned over to newly created land courts (*zemskie sudy*). As a result, it was considered superfluous to have voevodas in the uezds, and twenty-one *kommisary* were appointed instead. Each was in class VIII, received 540 rubles, and had between one and four clerks. Their responsibilities included the main-

tenance of order and the settlement of minor disputes, but the collection of the revenue was centralized in the provincial and gubernia
chanceries. All officials were subordinated to the governor, who had
the authority to dismiss them, but new appointments depended on the
Senate. Interpreters were added in the gubernia chancery; proceedings
there were conducted in Russian, and all decisions were published in
the Russian text with a Polish translation.[4] All these agencies were
replaced by a gubernia board, three chambers, and other local courts
prescribed by the Organic Law when the latter was introduced in
Bielorussia in the spring of 1778.

Russian troops were of course stationed in the region, but the size
of the deployment clearly showed that no high priority was involved.
Poland was no longer able to conduct offensive operations, and emergencies were met as in 1793-1795 by shifting troops from the Ukraine
and Lifland. For the year 1780 there is a reference to five garrison
battalions at Polotsk, Vitebsk, Rogachev, Skitki, and Bobruisk. *Shtatnye komandy* were introduced in 1773 and attached to each provincial
chancery and each *kommisar*. A customs guard of 213 was also established in 1783. Regular troops were commanded by Chernyshev, but
Passek was a civilian governor general. In the late 1770s the Sixth
Military Region (Bielorussian) consisted of four regiments of infantry
stationed in Pskov, Vitebsk, Nevezh, and Sebezh, two regiments of
carbineers in Velikie Luki-Toropets and Rezitsa, and one regiment of
hussars in Gomel and Chechersk.[5]

The original instruction sent to governors Kakhovskii and Krechetnikov emphasized that the primary aim of Russian administration in
Bielorussia was the introduction of order, "the soul of all administration," and an end to the "injustice, the robberies, and the murders"
which the Russians found were widespread upon their arrival. After
order came a more lenient administration of justice without "abominable tortures" in the investigation of crimes and without harsh punishments. Such an attitude, which was not a propaganda exercise
because it was intended to guide the conduct of officials on the spot,
shows that the Russians, not without reason, considered their penal
law less harsh than Poland's and believed that their occupation would
civilize Bielorussian life. The region indeed should not be conquered
by force of arms alone, but the hearts of its people ought to be won
over by a just and humane administration so that the "inhabitants

[4] PSZ, 1772, N. 13866, 13879; 1773, N. 14014; 1778, N. 14690 and 14693.

[5] PSZ, 1772, N. 13826; 1776, N. 14583 (TsGVIA, f. 52, op. 194, d. 131, 366); 1782,
N. 15349; 1783, N. 15664; 1795, N. 17419.

would have reason to consider their separation from the anarchy of the Polish Republic the first step in their [future] prosperity."

A two-tiered administration of justice was created. Private litigation (*lichnye dela*) would be handled in Polish in accordance with local laws and customs and in local courts, but only to the extent that this litigation did not affect Imperial prerogatives (*ne dotragivaiut do nashei vlasti*). Violations of peace and tranquility—the terms must have meant all serious crimes—had to be tried in agencies established by the Russian government, i.e., the provincial and gubernia chanceries. The creation of land courts systematized this broad distinction between civil and criminal jurisdiction. A land court was created in each province, consisting of a chairman (*prezus*) in class VIII and three members and two gubernia land courts consisting of a chief judge in class VIII and three members in Pskov gubernia and four members in Mogilev gubernia. In each uezd the *kommisar* examined civil suits if their value did not exceed twenty-five rubles and if no official document was included in the evidence. All other suits had to be brought before the provincial chancery, where proceedings were formal, but the *kommisar* decided after listening to oral pleadings. The gubernia court was probably both a court of appeal for the provincial courts and a court of first instance for the province containing the gubernia capital. The reform swept away these courts and replaced them with the full complement of judicial chambers, intermediate and lower courts. It seems that Polish was used in the lower courts, but the presence of an interpreter in the upper land court indicated that Russian must have been used as well, since the proceedings of the chambers and the gubernia board had to be conducted in Russian.[6]

It is quite obvious that the local nobility was well represented on the new courts, and the introduction of a uniform system of courts in Bielorussia did not so much mean an influx of Russian officials as the institutionalization of the social leadership exercised by the landed nobility. The judge of the court of equity was Ivan Khrapovitskii in Polotsk (where he had been chief judge of the land court) and Mikhail Tikhanovetskii in Mogilev; the chairman of the civil chamber was Vasilii Kakhovskii and Osip Lashkevich in Mogilev, Peter Bogomolets (who may have been Russian), and Stanislas Snarskii in Polotsk. Even the gubernia procurators bore Polish names like Semen Povaloshveikovskii, a relative of Passek, in Mogilev, and Anton Liubashchinskii in Polotsk, although the procurator there was for many years Ivan Mendeleev.

An essential question, one that cannot be answered here because

---

[6] PSZ, 1772, N. 13808; 1773, N. 14014; 1796, N. 17494, vol. 44², 264.

basic archival research still remains to be done, concerns the relationship between Russian and local law. The problem was not peculiar to
Bielorussia; it was also found in Little Russia and the Baltic provinces,
and only a few general comments may help to define the nature of the
problem. Civil suits and minor violations of public order—trespassing,
theft, small claims, fistfights—which came under the jurisdiction of
the lower courts were decided on the basis of local laws, and proceedings were in the local language. At the appellate level, however,
where questions of law were the essential consideration, it is difficult
to say whether definite guidelines existed. Finding the law in these
borderlands meant choosing a Russian, Polish, German, or Swedish
law—each different in its provisions yet equally applicable to the case—
or supplying the Russian law because there was no local law. The
most difficult question concerned the criteria governing the choice
between an equally applicable Russian or local law, and it needs to
be determined whether such criteria were purely subjective or whether
the secretaries in the Senate, the colleges, and later the judicial chambers developed a body of principles. Gradovskii, for example, refers
to an inheritance case—family law was the area where such conflicts
would be felt more acutely—to which the Kapnist family was a party.
The courts of Little Russia applied the Lithuanian Statute, but the
Senate divided the property in accordance with Great Russian law, on
the grounds that the Kapnists were not of Little Russian origin (they
were of Greek descent), even though they were a well-established
family in the Ukraine. If this criterion was later sustained in other
cases, it must have been of great importance, for it proclaimed that
the application of local law in a given borderland was restricted not
even to the local population but only to those who belonged to the
dominant ethnic group, while others came under Great Russian law.
In another and very different case, a retired major who had slapped
the Kiev land captain was sentenced by the Kiev criminal chamber to
degradation and banishment for life under Russian law, but Rumiantsev found extenuating circumstances and grounded in the Lithuanian Statute his commutation to detention in a fortress for three
months. In both cases a choice was made between Russian and Polish
law. In a third case the Senate invoked the Polish constitution of 1726,
Peter the Great's Code of Military Procedure, and the Organic Law
to decide that government *striapchie* should not be allowed to participate in the decision of financial cases in which they were either plaintiff
or respondent. Finally, Russian law could simply supersede local law:
fees charged during judicial proceedings (for stamp paper, etc.) had
to follow Russian law if the case began before 1772 but was terminated

after the annexation.[7] These few cases taken at random seem to indicate that it is quite likely that a body of jurisprudence developed, like the praetorian law of ancient Rome, combining Great Russian and local norms to form the foundations of an Imperial law in certain important areas such as property and family law.

The fiscal integration of Bielorussia began immediately after the annexation, a surprising development which can be explained only by the Imperial government's view of this new acquisition from the Polish-Lithuanian Commonwealth as being an integral part of Russia without the reservations marking its attitude toward the Baltic provinces and Little Russia. The symbol of the Great Russian fiscal system was the capitation, and the two governors were instructed in 1772 to begin immediately a census of souls and to introduce the capitation at the standard rate of seventy kopecks per soul. Part of the capitation was payable in kind in the form of one *chetverik* of rye flour valued officially at fifteen kopecks. To soften the introduction of this new tax among Bielorussians who were not used to "souls" being taxed, the capitation (*podushnaia podat'*) was called head tax (*pogolovnye dengi*). Jews were assessed at one ruble per head and townsmen at 1.20. Estimates for the two gubernias gave a total yield of 349,347 rubles, the largest single source of revenue. This revenue was assigned to the Commissary, as in Great Russia. The second source, estimated at 322,434 rubles, came from the sale of vodka. The landed nobility retained its right to distill vodka and to sell it freely, providing that each landowner paid a fee of fifty kopecks a year for every peasant "head" registered in his name. The nobility also retained the ownership of the inns (*korchmy*) in its possession at the time of the annexation, and governors were to see to it that their network be expanded in all towns and near churches. The price at which vodka as well as beer and mead were to be sold was fixed each year by decision of the landowners, confirmed by the land court and the governor. On state properties leased to landowners, the lessee likewise had to pay fifty kopecks per registered head. In the towns the sale of vodka was also free, but the *magistrat* had to pay the treasury 1.50 rubles for every townsman registered on the census. In *mestechki* belonging to landowners the rate was seventy-five kopecks. The revenue from the sale of vodka was scheduled to belong to the *Stats-Kontora* and to the Commissary.[8]

It soon became apparent, however, that these rates were much too

---

[7] Gradovskii, *Vysshaia admin.*, 205. A similar case, however, was decided on the basis of very different principles: see "Golos Elagina"; other cases are in TsGVIA, f. 44, d. 50, II, 201-204; PSZ, 1784, N. 15939; 1782, N. 15380; 1783, N. 15665.

[8] PSZ, 1772, N. 13808, pt. 15-17, 13865; 1774, N. 14204, 14119; 1781, N. 15288.

high. Reference has been made to the close relationship between capitation and vodka sales as the two major sources of revenue sustaining
the military establishment and to the sale of vodka as the readiest
source of cash for landowners. The government's concern for finding
a compromise between the farm system of Great Russia and local
privileges is evident in every borderland. Everywhere else, however,
the revenue depended on the proceeds from a sale, and the peasants
who purchased the vodka were still free agents. In Bielorussia their
contribution in the form of an additional capitation was a forced one,
distributed equally among those who drank and those who did not.
If the regular capitation was, as noted earlier, farmed out in all but
name among the estates and communities, the sale of vodka likewise
was farmed out in fact, not among a small number of tax farmers but
among the many estates and peasant communities. In both cases the
rationale was the reliability of the revenue. The result was that the
Bielorussian peasant was expected to pay a double capitation of 1.20
ruble in addition to the quitrent and in addition to his purchase of
vodka, produced and sold by the landowner at a price fixed in his
own interest. In Great Russia the profit of the treasury was the difference between the price at which the landowners sold a *vedro* of
vodka, administrative overhead, and the three rubles at which a *vedro*
was sold by the stores. In Bielorussia the treasury collected fifty kopecks, and the entire proceeds from the sale were pocketed by the
landowners.

It is not clear whether Chernyshev, acting in concert with the Bielorussian nobility, was responsible for such a system, but it was criticized
by Prince Viazemskii and Potemkin alike as serving only the interests
of the landowners, with grave implications for the security of a sensitive border area, despite the substantial concessions already made
by the government. As early as December 1772 the Empress announced
that the two new taxes would take effect on July 1 instead of January
1, 1773. In April 1773 the capitation was cut in half to thirty-five
kopecks, and the fifty-kopeck tax for the privilege of distilling vodka
was reduced to ten kopecks. In the towns the rates were reduced to
fifty kopecks and one ruble, respectively. Beginning in 1780 the ten
kopecks were raised to twenty kopecks, the fifty kopecks to sixty, and
the head tax on the Jews was reduced by half to fifty kopecks.[9] Thus,
on the eve of the reform of 1783, peasants paid a capitation of thirty-
five kopecks, including half a *chetverik* of flour valued at seven and
a half kopecks, the townsmen sixty kopecks, the Jews fifty kopecks;

---

[9] PSZ, 1772, N. 13923; 1773, N. 13973; 1774, N. 14113; 1778, N. 14689; 1779,
N. 14892; *Arkhiv Gos. Soveta*, I², 287.

the head tax for the privilege of distilling and selling vodka was twenty kopecks on private estates, still fifty kopecks on leased state properties and in *mestechki*, and one ruble in the towns.

The law of May 3, 1783, affected Bielorussia as well, and Governor General Passek was invited to join the debates of the Commission. In the end it was simply decided to "establish uniformity" with Little Russian conditions. All peasants were now required to pay the standard capitation of seventy kopecks, but the additional head tax for the right to distill and sell vodka was abolished. The delivery of flour in kind remained limited to half a *chetverik*, valued at seven and a half kopecks.[10] The same rate applied on privately owned *mestechki*. A quitrent of one ruble was imposed on peasants registered on state properties, whether belonging to the Court or the treasury or leased. In the towns the distinction between merchants and shopkeepers was also introduced, the former paying one percent of their declared capital and the latter the capitation of 1.20 rubles. Jews were to be taxed no longer as Jews but either as merchants or shopkeepers. The surtax of two kopecks per ruble also applied. The Commission was sharply critical of the social conditions in the towns, abetted by the production and sale of vodka. Townsmen were so called only in name; there was poverty everywhere, and trade and crafts were neglected because the townsmen found it more profitable to distill and sell vodka than to do anything else. The criticism seemed justified, since the towns of Bielorussia had not yet recovered from their long decline, but the solution, as in Little Russia, was such a transparent attempt to seal the monopoly of the nobility that class interests were obviously the guiding motive. Townsmen were forbidden to distill, and only the landed nobility and the treasury—either state distilleries or by contract with landowners—retained that right. The nobles would sell their vodka in their own villages, the treasury on its properties. In the towns the *magistrat*'s responsibility was limited to the *sale* of vodka, and its proceeds were to be used as in Little Russia for public construction and other needs.[11]

Bielorussia was the first territory annexed from the Polish-Lithu-

---

[10] Whether the tax was actually abolished is a moot point. The text says it was included in the capitation. Thus the increase in the rate of the capitation was 15 kopecks. Before the reform, the rate was 35 kopecks plus 20 kopecks: 55 kopecks less 7.5 kopecks commuted into a tax in kind (delivery of flour), a total cash payment of 47.5 kopecks. After the reform, the two forms of capitation were combined into a total tax of 70 kopecks less the 7.5 kopecks: 62.5 kopecks payable in cash. *Mestechki* occupied an intermediate position between towns and villages.

[11] *SIRIO*, I (1867), 304; PSZ, N. 15724, III; TsGADA, f. 16, d. 168, ch. 15, 218-221; on *starostva* see 1783, N. 15872.

anian Commonwealth, and it was considered by the Great Russian leadership to be an integral part of their historical patrimony. A more intolerant attitude toward local differences was noticeable there, and rapid steps were taken from the beginning to bring the new provinces into the administrative framework worked out for the Great Russian heartland.

THE BALTIC PROVINCES

The traveller who followed the immense arc from the shores of the Sea of Okhotsk to the banks of the Western Dvina encountered nothing but Slavic names at every stop, and only in New Russia did the abundance of Greek names remind him of the historic presence of immigrants from across the sea. Upon reaching the Dvina at Dünaburg in Bielorussia and entering Lifland past the town of Iakobstadt, he left the Slavic world for the easternmost corner of the Germanic lands, and alien world only recently acquired, largely autonomous within the Empire, drawn to Prussia by its language and religion, to Russia by the prospects of brilliant careers, yet socially and ethnically divided between the privileged Germanic minority and the native population.

What became at the end of the eighteenth century the three gubernias of Kurland, Lifland, and Estland had once before formed a political whole called Livonia, colonized and christianized by Germans. The area fell victim to the Polish-Swedish wars of the seventeenth century. Gustav-Adolf took Riga in 1621, and by 1625 Lifland and Estland were under Swedish administration. One hundred years later the treaty of Nystadt (1721) confirmed their annexation to the Russian Empire. Kurland retained an uncertain independence until 1795 and will be considered separately. The same treaty gave the Empire an area bound by the northern shore of the Gulf of Finland, Lake Ladoga, and a line following approximately the present boundary between the Soviet Union and Finland. The city of Vyborg became a gubernia capital. The treaty of Abo (1743) pushed this line further west and north, from the estuary of the Kiumen river, up and across Lake Saimaa to the old border above Lake Ladoga.[12]

The provincial administration was staffed with local nobles or foreigners in the Russian service. In Vyborg there was at first Major General Nikolai Nikolaevich Engelhardt (1765-1778), a vice-governor appointed in 1765 who was given the authority of a governor in 1769. He was not a relative of the Engelhardts of Lifland and Smolensk, but

---

[12] For general histories of the Baltic provinces, see Arbusow, Schmidt, and Bienemann, 53-135; and the article "Livonia" in *ES*, XVII^A (1896), 654-657.

the son of a German doctor, and probably owed his appointment to the Orlovs, with whom he took part in the coup of 1762. He was assisted by a single councillor (*Gubernamentsrat*) and two secretaries. There was no procurator. Among his successors were Evgenii Kashkin, who then became governor general in Tobolsk, and Major General Karl von Gintsel (1785-1793). The reform added a governor general, Friedrich Wilhelm, Prince von Würtemberg (1782-1787), a purely nominal appointment, but the gubernia was joined with that of Petersburg under Governor General Brius for the duration of the second Turkish war, when the situation along the Finnish border was extremely serious. There were two provincial chanceries, one for Vyborg and Keksholm provinces, the other for Kiumenegorsk province, with the usual comprehensive jurisdiction over general administration, judicial and fiscal affairs, and three *zemskie kommisary*, subordinated to each chancery, who maintained order and collected taxes. The three official languages were Russian, Swedish, and German.

In Estland it is surprising to find a governor general, Prince Peter von Holstein-Beck (1762-1775), in the rank of field marshal. The post was obviously a sinecure and a place of comfortable exile for the uncle of the defunct Peter III. After the reform the gubernia was combined with Lifland under the Riga Governor General. As in Vyborg, there was only a vice-governor, with the disproportionately high rank of lieutenant general, and the appointees all bore solid German-Swedish names: von Kadeus until 1768; Joachim von Sievers (1774-1778) after an interval during which there seems to have been no vice-governor at all; Georg Grotenhelm (1779-1786), who assumed the full title of governor in 1785; and Major General Andrei von Wrangel (1786-1796). The vice-governor was assisted by two *Gubernamentsräte* and two secretaries.

A similar organization existed in Riga; there, however, the governor general was not a figurehead but a courageous warrior who retained the trust and the affection of the Empress until his death in 1792 at the age of ninety-four. General George (Iuri) Brown was an Irishman forced to leave England by the discriminatory laws against Catholics. He entered Russian service in 1730, fought against the Turks, was taken prisoner and sold three times in Constantinople; he managed to escape with Turkish war plans against Russia and brought them to Petersburg. He fought the Prussians in the Seven Years War, while his relative commanded the artillery in Maria Theresa's armies. A full general in 1762, he was appointed by Peter III Governor General in Riga, where he remained for thirty years, the longest tenure of any governor or govenor general. Brown was also the only foreigner—excluding the two governors general just mentioned—to serve in this post under Catherine. All others, if they were not Russian, were at least born in the Empire. The vice-governor sat with two *Regierungsräte* and was also a lieutenant general: Reinhold Meiendorf (1765-1777) and Sebastian de Garvis (1778-1782). The post was replaced by that of a regular governor in 1783 and was filled by Major Generals Alexander Bekleshov (1783-1790), Ivan Rek (1791-1792), and Peter von der Pahlen (1793-1795). In all three gubernias the reform introduced the gubernia board, the procuracy, and the three chambers.[13]

Nowhere else was the Russian military presence so heavily concentrated as in the Baltic provinces, where its purpose was as much to serve as a strategic base of operations against Poland and Sweden as a reserve police force to maintain order in the provinces and to support the already substantial force stationed in Petersburg, in the event of disturbances affecting the security of the throne. In Vyborg alone there were four garrison battalions under a senior commandant. Regular troops consisted in the 1760s of four regiments of infantry in Vyborg, two in Fridriksham, and one regiment of carbineers in Keksholm. Brius still commanded five regiments of infantry, but after the Swedish war, during which troops engaged in Finland formed the Finland army under Valentin Musin-Pushkin, few troops remained in the area as more regiments were sent into operations against Poland. In Estland the Revel senior commandant was a major or lieutenant general: Ivan Benkendorf, grandfather of the future head of the Third Section, served in the post in the 1770s. Three battalions were stationed in the city and a fourth in Baltiiskii Port. The Estland Military Region was unusually large for such a small gubernia: three regiments of infantry in Revel, two in Weissenberg and Leal, one regiment of cuirassiers in Gapsal, and one of carbineers in Weissenstein. Its command, a sensitive one, was given to Nikolai Saltykov and Pavel Potemkin in the 1770s and 1780s. In Lifland there were no less than eight regiments of infantry and five of cavalry in the 1760s. Thus an unusually large force had been reduced to six regiments in the late 1770s, but the fact that it was commanded at the time by Marshal Golitsyn, the de facto governor general of Petersburg, pointed to its true purpose. In addition to the regular troops there were eight garrison battalions, four of which were in Riga under a senior commandant.[14]

The maintenance of order and the administration of justice in the countryside had been the responsibility of the nobility, and each gubernia had its own separate organization, despite some obvious sim-

---

[13] PSZ, 1783, N. 15776; on Vyborg gubernia, see 1771, N. 13693; 1797, N. 17838.
[14] PSZ, 1764, N. 12135; 1769, N. 13390; 1785, N. 16190; "Rospisanie (1763)"; TsGVIA, f. VUA, d. 234, f. 12, d. 235, 62.

ilarities. In Estland the maintenance of order was vested in the *Haken-richter*, who also watched over the condition of roads and bridges and collected the arrears; they conducted investigations and carried out judicial sentences. There were seven such judges before the reform, distributed among the four uezds. Land disputes and all criminal cases involving non-nobles residing in the countryside went before one of the *Manngerichte*, consisting of an elected judge and two assessors from the nobility. Appeals from these courts and all civil cases, if the value of the claim did not exceed 200 rubles, went before the *Land-gericht*, whose chairman was the marshal of the knights and whose membership consisted of the three *Mannrichter*, the seven *Haken-richter*, and three assessors. Attached to it was an orphan court. The provincial court (*Oberlandgericht*) consisted of twelve *Landräte* from the executive committee of the assembly of the nobility (*Landtag*); the chairman was the governor general or the vice-governor or a senior *Landrat*. This court, dominated not so much by the nobility as by the knights, elected the entire personnel of the lower courts and of the *Landgericht*. It received appeals from these courts and decided civil suits valued at no more than 200 rubles. Cases to which nobles and officials were a party began in this court. Meetings took place usually once a year, in the spring. Judges were paid from a separate fund consisting of revenue from the properties belonging to the *Landtag*.[15] In Lifland police functions were exercised by four *Ordnungsrichter* for Riga, Pernov, and Wenden uezds and Oesel Island. Each uezd had a *Landgericht* consisting of a judge, two assessors, and a *fiskal* (proc-urator) elected by the *Landtag* for three years. The highest court was the *Hofgericht*. Its chairman was appointed by the Empress; its vice-president, also a Lifland noble, was confirmed by the Senate from candidates submitted by the court; and its assessors and *ober-fiskal* were selected by the court itself. Appointments were for life, and vacancies were filled by cooptation. There were *magistraty* in all uezd centers except Wolmar.[16]

In Vyborg gubernia justice was administered by five uezd courts consisting of a judge (*Häradshövding*) and seven assessors elected in each parish (*Kirchspiel*) from well-to-do peasants who under Swedish law were free men. The judge, whose rank was not higher than lieu-tenant, had nevertheless once been appointed by the Swedish king but was now appointed by the College of Justice for Lifland, Finland, and Estland Affairs. These courts met usually twice a year in the winter in each parish, and received all criminal and civil cases in the uezd,

      [15] PSZ, 1797, N. 17845; 1798, N. 18675.
      [16] PSZ, 1766, N.. 12636 and 12653; 1797, N. 17846; Troshchinskii, "Zapiska," 105; PSZ, 1787, N. 16584.

including those to which Russian subjects were a party, except cases of lese majesty, treason, inheritance among noblemen, and crimes committed by office-holders: all such cases went directly to the College of Justice and the Third Department. Claims against the treasury were handled by the *statthalters*, the gubernia chancery, and the branch of the College of Revenue for Baltic Affairs. Appeals against the decisions of the uezd courts went to "the man who knew the law" (*Lagman*), who rode circuit in three places (Vyborg, Keksholm, and Wilmanstrand). In each place he met with seven peasant assessors elected locally. However, appeals in litigation involving bills of exchange (*vekseli*) and admiralty law (shipwrecks, riparian rights, pilots, and lighthouses) went directly to the College of Justice, and all criminal cases were automatically removed to it for review. Despite this narrowed jurisdiction the *Lagman* was a highly respected jurist who used to be chosen by the king from three candidates submitted by the nobility, the clergy, and the peasants. After the annexation he was appointed by the Senate and was in class VII. His decisions were appealed to the College of Justice only if the value of the claim exceeded sixteen rubles (fifty Silbermints thalers). There were *magistraty* only in Vyborg and Wilmanstrand; elsewhere justice was administered by the uezd courts. Appeals against the decisions of the *magistraty* went likewise to the College of Justice.[17]

This brief description of the local administration of the Baltic gubernias before the reform is enough to show its kinship with the new agencies created by the Organic Law of 1775. The separation of police, judicial, and fiscal administration, in marked contrast to the undifferentiated body of general administration prevailing in Great Russia, the distinction between civil and criminal justice, the election of judges and assessors by the local nobility and by peasants in Finland, the limits set on appeals from one court to another by the value of the claim, the three-tiered system of courts—all these passed in one form or another into the post-reform framework of local government. Zutis and Pavlova-Silvanskaia have studied in detail the extent of these borrowings from Baltic administration. What has been neglected is the second phase of the process of unification of Imperial legislation in local government. Once a standard text had been ironed out, "the original had to be made to fit the copy," as Brückner so aptly put it, and the reverse process created considerable resentment among the power-holders in the Baltic world, especially in Lifland.[18]

The central feature of the social organization of Livonia, outside

---

[17] PSZ, 1797, N. 17838; TsGADA, f. 16, d. 664, 2-10; instruction to the statthalter of oesel province in 1774, N. 14154.

[18] Zutis, 383-455; Pavlova-Sil'vanskaia, 302-372; Brückner, *Katharina*, 518-520.

the towns, was the distinction between the knights (*Ritterschaft, ry-tsarstvo*), whose genealogy was recorded in a special register, and other landowners (*Landschaft, zemstvo*). The introduction in 1787 of the Charter of Nobility, which recognized differences in social origins among the nobility but gave them no weight in the operation of the electoral law, followed the abolition of the executive committee of the *Landtag* the previous year. It was a frontal assault upon the privileged status of the knights, designed to create "equality" between the Baltic and Great Russian nobilities. The new electoral law "democratized" the election of the new land captains, uezd judges and their assessors, and gave the Russian government a more direct choice in the personnel of the highest courts in Lifland and Estland. In Vyborg gubernia the reform probably had the opposite effect. The *raspravy* were modelled after the Swedish courts, but the landed nobility now acquired a preponderance that it did not possess before. The native nobility, however, was not displaced but purged of its caste-forming tendencies and integrated into an Imperial nobility, the first step toward its remarkable achievement in the reign of Catherine's grandsons, when Germanic names were found in so many governmental posts. The wolves had ceased to long for the forest and had found a home. Among the chairmen of the judicial chambers we find an Ungern-Sternberg, a Mengden, a Budberg, and a Stackelberg. In Vyborg the former *Lagman* became the chairman of the civil chamber. The use of Russian was generalized at the gubernia level at least—another stage in the trend which probably began in the 1760s when the Senate ordered that preference in promotions be given to native secretaries who knew Russian. However, the complaint of the Vyborg governor in 1796 that gubernia level agencies were still using Swedish and German shows that progress was uncertain.[19]

The reform also affected municipal administration profoundly. As in Little Russia, the jurisdiction of the municipal agencies was restricted to the town limits, and town properties beyond became state domains. The *magistraty* were stripped of their police functions, at least in the larger towns. A new police board in Riga and Revel and the division of the two cities into districts and wards in 1786 followed the provisions of the Police Code. The introduction of the Municipal Statute of 1785 brought fresh air into the musty courtrooms, where the native Germanic population protected its exclusive privileges, not only against newcomers from other Germanic lands but worse still against the Latvian and Estonian townsmen toward whom it main-

[19] Dukes, 67, PSZ, 1787, N. 16584; 1769, N. 13376; 1787, N. 16477; 1796, N. 17516.

tained a haughty racial superiority. Twenty years earlier an accountant named Hefflein had sought to register among the Riga guild merchants, but the *magistrat* had rejected both his request and an order of the gubernia chancery, and appealed to the College of Justice, claiming that the knowledge of accountancy was not enough to make a merchant; his wife was a Latvian (even butchers, it asserted, were forbidden to marry Latvian women); their children would not be considered "free Germans"; and such status would cause "great offense" and "ineradicable dishonor" to the guild. In a stinging rebuke to the *magistrat*, the Senate ordered the immediate registration of Hefflein on the ground that membership in these corporations was regulated by Imperial law and not local prejudices, that a wife acquired the status of her husband, and that Hefflein's wife was even a free Latvian.[20] By creating a municipal society (*obshchestvo*) of merchants, shopkeepers, and craftsmen oblivious of social and ethnic origins, the Statute weakened the hold of the Germanic caste which had ruled the city and opened the doors of municipal government to people of other nationalities—including Russians. The reform of Baltic society and local government carried out by General Bekleshov, an upright and forceful man whose intemperate language unfortunately undermined his effectiveness in a sensitive operation, cracked but did not shatter completely the medieval shell of the German world in the Baltic provinces. The disarray (well described by Bienemann)[21] was not lasting. A counterattack followed after the recall of Bekleshov which would lead to the restoration, at least in part, of the old order under Paul.

The fiscal reform of 1783 also affected the Baltic provinces and provided evidence that the government was conscious of the link between Little Russia and the western borderlands or, to put it differently, that social conditions in those regions which had been under Polish or Swedish rule were showing increasing similarity to those of Great Russia and justified the extension of its fiscal regime. The capitation did not exist in Livonia but was replaced by a tax on land worked by peasants, some of whom were serfs of landowners, while others were still free men. This land tax was assessed on the basis of cadastral maps completed by the Swedish government at the end of the seventeenth century, which had become obsolete by the 1760s. The yield of the tax depended on the amount of land divided into *gaki* and the number of peasants settled on it, and its steady decline in the eighteenth century reflected both the process of absorption of peasant

---

[20] PSZ, 1786, N. 16404; 1787, N. 16584, 16154. The Hefflein case is in 1767, N. 12967. A very similar case, but one involving a Russian merchant, took place in 1774: see "Otkaz rizhskago magistrata."

[21] Bienemann, *passim*.

land into the landowners' personal properties, which were not taxed, and the abandonment by peasants of land registered in the cadastral surveys, either following the absorption of peasant land or on their own free will, to avoid the increasingly heavy burden borne by the remaining peasants. The growth of estates attacked the very foundations of the land tax, and the refusal of the Baltic nobility to acquiesce in a new survey made its abolition inevitable at a time when the Imperial government was looking for additional revenue from the borderlands. The introduction of the capitation of seventy kopecks and the surtax of two kopecks per ruble met no opposition from the nobility because it served their purpose in two ways. All peasants were required to pay it, to be sure, but the interests of the landowners were not affected since they continued to collect the same quitrent, and the social implications were alluring. Peasants, naturally bound to the lord in whose name they were registered in the Imperial census, could no longer move without his permission and without a passport; the many unattached individuals who could not register as townsmen were forced to register as serfs or state peasants. The expropriation of peasant land was at last officially encouraged. Protests came only from the towns, because only part of their properties had been divided into *gaki*. Not only were these properties considerably reduced in size, but the richer townsmen were now made to pay for the old, the sick, and those unable to work, who were nevertheless registered on the rolls of the capitation. The law of 1783 divided the townsmen into merchants and shopkeepers and imposed a tax on declared capital on the former and the capitation of 1.20 rubles on the latter. In Vyborg gubernia, however, there did exist a personal tax (*mantalskie, pogolovnye dengi*) of twenty-four kopecks (three *marki*) in the towns, sixteen to twelve kopecks in the countryside, payable, unlike the Russian capitation, by every male and female between the age of fifteen and sixty-three, excluding those unable to work (*driakhlye*). This tax was assessed on the basis of an annual census (*mantalskaia reviziia*).[22]

Other revenues from the Baltic provinces included rent from leased properties (*arendnye dengi*) and deliveries in kind of provisions for the army. Deliveries in kind (*stationnye dengi*) formed a complex system, and prices paid for them followed rates established as far back as the Swedish period and had become so unrealistic that the law of 1783 asked the three governors to submit proposals for revising them. The average price in Riga for 1773-1781 of a *chetvert* of rye was three

[22] PSZ, 1775, N. 14280; 1783, N. 15724, IV; 1784, N. 15965, 15870, pt. 9; Zutis, 298-300, 460-467, 504-505, 525-526, 535-544. For Vyborg gubernia, see "Pervyi opyt," 42-48; PSZ, 1783, N. 15891; 1778, N. 14706; 1783, N. 15655.

rubles, of barley 2.25 rubles, but the peasants who delivered these grains to military stores received only 1.50. For a *chetvert* of oats and fifteen *pud* of hay selling at 1.50 they received seventy-five and twenty-five kopecks, respectively. Prices varied from uezd to uezd, from estate to estate; in some places payments were made in *efimki*, in others in rubles; weights and measures were different in each of the three gubernias. The reform did away with this medieval particularism. Uniform provisions were introduced in 1784: Russian weights and measures became mandatory and fixed prices of two rubles, 1.85 and 1.10 for a *chetvert* of rye, barley, and oats, respectively, and five kopecks for a *pud* of hay became law. The Empress refused to commute these grain deliveries into cash payments, but their value, on each estate or state property, was deducted from the amount of the capitation due from the peasants who contributed the grain. The result was a complicated accounting, leaving much room for fraud.[23] The effect of the reform, it bears repeating, was not only to consolidate the social position of the nobility; it also wiped away for a while the medieval localisms of Baltic life, for which many felt a sentimental attachment but which also hindered the integration of the region into an Imperial framework.

It is a measure of the unity of the borderlands within an economic system marked by the triumph of serfdom that the law of 1783 addressed itself everywhere to the same two major sources of revenue: the capitation and the sale of vodka and beer. Swedish law knew two taxes on the sale of beverages: the *rekognitsionnaia podat'*, levied at least in Riga if not elsewhere on the entire amount of malt brewed into beer and on the vodka brought into the city from the estates of the landowners, and the *aktsiznye dengi*, collected from the sale in towns of beer, mead, wine, and cattle. The tax was collected by a brewing company, and its proceeds went to the state treasury. In Livonia the right to distill was the monopoly of the nobility in the countryside; in the towns the Swedish legislation of 1675 restricted the right to distill, brew, and sell to widows of merchants who could not continue the trade of their former husbands, to bankrupt merchants for four years to help them recover, to old and poor craftsmen and to their widows. Permits were given by the *magistraty*. These provisions were retained by the Russian government, which insisted that guild merchants were not allowed to share in the privilege. The law of 1783 extended to the Baltic provinces the same provisions as those enacted for Little Russia: the sale of vodka was given to the

[23] PSZ, 1784, N. 15906; Zutis, 538-539; see also 1781, N. 15179; 1783, N. 15782; 1786, N. 16731.

magistraty, and the proceeds were to be used for the public needs of the towns, but the law was not executed when Governor General Brown obtained the Empress's approval to retain the traditional system. In Vyborg gubernia the same Swedish legislation applied, although unfavorable agricultural conditions probably required that most of the vodka be imported. In Fridriksham, for example, wholesale and retail sale was the privilege of the merchants, but the sale in goblets (*charochnaia*) belonged to the poor and their widows who were allowed to make a profit of forty percent. In June 1782 an Imperial ukase gave Finnish peasants the right to distill ("a freedom they never had before") in return for a payment of twenty kopecks per registered soul, and the Liquor Code of 1781 providing for the farming out of the sale of vodka took effect in the towns on January 1, 1783. Townsmen were henceforth forbidden to distill and brew, and the twenty-kopeck tax did not apply to them. In the countryside the tax was assessed against the entire male population registered in the Imperial census, including the young, the old, and the "decrepit," and was collected as part of the capitation, which thus did not exceed fifty kopecks.[24]

THE ANNEXATIONS OF 1793-1795

We conclude with the territories annexed by the Empire as a result of the second and third partition of Poland. Their administration hardly belongs to Catherine's reign; placed at first under military rule until it could be certain that the annexation was permanent, their division into gubernias and uezds and the creation of agencies provided by the Organic Law was not complete until the summer of 1796, shortly before the death of the Empress. Yet, even a brief survey will indicate the direction that Russian policy was taking and establish the major achievements of the reform.

The territories acquired by the second partition were bound in the west by a line running from the Dvina upstream from Dünaburg through Pinsk to Khotin on the Dniestr; the third partition moved the Imperial boundary to the Nemen and the Western Bug. They contained over two million tax-paying souls (excluding Kurland), or about eleven percent of the population of the Empire registered in the 1795 census. The area was divided into six gubernias, created to replace the Polish *voevodstva*. Those of Vilno, Minsk, and Slonim were contained within

[24] "Pervyi opyt," 42-48, *Svedeniia o pit. sborakh*, 249-250, 257-259; PSZ, 1766, N. 12636, IV; 1782, N. 15621; 1783, N. 15724, IV; 1790, N. 16862. For Vyborg, see 1780, N. 14999; 1782, N. 15446.

the former Grand Duchy of Lithuania, and the three southern gubernias of Volhynia, Podolsk, and Bratslav contained largely Polish-
Ukrainian provinces. The history of the region was similar to that of
Bielorussia: flourishing trade and cultural centers in the sixteenth century, then a slow and inexorable decline beginning in the 1650s. Economic decline during the Russo-Polish wars and the Northern War
left towns deserted and consolidated an agrarian order marked by
serfdom and political anarchy.

Vilno and Slonim gubernias were placed under the jurisdiction of
the Governor General of Lifland and Estland, Prince Nikolai Repnin.
His instruction ordered him to liberate the Grand Duchy from its
internal enemies, to accept the oath of loyalty from the population,
to respect freedom of "religion and property," but to confiscate the
property of those who refused their allegiance and of Poles who had
left the Grand Duchy. The two gubernias were placed under military
administration. Uezds (*povety*) were administered by regimental and
brigade commanders who combined civil and military powers. In
Grodno, Repnin's headquarters, a "supreme government" (*verkhov-
noe pravlenie*) was created, consisting of three officers and a civilian
who headed four sections responsible for civil and criminal justice,
fiscal administration, and state domains. Repnin was advised to appoint Lithuanians in these sections and in his selection of sheriffs and
land captains to seek Lithuanians devoted to the Imperial cause. This
arrangement was obviously temporary. In August 1796 the governor
general was ordered to introduce the Organic Law in the two gubernias, but the new agencies were probably not open before the death
of the Empress.[25] The other four gubernias were placed under Lt.-
Gen. Timofei Tutolmin, who had spent the previous ten years as
Governor General of Olonets and Arkhangelsk and did not quite
possess Repnin's authority.

A substantial military presence was required in a territory where
centers of resistance remained very active. Moreover, these centers
were linked with others in parts of Poland occupied by Prussia and
Austria, with which Russia now had a common border. The table of
organization of the army dated December 6, 1796, shortly after the
death of the Empress, shows two regiments of infantry stationed in
Minsk, seven of infantry and three of cavalry deployed in the former
Grand Duchy and forming the Lithuanian Military Region. An additional ten regiments of infantry and four of cavalry were deployed

[25] On Repnin, see *RBS*, XVI (1913), 93-118; instruction in PSZ, 1794, N. 17264.
Russian policy toward the northwest is clearly stated in Bezborodko's letter to Repnin:
see Repnin, 57-61.

in the three southern gubernias forming the Ukrainian Region, bringing the total to twenty-six regiments, two of which stationed in Kiev. *Shtatnye komandy* were established in all gubernia and uezd capitals, but no information is available on the size and location of the garrisons at the time of Catherine's death.[26]

Polish courts in existence at the time of the annexation were at first retained with few changes. In the three southern gubernias they were similar to those on the left-bank Ukraine. In the former Grand Duchy, land courts in the uezds received civil litigation, and *grodskie* courts (also *starostinskie*) had jurisdiction over criminal cases. They consisted of a deputy of the voevoda in the provincial capitals or the deputy *starosta* in the uezd centers, sitting together with three elected judges and a clerk. *Magistraty* were also municipal courts. Civil and criminal appeals went to the Chief Lithuanian Tribunal, whose decisions were final. Its members, elected in provinces and uezds for one year, rode circuit in Vilno, Minsk, and Novogrudok. After the annexation the Tribunal was transformed into an upper land court to which a procurator was appointed; its decisions became subject to review in the supreme government, where final decisions were made by majority vote, the governor general casting the deciding vote in the event of a tie. By the summer of 1796 civil and criminal chambers, intermediate courts, and uezd courts were being established everywhere.[27]

Fiscal administration was systematized with no less rigor. The capitation of one ruble became law in all six gubernias, payable in both cash and grain. Repnin was ordered to conduct a census of all properties formerly belonging to the king of Poland (the so-called *stolovye imeniia*) or to the Catholic clergy, either deceased or residing outside Lithuania, as well as other properties granted to individuals for their lifetime, and to collect their revenues. In June 1794, as part of the tax measures to raise the national revenue, Jews in Minsk, Iziaslav, and Bratslav gubernias, as well as in Bielorussia, Little Russia, Ekaterinoslav gubernia, and Crimea, were required to pay double the rate of the capitation if they were shopkeepers and double the tax on declared capital if they were merchants, unless they wished to leave the Empire upon payment of a sum equivalent to three times the double tax. The production and sale of vodka was placed under the provisions of the law of 1783 for Little Russia and Bielorussia. Within a year the integration of the new territories had gone very far indeed.[28]

[26] PSZ, 1796, N. 17606, vol. 43', *kn. voen. sht.*, 3; 1796, N. 17494, vol. 44², 262-263; "Dnevnyia Zapiski o dvizhenii," 99-102, and Repnin, 218-220, 221-222.

[27] PSZ, 1794, N. 17264; 1796, N. 17494; on courts see ES, VIII^A (1893), 786-787 and IX^A (1893), 754, and Repnin, 471-474.

[28] PSZ, 1794, N. 17264, 17224; 1795, N. 17316, 17356. On the sale of vodka, see

The case of Kurland requires special consideration. The duchy occupied a strategic location between Lifland and Lithuania so that
Russian troop movements out of Lifland in the direction of Poland
required the tacit approval of the duke. When the Teutonic Order was
disbanded in 1561, one of its former leaders, a member of the Kettler
family, had assumed the title of duke and recognized the suzerainty
of Poland. A descendant married the niece of Peter the Great, the
future Empress Anna, in 1710. After his untimely death the following
year, his successor became the last member of that house to occupy
the ducal throne (1711-1737). Anna's favorite, Biron, was duke in
1737-1741, but the throne then remained vacant until 1758, when
Kurland was given to Karl, the son of the king of Poland. Biron
returned in 1763, reoccupied the ducal throne until 1769, and was
succeeded by his son Peter, who ruled until the annexation of 1795.

The central feature of Kurland political history was the growing
opposition of the nobility to ducal rule. Kurland was indeed a small
Poland, and the progress made by the Polish nobility in reducing to
insignificance the power of the king showed the Kurland nobility what
ought to be done. The preeminent position of the duke, sustained by
very extensive landed properties, was opposed by a dominant oligarchy
of nobles, organized into a corporation headed by a land marshal in
Mitava who controlled the administration and the judiciary. The conflict was over the duke's landed properties: many were leased to the
nobles, but Biron had two sons and fifteen grandchildren who needed
additional revenues to sustain their position, and the duke's intention
to conduct a new survey for his own benefit met with bitter opposition
from the corporation seeking to transform leases into legal title of
ownership and to obtain an even greater share of the ducal properties.
The parallel with Little Russia must be emphasized. The attempt made
by Razumovskii to review the legality of land grants made by his
predecessors had the same effect of striking at the vital interests of the
landed nobility, and both the hetman and the duke fell victim in the
end to the greed of powerful landowners who could not accept the
political pretensions of another landowner based on what they judged
to be an excessive share of the source of wealth. To achieve their ends
all parties took advantage of social tensions but did not create them.
Local parties financed by foreign money are not effective without a
social foundation, and if Kurland fell like a ripe plum in 1795, it was
because the Kurland *Landtag* had finally come to the conclusion in
March that the destruction of ducal power could be achieved only
with Russian support. Duke Peter was forced to abdicate in April, and

---

Arkhiv Gos. Soveta, I², 300, PSZ, 1795, N. 17327; on the border police, see 1795, N.
17373, 17419, vol. 44², 247-248.

the Empress distributed some two thousand peasant *dvory* among the Kurland nobility, whose privileges were confirmed. A governor general was appointed in Mitava, Lt.-Gen. Peter von der Pahlen, who had been governor in Riga for three years. Of Estonian origin, he had married the daughter of the Kurland land marshal. A strong supporter of union with the Empire, he epitomized in his family and his service the old union of Livonia in a single region dominated by Germanic influence.[29] A Lamsdorf in the post of governor, a von Stempel in the criminal chamber, and a von Heiking in the civil chamber guaranteed that the Kurland nobility would remain in control.

But even the voluntary union of Kurland with Russia did not dampen the Imperial government's passion for uniformity. Pahlen was instructed in May 1795 to collect statistics on the number of towns and on the revenue, to conduct a survey of the duke's holdings—one can only wonder in whose interest it was done—which now became the property of the Imperial treasury, to open customs houses in Vindava, Libava, and Polangen, and to create a border police in concert with Repnin. This latter measure was certainly intended to eliminate the piracy committed by the Kurlanders against Russian shipping, which Vorontsov compared in 1786 to the plundering of the caravans from Central Asia by the Kazakhs. Within a year Kurland had been divided into nine uezds. The *Mannrichter, Hauptmann,* and *Oberhauptmann* courts, elected by the nobility for three years, were replaced by uezd courts and an upper land court, and the *Oberhofgericht* was superseded by the judicial chambers.[30]

Any attempt to formulate a general assessment of Russian policy toward the borderlands after a survey emphasizing the bare facts must begin with an expression of doubt about the usefulness of such terms as autonomy and assimilation. These polar concepts conceal such a complexity of motives and developments that their indiscriminate use can only obscure our understanding of the historical evolution of the interaction between the core area and its dependencies. These relationships are not isolated phenomena but operate within an organic context of human interests, human emotions, and geographical limitation which form the texture of history. A territory which is also a human community is not autonomous because a legislative text or a treaty says it is, but because its natural leaders, whose power rests on their acceptance by the community, are able to create an environment

[29] On the history of Kurland, see Brückner, 245-250; Bil'basov, "Prisoedinenie," 3, 37-55; Mosolov, 43-58. Voldemar notes that the Kurland nobles wanted to obtain the rights of Russian noblemen (and not vice-versa): 394.

[30] PSZ, 1795, N. 17324, 17339, 17411; 1797, N. 17785; 1802, N. 20223; Vorontsov's statement in TsGADA, f. 16, d. 806, 30.

resistant to all outside pressures save the use of naked force. The degree of penetration of this environment and subversion of its individuality varies with the perception by the natural leaders of the relative worth of this organic context in which they and their predecessors have lived against that of another world whose dynamism is beginning to affect their traditional values. Assimilation likewise is not simply a one-way process of imposing one culture upon another. Ideas, patterns of thought and behavior, social attitudes are not received unless conditions have been created to receive them and to foster their growth. The terms cover a wide spectrum of activities, from the stationing of garrisons to the abolition of local customs and the banishment of the local language from the courts and the schools. Therefore it is more rewarding to examine the ever-changing relationships between Russia and its borderlands not as autonomy or assimilation, but as an evolving compromise reflecting social accommodation and geographical adjustments.

The advance of the frontier imposed such a geographical adjustment. The treaty of Kuchuk Kainardji revolutionized the strategic situation in the south and ended the traditional role of the Ukraine as the frontier region par excellence, at the very time when the social order created by that role was dying out, and a nobility born out of the free Cossack class was fashioning a new social order adapted to the peaceful life of a settled agrarian world. From the valley of the Dniepr to the Gulf of Finland, the race for the dispossession of the free peasant was accelerating, and the ownership of land and corvee labor became more than ever the criterion of economic and social power inimical to the retention of privileged status within the new ruling class, be it a hetman in Little Russia, the *Landtag* in the Baltic provinces, or a duke in Kurland. This perception of what was becoming the fundamental trend in the life of the southern and western borderlands—elsewhere the tension hardly existed yet—implied the rejection of traditional autonomy and a natural alliance with the ruling class of Great Russia, where the reforms of 1775-1785 created the institutional framework for the systematic exploitation of the peasantry. The institutions of the Baltic provinces—chiefly those which had reached a higher stage of development because they were nurtured by the need to protect the interests of the German nobility in a racially hostile environment—became the model for a complex of agencies of local government applied with hardly any modification to the entire Empire from the Prussian to the Chinese border. And this translation represented the essence of the compromise between Russia and its borderlands: institutional and procedural unification coupled with the retention of most of the substantive law. Fiscal reform likewise represented a compromise between

Great Russian legislation and economic conditions in some border-lands, but its central purpose was the refashioning of local societies in such a way that the enserfment of the peasantry would no longer be open to question.

Social convergence and administrative unification paved the way for the development of an Imperial nobility and an Imperial civil service.[31] It is true that the integration of local elites antedated the reign of Catherine, and the abundance of Turkic names among the leading families of the Empire is enough evidence that it had for long been traditional policy to receive into the community of believers the descendants of conquerors from the steppe who accepted Orthodoxy and made their peace with the Great Russian political order. From the Chinese border to the Caucasus, Russian civilization was advancing not so much by the use of force as by offering rewards and projecting power in such fashion that local elites found it in their interests to join a political order which confirmed their status and gave the ambitious among them the means to realize themselves. In only one area was the geographical environment inimical to the creation of a community of interest among the Russian nobility and the native elites. It is no coincidence that resistance to Russian penetration was nowhere so stiff as in the Caucasian mountains, which are the highest in Europe. Bestowing ranks, some as high as lieutenant general, on the native leaders underscored their equality with the Russians, and intermarriage in distant regions where Russian woman were still rare sealed the social equality of Russian and native.

This traditional policy continued in the reign of Catherine, but its beneficiaries were now men who grew up in a world fashioned by Polish civilization and to a much lesser extent by Swedish-German influences. Nowhere, perhaps, was the accommodation represented by Russian policy toward the borderlands so evident as in the fact that most of the men who carried out the reforms were not Great Russians but from those regions. Rumiantsev and Potemkin, of course, were Great Russians, and so was Repnin, but it may again have been no coincidence that the latter was sent to govern an area antagonistic to Russia, where, almost thirty years earlier, he had used military force to carry out Russian policy. However, the two Potemkins and Iakobi still exhibited marks of Polish influence; Gudovich was a Ukrainian, Igelstrom a Swedish-German, Brown an Irishman, and the men who carried out their orders were, if not Great Russians, natives of the region or of some other borderland. These governors general embodied the compromise binding Russia with its borderlands in the last quarter

[31] Raeff, "Uniformity," 109.

of the eighteenth century, yet their position was not always an easy one. A compromise implies that a common ground has been found, not necessarily that the tensions have disappeared. Brown certainly, who remained a foreigner, was caught between pressures from Petersburg and resistance from the *Landtag*, and the appointment of Bekleshov to carry out the reform in Lifland suggests that the Empress gave her preference not only to a younger man but also one more capable of enforcing the terms of the compromise in the face of whatever opposition remained. Rumiantsev spent thirty-two years in the Ukraine and was surrounded by Ukrainians to such an extent that he must have become very sensitive to the special interests of the region. Potemkin associated with Armenians, Greeks, and Wallachians, among many others, and this must have strengthened his awareness of New Russia as a separate world distinct from Great Russia. The very association of these governors general with the social elite of their territories was bound to make them responsive to the value of autonomy and suspicious of over-centralization, if not of administrative uniformity. Since the government of the Empress was characterized by extensive decentralization in all but the financial sphere, the tensions were minimized but could not be overlooked.

To emphasize the importance of social convergence and the development of a community of interests between the nobility of the southern and Baltic borderlands is only to provide a unifying theme in a very complicated story.[32] The student of Russian administrative history cannot fail to be impressed by the permanent contrast between the uniformity of central Russia and the individuality of each borderland. Languages were different; so were religions. Social customs, dress, even the shape of houses, varied from place to place. In the middle years of the reign, when the administration of the Empire was divided between Potemkin and Prince Viazemskii, the latter assumed direct responsibility for the administration of central Russia, while the former, combining functional and territorial commands, became the major figure in the administration of the borderlands. The contrast was felt even by those who embodied the Imperial idea. The Empress spoke of it in her instruction to the Procurator General, and borderlands were still called "countries" in the early years of the nineteenth century. Therefore, the study of the borderlands during the reign of Catherine teaches two lessons. Social convergence sustained by the evolution of an agrarian order which had so much in common in central Russia and the borderlands, at least in European Russia, acted as a centripetal force for the union of these constituent parts of the Empire. Ethnic,

[32] von Rauch touches upon this briefly in *Russland*, 46-47.

religious, and linguistic differences, which could not be erased, no matter how intensive an assimilative policy might be, created centrifugal forces keeping permanently alive a second allegiance, unknown and impossible in central Russia. Perhaps it was this dual allegiance rather than the proximity of the Western lands and of the sea which made life in the borderlands freer than in Great Russia. At any rate, the inevitable tensions between these two forces, not a static phenomenon but a fugue-like evolutionary process, constitutes one of the central themes of modern Russian history. Only in the borderlands could a man cherish a double allegiance, to the community shaped by forces different from those which fashioned Great Russia and to an Empire which alone provided the possibility of a liberating integration into a wider world.

CONCLUSION

Much was achieved in the domestic administration of the Russian Empire during the thirty-four years of Catherine's reign, but the solid accomplishments of the reform which brought an historical period to an end also raised unsettling questions for the future.

The Empire in the 1760s still consisted of a Great Russian heartland and poorly integrated satellite territories anchored in a different past, but governed by a ruling class gravitating toward Petersburg and Moscow. The heartland, despite its size, possessed a remarkable unity forged by a peculiar fusion of ethnicity, religion, and political self-righteousness. This unity fostered centripetal forces and supported the leadership of a ruling class open to penetration from the socially dependent classes, but at a rate determined, on the one hand, by the leaders' growing responsibilities and by the evolution of serfdom, on the other. The social nucleus of the ruling class was the officer corps; it formed the school of the nation, shaped its thought, and supplied the political personnel at all levels. The political nucleus was comprised of those who occupied positions in the first eight classes and filled the leadership and management positions. Its executive functions were carried out either by subordinate officers or by men who had been coopted into the secretarial ranks. The purely clerical staff still remained outside it. The officer corps continued to look down upon secretaries and clerks, indeed upon the civil service in general, and to view the exercise of the political function as an essentially military activity marked by respect for hierarchy and a demand for unconditional obedience.

The officer corps was not a bureaucracy, but a political association of the ruling families in the capitals and their clients in the regiments. These families formed, together with the ruling house, to which they were inextricably related by marriage ties, a dynamic ruling class conscious of its privileges and intent upon maintaining its monopoly over the exercise of the political function. Save for the Secret Expedition, which had but a small staff, as far as we can tell, and no local agencies, the ruling class needed no specialized police apparatus because its basic internal unity precluded threats to a conservative ideology for which the existence of serfdom was inseparable from the political supremacy of the nobility, the legitimacy of the ruling house, and the destiny of Great Russia.

The position of the officer corps as the bearer of that ideology was legitimized by the fact that the army was the very place where the symbiosis between ruling class and society took place on a permanent basis. Wars that became bloodier as the century wore on created a world of experiences shared by officers and men and facilitated social mobility from the folk-society into the ruling class. If Peter was the first to insist upon the westernization of the ruling class, the movement did not gather momentum until Elizabeth, and then only in the two capitals. In the army the need to command obedience in battle, as well as in the drudgery of camp life, created a sentiment of mutual dependence that sustained the dynamism of the ruling class.

By the 1760s, however, certain issues had taken on an urgency that required the special attention of the leadership. The spread of the secular message of the Enlightenment, accelerated by the disposition of a foreign born ruler who did not share the religious beliefs of Anna Ioanovna, let alone of Elizabeth, raised everywhere the issue of legitimacy: that of the ruler who had to appeal to the general good without yet knowing what it entailed, and that of the ruling class vis-à-vis the rest of society. Catherine's legitimacy was assured by the acceptance of serfdom and by a successful program of territorial expansion which brought fame and spoils to the entire ruling class. To maintain the legitimacy of the nobility's position now that participation in the exercise of the political function was no longer mandatory was more difficult. On the one hand, westernization required the absorption of the alien manners, dress, and languages which marked off the ruling class from the socially dependent in the most glaring fashion; it thus threatened to bring about the existence of two cultures, hostile to each other because the national culture was of foreign origin, and to undermine the process of cooptation by which the ruling class replenished itself. On the other hand, westernization also implied efficiency in governmental operations, both to improve the performance of the army and to advance toward that state of general welfare which now became the goal of political action.

The internal constitution of the Empire was anything but efficient in the 1760s. The territorial division was obsolete and could not support an efficient administration. Local government by voevoda was a legacy of the seventeenth century; by the 1760s contemporaries could only deplore the insignificance of public power in the countryside. A voevoda with a deputy and perhaps a dozen clerks was hardly adequate to administer in the large uezds a population of several tens of thousand souls, and this without any effective executive police. In the east, where colonization was advancing at a rapid pace, large areas lacked a single voevoda. Taxes were still collected with substantial arrears, brigandage was rampant everywhere, and the administration of justice was undermined by the absence of a coercive power strong enough to bring the parties to court. The exercise of the political function was still largely restricted to the two capital cities, where a large bureaucratic apparatus handled the administrative business of the Empire.

Hence there was the near absence of a hierarchy of responsibilities to keep the trivia of day-to-day administration from reaching the higher levels of government. Uezd voevodas, provincial voevodas, governors, and colleges were all subordinated to the Senate and even to the Empress herself. This practice, reflecting an ingrained cultural conservatism which hallowed tradition and distrusted innovation, was at the root of the maxim that virtually no legislation, understood in the broadest possible terms, could be amended without the sanction of the ruler, and all doubts had to be referred to higher authority on pain of severe fines. As a result, autocratic Russia was not so much a country in which orders were handed down from above and carried out with the precision of eighteenth-century military drill as one in which a political tradition and social convention acted in concert to channel upward the final decision in all but the most insignificant disputes. The Russian political class was animated by a centripetal dynamism which imposed a powerful internal discipline, blocking initiative but transmitting to the leadership the doubts, the concerns, and the needs of the rank and file.

Even that apparatus of central government was not efficient. Despite their subordination to the Senate, the colleges had become autonomous bodies, poorly responsive to coordination and integration, and the emergence of a bureaucratic threat to the freedom of action of the ruling class and even of the ruler was a distinct possibility. The colleges naturally were the main beneficiaries of the practice of referring administrative decisions to the center, and their very existence gave the Russian state of the eighteenth century a certain systematic orderliness. However, the criteria chosen for the distribution of government business among them suffered from faulty assumptions. Legislation assigning each college a sector to administer, with a comprehensive jurisdiction combining judicial and fiscal powers, gave it the means to perpetuate an autonomous existence. The collegial system did not create a network of interdependent relationships but abetted the selfish pursuit of departmental interests.

This excessive administrative concentration took place at a time when the spread of colonization favored the dispersion of the ruling class. As estates multiplied and their distances from Moscow, let alone from Petersburg, grew, obtaining redress became a luxury accessible only to the wealthy and well connected; and the retention of traditional methods caused such clogging, delays, and expense that the ruling class, and with it the townsmen and peasants upon whom it depended, had to devise a more satisfying procedure to settle differences. Moreover, the nightmare of financial administration made it impossible even to know how much revenue was collected.

All substantial administrative reforms, perhaps, are motivated by the same idea: to make the existing system more efficient. They also have a social content which must not be overlooked. The search for efficiency led the reformers in two directions. The officer corps, demobilized in 1762 and again in 1775, vastly expanded its role in the civilian administration of the country. The reform to a large extent transplanted the military hierarchy in the gubernias and uezds, so much so indeed that we may very well ask whether the militarization of government which John Keep saw as a characteristic feature of the reign of Paul[1] did not in fact begin a generation earlier. There was one major difference, however: Catherine's army was a decentralized one in which regional commanders-in-chief exercised vast powers, without much coordination by a central authority. This deconcentration of leadership, even in the army, which had always been the epitome of rigid hierarchy, was symptomatic of the redistribution of authority taking place within the ruling class—a rare phenomenon in Russian history and one that may be peculiar to Catherine's reign. Its first purpose was to create spoils in the form of new positions paid for by the treasury for demobilized officers and landowners. Its second purpose was to create an administrative framework for the supply of essential services—the restoration of order, the ensuring of justice, the improvement of municipal administration—and for better control of the townsmen and peasants. And the reform also sought to achieve a compromise with the socially dependent by giving them their own courts. These bodies were associations at the periphery of the leadership—between landowners and the "best men." They operated as channels through which authority was routinized and subordination legitimized. The consequence of this reform was to break up the bureaucracies of clerks which fifty years of neglect of the provinces had allowed to grow to a point where the leadership of the ruling class was in danger of being thwarted.

This movement found a leader in Potemkin, whose origin and influence promised a successful completion. It carried out a territorial division of the Empire that became the most lasting achievement of the reform. The new gubernias were compact territories, their capitals had a central location, and their population was of a size facilitating "enlightened" government. The unity of administration in the person

[1] Keep, "Militarization."

of the uezd voevoda was abandoned, and his responsibilities were distributed among the sheriff, the land captain, and the uezd court, and even a court for state peasants. Three intermediate courts were also created in each gubernia, one for each of the three major groups of society—the nobility, the townsmen, and the state peasants—the serfs, about half the total population, having no legal person in need of protection. The unity of administration at the gubernia level was likewise, if not abandoned, at least diluted by the creation of three chambers for judicial and fiscal affairs, while the governor retained powers of supervision over the observance of legality. Each agency was given a jurisdiction bound territorially by the limits of the uezd and the gubernia and vertically by that of the next higher agency. Court decisions were now final if the value of the suit did not exceed a certain limit. Direct links between the uezd and the central government were discontinued, and gubernia agencies became effective co-ordinating bodies for governmental activities in the entire gubernia. This resulted in a considerable improvement in fiscal administration and eliminated the fragmentation which had been such an obstacle to the compilation of reliable statistics.

The provincial nobility now possessed the means to guarantee its unhindered exploitation of the serfs, and by extension of the state peasantry as well. The creation of the *raspravy* was opposed by the nobility and was made possible by the insistence of the Empress.[2] One cannot assume that they were very effective in protecting the state peasants against abuses and exploitation. A biographer of Potemkin has noted the contrast symptomatic of the reign between a passion for grandiose projects and solicitude for the welfare of the fatherland, on the one hand, and contempt for the "good of the state" if its pursuit was an obstacle to the realization of personal profit. The reign was indeed marked by a passionate search for landed property and for peasants because they provided the only two sources of the cash that gave an economic and cultural foundation to status—the quitrent and the proceeds from the sale of vodka to the treasury.[3]

But the reform also led in another direction, and Prince Viazemskii was undoubtedly the leader here. The need was very pressing to identify the sources of revenue, to tabulate their yields, and to create a network of agencies facilitating the flow of cash to disbursing agencies and securing greater accountability. The conclusion was reached sometime in the late 1760s that the financial autonomy of the colleges was

[2] Pavlova-Sil'vanskaia, "Uchrezhdenie," 373-375.
[3] "Potemkin," in *RBS*, XIV (1905), 667. Orlov Davydov (199) notes that the emphasis among landowners was not so much on cultivating their land as in acquiring more and more land.

incompatible with the preparation of a national budget, and the creation of the Expedition of State Revenues was a major innovation. It was not truly subordinated to the Senate, as the colleges had been because its chief was the Procurator General himself, the head of the entire chancery of the Senate, responsible to the Empress alone. Deference to the First Department was maintained when doubts arose about the interpretation of the law and when orders had to be sent to governors and treasury chambers, but the Expedition was in fact the embryo of a modern ministry of finance. The consequences were striking. The financial colleges became obsolete and were closed. The preparation of extensive financial documentation was vested in the treasury chambers, where tax collection, accounting, and audit were concentrated for the entire gubernia, so that only twenty-six financial reports (for central Russia alone) formed the basic elements used by the Expedition to prepare the budget. An entire code of financial procedure was published—while none saw the light for judicial procedure—and beginning in 1781, regular budgets, whatever their defects, were prepared. The pressures for such a comprehensive reform of financial administration, generated both by objective needs and by the ambitions of the Procurator General, merged with those exerted by the provincial nobility to decentralize the administration of justice, and brought about the abolition of the executive branch of government.

The reform went too far and raised fundamental questions about the continued viability of the Imperial government. Although Petersburg had been definitely established as the political capital of the Empire by the 1730s, Moscow remained its no less important administrative and social capital. The closing of the colleges terminated its administrative role and completed the pattern of territorial and administrative unity imposed by the Organic Law upon the whole of central Russia. It left Petersburg, still tucked away in the middle of swamps, 763 kilometers north of Moscow, the undisputed capital of the Empire—this at a time when the boundaries of the Empire were advancing deeper into the south and the southeast. It would take another generation before the results could be felt, as Moscow remained the social capital and a refuge for influential members of the ruling class dissatisfied with the policies of the government. Distances made contacts with the Tsar and the Court more difficult, the flow of cash was complicated by unnecessary detours, and the physical isolation of the northern capital restricted the diffusion of ideas received from the outside world. Only four of the other twenty-two gubernia capitals (Pskov, Novgorod, Petrozavodsk, and Arkhangelsk) were closer to Petersburg than to Moscow, and they were hardly the most important. Great Russia continued to gravitate willy-nilly around Moscow, while the northern capital increasingly assumed the trappings of bureaucratic power. There was of course an indisputable logic in this situation both during and after the reign of Catherine. The foundations of bureaucratic government had been undermined by the consolidation of the social position of the provincial nobility, its assumption of power over the provincial police and judiciary, and the enormous sums with which its position was subsidized by the exemption of its peasants from the state-collected quitrent—the proceeds of which went to maintain an apparatus of governmental and military institutions of which noblemen were the main beneficiaries. The closing of the colleges and the isolation of Petersburg were the expression of a strong centrifugal current characteristic of the second half of the reign.

What had been a mixture of government by political clans and bureaucratic agencies became more than ever a government of men. A governmental structure consisting of colleges, with permanent paid officials, procedures, and governmental quarters, subordinated to committees of senators (departments) reporting to the Empress through the Procurator General, was replaced by the Expedition of State Revenues and the chancery of the Procurator General, who combined in his person responsibility for the police, the administration of justice and finance and the treasury. The central government of the Empire after 1775 was to a large extent concentrated in three agencies—the Secretariat, the College of War, and the Procurator General's office—whose orders were carried out not by bureaucratic agencies but by some fifteen governors general in central Russia and another seven in the borderlands.

The extent of the deconcentration of governmental functions achieved by the reform was unprecedented. Not only the management of the salt monopoly—an already fairly complex operation—was removed to the jurisdiction of the treasury chambers, but even the management of the Ural mines and the administration of the custom houses. One can only wonder who the guardians of the state idea were among the vice-governors, directors of economy, and mining, salt, vodka, and custom councillors in distant provincial capitals, where the well-born dispensed favors and amenities, neutralized overzealous officials and even declared them insane. It is quite clear that the entire structure of domestic administration was kept together by the diligence of the Empress, Bezborodko, and Prince Viazemskii. Since the responsibilities of the Empress and her secretary went far beyond domestic affairs, it was the Procurator General who carried the largest share of the burden. The reluctance of the Empress to part with him until overwork and illness destroyed him, and the feeling that he was doing the work of four men, underscored the extent to which the functioning of the machinery of government had become dependent on one man. In a bureaucratic system ministers are not indispensable, even if some are better than others, because a complex of established relationships and procedures sustains the qualities and tempers the defects of the new men. The retirement of Prince Viazemskii and the weakening of the Empress left an institutional void at the center of the Imperial government at a time when provincial bodies were in charge of all its important functions. By the end of 1796, in the general context of a tense international situation and debilitating inflation at home, the Imperial government was facing a momentous crisis.

There were other issues, broader than that of the institutional viability of the new system, but no less disturbing to the contemporary observer. The ruling class itself was undergoing change. The merger of the Great Russian nobility with the landed elite of the Baltic and Ukraine into a single Imperial ruling class governed by the same charter of 1785 dislocated at the same time the internal unity of that class, still so strong in the 1760s. It brought into play forces generated by ethnic and regional differences and even by religious antagonisms, and it indicated the pluralization of the elite, a phenomenon bound to clash in the long run with the traditional insistence on the monolithic exercise of power and leadership.

The reform also kept alive the issue of legitimacy. The creation of such a large number of new positions in provincial administration gave many retired officers an opportunity to participate in the exercise of the political function, a more satisfying activity than the dreary existence of a pensioner assigned to a monastery. But the aggressive policy of the Russian government in Poland and the Caucasus, together with the perception that war with France was inevitable, kept the army on a war footing; it also kept in suspense the question of where the new officers would be appointed when they retired, now that positions had been filled in the provinces. Worse still, the fragmentation of the army into separate commands without firm central leadership, the nefarious influence of the incompetent and corrupt Zubov brothers, the breakdown of any uniform promotion system coupled with the spread of favoritism, created a deep unease in the officer corps, and many began to yearn for the firm hand of a ruler capable of rising above the crippling influence of clans and favorites.

If the legitimacy of Catherine's government was undermined among the political leadership in the last three or four years of the reign— Rostopchin's poisonous pen was probably no exception—what are we to think of the legitimacy of the ruling class in its relationship with the socially dependent? A social contract is not valid for all time but is being constantly renegotiated, even in a society where the dominion of a ruling class is taken for granted. The reforms introduced basic services and built an institutional bridge between noble, on the one hand, townsman and peasant, on the other. It also facilitated the collection of taxes and created an apparatus to punish delinquents. It formalized the exploitation of both serfs and peasants, sometimes called in the sources "state peasants" but more often "peasants of the treasury," i.e., those kept in trust for the needs of the ruling class as a whole. Exploitation can be legitimate when it is accepted, when a complex of social, economic, and cultural circumstances provide no alternative and stir no expectations of a better life. But the increased exploitation came at the very time when the legitimacy of serfdom was being challenged—even if Radishchev's *Journey* was still an isolated appearance—and when the ruling class was fashioning a national culture disdainful of the folk tradition. Exemption from the capitation and from corporal punishment, powdered wigs and buckled shoes, conversations in French and German, created a feeling of alienation, a sense of moral injury on the part of the toiling peasant which undermined his allegiance to a social order whose foundations were beginning to be sapped by the slow progress of capitalism. Within the ruling class itself belief in westernization had become so dogmatic that wearing peasant dress could draw the attention of the Secret Expedition.

The unease widely felt at the end of Catherine's reign was a result of the convergence of these several issues, rather than of the challenge flung by the French Revolution. Like all major historical periods the reign marked the culmination of trends that had been evolving for several generations and the beginning of new ones that rejected traditional assumptions. The reform took place at a time when serfdom was reaching its apogee; its consequences became visible when questions were already being raised as to whether the efficiency of the Imperial government was really compatible with the continued existence of serfdom. It gave license to officers and landowners to administer not in the name of the general good but for systematic greed and extortion. It dismantled the central government apparatus and transformed the provincial government into an instrument of class rule. In so doing it forced into people's consciousness a realization that the interest of the ruling class was not necessarily identical with that of the collectivity. No wonder that the reaction began immediately after the death of the Empress.

How else are we to understand the reforms of Paul—which set the stage for those of his two sons—but as a reassertion of the idea of "state interest" against the claims of the landed nobility? There was certainly much more than a psychological reason for his determination to undo his mother's work. The reaction exposed a fissure within the ruling class and between the ruling class and the clerks, whose yearning for status naturally supported the restoration of a central bureaucracy. It sought first to enhance the autonomy of the ruling house. The marriage of the tsar with foreign princesses, henceforth to become a tradition, and the proclamation of a succession law, together with the availability of healthy sons to take up the relay at the death of every ruler, strengthened immeasurably the authority of the Romanov house in the politics of the ruling class. The new tsar found support among some of the ruling families, but his political base was in the upstart officers who had served him at Gatchina and who now displaced at various levels in the army the commanders from established families. If Potemkin was the symbol of the rank and file of the officer corps in the middle years of Catherine's reign, Arakcheev—and what a difference!—became that of a new group pressing for recognition. In the capital itself, the clanking of spurs, so offensive to contemporary ears, which replaced the rustling of silk in the corridors of the Winter Palace, heralded the arrival of these new men. Paul, however, went too far too quickly in challenging the prerogatives of the established political leadership, and it cost him his life, but the reaction continued in milder form because it was solidly grounded in an objective situation.

The concern for the general welfare bequeathed by the Enlightenment had to become the property of the educated public and the conviction of the ruling class before it could be translated into a concrete program of action. Certainly the reform familiarized large numbers of officers with the needs of the towns and countryside, and the opening of "public" (*narodnye*) schools prepared a new generation to handle documents and figures with greater competence. But the very deconcentration of economic management, which placed primary responsibility for the creation of an industrial infrastructure in various local "expeditions," precluded the elaboration of a consistent economic policy, of which the construction of canals and the protection of "state peasants," begun so soon after the accession of Paul, were two important components.

The formulation of a program designed to improve the condition of the Empire was dictated, as in the early years of Catherine's reign, by the search for legitimacy, for spoils, and for efficiency, in view of the certainty of Russia's participation in a European conflict that would tax the resources of the Empire much more severely than war with the Turks ever had. The restoration of some colleges, the creation of a new ministry (for Crown properties), and the systematic reconcentration of government functions—a difficult task not completed until

1811—began as early as 1797. The core of a new bureaucracy, already shaped by Prince Viazemskii's efforts, began to expand, a new bureaucracy which by its social origins, allegiance, and concentration in the northern capital would within two generations develop into a body autonomous from society—a development diametrically opposed to that characteristic of the reign of Catherine, yet equally defective in its excessive scope. In the provinces governors general were abolished, the intermediate courts were closed, and the financing of other class agencies was shifted from the state budget to the responsibility of noblemen and townsmen. Paul's cutting remark that a man was noble only so long as he spoke to him was not a figure of speech but an assertion that the interest of the ruling house, and with it that of the whole, took precedence over that of the dominant class.

All this, however, does not belong to the subject of this book; it is only a glance at the next reign, when regimentation and intolerance set the tone of political life. That Catherine's reign was suffused with a totally different atmosphere is obvious from the fact that perhaps no other reign was so rich in remarkable personalities. The Empress remains the finest gift of the German lands to her adopted country. Intelligent, educated, charming, and ruthless, she is one of the greatest figures in European history, and the obsession with her nocturnal activities which has filled one biography after another is the most telling commentary on our ignorance of Russian domestic history. One of her qualities was the ability to choose outstanding collaborators among the political families that sustained her power. Potemkin, whose vision created a legend, was the best known, but Prince Viazemskii, elusive behind the charm of his appearance and the ruthless exercise of his considerable power, remains an unfamiliar figure. The one, by his origin, represented the rank-and-file nobility who administered the Empire and the ambitious elements in the polonized borderlands who sought integration into it; by his associations and by necessity, he became the leader of a military- and foreign-policy establishment supporting the subjection of Poland and expansion into the empty lands of the south. The other, by virtue of his intelligence, hard work, and the post he occupied, assumed the leadership of the two most powerful families in domestic administration. Each of them in turn governed with the help of governors and governors general, many of whom left their mark on administrative history: Chicherin and Kashkin in Tobolsk, Iakobi in Irkutsk, Igelstrom in Orenburg, Gudovich in the Caucasus, Rumiantsev in the Ukraine, Brown in Riga; Sievers in Novgorod, Krechtnikov in Tula, Tutolmin in Petrozavodsk, Repnin in Smolensk. None of these men was the faceless bureaucrat usually associated with Russian administrators. They were passionate men, symbols of an

aristocratic age which believed in fame, dash, and color. The reverence
with which older men later spoke of the age of Catherine showed that
it was indeed the golden age of the Russian nobility.[4] Whatever its
shortcomings, the reign remains one of the richest, most dynamic, and
vibrant episodes in the unfolding destiny of a great people.

[4] Dolgorukov, "Zapiski," 1914, N. 8 (Dec.), 33; Chichagov, 64-65. Chechulin, *Rus.
prov. obshchestvo*, is a welcome antidote to the usual dark picture of local society
inherited from Semevskii. See also Golitsyn, 1279, 1318; Turgenev, 1885, IV, 480,
1886, I, 60-62; De Sanglin, 443ff.

APPENDICES

APPENDIX A.

GENEALOGICAL TABLES

These tables include only individuals mentioned in the text (italics) and those necessary to establish a genealogical link.

* Fieldmarshal

** Procurator General

† Boyar

1. Anna Saltykova married Lev Naryshkin and then Boris Sheremetev.

2. The Empress Elizabeth

3. Niece of D. Menshikov, Peter the Great's favorite.

4. Nikita Panin was only engaged to Anna Sheremeteva: the bride-to-be died before the wedding.

5. Iuri Trubetskoi then married Olga Golovina; Dolgorukov does not specify which wife was the mother of the four children.

6. Nikita Trubetskoi then married Anna Kheraskova; which wife was the mother of the four children is unknown.

7. Praskovaia Iaguzhinskaia was the daughter of the first procurator general, Pavel Iaguzhinskii (1722-1726, 1730-1731).

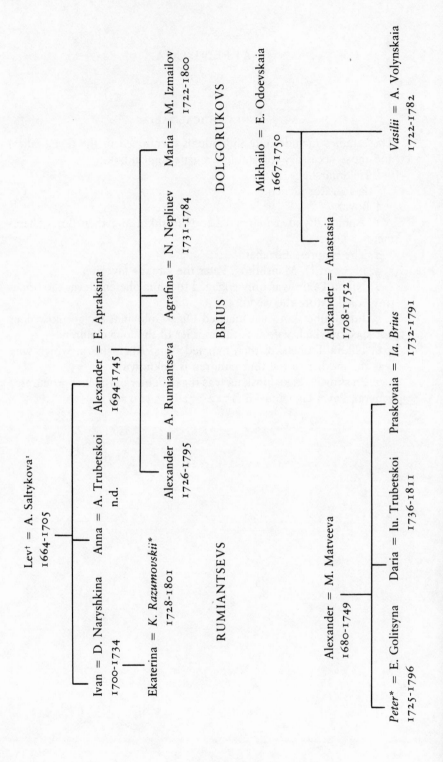

NARYSHKINS

Lev† = A. Saltykova'
1664-1705

Ivan = D. Naryshkina
1700-1734

Anna = A. Trubetskoi
n.d.

Alexander = E. Apraksina
1694-1745

Maria = M. Izmailov
1722-1800

Ekaterina = K. *Razumovskii**
1728-1801

Alexander = A. Rumiantseva
1726-1795

Agrafina = N. Nepliuev
1731-1784

RUMIANTSEVS

BRIUS

DOLGORUKOVS

Mikhailo = E. Odoevskaia
1667-1750

Alexander = Anastasia
1708-1752

Vasilii = A. Volynskaia
1722-1782

Alexander = M. Matveeva
1680-1749

Daria = Iu. Trubetskoi
1736-1811

Praskovaia = *Ia. Brius*
1732-1791

*Peter** = E. Golitsyna
1725-1796

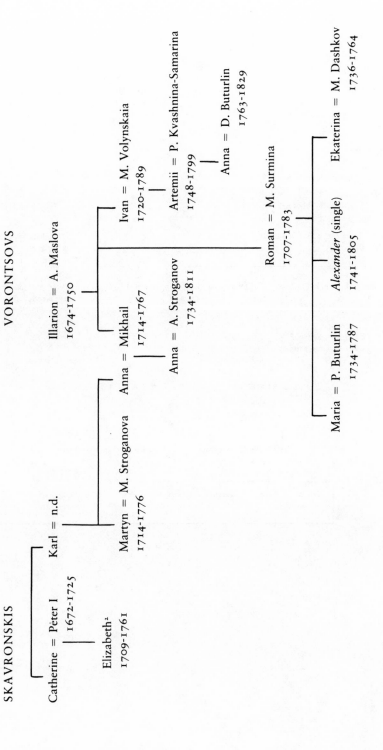

SKAVRONSKIS

VORONTSOVS

Catherine = Peter I
1672-1725

Karl = n.d.

Elizabeth² 1709-1761

Martyn = M. Stroganova
1714-1776

Illarion = A. Maslova
1674-1750

Anna = Mikhail
1714-1767

Ivan = M. Volynskaia
1720-1789

Anna = A. Stroganov
1734-1811

Artemii = P. Kvashnina-Samarina
1748-1799

Anna = D. Buturlin
1763-1829

Roman = M. Surmina
1707-1783

Maria = P. Buturlin
1734-1787

Alexander (single)
1741-1805

Ekaterina = M. Dashkov
1736-1764

CHERNYSHEVS

Grigorii = E. Rzhevskaia
1670-1745

Petr = E. Ushakova   *Ivan* = E. Efimovskaia   *Zakhar* = A. Vedel   M. Vedel = *Peter*   Anna = *I. Nepliuev*
1712-1773   1726-1797   1722-1784   1721-1789   1693-1773

Daria = *I. Saltykov*
1730-1805

PANINS

Ivan = A. Everlakova[3]
1673-1736

Anna = *M. Lunin*
n.d.

SHEREMETEVS

Boris[†]* = A. Saltykova[1]
1652-1719

Peter = V. Cherkasskaia
1713-1788

RAZUMOVSKIIS

*Kiril** = E. Naryshkina
1728-1803

Nikita[4] = Anna   Varvara = Alexei   Praskovaia = *I. Gudovich*
1718-1783   1748-1822   1741-1820

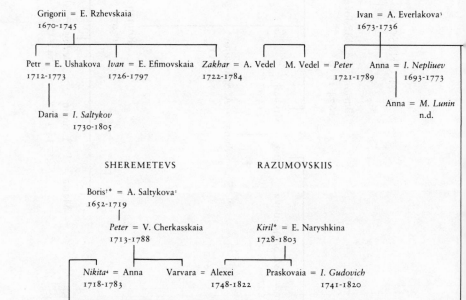

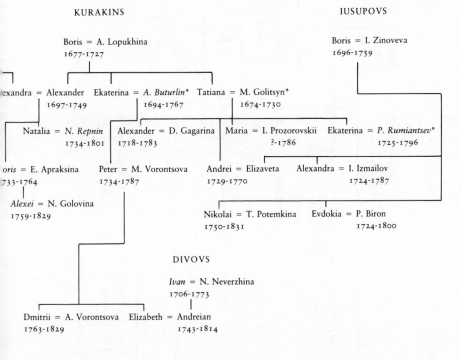

KURAKINS   IUSUPOVS

Boris = A. Lopukhina   Boris = I. Zinoveva
1677-1727   1696-1759

exandra = Alexander Ekaterina = *A. Buturlin** Tatiana = M. Golitsyn*
       1697-1749   1694-1767   1674-1730

Natalia = *N. Repnin* Alexander = D. Gagarina Maria = I. Prozorovskii Ekaterina = *P. Rumiantsev**
    1734-1801   1718-1783   ?-1786   1725-1796

oris = E. Apraksina Peter = M. Vorontsova Andrei = Elizaveta Alexandra = I. Izmailov
733-1764   1734-1787   1729-1770   1724-1787

Alexei = N. Golovina
1759-1829   Nikolai = T. Potemkina Evdokia = P. Biron
                               1750-1831   1724-1800

DIVOVS

Ivan = N. Neverzhina
1706-1773

Dmitrii = A. Vorontsova Elizabeth = Andreian
1763-1829   1743-1814

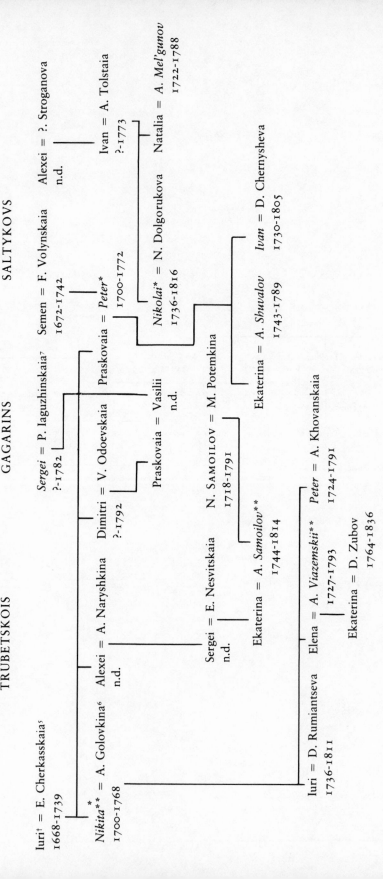

APPENDIX B

SALARY SCALES

Class	Salary	Position
I	7,000	Fieldmarshal
II	3,600	Full General; governor general[1]
III	2,160	Lt.-General; governor general[1]
IV	1,875	President of certain colleges; [2] governor before 1775
	1,800	Major General; governor after 1775;[3] heads of the four expeditions of the Expedition of State Revenues
V	1,875	Heads of the two central treasuries after 1780; member of the Expedition of State Revenues
	1,350	Vice-President of certain colleges[4]
	1,200	Vice-Governor
	840	Brigadier; chairmen of chambers
	600	Governors' deputies (before 1775)
VI	1,000	Director of economy
	600	Army colonel; councillor of college; provincial voevoda; councillor of chambers; gubernia procurator; judge of the equity court; chairman of upper land court
	450	Gubernia procurator (before 1775)
VII	450	Councillor in college (*nadvornyi sovetnik*)
	360	Lt.-Colonel; gubernia *striapchii*; procurator of upper land court; noble assessors in equity court; chairmen of gubernia *magistrat* and upper *rasprava*
VIII	375	Assessor in colleges; provincial procurator; voevodas in towns and uezds
	300	Premier-major; assessor of chamber; gubernia treasurer; *striapchii* of upper land court; procurator of gubernia *magistrat* and upper *rasprava*; sheriff; uezd judge
	260	Second-major
IX	250	Assessor of uezd court; uezd treasurer; land captain; judge of lower *rasprava*
	200	Army captain
X	200	Secretary of college;[5] municipal assessors in equity court and gubernia *magistrat*; *striapchii* of gubernia *magistrat* and upper *rasprava*; noble assessors of lower land court

	120	First lieutenant
XI	250	Secretary of gubernia board and chambers
	150	Uezd *striapchii*
XII	250	Secretary of upper land court; gubernia *magistrat* and upper *rasprava*
	120	Burgomasters
	100	Second lieutenant
XIII	100	Ensign; *ratmany*
XIV	200	Secretary of uezd court, lower land court and lower *rasprava*

Source: PSZ, 1763, N. 11991, vol. 44², 61-62, 1796, N. 17494, vol. 44², 253-257, and TsGVIA, f. VUA, d. 16221, fol. 13. Officers' salaries do not include the so-called "rations."

¹ An additional 6,000 rubles for entertainment expenses.

² 2,250 rubles if stationed in Petersburg.

³ An additional 1,200 rubles for entertainment expenses.

⁴ 1,875 rubles if stationed in Petersburg.

⁵ In a college a secretary received 375 rubles (450 in Petersburg), in the Senate 600 rubles (750 in Petersburg).

THE IMPERIAL GOVERNMENT IN THE 1760S

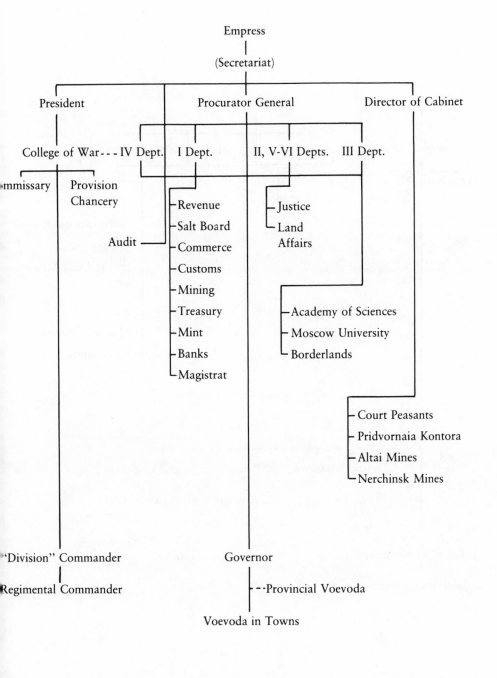

THE IMPERIAL GOVERNMENT IN THE 1780S

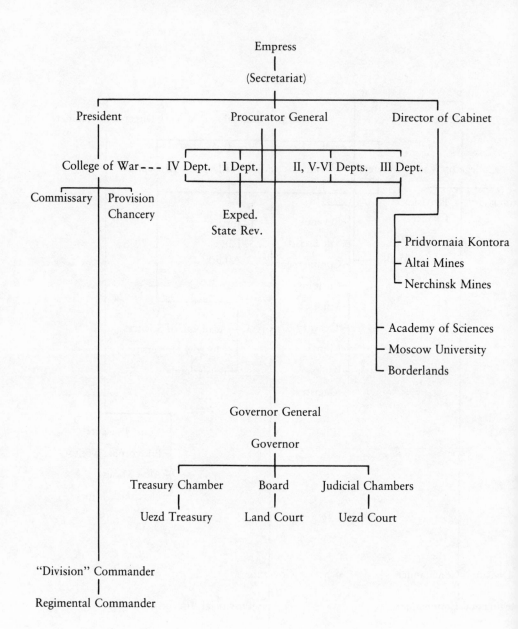

FINANCIAL AGENCIES IN THE 1780S

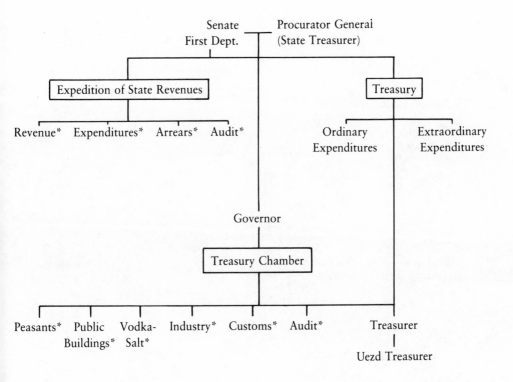

Senate First Dept. — Procurator General (State Treasurer)

Expedition of State Revenues

Revenue* Expenditures* Arrears* Audit*

Treasury

Ordinary Expenditures Extraordinary Expenditures

Governor

Treasury Chamber

Peasants* Public Buildings* Vodka-Salt* Industry* Customs* Audit* Treasurer

Uezd Treasurer

* Expeditions

GLOSSARY

chetvert'	measure of capacity; equals two hectoliters.
chetverik	measure of capacity; equals 1/8 of a chetvert'.
desiatskii	"tensman" (responsible for ten males).
gak	German Haken. A cadastral division whose size varied according to the quality of the soil.
kul'	measure of weight; equals nine pudy.
magistrat	municipal council. After the reform its functions became chiefly judicial, except in small towns where they remained unchanged.
meshchane	shopkeepers. A difficult term to translate. "Shopkeepers" were not merchants but were often classified separately from craftsmen; engaged in retail trade.
nadvornyi	name given to a court created by the reform in only a few cities with jurisdiction over individuals not belonging to the established social categories.
nakazy	instructions given by nobles, townsmen, and state peasants to their delegates to the Legislative Commission.
Nakaz	Catherine's Great Instruction; intended to guide the deliberations of the Legislative Commission.
namestnichestvo	synonymous with gubernia.
oblast'	territorial subdivision after the reform, between the gubernia and the uezd.
odnodvortsy	service people assigned to defend the southern border and given one homestead (dvor) for their support.
pristav	after the reform a deputy sheriff or officer in charge of a district in a town.
pud	measure of weight, equals 16.4 kg.
rasprava	peasant court created by the reform, with jurisdiction over state peasants only.

ratmany	municipal councillors (together with burgomasters).
ratusha	municipal council in very small towns.
raznochintsy	individuals, subject to personal taxes, belonging neither to meshchane not to craftsmen, such as sons of personal nobles, retired soldiers and clerks, etc.
shtatnye komandy	local police forces created in 1763; staffed with old soldiers.
sloboda	quarter in a town populated by an ethnic minority or a definite occupational group; also a village in certain parts of the country, notably the north and New Russia.
sotskii	"hundredsman" (responsible for 100 males).
starosta	headman in a village or a town.
starshina	usually Cossack superior officers forming a separate social group; also the social leadership in some borderlands.
striapchii	deputy procurator; in the uezd the procurator himself.
Ulozhenie	Code of Laws, published in 1649.
upravitel'	appointed official who administered the peasants of the Court.
vedro	measure of capacity; equals 12.3 liters.
vybornye	elected representatives of the peasantry who administered village affairs; in towns elected members of the oral courts.

BIBLIOGRAPHY

I. ARCHIVAL MATERIALS

A. *Tsentral'nyi Gosudarstvennyi Arkhiv Drevnikh Aktov (TsGADA)*

fond 10, opis' 1

delo 545: Prosheniia podannyia na imia imperatritsy Ekateriny II i nakhodivshiiasia v deloproizvodstve u S.M. Koz'mina, chast' 18, 1775 god.

fond 16 Vnutrennee upravlenie

delo 168: Vysochaishiia poveleniia i vsepoddaneishie doklady i raporty Senata i general-prokurora po Senatskim delam, ch. 15 (1780s).

delo 189: Proekty i predstavleniia Pallasa i raznykh drugikh lits kasatel'no vnutrennago upravleniia i gos. khoziaistva Rossii, 1761-1802 gg., ch. I.

delo 190: Pis'mo Nikolaia Vonliar-Liarskago o ispravlenii sudoproizvodstva v Rossii, 1762.

delo 192: Otchet grafa Petra Saltykova s viedomostiu o vykupe arestantov, soderzhashikhsia za kazennye i chastnye dolgi, 1765.

delo 196: O voprosakh budto by zadannykh ot Moskovskoi iustitsii kasatel'no telesnykh nakazanii, 1774.

delo 197: Donesenie Remera o poriadke proizvodstva grazhdanskikh i ugolovnykh del, 1774.

delo 200: O voprosakh, voznikavshikh po sudebnym delam v namestnichestvakh, 1776-1780.

delo 208: Spiski i shtaty gorodskikh politsii (1764?).

delo 216: Proekty ukazov ob uchrezhdenii gubernskikh reketmeisterov i zapiski kasaiushchiasia do dolzhnosti General-Reketmeistera s sobstvennoruchnoi rezoliutsieiu Imp. Ekateriny II, n.d.

delo 334: Predstavleniia po Iustits-Kollegii, 1742-1781.

delo 340: Perepiska po Revizion Kollegii 1733-1799.

delo 374: Predstavlenie gubernatorov A. Maslova, N. Beketova, E. Shcherbinina i A. Kvashnina-Samarina o razshirenii gubernatorskoi vlasti po nekotorym chastiam gubernskago upravleniia, 1768.

delo 384: O nedostatkakh, zamechennykh senatorami grafom A. Vorontsovym i A. Naryshkinym pri osmotre gubernii Pskovskoi, Polotskoi, Smolenskoi, Mogilevskoi, Kievskoi, Chernigovskoi, Novgorod-Severskoi, Orlovskoi i Moskovskoi, 1785.

delo 500: Doneseniia kniazia Alexandra Golitsyna o sostoianii Peterburga i o raspolozhennykh tam voiskakh, 1775-1783.

delo 532: O snabzhenii Peterburga khlebom, 1786.

delo 632: Doneseniia general-gubernatora Alexandra Glebova o
Bel'gorodskoi i Smolenskoi guberniiakh, 1773-1776.

delo 664: Doneseniia Vyborgskago gubernatora Nikolaia Engel'-
gardta, 1766-1775.

delo 778: Doneseniia general-gubernatora Ivan Rebindera o Nizhe-
gorodskoi i Penzenskoi guberniiakh, 1783-1792.

delo 804: Doneseniia gubernatora Timofeia Tutolmina o guberniiakh
Olonetskoi i Arkhangel'skoi, 1784-1795.

delo 806: Donesenie senatora grafa Alexandra Vorontsova i Alexeia
Naryshkina ob osmotre Olonetskoi gubernii, 1786.

fond 19 Finansy

delo 154: Razsuzhdenie o monetakh voobshche i osobenno o rossiiskikh, 1763.

delo 160: O chervonnykh, delannykh na manere Gollandskikh, 1770.

delo 161: O umnozhenii Moskovskago monetnago Departamenta i
uvelichenii shtata monetnago Departamenta v S.-Peterburge, 1774.

delo 164: O vysokom kurse inostrannoi monety-talera, 1780.

delo 166: Proekt ukazu grafu Bezborodke o zapreshchenii vvoza i
vyvoza iz zagranitsy assignatsii, 1788.

delo 168: O upotreblenii kabinetskago zolota na delanie poluimpe-
rialov, 1795.

delo 344: Zamechaniia kn. A.A. Bezborodko ob uvelichenii gosudarstvennykh dokhodov i uluchenie finansov. Mnenie grafa Bezborodko ob obraze upravleniia finansov ili gosudarstvennago khoziaistva. O sostoiania Kabineta v razsuzhdenii ego dokhodov i
raskhodov, n.d.

fond 248 Senate

delo 6507: Dela po Voronezhskomu Namestnichestvu, 1780-1792.

delo 6513: Dela po Tambovskomu Namestnichestvu, 1780-1792.

delo 6519: Dela po Vologodskomu Namestnichestvu, 1781-1792.

delo 6523: Dela po Nizhegorodskomu Namestnichestvu, 1780-1792.

delo 6512 and 6602: Dela po Saratovskomu Namestnichestvu, 1780-
1789.

delo 6560: Dela po Kurskomu namestnichestvu, 1783-1792.

delo 6563: Dela po Vladimirskomu Namestnichestvu, 1780-1792.

fond 291 Glavnyi Magistrat

delo 14358: Po chelobit'iu kapitana Spitsyna.

delo 14379: Po reportu Lifliandskoi General Gubernskoi Kantseliarii.

delo 14454: Po promemorii Glavnoi Proviantskoi Kantseliarii.

delo 14494: Po prosheniu kapitana Khitrovo.

delo 14501: Po promemorii Iustits-Kollegii.

delo 15405: Po soobshcheniu Moskovskago Gubernatora Iushkov.

delo 20521: O promemorii Komissariata.

delo 21085: Po promemorii Komissariata.

fond 370: opis' 1 Dela otnosiashchiesia do obrazovaniia razlichnykh gosudarstvennykh uchrezhdenii

delo 21: Vsepoddaneishii doklad Senata s predstavleniem mneniia DTS kniazia Shakhovskago o preobrazovanii grazhdanskikh shtatov, 1762.

delo 22: Mnenie DTS senatora kn. Shakhovskago o preobrazovanii grazhdanskikh shtatov.

delo 27: Punkty, predstavlennye grafom A. P. Bestuzhevym-Riuminym v Komissiu o svobode dvorianstva.

delo 31: Dela otnosiashchiesia do Senatskoi Kontory, 1763.

delo 33: Vsepoddaneishii doklad Senata o preobrazovaniiakh gubernskikh i uezdnykh prisutstvennykh mest, 1764.

delo 39: Mnenie Novgorodskago gubernatora Sivers o Dvorianskoi Gramote, n.d.

delo 42: Proekt ob uchrezhdenii poriadka ugolovnogo sudo proizvodstva, n.d.

delo 44: Komissia blagochiniia ili politsii, n.d.

delo 50: Komissia o obraze sborov i obraze raskhodov, n.d.

delo 57: Raznye proekty inostrannye, n.d.

fond 393 Reketmeisterskaia Kontora

delo 631: Po presheniu Zasetskago.

delo 731: Po prosheniu Smirnova.

delo 1011: Po prosheniu Dubroviny.

delo 1049: Po prosheniu Medvedeva.

delo 1062: Po prosheniu Cheremisinova.

B. Tsentral'nyi Gosudarstvennyi Voenno-istoricheskii Arkhiv (TsGVIA)

fond VUA (Voenno-Uchenyi Arkhiv)

delo 117: Rasporiazheniia gosudarstvennoi Voennoi Kollegii po snabzheniiu armii kommisariatskimi i artilleriiskimi veshchami, 1769.

delo 228: Vysochaishie reskripty grafu Rumiantsevu s 1780 po 1788.

delo 234: Rospisanie kvartiram polkov (1770s and 1790s).

delo 16193: Raznye postanovleniia i ukazy v tsarstvovanie Ekateriny II s 1763 po 1789.

delo 16221: Polnyi spisok vsei Rossiiskoi armii soglasno nastoiashchemu eia sostavu v tsarstvovanie imp. Ekateriny II, 1769.

fond 12 (Commissary)

opis' 3/62, delo 235: (Commissary budget for 1780).

opis' 3/62, delo 251: (Various Commissary materials for 1786).

opis' 11, d. 39: General'noi otchet za 1793 god o summakh glavnago kommissariata.

opis' 8, d. 46 (Various Commissary materials for 1774-1777).

opis' 11, d. 48: O uchinenii general'nago rospisaniia o potrebnoi na budushchii 796-i god Kommisariatskago vedomstva denezhnoi kazne.

fond 18 (Provisions Chancery)

opis' 2/69, delo 184 (Various materials including contracts for the provisioning of troops).

opis' 3/70, delo 3/196: O assignovanii v proviantskoe vedomstvo na budushchei 1791 god na prevyshenie na proviant i furazh shtat-nykh tsen summy.

fond 44

opis' 193, d. 50 (Various orders to and correspondence with Ru-miantsev, 1786).

fond 52

opis' 194, delo 31 (Reports of the Military Commission).

opis' 1/194. dela 123-125 (Various correspondence with Potemkin, 1775-1776).

opis' 1/194, delo 342 (Correspondence between commissary commis-sions, the Commissary and Potemkin, 1785-1786).

fond 410

delo 14: Ordera Khrushcheva Vul'fu, 1793.

delo 20: Les bons et derniers avis de Catherine II à Paul I, trouvés parmi les papiers de l'Impératrice après sa mort, 1796.

II. PUBLISHED WORKS OF GENERAL INTEREST AND ON CENTRAL RUSSIA

For the sake of brevity, this bibliography does not include books listed in de Madariaga's bibliography, except those to which reference is made in the text.

Absoliutizm v Rossii (XVII-XVIII vv.). Sbornik statei, Moscow, 1964.

Adres' Kalendar. See *Mesiatseslov*.

Afanas'ev, A., "Cherty russkikh nravov XVIII stoletiia," *RV*, Aug. 1857, 623-644.

Alexander, J., "Catherine II, Bubonic Plague, and the Problem of Industry in Moscow," *AHR*, 79:3 (June 1974), 637-671.

Alexandrov, V., *Sel'skaia obshchina v Rossii (17-nachalo 19 vv.)* Mos-cow, 1976.

Amburger, E., *Geschichte der Behördenorganisation Russlands von Peter dem Grossen bis 1917*, Leiden, 1966.

———, "Statthalterschaftsverfassung und Städtegründung in Russland im letzten Viertel des 18 Jahrhunderts," *JGO*, 28:1 (1980), 17-30.

Ardant, G., *Théorie sociologique de l'impôt*, 2 vols., Paris, 1965.

Arkhiv Gosudarstvennago Soveta, vol. I (1768-1796), SPb, 1869.

Arkhiv Senata, vols. XIV-XV.

Aron, R., "Social Structure and the Ruling Class," *The British Journal of Sociology*, I (1950), 1-16, 126-143.

Arsen'ev, K., *Statisticheskie ocherki Rossii*, SPb, 1848.

Aucoc, L., "Les controverses sur la décentralisation administrative," *Revue politique et parlementaire*, 1895, IV, 7-34, 227-254.

Augustine, W., "Notes Toward a Portrait of the Eighteenth Century Russian Nobility," *CSS*, IV:3 (Fall 1970), 373-425.

Babkin, D., *Protsess A.M. Radishchev*, Moscow-Leningrad, 1952.

Bak, I., *Antifeodal'nye ekonomicheskie ucheniia v Rossii vtoroi poloviny 18 v.*, Moscow, 1958.

Bantysh-Kamenskii, D., *Slovar' dostopamiatnykh liudei russkoi zemli*, 5 chasti, Moscow, 1836-1847.

Bar, C. L. von, et al., *A History of Continental Criminal Law*, Boston, 1916.

Barsov, N., "Arsenii Matseevich, Metropolit Rostovskii," *RS*, 1876, I (Jan.-April), 721-756.

Barsov, T., "O dukhovnoi tsenzure v Rossii," *Khristianskoe Chtenie*, May 1901, 691-719, June, 966-998, July, 108-130, Aug., 238-257, Sept., 390-404.

Beccaria, *On Crimes and Punishments*, New York, 1963.

Beskrovnyi, L., *Russkaia armiia i flot v 18 veke*, Moscow, 1958.

Bezrodnyi, A., "Proshlyi vek v ego nravakh, obychaiakh i verovaniiakh," *RS*, 1897, II (April-June), 282-298.

Belavskii, M., *Krestianskii vopros v Rossii nakanune vosstaniia E.I. Pugacheva*, Moscow, 1965.

Bilbasov, V., *Istoriia Ekateriny vtoroi*, 2 vols., London, 1895.

"Bilet izvozchiku v 1794 godu," *RS*, 1896, I (Jan.-March), 122-124.

Blank, P., "Ekaterinskaia Kommissiia 1767-1769," *RV*, Jan., 126-172; Feb., 512-566; March, 5-49; April, 549-585; May, 194-227; June, 711-744.

Blinov, I., Gubernatory. *Istoricheskii-iuridicheskii ocherk.*, SPb, 1905.

——— "Iz istorii dolzhnosti gubernatora posle uchrezhdeniia o guberniiakh 1775 goda," *VP*, 1903, IV (April), 120-170.

——— "Nadzor za deiatel'nost'iu gubernatorov," *VP*, 1902, N. 7 (Sept.), 37-77.

Blum, J., *Lord and Peasant in Russia*, Princeton, 1962.

Blum, K., *Ein russischer Staatsmann. Des Grafen Jakob Johann Sievers Denkwürdigkeiten zur Geschichte Russlands*, 4 vols., Leipzig and Heidelberg, 1857-1858.

Bogoiavlenskii, S., "Rossia, Frantsiia v 1789-1792 gg., *LN*, N. 33-34 (1939), 25-48.

Bolotov, A., *Zhizn' i prikliucheniia A.A. Bolotova 1738-1795*, 4 vol., Moscow, Russkaia Starina, 1870-1873 (reprinted by Oriental Research Partners, Cambridge, England, 1973).

Borovoi, S., *Kreditnaia politika i banki Rossii v XVIII veke*, Odessa, 1957.

Brückner, A., *Katharina die Zweite*, Berlin, 1883.

—— (Brikner) "Vskrytie chuzhikh pisem i depesh pri Ekaternie II," *RS*, 1873, I (Jan.-June), 75-84.

Bulygin. I., *Polozhenie krest'ian i tovarnoe proizvodstvo v Rossii— vtoraia polovina XVIII veka*, Moscow, 1966.

"Bumagi grafa A.R. Vorontsova," *Arkhiv kniazia Vorontsova*, V, 1872.

"Bumagi, otnosiashchiiasia do N.I. Novikova," *Chteniia*, 1867, IV (Oct.-Dec.), smes', 40-62.

Bushkovitch, P., "Taxation, Tax Farming, and Merchants in Sixteenth-Century Russia," *SR*, 37:3 (Sept. 1978), 381-398.

B-va, S., "Obshchestvennye idealy v Ekaterinskuiu epokhu," *VE*, 1876, I (Jan.), 49-83.

Carlyle, R. W., and A. J., *A History of Medieval Political Theory in the West*, 5 vols., London, 1962.

Chebotarev, Kh., *Istoricheskoe i topograficheskoe opisanie gorodov Moskovskoi gubernii s ikh uezdami*, Moscow, 1787.

Chechulin, N., *Russkoe provintsial'noe obshchestvo vo vtoroi polovine XVIII veka*, SPb, 1889.

—— *Ocherki po istorii russkikh finansov v tsarstvovanie Ekateriny II*, SPb, 1906.

—— *Ekaterina II v bor'be za prestol*, Leningrad, 1924.

—— "Proekt imperatorskago soveta v pervyi god tsarstvovaniia Ekateriny II," *ZhMNP*, 1894, March, 68-87.

—— "Vypusk pervykh sta millionov rublei assignatsiiami," *Iuzhno-Russkii Almanakh*, 1902, 1-12.

—— ed., *Nakaz Imperatritsy Ekateriny II, dannyi Kommissiu o sochinenii proekta novago Ulozheniia*, SPb, 1907.

"Chelobitnaia kirasira Popova," *Chteniia*, 1863, II (April-June), smes', 65-66.

Chernov, A., *Gosudarstvennye uchrezhdeniia Rossii v XVIII veke. Zakonodatel'nye materialy*, Moscow, 1960.

Chichagov, *Arkhiv admirala P.V. Chichagova*, SPb. 1885.

Chicherin, B., *Oblastnyia uchrezhdeniia Rossii v XVII-m veke*, Moscow, 1865.

Chulkov, M., *Istoricheskoe opisanie rossiiskoi kommertsii pri vsekh portakh i granitsakh*, 7 vols., SPb, 1781-1786.

Chulkov, N., "F.V. Krechetov—zabytyi radikal'nyi publitsist XVIII veka," *LN*, N. 9-10 (1933), 453-470.

Confino, M., *Domaines et seigneurs en Russie vers la fin du XVIII siècle*, Paris, 1963.

Cracraft, J., *The Church Reform of Peter the Great*, London, 1971.

Crisp, O., *Studies in the Russian Economy Before 1914*, London, 1976.

Daniel, W., "The Merchant's View of the Social Order in Russia As Revealed in the Town Nakazy from Moskovskaia *Guberniia* to Catherine's Legislative Commission," *C-ASS*, XI:4 (Winter 1977), 503-522.

"Dela XVIII veka," *RA*, 1902, III (N. 9-12), 401-409.

"Delo o Baibakove, po pis'mu Sofiiskago gorodnicheskago G. Tokareva," *Chteniia*, 1867, II (April-June), smes', 36-39.

"Delo o professore Mel'mane," *Chteniia*, 1861, IV (Oct.-Dec.), 199-200.

"Delo o professore Moskovskago Universiteta I. V. Mel'mane," *Chteniia*, 1863, II (April-June), smes', 86-120.

Delperée, A., "Deconcentration et décentralisation fonctionelles," *Respublica*, V (1963), N. 4, 375-380.

Derzhavin, G., *Zapiski* in *Sochineniia*, VI, SPb, 1871 (reprinted by Oriental Research Partners, 1973).

De Sanglin, "Zapiski De Sanglena, 1776-1831," *RS*, 1882, IV (Oct.-Dec.), 443-498.

Ditiatin, I., *Ustroistvo i upravlenie gorodov Rossii*, I, SPb, 1875.

Dmitriev, A., "Permskie zemlevladel'tsy Lazarevy i ikh preemniki kniazia Abamelik," *IV*, 1893, II (April-June), 425-447.

Dmitriev, F., *Istoriia sudebnykh instantsii i grazhdanskago appelliatsionnago sudoproizvodstva ot Sudebnika do Uchrezhdeniia o Guberniiakh*, Moscow, 1859.

"Doklad kn. Potemkina o prostupkakh serzhanta Zolotokhina 1788 g.," *RS*, 1875, II (May-Aug.), 148-149.

"Doklad grafa Ia.E. Siversa o sostoianii Novgorodskoi gubernii, 1764," *RA*, 1892, III (Sept.-Dec.), 169-198.

Dolgorukov, I., *Kapishche moego serdtsa*, Moscow, 1890.

———— "Zapiski kn. I. M. Dolgorukova," *Russkii Bibliofil'*, 1913-1916.

Dolgorukov, P., *Rossiiskaia Rodoslovnaia Kniga*, 4 vols., SPb, 1854-1857.

Donnert, E., *Politische Ideologie der russischen Gesellschaft zu Beginn der Regierungszeit Katharinas II*, Berlin, 1976.

Dorn, W., *Competition for Empire 1740-1763*, New York, 1940.

Drizen, N., "Ocherki teatral'noi tsenzury v Rossii v XVIII v.," *RS*, 1897, II (April-June), 539-568.

Dubasov, I., "Iz istorii otzhivshago chinovnichestva," *RA*, 1878, I (N. 1-4), 30-39.

Dubrovin, N., "Russkaia zhizn' v nachale XIX veka," *RS*, 1898, IV (Oct.-Dec.), 481-516; 1899, I (Jan.-March), 3-38, 241-264, 539-569; II (April-June), 53-75, 481-508.

Dukes, P., *Catherine the Great and the Russian Nobility*, Cambridge, 1967.

"Dukh Ekateriny II," *RA*, 1865, 1278-1293.

Duran, J., "The Reform of Financial Administration in Russia during the Reign of Catherine II," *CSS*, IV:3 (Fall 1970), 485-496.

Dvukhsotletie Intendantstva 1700-1900, SPb, 1900.

Dvukhsotletie Kabineta Ego Imperatorskago Velichestva 1704-1904, SPb, 1911.

Dvorianstvo i krepostnoi stroi Rossii 16-18 vekov. Sb. statei posviashchennykh pamiati prof. A. A. Novosel'skago, Moscow, 1975.

Eeckaute, D., "Les brigands en Russie du XVII au XVIII siècle: mythe et réalité," *RHMC*, XII, Juillet-Sept. 1965, 161-202.

Efremov, P., "S.I. Sheshkovskii," *RS*, 1870, II (July-Dec.), 510-512.

Eisenstadt, S., *The Political System of Empires*, New York, 1963.

Eroshkin, N. *Istoriia gosudarstvennykh uchrezhdenii dorevoliutsionnoi Rossii*, 2nd ed., Moscow, 1968.

Esipov, G., *Liudi starago veka*, SPb, 1880.

Esmein, A., *A History of Continental Criminal Procedure*, Boston, 1913.

Esper, Th., "The Odnodvortsy and the Russian Nobility," *SEER*, XLV:104 (Jan. 1967), 124-134.

Feldshtein, G., *Glavnyia techeniia v istorii nauki ugolovnago prava v Rossii*, Iaroslavl', 1909.

Fesler, J., *Area and Administration*, University (Alabama), 1964.

Filimonov, D., "Kreditnyia uchrezhdeniia Moskovskago Vospitatel'nago Doma," *RA*, 1876, I, 265-276, II, 219-224.

Filippov, M., "Tiur'my v Rossii. Sobstvennoruchnyi proekt imp. Ekateriny II," *RS*, 1873, II (July-Dec.), 60-86, 812.

Firsov, N., *Pravitel'stvo i obshchestvo v ikh otnosheniakh k vneshnei torgovle Rossii v tsarstvovanie imp. Ekateriny II*, Kazan, 1902.

Fortunatov, F., "Zametki i dopolneniia Vologzhanina k stat'e ob A.P. Mel'gunova," *RA*, 1865, 1459-1504.

Frumenkov, G., *Uzniki Solovetskogo monastyria. Politicheskaia ssylka v Solovetskii monastyr' v XVIII-XIX vekakh*, Arkhangelsk, 1965.

Gagliardo, J., *Enlightened Despotism*, New York, 1967.

Gay, P., *The Enlightenment: An Interpretation*, 2 vols., New York, 1966-1969.

Gernet, M., *Istoriia tsarskoi tiurmy*, 5 vol., Moscow, 1960-1961.

——— "Politicheskii sysk v Rossii v gody frantsuzskoi revoliutsii," *Sovetskaia iustitsiia*, 1939, N. 15-16 (August), 26-31.

Geyer, D., " 'Gesellschaft' as staatliche Veranstaltung. Bemerkungen zur Sozialgeschichte der russischen Staatsverwaltung im 18. Jahrhundert," *JGO*, 1966, XIV:1 (March), 21-50.

——— "Staatsausbau und Sozialverfassung. Probleme des russischen Absolutismus am Ende des 18. Jahrhunderts," *CMRS*, 1966, VII:3 (July-Sept.), 366-377.

Givens, R., Servitors or Seigneurs: The Nobility and the Eighteenth Century Russian State, unpublished Ph.D. dissertation, California, Berkeley, 1975.

Glasenapp, I., *Staat, Gesellschaft und Opposition in Russland im Zeitalter Katharinas der Grossen*, Munich, 1964.

Glebov, I., *Administrativnaia deiatel'nost imperatritsy Ekateriny II*, Vil'na, 1905.

Goertz, J. von, *Mémoire sur la Russie (1786)*, Wiesbaden, 1969.

Golitsyn. "Zapiski kniazia Fedora Nikolaevicha Golitsyna," *RA*, 1874, I, 1271-1336.

Gol'tsev, V., "Politika nravov po russkomu zakonodatel'stvu XVIII veka," *IuV*, 1884, X, 218-257.

———, "Nravy russkago obshchestva v tsarstvovanie Ekateriny II, *IuV*, 1886, II, 215-217.

Gorodskiia poseleniia v Rossiiskoi Imperii, 7 vols., SPb, 1860-1864.

Got'e, Iu., *Istoriia oblastnago upravleniia v Rossii ot Petra I do Ekateriny II*, 2 vols., Moscow, 1913-1941.

———, *Zamoskovnyi krai v 17 veke*, 2nd ed., Moscow, 1937.

———, "Iz istorii peredvizheniia naseleniia v XVII v.," *Chteniia*, 1908, I, 3-26.

Gradovskii, A., *Vysshaia administratsiia Rossii XVIII st. i general-prokurory*, SPb, 1866.

———, "Istoricheskii ocherk uchrezhdeniia general-gubernatorstv v Rossii," *RV*, 1869, Nov., 5-31; Dec., 396-413.

Gribovskii, A., *Zapiski o Ekaterine Velikoi*, Moscow, 1864.

Gribovskii, V., ed., *Materialy dlia istorii vysshago suda i nadzora v pervuiu polovinu tsarstvovaniia Ekateriny vtoroi*, SPb, 1901.

Griffiths, D., "Eighteenth-Century Perceptions of Backwardness: Projects for the Creation of a Third Estate in Catherinean Russia," *C-ASS*, 13:4 (Winter 1979), 452-472.

Grigor'ev, V., *Reforma mestnago upravleniia pri Ekaterine II*, SPb, 1910.

———, "Zertsalo upravy blagochiniia," *RIZh*, I, 3-4, (1917), 73-103.

Gur'ev, *Denezhnoe obrashchenie v Rossii v 19 stoletii*, SPb, 1903.

Hassell, J., "The Implementation of the Russian Table of Ranks during the Eighteenth Century," *SR*, 29:2 (June 1970), 283-299.

———, "Catherine II and Procurator General Vjazemskij," *JGO*, 24:1 (1976), 23-30.

Ho, Ping-ti, *The Ladder of Success in Imperial China*, New York, 1962.

Huizinga, J., *The Waning of the Middle Ages*, New York, 1954.

Iasnopol'skii, L., *Ocherki russkago biudzhetnago prava*, I, Moscow, 1912.

Ikonnikov, V., "Arsenii Matseevich, istoriko-biograficheskii ocherk," *RS*, 1879, I (Jan.-April), 731-752; II (May-Aug.), 1-34, 557-608; III (Sept.-Dec.), 1-34, 177-198.

Ilovaiskii, *Sochineniia D.I. Ilovaiskago*, 2 vols., Moscow, 1884-1887.

"Istoricheskie razskazy i anekdoty, zapisannye so slov imenityk liudei P.F. Karabanovym," *RS*, 1872, I (Jan.-March), 129-147, 457-468, 670-680, 767-772.

Istoriia Pravitel'stvuiushchago Senate za dvesti let, 1711-1911, 5 vols., SPb, 1911, vol. II.

Iudin, P., "Zhaloba Saratovskikh krest'ian na zemskii sud," *RA*, 1908, III (N. 9-12), 215-217.

———, "K delu Mirovicha," *RS*, 1912, IV (Oct.-Dec.), 340-341.

Ivanov, P., *Opyt biografii general-prokurorov i ministrov iustitsii*, SPb, 1863.

"Iz bumag general-prokurorova kniazia A.A. Viazemskago," *RA*, 1878, II (May-Aug.), 472.

"Iz bumag Nikolaia Petrovicha Arkharova," *RA*, 1864, 873-926.

"Iz proshlago. Proshenie kupchikhi Neishteterovoi," *DNR*, 1879, I (Jan.-April), 261-264.

"Iz rozysknago dela o tragedii Kniazhnina Vadim," *RA*, 1863, 467-473.

"Izustnyi ukaz imp. Ekateriny II o pokupke dlia armii sukon s rossiiskikh fabrik 1766," *RS*, 1878, III (Sept.-Dec.), 716.

Johnson, H., *Frederick the Great and His Officials*, New Haven, 1975.

Jones, R., *The Emancipation of the Russian Nobility 1762-1785*, Princeton, 1973.

———, "Catherine II and the Provincial Reform of 1775: A Question of Motivation," *CSS*, IV:3 (1970), 497-512.

―――, "Jacob Sievers, Enlightened Reform, and the Development of a 'Third Estate' in Russia," *Russian Review*, 36:4 (1977), 424-437.

Kabuzan, V., *Izmeneniia v razmeshchenii naseleniia Rossii v 18-pervoi polovine 19 v.*, Moscow, 1971.

Kahan, A., "The Costs of 'Westernization' in Russia: The Gentry and the Economy in the Eighteenth Century," *SR*, 35:1 (1966), 40-66.

Kartavtsev, E., "Nashe zakonodatel'stvo o narodnom prodovolstvii. Istoricheskii ocherk," *VE*, 1892, I (Jan.-Feb.), 628-678.

"Kartinki proshlago veka," *RA*, 1902, III (N. 9-12), 236-244.

Kashin, N., "Novyi spisok biografii A. N. Radishcheva," *Chteniia*, 1912, II, smes', 1-26.

Kashkin, N., *Rodoslovnye razvedki*, 2 vol., SPb, 1912-1913.

Kazantsev, B., "Zakonodatel'stvo russkogo tsarizma po regulirovaniu krest'ianskogo otkhodu v XVII-XIX vv.," *VI*, N. 6 (1970), 20-31.

K bytovoi istorii Rossii v XVII-XVIII vv., *Chteniia*, 1908, III, 22-40.

Keep, J., "Light and Shade in the History of the Russian Administration," *C-ASS*, VI:1 (1972), 1-9.

―――, "Paul I and the Militarization of Government," *C-ASS*, VII:1 (1973), 1-14.

―――, "From the Pistol to the Pen: The military memoir as a source on the social history of pre-Reform Russia," *CMRS*, XXI:3-4 (1980), 295-320.

―――, "Catherine's Veterans," *SEER*, 59:3 (1981), 385-396.

"K istorii tsarstvovaniia imperatritsy Ekateriny II," *RS*, 1896, IV (Oct.-Dec.), 447-462.

Kizevetter, A., *Posadskaia obshchina v Rossii XVIII stoletii*, Moscow, 1903.

Klingshtet, von, "Plan o privedenii rossiiskoi torgovli v luchshee so-stoianie 1765," *Chteniia*, 1863, II (April-June), 45-56.

Klokman, Iu., *Sotsial'no-ekonomicheskaia istoriia russkago goroda*, Moscow, 1967.

Korelin, A., *Dvorianstvo v poreformennoi Rossii 1861-1904 gg.*, Moscow, 1979.

Korff, S., "Ocherki istoricheskago razvitiia gubernatorskoi dolzhnosti v Rossii," *VP*, 1901, N. 9 (Nov.), 130-148.

Korkunov, N., "Proekt verkhovnago sovestnago suda," *ZhMIu*, 1895, N. 2 (Feb.) 135-138.

―――, "Proekt ustroistvu Senata G.R. Derzhavina," *ZhMIu*, 1896, N. 10 (Dec.), 1-14.

Korolenko, V., "Russkaia pytka, Istoricheskii ocherk," *RB*, N. 1 (Jan. 1912), 127-146.

Korol'kov, M., "Poruchik Fedor Krechetov—Shlisselburg uznik XVIII stoletiia," *Byloe*, 1906, N. 4 (April), 43-60.

Korsakov, A., "Stepan Ivanovich Sheshkovskii (1727-1794)," *IV*, 1885, IV (Oct.-Dec.), 656-687.

————, "Dela davno minuvshikh let," *IV*, 1888, IV (Oct.-Dec.), 176-201.

Kostomarov, N., "Bytovye ocherki iz russkoi istorii XVIII veka," *IV*, 1883, I (Jan.-March), 5-24, 481-494.

"Kratkaia vedomost' o vsekh, delannykh na monetnykh dvorakh, rossiiskikh zolotykh i serebriannykh monetakh," *Chteniia*, 1864, III (July-Sept.), 101-104.

Krest'ianskaia voina 1773-1775 gg. v Rossii. Dokumenty iz sobranii gos. istor. muzeia, Moscow, 1973.

Krieger, L., *Kings and Philosophers 1689-1789*, New York, 1970.

Kulakova, L., et al., *Radishchev v Peterburge*, Leningrade, 1976.

Kulomzin, A., "Finansovoe upravlenie v tsarstvovanie Ekateriny II," *IuV*, Feb. 1869, 3-28, March, 3-38.

————, "Gosudarstvennye dokhody i raskhody v Rossii XVIII-go stoletiia," *VE*, May 1869, 336-351.

————, "Gosudarstvennye dokhody i raskhody v tsarstvovanie Ekateriny II (1762-1780), *RV*, Nov. 1869, 108-151 (1762-1769); Oct., 1870, 373-425 (1769-1780).

————, ed., "Gosudarstvennye dokhody i raskhody v tsarstvovanie Imp. Ekateriny II," *SIRIO*, V (1870), 219-294, VI (1871), 219-304.

————, "Assignatsii v tsarstvovanie Ekateriny II," *RV*, May 1869, 216-243.

Kurilov, A., *Literaturovedenie v Rossii XVIII veka*, Moscow, 1981.

Langeron, A., "Russkaia armiia v god smerti Ekateriny II," *RS*, 1895, March, 147-166, April, 145-177; May, 185-202.

Lappo-Danilevskii, A., *Ocherki unutrennei politiki imperatritsy Ekateriny II*, SPb, 1898.

————, "Sobranie i svod zakonov Rossiiskoi imperii, sostavlennye v tsarstvovanie imp. Ekateriny II," *ZhMNP*, 1897, Jan. 1-59, March, 132-168, May, 60-82, Dec., 365-390.

Lazovskii, V., "Rozysknaia Ekspeditsiia pri Moskovskoi Gubernskoi Kantseliarii 1763-1782 g.," *Opisanie dokumentov i bumag, khraniashchikhsia v Moskovskom Arkhive Ministerstva Iustitsii*, kn. 4, Moscow, 1884, 136-192.

Lebedev, A., "O brachnykh razvodakh po arkhivnym dokumentam

Khar'kovskoi i Kurskoi dukhovnykh konsistorii," *Chteniia*, 1887, II 1-31.

LeDonne, J., "The Provincial and Local Police under Catherine the Great, 1775-1796," *CSS*, IV:3 (1970), 513-528.

———, "The Judicial Reform of 1775 in Central Russia," *JGO*, 21:1 (1973), 29-45.

———, "Indirect Taxes in Catherine's Russia. I. The Salt Code of 1781," *JGO*, 23:2 (1975), 161-190; II. "The Liquor Monopoly," *JGO*, 24:2 (1976), 173-207.

———, "Appointments to the Russian Senate," *CMRS*, XVI:1 (1975), 27-56.

———, "The Evolution of the Governor's Office, 1727-1764," *C-ASS*, 12:1 (1978), 86-115.

———, "Catherine's Governors and Governors General 1763-1796," *CMRS*, XX:1 (1979), 15-42.

———, "The Territorial Reform of the Russian Empire, 1775-1796. I. Central Russia, 1775-1784," *CMRS*, XXIII: 2 (1982), 147-185; II. The Borderlands, 1777-1796, *CMRS* (forthcoming).

Levenstim, A., "Sledy proshlago v Svode Zakonov," *VP*, 1900, N. 2 (Feb.), 45-83, N. 3 (March), 48-90.

Liashchenko, P., *History of the National Economy of Russia to the 1917 Revolution*, New York, 1949.

Lipinskii, M., "K istorii russkago ugolovnago prava XVIII v.," *ZhGUP*, Dec. 1885, 1-54.

Liubavskii. *Sbornik statei v chest' M.K. Liubavskago*, Petrograd, 1917.

Lodyzhenskii, K., *Istoriia russkago tamozhennago tarifa*, SPb, 1886.

Longinov, M., "Neskol'ko izvestii o Penzenskom pomeshchike Struiskom," *RA*, 1865, 481-488.

———, "Neskol'ko izvestii o pervykh posobnikakh Ekateriny Velikoi," *OV*, III (1869), 343-355.

———, "Materialy dlia istorii russkago prosveshcheniia i literatury v kontse XVIII veka," *RV*, 1858, Feb., 715-732, 1859, Aug., 357-386, 1860, Feb., 631-650.

Lopukhin, I., *Zapiski*, London, 1860 (reprinted by Oriental Research Partners, 1976).

———, "Vopl' starinnago sud'i. O delakh dvukh staroobriadtsev," *Chteniia*, 1862, II (April-June), 153-155.

Lutskii, V., "Ekaterina II i sekretar' Pozdniak," *RS*, 1874, III (Sept. Dec.), 370-371.

Madariaga, I. de, "Catherine II and the Serfs: A Reconsideration of Some Problems," *SEER*, LII:126 (Jan. 1974), 34-62.

———, *Russia in the Age of Catherine the Great*, New Haven, 1981.

Maier, N., *Die ältere deutsche Staats- und Verwaltungslehre (Polizeiwissenschaft)*, Neuwied, 1966.

Makogonenko, G., *Nikolai Novikov i russkoe prosveshchenie 18 veka*, Moscow-Leningrad, 1951.

Maslovskii, D., "Russkaia armiia Ekateriny Vtoroi," *VS*, CCV, N. 5 (May), 5-49, N. 6 (June), 231-271.

"Materialy k ego (Volkova) biografii," *RS*, 1874, III (Sept.-Dec.), 478-496.

Meehan-Waters, B., "The Muscovite Noble Origins of the Russians in the Generalitet of 1730," *CMRS*, XII: 1-2 (Jan.-June 1971), 28-75.

Merton, R., ed., *Reader in Bureaucracy*, New York, 1952.

Mesiatseslov s rospis'iu chinovnykh osob v gosudarstve na let ot rozhdeniia Khristova, SPb, 1765-1796.

Mikhnevich, V., "Iz starykh bumag," *IV*, 1897, I (Jan.-March), 750-755.

Milov, L., *Issledovanie ob "ekonomicheskikh primechaniakh" k general'nomumezhevaniu*, Moscow, 1965.

Minkh, A., "Iz starinnykh obychaev v gorode Saratove," *RS*, 1903, II (April-June), 306.

"Mnenie, kakoe, po Vysochaishemu Eia Imp. Velichestva poveleniu sobravshiesia General-Gubernatory i praviashchie ikh dolzhnost' polozhili, k preduprezhdeniiu nedostatkakh v khlebe, po prichine nyneshniago neurozhaia," *Chteniia*, 1865, II (April-June), smes', 71-74.

Montesquieu, *The Spirit of the Laws*, New York, 1949.

Moore, Barrington, Jr., *Injustice: The Social Bases of Obedience and Revolt*, White Plains, N.Y., 1978.

Morrison, K., "Catherine II's Legislative Commission: An Administrative Interpretation," *CSS*, IV:3 (1970), 464-484.

Mosca, G., *The Ruling Class*, New York, 1939.

"Moskva 1785 goda," *SA*, 1968, N. 5, 63-65.

Mustafin, V., "Gosudarevo 'slovo i delo' i kadet Zemtsov," *RS*, 1893, IV (Oct.-Dec.), 644-646.

Nol'ken, A., "Sudebnaia Reforma 1864 i Pervyi Departament Pravitel'stvuiushchago Senata," *ZhMIu*, 1905, N. 2 (Feb.), 107-143.

"Novye dokumenty po delu Novikova," *SIRIO*, II, 1868, 96-158.

Obrebski, J., *The Changing Peasantry of Eastern Europe*, Cambridge, Mass., 1976.

"Obriad kako obvinenyyi pytaetsia," *RS*, 1873, II (July-Dec.) 58-59.

Omel'chenko, O., "Politicheskaia teoriia v 'Nakaze komissii o sostavlenii proekta novogo Ulozheniia' Ekateriny II," *VMU*, 1977, N. 1, 77-92.

"O nagovornoi soli (Iz deloproizvodstva kontsa XVIII veka)," *Chteniia*, 1904, IV, smes', 20-26.

Opis del arkhiva Vladimirskago gubernskago pravleniia, Vladimir, 1902.

Orlov, A., *Volneniia na Urale v seredine XVIII veka*, Moscow, 1979

Orlov-Davydov, V., "Biograficheskii ocherk grafa V. G. Orlova," *RA*, 1908, II (N. 5-8), 301-395, 429-506, III (N. 9-12), 145-214, 303-366, 465-506.

Osteuropa in Geschichte und Gegenwart. Festschrift für Gunther Stökl zum 60. Geburtstag, Köln-Wien, 1977.

Pamiatniki novoi russkoi istorii. Sb. istoricheskikh statei i materialov, ed. V. Kashpirev, 3 vols., SPb, 1871-1873.

Papmehl, K., "The Problem of Civil Liberties in the Records of the 'Great Commission,' " *SEER*, XLII (June 1964), 274-291.

Pardalotskii, F., "Valdaiskaia starina," *RS*, 1890, I (Jan.-June), 775-789.

Pavlova-Sil'vanskaia, M., "Uchrezhdenie o guberniiakh' 1775 goda i ego klassovaia sushchnost'," Candidate dissertation, Moscow, 1964.

———, "Sozdanie v 1775 godu soslovnykh sudov dlia krest'ian," *VMU*, 1963, 3, 69-73.

"Pervyi opyt obshchei rospisi gosudarstvennykh dokhodov Rossii (za 1769 god)" in *Sbornik svedenii . . .*, 1866, III, kn. 10, 23-57.

"Peterburg v 1781-1782 gg. Pis'mo Pikara k kniaziu A.B. Kurakinu," *RS*, 1870, I (Jan.-June), 128-152.

Peterson, C., *Peter the Great's Administrative and Judicial Reforms*, Stockholm, 1979.

Petrov, N., "Evgenii Petrovich Kashkin," *RS*, 1882, III (July-Sept.), 1-40.

Petrova, V., "Politicheskaia bor'ba vokrug senatskoi reformy 1763 goda," *VLU*, vyp. 2 (N. 8), 1967, 57-66.

Pintner, W., and Rowney, D., *Russian Officialdom. The Bureaucratization of Russian Society from the Seventeenth to the Twentieth Century*, Chapel Hill, 1980.

Piontkovskii, S., "Arkhiv tainoi ekspeditsii o krest'ianskikh rastroeniakh 1774 g.," *Istorik-Marksist*, kn. 7 (47), 1935, 91-100.

Pipes, R., *Russia under the Old Regime*, New York, 1974.

"Pis'ma imp. Ekateriny Velikoi k fel'dmarshalu grafu P.S. Saltykovu 1762-1771," *RA*, 1886, III (N. 9-12), 5-105.

"Pis'mo general-prokurora kniazia A.A. Viazemskago," *RA*, 1889, I (Jan.-April), 397.

"Pis'mo grafa F. V. Rostopchina o sostoianii Rossii v kontse Ekaterinskago tsarstvovaniie," *RA*, 1878, I (N. 1-4), 292-298.

"Pis'mo imp. Ekateriny II k P.P. Konovnitsynu 1785," *RA*, 1877, III (Sept.-Dec.), 333.

"Pis'mo Tauberta k Kozitskomu i proshenie ego k Imperatritse o myze, a takzhe proshenie vdovy ego," *Chteniia*, 1867, III (July-Sept.), 4-8.

Pobedonotsev, K., "Utverzhdenie krepostnago prava v Rossii v XVIII stoletii," *RV*, Sept. 1861, 223-253.

"Podmetnoe pis'mo imp. Ekaterine II 1791 goda," *Chteniia*, 1860, IV (Oct.-Dec.), smes', 274-279.

"Podlinnye reestry knigam, vsiatym po Vysochaishemu poveleniu iz palat N.I. Novikova v Moskovskuiu Dukhovnuiu i Svetskuiu Tsenzuru," *Chteniia*, 1871, III (July-Sept.), smes', 17-48.

Podvysotskii, A., "Popytka osveshcheniia ulits v Arkhangel'sk v 1767-1768 gg.," *RS*, 1879, III (Sept.-Dec.), 101-102.

Pokrovskii, I., "Gavril', metropolit Novgorodskii i St. Peterburgskii, kak tserkovno-obshchestvennyi deiatel'," *Khristianskoe Chtenie*, 1901, Oct., 482-510; Nov., 687-718.

Polenov, A., "O krepostnom sostoianie krest'ian v Rossii," *RA*, 1865, 287-318.

Polianskii, F., *Gorodskoe remeslo i manufaktura v Rossii v 18 v.*, Moscow, 1960.

Polnoe Sobranie Zakonov Rossiiskoi Imperii 1649-1913, 234 vols., SPb, 1830-1916.

"Pomest'e Saltychikhi," *RA*, 1281-1286.

Ponomarev, P., "Odna is zamechatel'nykh russkikh zhenshchin," *IV*, II (April-June), 90-136.

"Prakticheskoe opisanie monetnago proizvodstva v Ekaterinburge 1780," *Chteniia*, 1907, II, smes', 1-29.

"Proekt kn. M.N. Volkonskago o luchshem uchrezdenii sudebnykh mest, podannyi imperatritse Ekaterine II v 1775 g.," *SIRIO*, V (1870), 122-127.

Prokhorov, M., "Opyt sostavleniia svodnykh tablits vystuplenii pomeshchich'ikh krest'ian Rossii 1760-1773 gg.," *AE*, 1972, 126-134.

"Proshenie (Karachevskikh) ekonomicheskikh krest'ian orlovskago namestnichestva general-gubernatoru A. A. Bekleshovu," *RS*, 1875, I (Jan.-April), 402-405; also published in *RA*, 1871, 1527-1532, and *RA*, 1891, II (N. 5-8), 298-302.

"Proshenie k imperatritse Kiriiaka Kontratovicha," *Chteniia*, 1867, III (July-Sept.), 9-10.

Puparev, A., "Iz pomeshchich'iago byta kontsa XVIII v.," *RS*, 1892, III (July-Sept.), 225-237, 496-502.

Radishchev, A., *A Journey from St. Petersburg to Moscow*, tr. L. Wiener, Cambridge, 1958.

Radzinowicz, L., *A History of English Criminal Law and Its Administration Since 1750*, vol. I, London, 1948.

Raeff, M., *Origins of the Russian Intelligentsia: The Eighteenth Century Nobility*, New York, 1966.

———, ed., *Catherine the Great: A Profile*, New York, 1972.

———, ed., *Plans for Political Reforms in Imperial Russia 1730-1905*, Englewood Cliffs, 1966.

———, "L'Etat, le gouvernement et la tradition politique en russie impériale," *RHMC*, 1962, Oct.-Dec., 295-307.

———, "The Well-Ordered Police State and the Development of Modernity in Seventeenth- and Eighteenth-Century Europe: An Attempt at a Comparative Approach," *AHR*, 80:5 (Dec. 1975), 1221-1243.

———, "Russia's Autocracy and Paradoxes of Modernization," in *Ost-West-Begegnung in Osterreich. Festschrift für E. Winter zum 80. Geburtstag*. Vienna, 1976, 275-284.

———, "The Domestic Politics of Peter III and his Overthrow," *AHR*, 75:5 (June 1970), 1289-1310.

Ransel, D., *The Politics of Catherinian Russia. The Panin Party*, New Haven, 1975.

———, "Nikita Panin's Imperial Council Project and the Struggle of Hierarchy Groups at the Court of Catherine II," *CSS*, IV:3 (Fall 1970), 443-463.

———, "Catherine II's Instruction to the Commission on Laws: An Attack on Gentry Liberals?" *SEER*, L:118 (Jan. 1972), 10-28.

Ravich, N., *Dve stolitsy. Istoricheskii roman*, Moscow, 1975.

"Razgovor uezdnykh dvorian o vybore sud'i," *RA*, 1902, II (N. 5-8), 489-491.

"Razmyshlenie o neudobstvakh v Rossii dat' svobodu krest'ianam i sluzhiteliam ili zdelat' sobstvennost' imenii," *Chteniia*, 1861, III (July-Sept.), smes', 98-134.

Reisner, M., "Dukhovnaia politsiia v russkom tserkovnom stroe," *RB*, 1907, N. 9 (Sept.), 132-165, N. 11 (Nov.), 107-137.

"Reskript imp Ekateriny Velikoi senatoru Mavrinu po povodu zloupotreblenii v Viatskom namestnichestve," *RA*, 1896, I (Jan.-April), 321-325.

"Reskript i nakaz imp Ekateriny II kniaziu M. Volkonskomu pri naznachenii ego Glavnokomanduiushchim v Moskve," *RA*, 1915, III, 209-215.

Romanovich-Slavatinskii, A., *Dvorianstvo v Rossii ot nachala XVIII veka do otmeny krepostnago prava*, SPb, 1870.

Romanovich-Slavatinskii, A., "Goloda v Rossii i mery pravitel' stva protiv nikh," *Universitetskiia izvestiia (Kiev)*, 1892, N. 1 (Jan.), 27-68.

"Rospisanie russkikh voisk v 1763 godu" in *Stoletie Voennago Ministerstva, 1802-1902*, 13 vol, SPb, 1902-1914, IV (1902), Glavnyi Shtab, Introduction, 35-41.

Rozman, G., *Urban Networks in Russia 1750-1800 and Premodern Periodization*, Princeton, 1976.

Rubinshtein, N., "Vneshniaia torgovlia Rossii i russkoe kupechestvo vo vtoroi polovine XVIII v.," *IZ*, 54 (1955), 343-361.

Rummel, V., and Golubtsov, V., *Rodoslovnyi sbornik russkikh dvorianskikh familii*, 2 vols., SPb, 1886-1887.

Rüss, H., *Adel und Adelsopposition in Moskauer Staat*, Wiesbaden, 1975.

Russkii Biograficheskii Slovar', 25 vols., SPb, 1896-1918.

Salias, E., "Poet Derzhavin, pravitel' Namestnichestva (1785-1788)," *RV*, Sept. 1876, 66-120, Oct., 567-627.

"Saltychikha," *RA*, 1865, 247-255.

Samoilov, A., "Zhizn' i deianiia general-fel'dmarshala kniazia G.A. Potemkina-Tavricheskago," *RA*, 1867, 575-606, 993-1027, 1203-1262, 1537-1578.

Sbornik istoricheskikh materialov i dokumentov, otnosiashchikh k novoi russkoi istorii XVIII i XIX veka, ed. M. Mikhailov, SPb, 1873.

Sbornik svedenii i materialov po vedomstvu Ministerstva Finansov, 10 vols., SPb, 1866-1867.

Schmidt, S., "La politique intérieure du tsarisme au milieu du XVIII siècle," *Annales*, 1966, N. 1 (Jan.), 95-110.

"Sekretnyi ukaz imp. Ekateriny Velikoi izdannyi po sluchaiu dorogovizny khleba i naslannyi chrez Prav. Senat voevode goroda Balakhny Krapivinu," *Chteniia*, 1847, I, smes', 20-21.

Selifontov, N., "Ivan Konstantinovich Boshniak, komendant goroda Saratova v 1774 g.," *RS*, 1879, III (Sept.-Dec.), 198-216.

Semenov, A., *Izuchenie istoricheskikh svedenii o Rossiiskoi vneshnei torgovie i promyshlennosti s poloviny XVII-go stoletiia po 1858 godu*, 2 vols., SPb, 1959.

Semevskii, V., *Krest'ianskii vopros v Rossii v XVIII i pervoi polovine XIX veka*, 2 vols., SPb, 1888.

———, *Krest'iane v tsarstvovanie Ekateriny II*, 2 vols., SPb, 1901.

———, "Volneniia krepostnykh krest'ian pri Ekaterine II 1762-1789," *RS*, 1877, I (Jan.-April), 193-226.

———, "Sel'skii sviashchennik vo vtoroi polovine XVIII veka," *RS*, II (May-Aug.), 501-538.

Shchepetov, K., *Krepostnoe pravo v votchinakh Sheremetevykh (1708-1885)*, Moscow, 1947.

———, *Iz zhizni krepostnykh krest'ian Rossii 18-19vv*, Moscow, 1963.

Shcherbatov. *Sochineniia kniazia M.M. Shcherbatova*, 2 vols., SPb., 1896-1898.

———, *Neizdannye sochineniia*, Moscow, 1947.

Sipovskii, P., "Russkaia zhizn' XVIII v. po romanam i povestiam," *RS*, 1906, II (April-June), 378-400, 523-548.

SIRIO. Sbornik Imperatorskago Russkago Istoricheskago Obshchestva, 148 vols., SPb, 1867-1916.

Sivkov, K., Ocherki po istorii politicheskikh protsessov v Rossii v poslednei treti XVIII veka, Candidate dissertation, Moscow, 1943.

———, "Podpol'naia politicheskaia literatura v Rossii v poslednei treti XVIII veka," *IZ*, N. 19 (1946), 63-101.

Sjoberg, G., *The Preindustrial City: Past and Present*, New York, 1960.

Slezkinskii, A., "Volokita starorusskago magistrata," *RS*, 1899, II (April-June), 475-480.

———, "Bytovye cherty iz zhizni chinovnika kontsa proshlago stoletiia," *RS*, 1897, IV (Oct.-Dec.), 223-224.

Sobornoe Ulozhenie 1649 goda. Uchebnoe posobie dlia vysshei shkoly, Moscow, 1961.

"Sobstvennoruchniaia pis'ma i zapiski imp. Ekateriny II-i k A.V. Khrapovitskomu 1783-1793," *RA*, 1872, 2062-2079.

Sokolovskii, M., "Ekaterina Velikaia kak blagotvoritel'nitsa," *RA*, 1904, II, 313-341.

Solov'ev, S., "Moskva v 1770 i 1771 gg.," *RS*, 1876, III (Sept.-Dec.), 189-204.

Soloveytchik, G., *Potemkin*, New York, 1947.

"Son, vidennyi v 1765 godu," *RA*, 1873, II (July-Dec.), 1910-1928.

"Sotvorenie sekretaria (satira XVIII stoletiia)," *RS*, 1884, IV (Oct.-Dec.), 222.

"Sovremennoe pis'mo o Saltychikh," *OV*, IV (1869), 94-96.

Stavrovskii, A., "Desiat' pisem G. R. Derzhavina k V. S. Popovu," *RA*, 1865, 349-363.

Stein. L. von, *The History of the Social Movement in France, 1789-1850*, ed. K. Mengelberg, Totowa, 1969.

St.-Peterburgskaia stolichnaia politsiia i gradonachal'stvo. Kratkii istoricheskii ocherk, SPb, 1903.

Stroev, V., "Krest'ianskii vopros v Ekaterinskoi kommissii dlia sostavleniie Ulozheniia," *RS*, IV (Oct.-Dec.), 165-182.

Studenkin, G., "Saltychikha, 1730-1801," *RS*, 1874, II (May-Aug.), 497-548.

Sudebnaia Reforma, ed. N. Davydov and N. Polianskii, Moscow, 1915.

"Sumerechnye raskazy starushki," *RA,* 1889, III (N. 9-12), 397-403

Svedeniia o piteinykh sborakh v Rossii, 5 *chasti,* SPb, 1860-1861.

Szamuely, T., *The Russian Tradition,* New York, 1974.

Tankov, A., "K istorii vziatochnichestva," *IV,* 1888, IV (Oct.-Dec.), 240-245.

Tankov, N., "Orlovskie razboiniki v 1765 godu," *RS,* 1897, I (Jan.-March), 191-192.

Tarasov, I., "Politseiskii arest v Rossii v XVIII stoletii," *ZhGUP,* 1885, N. 7 (Sept.), 61-86.

Tilly, Ch. ed., *The Formation of National States in Western Europe,* Princeton, 1975.

Timofeev, A., "Telesnyia nakazaniia," *ES,* XXXIV (1902), 290-295.

Tolstoi, D., *Istoriia finansovykh uchrezhdenii Rossii so vremeni osnovaniia gosudarstva do konchiny Imp. Ekateriny II,* SPb, 1848.

Trefolev, L., "A.P. Mel'gunov, General-Gubernator Ekaterinskikh vremen," *RA,* 1865, 931-978.

———, "Iaroslavskaia starina," *RA,* 1896, I (Jan.-March), 206-219, II (April-June), 147-155, III (July-Sept.), 88-100, 1897, I (Jan.-March), 189-212.

———, "Zaplechnyi master," *RA,* 1868, 1064-1068.

———, "Razskazy ob Iaroslavskoi starine," *RA,* 1876, III (N. 9-12), 314-344.

Troitskii, S., *Finansovaia politika russkogo absoliutizma v XVIII veke,* Moscow, 1966.

———, *Russkii absoliutizm i dvorianstvo v 18 veke. Formirovanie biurokratii,* Moscow, 1974.

———, "O nekotorykh spornykh voprosakh istorii absoliutizma v Rossii," Istoriia *SSSR,* 1969, 3 (May-June), 130-149.

———, "Sotsial'nyi sostav i chislennost' biurokratii Rossii v seredine XVIII veka," *IZ,* 89 (1972), 295-352.

———, "Dvorianskie proekty ukrepleniia gosudarstvennykh finansov v Rossii v seredine XVIII veka," *VI,* 1958, N. 2 (Feb.), 60-75.

———, "Novyi istochnik po istorii ekonomicheskikh mysli v Rossii v seredine XVIII v.," *AE za* 1966 (1968), 425-436.

———, "Iz istorii sostavleniia biudzheta v Rossii v seredine XVIII v.," *IZ,* 78 (1965), 181-203.

Troshchinskii, "Zapiska D. P. Troshchinskago o ministerstvakh," *SIRIO,* III (1868), 1-162.

"Dmitri Prokof'evich Troshchinskii, 1754-1829," *RS,* 1882, II (April-June), 641-682.

"Tsena liudei v Rossii sto let nazad," *Chteniia,* 1896, II, smes', 7-11.

Tsvetaev, D., "Iz arkhiv Khar'kovskago Namestnichestva," *RA*, 1887, II (N. 5-8), 145-157.

Turgenev. "Zapiski Aleksandra Mikhailovicha Turgeneva 1772-1823," *RS*, 1885, III (July-Sept.), 365-390; IV (Oct.-Dec.), 55-82, 247-282, 473-486, 1886; I (Jan.-March), 39-62; IV (Oct.-Dec.) 45-76, 259-284, 1887; I (Jan.-March), 77-106, 329-342.

Turkestanov, M., *Gubernskii sluzhebnik ili spisok general-gubernatoram, praviteliam, poruchikam pravitelia, predsedateliam ugolovnoi i grazhdanskoi palat i dvorianskikm prevoditeliam v 47 namestnichestvakh 1777-1796 gg.*, SPb, 1869.

"Ukazy grava P.B. Sheremeteva ego upraviteliam," *RA*, 1898, I (N. 1-4), 509-522, II (N. 5-8), 275-288, 445-452, III (N. 9-12), 5-35.

Veinberg, L., "Ocherki starodavnago mestnago byta," *RA*, 1887, II (N. 5-8), 288-306, III (N. 9-12), 416-423.

Veretennikov, V., "Iz istorii instituta prokuratury nachala Ekaterinskago tsarstvovaniia," *RIZh*, V (1918), 86-100.

Vernadskii, G., *The Tsardom of Muscovy 1547-1682*, New Haven, 1969.

Veselovskii, S., *Trudy po istochnikovedeniiu i istorii Rossii perioda feodalizma*, Moscow, 1978.

Veshniakov, V., *Proekt imperatritsy Ekateriny II ob ustroistve svobodnykh sel'skikh obyvateliakh*, SPb, n.d.

Villain, J., *Le Recouvrement des impôts directs sous l'Ancien Régime*, Paris, 1952.

Vitkorskii, S., "Istoriia smertnoi kazni v Rossii i sovremennoe eia sostoianie," *UZIMU*, vyp. 41, Moscow, 1912.

Vladimirskii-Budanov, M., *Obzor istorii russkago prava*, 6th ed., SPb, 1909.

Vlasov, V., "Arestant Vasilii Briagin 1788," *RS*, 1873, II (July-Dec.), 86-87.

"Dmitri Vasil'evich Volkov," *RS*, 1874, I (Jan.-April), 163-174.

Vorontsov, A., "Primechaniia na nekotoryia stat'i, kasaiushchiasia do Rossii, grafa A.R. Vorontsova, Imperatoru Aleksandru I-mu predstavlenyyia," *Chteniia*, 1859, kn. I (Jan.-March), smes', 89-102.

"Vsepoddaneishii doklad Pravitel'stvuiushchago Senata po d elu kapitana Golokhvastova v zakliuchenii ego v ostorg Novgorodskim gubernatorom Siversom," *SIRIO*, II (1868), 419-424.

Ware. T., *The Orthodox Church*, New York, 1963.

Weber, M., *The Theory of Social and Economic Organization*, New York, 1947.

Williams, E., *The Ancien Regime in Europe: Government and Society in the Major States 1648-1789*, New York, 1970.

Wittfogel, K., *Oriental Despotism*, New York, 1981.
Wolzendorff, K., *Der Polizeigedanke des modernes Staates*, Breslau, 1918.
Wortman, R., *The Development of Russian Legal Consciousness*, Chicago, 1976.
Yaney, G., *The Systematization of Russian Government. Social Evolution in the Domestic Administration of Imperial Russia, 1711-1905*, Urbana, 1973.
Zaitsev, K., *Ocherki istorii samoupravleniia gosudarstvennykh krest'ian*, SPb, 1912.
"Zapiska imp. Ekateriny Velikoi o Roslavl'skom konnom polku ili Riazanskikh dragunakh," *RA*, 1886, III (N. 9-12), 106-110.
Zapiski L'va Nikolaevicha Engelgardta 1766-1836, Moscow, 1868.
"Zapiski Mertvago, 1760-1824," *RA*, 1867, 1-335.
"Zapiski Vinskago," *RA*, 1877, 76-123, 150-197.
"Zhaloba krest'ian Tambovskago namestnichestva," *RA*, 1875, III (N. 9-12), 397-398.
Zheludkov, V., *Gubernskaia reforma 1775 goda*. Candidate dissertation, Leningrad, 1963.
Zhidkov, G., *Kabinetskoe zemlevladenie (1747-1917 gg.)*, Novosibirsk, 1973.
"Zhurnal reliatsii k Eia Imp. Velichestva 1782 i 1787 godov Tul'skago, Riazanskago i Kaluzhskago General-Gubernatora M.N. Krechetnikov," *Chteniia*, 1863, IV (Oct.-Dec.), i-xiii, 1-20.

III. Published Works on the Borderlands

Abramov, N., "Petr Alexeevich Slovtsov," *Chteniia*, 1871, IV, (Oct.-Dec.), smes', 84-103.
———, "O byvshem Tobol'skom Namestnichestve, 1782-1797 g., *Chteniia*, 1869, I (Jan.-March), smes', 15-22.
Aksakov, I., "Ukrainskiia iarmarki," *RBa*, 1858, II, 87-158.
Andreev, "Domovaia letopis' Andreeva, po rodu ikh, pisannaia kapitanom Ivanom Andreevym v 1789," ed., G. Potanin, *Chteniia*, 1870, IV (Oct.-Dec.), smes', 63-176.
Appolova, N., *Ekonomicheskie i politicheskie sviazi Kazakhstana i Rossiei v 18-nachale 19 vv.*, Moscow, 1960.
Arbusow, L., *Grundriss der Geschichte Liv-, Est- und Kurlands*, Riga, 1908.
"Arkhiv grafa Igel'stroma," *RA*, 1886, III (N. 9-12), 341-371, 480-496.
Auerbach, H., *Die Besiedelung der Südukraine in den Jahren 1774-1787*, Wiesbaden, 1965.

Baskakov, N., *Russkie familii Tiurkskogo proiskhozhdeniia*, Moscow, 1979.

Bentkovskii, I., "Grebentsy," *Chteniia*, 1887, III, 1-33.

Bienemann, F., *Die Statthalterschaftszeit in Liv- und Estland, 1783-1796*, Leipzig, 1886.

Bil'basov, V., "Prisoedinenie Kurliandii," *RS*, 1895, I (Jan.-March), 3-55.

Bodianskii, O., "Tri propovedi P.A. Slovtsova," *Chteniia*, 1873, III (July-Sept.), smes', 141-153.

Brikner, A., "Puteshestvie imp. Ekateriny II v Mogilev v 1780 godu," *RV*, August 1881, 459-509, Sept., 311-367.

———, "Puteshestvie Ekateriny II v Krym," *IV*, 1885, III (July-Sept.), 5-23, 242-264, 444-509.

———, "Kniaz' G.A. Potemkin (po zapiskam grafa Lanzherona khraniashchimsia v Parizhskom arkhive), *IV*, 1895, IV (Oct.-Dec), 817-842.

"Bumagi, do upravleniia Malorossieiu grafa P.A. Rumiantseva-Zadunaiskago otnosiashchiesia," *Chteniia*, 1861, I (Jan.-March), 137-165.

Chumikov, A., "Ostzeiskoe dvorianstvo i dvorianskaia zhalovannai gramota," *RS*, 1885, II (April-June), 193-204.

Dmitriev-Mamonov, A., "Pugachevshchina v Sibirii," *Chteniia*, 1898, IV, 1-152.

"Dnevniania zapiska o dvizhenii i deistviiakh voisk russkikh v Vel. Kn. Litovskom i Pol'she v 1792 godu, nakhodiashchsia pod nachal' stvom Gen.-Anshefa M.N. Krechetnikova," *Chteniia*, 1863, IV (Oct.-Dec.), 21-104.

Don i stepnoe Predkavkaz'e XVIII-pervaia polovina XIX v., Zaselenie i khoziaistvo, Rostov/Don, 1977.

Donnelly, A., *The Russian Conquest of Bashkiria 1552-1740*, New Haven, 1968.

Dubrovin, F., "Brat'ia Potemkiny na Kavkaze," *RV*, Nov. 1878, 5-55, Dec., 483-561, Jan. 1879, 65-102, April, 825-883.

Dubrovin, P., "Pred nachalom Pugachevskago bunta," *RV*, 1881, April, 469-511; May, 39-93; June, 519-583; July, 101-153; Aug., 647-700.

Elagin. "Golos Senatora I.P. Elagina o razdele imeniia grafov Vorontsovykh s ikh nevestkoiu, grafinineiu A. K. Vorontsovoiu zh, urozhdennoi Skavronskoiu," *Chteniia*, 1861, II (April-June), 144-158.

Engelhardt, N., *Die Beschreibung des russischen Kaiserlichen Gouvernements von Wiburg (1767)*, Helsinki, 1973.

Evarnitskii, D., "Pervyi Ekaterinoslavskii gubernator," *IV*, 1887, II
    (April-June), 630-638.
—— "I.M. Sinel'nikov pered sudom istorii," *IV*, 1896; II (April-
    June), 317-320.
Gajecky, G., *The Cossack Administration of the Hetmanate*, 2 vols.,
    Cambridge (Mass.), 1978.
Gazenvinkel', K., "Sibirskii gubernator D. I. Chicherin," *IV*, 1893; II
    (April-June), 783-790.
Gol'denberg, L., *Fedor Ivanovich Soimonov (1692-1780)*, Moscow,
    1966.
Goroda Sibiri. Epokha feodalizma i kapitalizma, Novosibirsk, 1978.
Goroda Sibiri: ekonomika, upravlenie i kultura v dosovetskii period,
    Novosibirsk, 1974.
Gritskevich, A., *Chastnovladel'cheskie goroda Belorussii v 16-18 vv.*,
    Minsk, 1975.
Gromyko, M., *Zapadnaia Sibir' v XVIII v.*, Novosibirsk, 1965.
Gur'ev, V., "Ispovednyi shtraf v Sibiri v techenie proshlago XVIII
    veka," *RV*, Jan., 1882, 5-38.
Gurevich, B., *Mezhdunarodnye otnosheniia v Tsentral'noi Azii v XVII-
    pervoi polovine XIX v.*, Moscow, 1979.
Hrushevsky, M., *A History of the Ukraine*, New Haven, 1941.
Istoriia gorodov Sibiri dosovetskogo perioda (XVIII-nachalo XX v.,
    Novosibirsk, 1977.
Iudin, P., "Baron O.A. Igel'strom v Orenburgskom krae (1784-1792,
    1796-1798)," *RA*, 1897 (N. 1-4), 513-555.
Iudin, P., "S Volgi na Terek (k istorii zaseleniia Povolzh'ia i Kavkaza),"
    RA, 1901, II (5-8), 531-544.
——, "Iz Astrakhanskoi zhizni Suvorova," *RS*, 1912, IV, (Oct.-
    Dec.), 590-596.
"Iz dnevnika M.S. Rebelinskago," *RA*, 1897, I (N. 1-4), 464-481.
"K istorii krest'ian v Estliandskoi gubernii," *RS*, 1895, III (July-Sept.),
    203.
"K istorii Sibiri v kontse XVIII veka. Vospominaniia T. P. Kalashni-
    kova," *RA*, 1904, III, 145-183.
Kabuzan, V., *Zaselenie Novorossii v 18-pervoi polovine 19-go veka:
    Ekaterinoslavskoi i Khersonskoi gubernii, 1719-1858*, Moscow,
    1976.
Karatygin, P., "Graf Pavel Sergeevich Potemkin," *IV*, III (July-Sept.),
    354-371.
Karpov, G., "O krepostnom prave v Malorossii," *RA*, 1875, II (N. 5-
    8), 229-232.
*Kazakho-russkie otnosheniia v XVIII-XIX vekakh (1771-1867 gody).
    Sb. dokumentov i materialov*, Alma-Ata, 1964.

Kohut, Z., The Abolition of Ukrainian Autonomy 1763-1786, un-published Ph.D. dissertation, University of Pennsylvania, 1975.

"Kratkoe izlozhenie predmetov, vziatoe is prav, v Maloi Rossii ipo-trebliaemykh, po kotoromu sleduet izobrazit' te prava, soglasno planu Vysochaishe konfirmovannomu," Chteniia, 1861, II (April-June), 69-75.

Kul'sharipov, M., Politika tsarizma v Bashkirii 1775-1800 gg., Candidate dissertation, Moscow, 1971.

Laidinen, A., Ocherki istorii Finliandii vtoroi poloviny XVIII v., Leningrad, 1972.

Lazarevskii, A., "Ocherk malorossiiskikh familii. Materialy dlia istorii obshchestva v XVII i xviii vekakh," RA, I (N. 1-4), 91-97, 311-325, 439-452; II (N. 5-8), 248-264, 402-409; III (N. 9-12), 299-308, 1876; III (N. 9-12), 437-455.

Lehtonen, U., Die polnischen Provinzen Russlands unter Katharina II in den Jahren 1772-1782, Berlin, 1907.

Ligi, Kh., Feodalnye povinnosti estonskikh krest'ian (do nachala XIX veka), Tallin, 1968.

Longworth, Ph., The Cossacks, London, 1971.

Maksimovich, G., Deiatel'nost' Rumiantseva-Zadunaiskago po upra-vleniiu Malorossiei, vol. I, Nezhin, 1913.

Maksimovich, M., "O G. N. Teplov i ego zapiske 'o neporiadkakh Malorossii', " RBa, 1857, IV, 61-78.

Maksimovich, S., Sibir' i katorga, SPb, 1871.

Makushev, V., "Rossiia i Pol'sha v XVII veke.Po reliatsiiam vene-tsiiantsa D. Dol'fina i gennestsa S. Rivaroly," RV, May 1870, 5-25.

Miakotin, V., Ocherki sotsial'noi istorii Ukrainy v XVII-XVIII v., vol. I, 3 parts, Prague, 1924-1926.

"Mikhail Pavlovich Miklashevskii," RBa, 1856, I, Appendix, 1-50.

Miller, O., "O nashem krepostnom prave v XVIII stoletii," RA, 1875, III (N. 9-12), 82-89.

Milov, L., "O tak nazyvaemykh agrarnykh gorodakh Rossii XVIII veka," VI, 1968, N. 6 (June), 54-64.

"Mnenie, na kakom by osnovanii zavesti poriadok v dache chinov armeiskikh Malorossiiskim starshinam," Chteniia, 1861, II, April-June), 76-77.

Mochul'skii, "Russkiia prava na Pribaltiiskii krai (istoricheskii o-cherk)," RV, Sept. 1894, 159-190; Oct., 40-67.

Mosolov, A., "Kurliandiia pod upravleniem Ekateriny Velikoi (1795 god)," RV, May 1870, 26-60.

"Nastavlenie, dannoe grafu P. Rumiantsevu, pri naznachenii ego Ma-

lorossiiskim general-gubernatorom, s sobstvennoruchnymi pri-
bavkami Ekateriny II, 1764," *SIRIO*, VII (1871), 376-391.

"Nastavlenie vybornomu ot Malorossiiskoi Kollegii v Kommissiiu o
sochinenii proekta novago Ulozheniia d. koll. sovetniku i chlenu
toi Kollegii Dm. Natalinu," *Chteniia*, 1858, III (July-Sept.), 5-70.

Nolde, B., *La formation de l'Empire russe*, 2 vols., Paris, 1952-1953.

O rasporiadkakh Chicherina v Tobol'sk, Tobol'sk, 1891.

"O rasprostranenii torga s oblastiami Khivinskoiu, Bukharskoiu i in-
deiskimi, 1787," *Chteniia*, 1863, II (April-June), 57-64.

"O vyplavke na Nerchinskikh zavodakh serebra s 1704 po 1768,"
Chteniia, 1864, III (July-Sept.), 94-100.

Ogloblin, N., "Naezd (Ocherk iz zhizni Malorossii kontsa xviii v.),"
IV, 1893; II (April-June), 732-746.

Oglobin, O., *Liudi staroi Ukrainy*, Munich, 1959.

"Otkaz rizhskago magistrata v priniatii byvshago viazemskago kuptsa
Iv. Fatova v meshchanstvo I-i gildii," *Chteniia*, 1896, III, smes',
42-58.

"Otgoloski Pugachevskago bunta," *RS*, 1905, II (April-June), 662-
670.

Pashuk, A., *Sud i sudochynstvo na livoberezhny Ukrajini v XVII-
XVIII st. (1648-1782)*, L'vov, 1967.

Pishkevich, A., "Zhizn' A.S. Pishkevicha, im samim opisannaia, 1764-
1805," *Chteniia*, 1885, I (Jan.-March), 1-112; II (April-June),
113-273.

Pishkevich, S., "Izvestiia o pokhozhdeniiakh S.S. Pishkevicha," *Chteniia*, 1881, IV (Oct.-Dec.), 1-320, 1882, II (April-June), 321-481,
1883, II (April-June), 482-561.

"Pis'ma imp. Ekateriny II-i k T. I. Tutolminu," *RA*, 1873, II, 2274-
2317.

"Pis'ma i ukazy Ekateriny Velikoi k sibirskomu Gubernatoru D.I.
Chicherinu," *RA*, 1891, II (May-Aug.), 6-13.

"Pis'ma k generalu i kavaleru M. N. Krechetnikovu grafa Chernysheva
i drugikh s 1769 po 1785," *Chteniia*, 1863, IV (Oct.-Dec.), 1-
63.

"Pis'ma k General Maioru i kavaleru P.N. Krechetnikovu," *Chteniia*,
1863, III (July-Sept.), 1-114.

"Pis'mo imp. Ekateriny II k grafu Braunu, general-gubernatoru Est-
liandii i Lifliandii," *RS*, 1895, I (Jan.-March), 217-219.

"Plakat Belorusskago General-Gubernatora, Grafa Chernysheva 1772,"
Chteniia, 1863, I (Jan.-March), 165-171.

Pogosian, F., *Sudebnik Astrakhanskikh armian*, Erivan, 1968.

Pokhilevich, D., *Krest'iane Belorussii i Litvy vo vtoroi polovine XVIII
veka*, Vilna, 1966.

Pokrovskii, N., *Antifeodal'nyi protest Uralo-Sibirskikh krest'ian-staroobriadtsev v 18 v.*, Novosibirsk, 1974.

Popov, N., "Voennyia poseleniia Serbov v Avstrii i Rossii," *VE*, 1870, N. 6 (June), 584-614.

Pronshtein, A., *Zemlia Donskaia v XVIII veke*, Rostov/Don, 1961.

Rabtsevich, V., Mestnoe upravlenie Zapadnoi Sibirii v 80-kh godakh XVIII-pervoi chetverti XIX stoletii, Candidate dissertation, Novosibirsk, 1973.

Polons'ka-Vasilenko, N., *Istoriia Ukraini*, 2 vols., Munich, 1972-1976.

Raeff, M., "Uniformity, Diversity, and the Imperial Administration in the Reign of Catherine II," in *Osteuropa in Geschichte und Gegenwart*, 97-113.

———, "The Style of Russia's 'Imperial' Policy and Prince G. A. Potemkin," in G. Grob, ed., *Statesmen and Statecraft of the Modern West*, Barre, Mass., 1967, 1-51.

Rafienko, L., Upravlenie Sibiriu v 20-80 gg. XVIII veka, Candidate dissertation, Novosibirsk, 1968.

Rauch, G. von, *Russland: Staatliche Einheit und nationale Vielfalt*, Munich, 1953.

"Razyne bumagi General-Maiora Tevkeleva ob Orenburgskom krae i o Kirgiz-Kaisatskikh ordakh 1762 goda," *VIRMO*, XIII (1852), smes' 15-19.

Repnin. "Bumagi kn. N. V. Repnina za vremia upravleniia ego Litvoiu," *SIRIO*, XVI (1875).

Reshetinskii, V., "Graf Rumiantsev-Zadunaiskii kak administrator," *RA*, 1914, I, 488-500.

Rovinskii, K., "Delo o tridtsati shesti nezakonnykh brakakh," *RA*, 1909, II, (N. 5-8), 161-181.

Rumiantsev. "Mnenie Gen-Anshefa, Malorossiiskago Gen-Gubernatora i kavalera, Grafa Rumiantseva, o skuple v Maloi Rossii kazach'ikh imenii, o svobodnykh pospolitykh i o zhivushchikh v poddanstve Kozakakh, kak im nyne byt' i vpred ostavat'sia," *Chteniia*, 1861, II (April-June), smes', 59-68.

Rychkov, N., *Dnevnyia Zapiski puteshestviia kapitana Nikolaia Rychkova v Kirgiz-Kaisatskoi stepi 1771 godu*, SPb, 1772.

R-n, N., "Zapiski o iuzhnoi Rusi izd. P.A. Kulisha," *RBa*, IV, 1857, 1-21.

Sakovich, P., "Istoricheskii obzor deiatel'nosti grafa Rumiantseva-Zadunaiskago i ego sotrudnikov: kniazia Prozorovskago, Suvorova i Brinka, s 1775 po 1780," *RBa*, 1858, IV, 173-260.

Schmidt, O., *Rechtsgeschichte Liv-, Est- und Curlands*, Dorpat, 1894.

"Serebro v Osetii (k istorii gornopromyshlennosti na Kavkaze)," *RA*, 1915, II (N. 5-8), 55-67.

Shishkov, A., "Golos o neobkhodimosti imet' odinakovye zakony i Pribaltiiskim Guberniiam s zakonami Rossiiskoi Imperii," *Chteniia*, 1867, IV (Oct.-Dec.), 83-95.

Shteingel, V., "Sibirskie satrapy 1765-1819," *IV*, 1884, III (July-Sept.), 366-386.

Shtrandman, N., "Sibir' i eia nuzhdy v 1801 godu," *RS*, 1879, I (Jan.-April), 150-156.

"Sibirskii Gubernator D.I. Chicherin 1773-1776 gg.," *RS*, 1891, III (July-Sept.), 179-182.

Sladkovskii, M., *Istoriia torgovo-ekonomicheskikh otnoshenii narodov Rossii s Kitaem (do 1917 g.)*, Moscow, 1974.

Slavutinskii, S., "Iz Ostrogozhskoi khroniki," *DNR*, 1877, I (Jan.-April), 125-126.

Slovtsov, P., *Istoricheskoe obozrenie Sibiri*, 2 vols., SPb, 1886.

Ssylka i katorga v Sibiri 18-nachalo 20 vv., Novosibirsk, 1975.

Ssylka i obshchestvenno-politicheskaia zhizn' v Sibiri (XVIII-nachalo XX v.), Novosibirsk, 1978.

Sulotskii, A., "Petr Andreevich Slovtsov," *Chteniia*, 1873, III (July-Sept.), smes', 130-140.

"Svedeniia o rode Tevkelevykh i o sluzhbe General-Maiora Alexeia Ivanovicha Tevkeleva," *VIMO*, XIII (1858), smes', 19-22.

Sychevskii. "Istoricheskaia zapiska o kitaiskoi granitse," *Chteniia*, 1875, II (April-June), 1-292.

Timkovskii. "Zapiski Il'i Fedorovicha Timskago," *RA*, 1874, I, 1377-1466.

Tishchenko, D., *Politika russkogo tsarizma na Ukraine pri Ekaterine II*. Candidate dissertation, Moscow, 1946.

Tolstoi, M., "Sviatel' Pavel, Metropolit Tobol'skii i Sibirskii," *Chteniia*," 1870, II (April-June), smes', 158-168.

Vitevskii, V., "Proiskhozhdenie Ural'skago voiska," *DNR*, 1879, May-Sept., 206-216.

Vol'demar, "Ocherk istorii Kurliandii," *RV*, Dec. 1869, 367-395.

"Vospominaniia senatora barona Karla Geikinga," *RS*, 1897, III (July-Sept.), 291-308, 517-537, IV (Oct.-Dec.), 121-138, 405-424, 591-614.

"Vozrazhdenie deputata Grigoriia Politiki na nastavlenie Malorossiiskoi Kollegii Dm. Natalinu," *Chteniia*, 1858, III (July-Sept.), 71-102.

"Zaboty imp Ekateriny Velikoi o Lifliandskoi Gubernii," *RA*, 1907, III (Sept.-Dec.), 5-10.

"Zamechaniia, do Maloi Rossii prinadlezhashchiia," *Chteniia*, 1848-1849, I, 1-35.

"Zapiska Orenburgskago gubernatora Reinsdorfa nedostatkakh vverennoi ego upravleniiu gubernii 1770 g.," *VIRGO*, 1859, N. 10, 90-104.

"Zapiska Dmitriia Volkova ob Orenburgskoi gubernii 1763 g.," *VIRGO*, 1859, N. 9. 49-60.

"Zapiski Donskago Atamana Denisova 1763-1841," *RS*, 1874, II (May-August), 1-45, III (Sept.-Dec.), 379-410, 601-641.

"Zapiski iz dela, proizvedennago v Komitete Vysochaishe utverzhdannom pri Pravitel'stvuiushchem Senate, kasatel'no prav na dvorianstvo byvshikh Malorossiiskikh chinov," *Chteniia*, 1861, II (April-June), 80-139.

Zapiski o Slobodskikh polkakh s nachala ikh poseleniia do 1766 goda, Khar'kov, 1812.

"Zemel'nye akty Ufimskikh bashkir-votchinnikov," *Chteniia*, 1900, IV, 28-29.

Zutis, Ia., *Ostzeiskii vopros v 18 veke*, Riga, 1946.

This book comprises part of the
STUDIES OF THE HARRIMAN INSTITUTE,
successor to:

STUDIES OF THE RUSSIAN INSTITUTE

ABRAM BERGSON, *Soviet National Income in 1937* (1953).

ERNEST J. SIMMONS, JR., ed., *Through the Glass of Soviet Literature: Views of Russian Society* (1953).

THAD PAUL ALTON, *Polish Postwar Economy* (1954).

DAVID GRANICK, *Management of the Industrial Firm in the USSR: A Study in Soviet Economic Planning* (1954).

ALLEN S. WHITING, *Soviet Policies in China, 1917-1924* (1954).

GEORGE S.N. LUCKYJ, *Literary Politics in the Soviet Ukraine, 1917-1934* (1956).

MICHAEL BORO PETROVICH, *The Emergence of Russian Panslavism, 1856-1870* (1956).

THOMAS TAYLOR HAMMOND, *Lenin on Trade Unions and Revolution, 1893-1917* (1956).

DAVID MARSHALL LANG, *The Last Years of the Georgian Monarchy, 1658-1832* (1957).

JAMES WILLIAM MORLEY, *The Japanese Thrust into Siberia, 1918* (1957).

ALEXANDER G. PARK, *Bolshevism in Turkestan, 1917-1927* (1957).

HERBERT MARCUSE, *Soviet Marxism: A Critical Analysis* (1958).

CHARLES B. MCLANE, *Soviet Policy and the Chinese Communists, 1931-1946* (1958).

OLIVER H. RADKEY, *The Agrarian Foes of Bolshevism: Promise and Defeat of the Russian Socialist Revolutionaries, February to October, 1917* (1958).

RALPH TALCOTT FISHER, JR., *Pattern for Soviet Youth: A Study of the Congresses of the Komsomol, 1918-1954* (1959).

ALFRED ERICH SENN, *The Emergence of Modern Lithuania* (1959).

ELLIOT R. GOODMAN, *The Soviet Design for a World State* (1960).

JOHN N. HAZARD, *Settling Disputes in Soviet Society: The Formative Years of Legal Institutions* (1960).

DAVID JORAVSKY, *Soviet Marxism and Natural Science, 1917-1932* (1961).

MAURICE FRIEDBERG, *Russian Classics in Soviet Jackets* (1962).

ALFRED J. RIEBER, *Stalin and the French Communist Party, 1941-1947* (1962).

THEODORE K. VON LAUE, *Sergei Witte and the Industrialization of Russia* (1962).

JOHN A. ARMSTRONG, *Ukrainian Nationalism* (1963).

OLIVER H. RADKEY, *The Sickle under the Hammer: The Russian Socialist Revolutionaries in the Early Months of Soviet Rule* (1963).

KERMIT E. MCKENZIE, *Comintern and World Revolution, 1928-1943: The Shaping of Doctrine* (1964).

HARVEY L. DYCK, *Weimar Germany and Soviet Russia, 1926-1933: A Study in Diplomatic Instability* (1966).

(*Above titles published by Columbia University Press.*)

HAROLD J. NOAH, *Financing Soviet Schools* (Teachers College, 1966).

JOHN M. THOMPSON, *Russia, Bolshevism, and the Versailles Peace* (Princeton, 1966).

PAUL AVRICH, *The Russian Anarchists* (Princeton, 1967).

LOREN R. GRAHAM, *The Soviet Academy of Sciences and the Communist Party, 1927-1932* (Princeton, 1967).

ROBERT A. MAGUIRE, *Red Virgin Soil: Soviet Literature in the 1920's* (Princeton, 1968).

T. H. RIGBY, *Communist Party Membership in the U.S.S.R., 1917-1967* (Princeton, 1968).

RICHARD T. DE GEORGE, *Soviet Ethics and Morality* (University of Michigan, 1969).

JONATHAN FRANKEL, *Vladimir Akimov on the Dilemmas of Russian Marxism, 1895-1903* (Cambridge, 1969).

WILLIAM ZIMMERMAN, *Soviet Perspectives on International Relations, 1956-1967* (Princeton, 1969).

PAUL AVRICH, *Kronstadt, 1921* (Princeton, 1970).

EZRA MENDELSOHN, *Class Struggle in the Pale: The Formative Years of the Jewish Workers' Movement in Tsarist Russia* (Cambridge, 1970).

EDWARD J. BROWN, *The Proletarian Episode in Russian Literature* (Columbia, 1971).

REGINALD E. ZELNIK, *Labor and Society in Tsarist Russia: The Factory Workers of St. Petersburg, 1855-1870* (Stanford, 1971).

PATRICIA K. GRIMSTED, *Archives and Manuscript Repositories in the USSR: Moscow and Leningrad* (Princeton, 1972).

RONALD G. SUNY, *The Baku Commune, 1917-1918* (Princeton, 1972).

EDWARD J. BROWN, *Mayakovsky: A Poet in the Revolution* (Princeton, 1973).

MILTON EHRE, *Oblomov & His Creator: The Life and Art of Ivan Goncharov* (Princeton, 1973).

HENRY KRISCH, *German Politics Under Soviet Occupation* (Columbia, 1974).

HENRY W. MORTON and RUDOLPH L. TÖKÉS, eds., *Soviet Politics and Society in the 1970's* (Free Press, 1974).

WILLIAM G. ROSENBERG, *Liberals in the Russian Revolution* (Princeton, 1974).

RICHARD G. ROBBINS, JR., *Famine in Russia, 1891-1892* (Columbia, 1975).

VERA DUNHAM, *In Stalin's Time: Middleclass Values in Soviet Fiction* (Cambridge, 1976).

WALTER SABLINSKY, *The Road to Bloody Sunday* (Princeton, 1976).

WILLIAM MILLS TODD III, *The Familiar Letter as a Literary Genre in the Age of Pushkin* (Princeton, 1976).

ELIZABETH VALKENIER, *Russian Realist Art. The State and Society: The Peredvizhniki and their Tradition* (Ardis, 1977).

SUSAN SOLOMON, *The Soviet Agrarian Debate* (Westview, 1978).

SHEILA FITZPATRICK, ed., *Cultural Revolution in Russia, 1928-1931* (Indiana, 1978).

PETER SOLOMON, *Soviet Criminologists and Criminal Policy: Specialists in Policy-Making* (Columbia, 1978).

KENDALL E. BAILES, *Technology and Society under Lenin and Stalin: Origins of the Soviet Technical Intelligentsia, 1917-1941* (Princeton, 1978).

LEOPOLD H. HAIMSON, ed., *The Politics of Rural Russia, 1905-1914* (Indiana, 1979).

THEODORE H. FRIEDGUT, *Political Participation in the USSR* (Princeton, 1979).

SHEILA FITZPATRICK, *Education and Social Mobility in the Soviet Union, 1921-1934* (Cambridge, 1979)

WESLEY ANDREW FISHER, *The Soviet Marriage Market: Mate-Selection in Russia and the USSR* (Praeger, 1980).

JONATHAN FRANKEL, *Prophecy and Politics: Socialism, Nationalism, and the Russian Jews, 1862-1917* (Cambridge, 1981).

ROBIN FEUER MILLER, *Dostoevsky and the Idiot: Author, Narrator, and Reader* (Harvard, 1981).

DIANE KOENKER, *Moscow Workers and the 1917 Revolution* (Princeton, 1981).

PATRICIA K. GRIMSTED, *Archives and Manuscript Repositories in the USSR: Estonia, Latvia, Lithuania, and Belorussia* (Princeton, 1981).

EZRA MENDELSOHN, *Zionism in Poland: The Formative Years, 1915-1926* (Yale, 1982).

HANNES ADOMEIT, *Soviet Risk-Taking and Crisis Behavior* (George Allen & Unwin, 1982).

SEWERYN BIALER and THANE GUSTAFSON, eds., *Russia at the Crossroad: The 26th Congress of the CPSU* (George Allen & Unwin, 1982).

ROBERTA THOMPSON MANNING, *The Crisis of the Old Order in Russia: Gentry and Government* (Princeton, 1982).

ANDREW A. DURKIN, *Sergei Aksakov and Russian Pastoral* (Rutgers, 1983).

BRUCE PARROTT, *Politics and Technology in the Soviet Union* (MIT Press, 1983).

SARAH PRATT, *Russian Metaphysical Romanticism: The Poetry of Tiutchev and Boratynskii* (Stanford, 1984).

STUDIES OF THE HARRIMAN INSTITUTE

ELIZABETH KRIDL VALKENIER, *The Soviet Union and the Third World: An Economic Bind* (Praeger, 1983).

INDEX

LIBRARY OF CONGRESS CATALOGING IN PUBLICATION DATA

LeDonne, John P., 1935-
    Ruling Russia.

    (Studies of the Harriman Institute)
    Bibliography; p.
    Includes index.
    1. Soviet Union—Politics and government—1689-1800. 2. Administrative
agencies—Soviet Union—History—18th century. 3. Soviet Union—History—
Catherine II, 1762-1796. 4. Soviet Union—Executive departments—History—18th
century. I. Title. II. Series.
JN6524.L42   1984   947'.06   84-2168
ISBN 0-691-05425-8